AF615079

Dedicated to Earth Trustees Everywhere

Star of Hope

Published by
SWAN BOOKS

First Edition

This book was designed, printed
and manufactured in the United States
by Astoria Graphics, New York

The cover design is by
Erling I. Saevarsson

Editorial Advisor: Anji Janitschek

International Standard Book Number:
0-9785258-0-9

Printed and manufactured in the United States of America

SWAN BOOKS
Post Office Box 953
Pine Plains, NY 12567
USA

Contents

Acclaim for John McConnell

John McConnell was well known at the United Nations as someone courageous with ideas, a diplomat for the Earth. And he never gave up.
– Robert Muller, United Nations Assistant Secretary-General

I always admired John McConnell's strength and individuality.
– Maurice Strong, United Nations Under-Secretary-General

John McConnell is a man of vision who helped shape my understanding of the global threats to our survival.
– G. P. Koirala, Prime Minister of Nepal

John McConnell is totally dedicated and committed to the concept of peace building through the environment. Anna was an integral part to his existence.
– U.S. Ambassador John McDonald

John McConnell supported peace movements and added his voice as an outstanding citizen.
– Mark O. Hatfield, former U.S. Senator

John McConnell is the most dedicated man I've ever known.
– Edward Abramson, former Majority Whip of the New York State Assembly

John McConnell is a visionary and a very determined person who doesn't let go of an important idea – care for the environment.
– Edwina Sandys, artist and granddaughter of Sir Winston Churchill

John McConnell is a personal hero because he never gave up on the fight for a better way for all of us to take care of Mother Earth. He is a modern day Saint Francis, and I love him for it.
– Angela Alioto, civil rights trial attorney, former president of the San Francisco Board of Supervisors, and daughter of former San Francisco mayor Joseph Alioto

John McConnell is among the leading world figures in the search for world peace.
– Norman Corwin, author, screenwriter, producer, essayist and educator

John McConnell always struck me as a very sincere individual. Very idealistic. Very much concerned about the future of mankind.
– S. Fred Singer, President of The Science & Environmental Policy Project

John McConnell is one of those amazing people. He keeps doing good things and is very little known. He's a very fine man, and I admire him a great deal.
– Frank O. Braynard, director of Operation Sail 1976

Foreword

John McConnell is an idealist, a visionary, a peacemaker.
Those are the people needed today, for our future.
– George Gallup, Jr., interview by author 1 August 2005

POLARIZATION IN OUR COUNTRY and in other parts of the world – and this is true of extremist groups on the left and the right – comes from misinformation. As pollsters, we want to demonstrate to people that there is a certain level of knowledge and understanding that gives our societies a strong sense of unity. Or, as John McConnell would say, people would forego their intolerances and conflicts if they would only recognize their common interests.

Our polls have shown that most people in the world want the three things to which John McConnell has devoted his life, "peace, justice and the care of Earth." In spite of incredible disruptions, pain and turmoil, people on all sides are working energetically on the world's problems. They are united at a deep level because they know that when people have their needs met, they are more wiling to accept the customs and points of view of others. When people sincerely live out their faith, they learn not to favor one person over another. But that transformation from a state of war and terror toward peace and tolerance takes faith and prayer.

We also found that crisis brings people into a greater awareness of their needs. People look out for their family, and they turn to God for guidance and comfort. Secondly, people turn to the leaders of their nation for calming strength. And, then, they turn to their support groups, their extended family.

The environment is another important matter. In an international survey, we asked general questions and specific questions about global warming, recycling and other environmental issues. We found that the environment comes to the fore when people relate it to health concerns, such as the human detriment that comes from polluting factories or burning forests. And people blame pollution on underdeveloped countries as much as on developed countries.

Because of these surveys, I think that people – if they knew more about John McConnell – would appreciate him as a visionary, as a peacemaker, and as somebody who seeks justice in our world.

George Gallup, Jr.

George Gallup, Jr. of The Gallup Organization, Princeton, New Jersey, is the author of *Surveying the Religious Landscape: Trends in U.S. Beliefs* and other works about American public opinion. He is currently writing a biography about his father, George Gallup, Sr., one of the originators of the opinion poll.

Preface

Dear Heavenly Father, we pray that you will be with us to inspire and direct our thoughts and words.
– John McConnell, prayer at the beginning of interview by author, 25 August 2004

I wrote John McConnell's biography because I believe in his message of "peace, justice and the care of Earth," which he intoned as a triad – in that prerequisite order.

"Peace," John said, "is not merely the absence of war; that's an armistice or a ceasefire. Rather, peace comes from an honest understanding of another person's point of view, whether that person is a part of your family, a neighbor or a perceived enemy. Justice is not an eye for an eye and a tooth for a tooth; that's legalized revenge. Rather, justice is an equal sharing of all the world's natural resources by all the world's people. When we have peace and justice, people will take care of Earth as their right and responsibility. We must have all three," he said, "if we are to continue the human adventure on our nest in the stars with its wonderful web of life."

John's eloquence, wit, charm and devotion to his cause, in spite of adversities, captured my admiration. Also, I enjoy writing about people who have not received adequate acclaim for their contributions, and John fit that parameter. In that regard, he was like the rest of us with our ideas, hopes, desires and wishes; we do the best we can with the skills and situations given us.

I came to appreciate Anna McConnell, John's wife of thirty-eight years, for her love, support and dedication to her husband and his cause as well as her cooperative, yet independent, spirit. I saw, as many of the McConnells' long-time friends pointed out, that Anna was a saint. Therefore, this biography is a tribute to her as well.

At times, I felt humbled by the magnitude of this project. I questioned myself most often as I researched and wrote in the archives of the Swarthmore College Peace Collection, housed within the Swarthmore College library near Philadelphia, Pennsylvania. The Peace Collection was established about 1930 when Jane Addams of Hull House in Chicago, Illinois, donated her papers and books relating to peace and justice to Swarthmore College. Since then, the Peace Collection has gathered and preserved records of organizations and individuals who have worked for nonviolent social change, disarmament and conflict resolution. The Peace Collection contains over 200 major document groups, 3,000 smaller collections, over 12,000 books and pamphlets, thousands of periodicals, and over 1,700 reels of microfilm.

John and Anna added thousands of paper documents, audio tapes and video tapes to this collection in 2002. The John McConnell Document Group (#212), stored in archive boxes, occupies more than thirty-five feet of shelf space. Within the year of November 2004 through December 2005, I invested six months there with my computer and document scanner. It was a daunting task made even more formidable by the fact that, daily, I walked past shelves and shelves of tomes about peace and war and about human relations and international relations. Why was I adding one more volume to this collection? I wondered.

In those moments, I felt John McConnell's frustration – even his admission of failure – when he felt his message had not been heard and his vision not accepted to the extent he hoped it would be. I appreciated John's anger when the forty-third president of his country, George W. Bush of the United States of America, attacked the sovereign nation of Iraq on 20 March 2003 – Earth Day, the vernal equinox, a holy day of peace and brotherhood in the Middle East – and the very day that John strove to make a symbol of international peace and environmental justice. Of what value is Earth Day, a global holiday, if the world's most powerful political leader chooses that day to thumb his nose at peace through understanding? Of what value is one more book among so many?

Then a friend reminded me of the balance of human energy and the need for determination. "John McConnell's biography could be the one book that raises the critical mass of peace consciousness to a higher level and tips the balance of power from discord to harmony, from war to peace, from conflict to understanding," my friend said. As I thought about that statement, I began to understand and appreciate John and Anna McConnell's persistence. Many times in their lives, they could have given up and become, even through non-involvement, part of the problem rather than part of the solution. But they didn't give up. As Anna said, "We need visionaries on Planet Earth to point the way to a better future."

Armed and buoyed by that attitude, John McConnell, a global visionary, has given to the world the *original* Earth Day, the Earth Flag, a Minute for Peace, the Earth Society Foundation, the concept of Earth Rights, the Sea Citizens program, the Earth Trustee Agenda, the Earth Day Proclamation, the original Earth Charter, 77 Theses on the Care of Earth, the Earth Magna Charta, numerous essays, and the newspaper editorial that launched him into the international arena – Star of Hope.

As John McConnell, in his 89th and 90th years, told me his life story, he revealed great recall for poetry and lyrics, some of which he sang. He expounded on philosophy. But he remembered dates not at all and periods of time only in general terms. Many of the newspaper clippings in his files contained circles to lead readers' eyes to key information but lacked the paper's banner and date of publication. Obviously, knowing *when* an event occurred was not as important as knowing the event *did* occur or that he helped make it happen. Chronology, in John's mind, was a detail that got in the way of concepts. Even planning was, enigmatically, a detail that got in the way of intended accomplishment.

As we talked, his train of thought ran freely from one recollection, often unfinished, to another. The topics of conversation looped and spun for hours until warp and weft finally wove back and formed connections, then assumed texture, color and beauty. This book, the biography of John McConnell, is organized in the same fashion. It is chronological, but not strictly so. Rather, each chapter reveals a theme, related through events that propelled John further into his calling.

Through his discourse, John revealed himself as a romantic visionary with a keen interest in current world events, able to see the future as few others can, while often being unable – or unwilling – to view present requirements without the aid of others. John met many of these others – organizers, planners, executives, attorneys, accountants, communicators, scientists, naturalists, volunteers with various skills, and especially Anna – who believed in his cause and helped him clerk his concepts into accomplishment.

In his octogenarian years, the names of some of these people slipped out of the arena of instant recall, a characteristic of aging that John experienced with regret. At the same time, he freely expressed gratitude for Anna, who spent many months organizing his papers. "Maybe Anna will remember," John often said, in response to my questions about time or a name.

John and Anna deserve great credit for having preserved so many documents, most of them at Swarthmore, that provided details and dates to confirm their recollections. Without those papers, this book would be much different, if not impossible to write. And because of them, I was able to quote John extensively, allowing the beauty of his writing to shine forth.

If you gain nothing else from this book, please take with you John's message that "peace, justice and the care of Earth" are inextricably bound. If you gain that knowledge, you will add your brilliance to the beacon – the Star of Hope – that is John McConnell.

Robert M. Weir

Robert M. Weir
Kalamazoo, Michigan
March 20, 2006 (Earth Day)

1

In Pursuit of Justice

(pre-1915 to present)

Flatland vision is caused by closing one eye – the eye of the heart. If we will open it and look at the whole world – with full vision – we will see new depths of love and new promises of peace.
– John McConnell, "Flatland," 1975

John McConnell's mind riveted on his idea. Earth Day. A global holiday. An event for all people of all nations. But when? What moment? What day? What period of time would, by its nature, gain universal appeal? When?

John pondered this question in his home in New York City and as he walked the halls of the United Nations. He considered it during a five-day train trip to visit his mother in Oakland, California. He posed it to his wife Anna who accompanied him, as she often did, especially on trips that involved family. He mulled over this date and that. When?

The answer came to him in a book about the Druids and their magnificent astronomic megaliths at Stonehenge. There, at the moment of sunrise on the first day of spring, the sun – Earth's great celestial star – rises from behind one key stone, outside the sarsen circle, when viewed from one of four primary station stones within the circle. [1]

---

[1] *Observing from the Stonehenge* [online]. National University of Singapore, Department of Mathematics. [cited 12 December 2004]. Available from

Yes. Earth Day would be the first day of spring, the vernal equinox, one of two days each year when the Northern Hemisphere and the Southern Hemisphere share equal sunlight. When the sun sets at the South Pole and rises at the North Pole. When people standing on the Equator do not cast a shadow.

John considered the comparable autumnal equinox, which has the same characteristics, but the Northern Hemisphere has a larger land mass and greater population. Earth Day on the vernal equinox would appeal to more people.

The vernal equinox. The Druids. Ancient Roman calendars began on March 1. [2] Persians observed the new year with Noruz, which means "New Day," on March 21. [3] Europeans in the Middle Ages celebrated the new year on March 25, the Christian feast of Annunciation. [4] The Roman Catholic Church set Easter, the commemoration of Christ's resurrection, as the first Sunday after the first full moon of spring. [5] These thoughts raced through John McConnell's mind as dilemma transformed into determination. From his mother's living room, John shouted, "Anna! Anna! I've got it. I know when Earth Day will be."

Hearing him, his wife moved through the kitchen in his direction. "Oh, John, when?"

"We're going to have Earth Day on the spring equinox."

At that moment on 1 October 1969, the City of Oakland shook beneath their feet. John and Anna looked at each other, and he felt the Lord, speaking through that minor earthquake, was supporting his decision. [6]

Such a message from God was not the first, nor would it be the last, in John McConnell's life.

***

---

www.math.nus.edu.sg/aslaksen/gem-projects/hm/0102-1-stonehenge/others.htm.

[2] *The New Year* [online]. World Book [cited 8 August 2004]. Available from www2.worldbook.com/features/holidays/html/new_year.htm.

[3] Ibid.

[4] Ibid.

[5] Frederick G. Holweck. *Easter* [online]. The Catholic Encyclopedia [cited 4 February 2006]. Available from www.newadvent.org/cathen/05224d.htm.

[6] John McConnell, journal, 1 October 1969. John and Anna McConnell, interview by author, Denver, Colorado, August 2004.

John McConnell's father, John Saunders McConnell – known as J. S. – was born in Seattle, Washington, on 9 January 1892, the youngest of five children of Frances Isabelle (Belle) Saunders and the Rev. Theodore Ward (T. W.) McConnell. After a brief, yet successful, career in real estate, which he began at age 19, J. S. answered the call to Christ. Charismatic, fearless and not officially ordained, he began to hold street meetings where he preached proof through action and quickly became known as "the fiery Irishman" and "the boy evangelist."

John's mother, Hattie MacLaughlin, was born 17 December 1892 in Shannon, Texas. She was a beautiful young woman who played piano for a revival at which J. S. preached. Enamored with the vision of Hattie forever by his side, J. S. overrode his previous declaration that he would never marry. They wed on 15 December 1912, and she followed him from Shannon on a nearly continuous journey, traversing the continent from southern California to British Columbia, to Ontario and New York, and south to Florida. Their choice of direction was consistent with what J. S. believed was his calling to serve the Lord as an independent Pentecostal evangelist. [7]

From the beginning, J. S. found himself captivated by teachings of the Assemblies of God, a new religion of the early 1900s, which had its roots in tent revivals of the late 1800s. This religious movement had experienced a groundswell of support due to a gathering at Bethel Bible College in Topeka, Kansas, on New Year's Day 1901. Inspired, preachers began a massive revival that quickly spread to Missouri, Texas, and other states. [8] Beginning in 1906, [9] this rolling religious thunder reached climactic proportions during a three-year revival meeting at Azusa Street Mission in Los Angeles, attended by people from across the nation and overseas, [10] including T. W. McConnell.

T. W. had come to his evangelical calling from a path of violence. In a testimony he wrote while at Azusa Street in September 1906, T. W. confessed, "About 28 years ago, I went to a meeting to break it up and the

---

[7] John McConnell, interview by author, Denver, Colorado, August 2004.

[8] *Our History* [online]. General Council of the Assemblies of God [cited 24 December 2004]. Available from www.ag.org/top/about/history.cfm.

[9] *Azusa Street Mission* [online]. The Latter Rain [cited 24 December 2004]. Available from latter-rain.com/eccle/azusa.htm.

[10] *Our History* [online]. General Council of the Assemblies of God [cited 24 December 2004]. Available from www.ag.org/top/about/history.cfm.

Lord broke me up. My conversion I could never doubt. I was called to preach and refused, and went on for a number of years trying to get away from the call. … Finally I obeyed the Lord. … The Lord sanctified my soul. … The Lord appeared to me in a dream. … He told me to give up my business, and make my wants known to Him, and not to man. I obeyed. The Lord supplied my every need, and was with me in revival meetings and in healing many that I prayed for."

Of "the old barn-like building on Azusa Street," T. W. called it "the plain old plank beside which they kneeled in the sawdust when God saved, sanctified and baptized them with the Holy Ghost. Those who know God feel His presence as soon as they cross the threshold." Calling that long-running revival "the Nazareth of Los Angeles," T. W. recounted, "The work began among the colored people," then he told of "the first white woman to receive the Pentecost," and of "multitudes who have come." He concluded his message with a theme of ethnic equality that his grandson, John McConnell, would later espouse in his campaign for world peace and justice. "God makes no difference in nationality. Ethiopians, Chinese, Indians, Mexicans and other nationalities worship together," T. W. wrote. [11]

Inspired by his father's lead, J. S. McConnell, then 22, and his bride were among 300 enthusiastic preachers and laymen from twenty states and several foreign countries [12] who attended a revival conference at the Grand Opera House in Hot Springs, Arkansas, eight years later on 2 April 1914. Called together by Eudorus N. Bell, a former Southern Baptist pastor who published *Word and Witness* magazine and was later elected as the first chairman of the Assemblies of God, [13] this group believed, to the person, in baptism of the Holy Spirit and the power to speak in tongues, have visions and perform miracles, including divine healings. [14]

---

[11] T. W. McConnell, "Apostolic Faith," Vol. 1. No. 1, Los Angeles, CA, (September 1906).

[12] *Our History* [online]. General Council of the Assemblies of God [cited 24 December 2004]. Available from www.ag.org/top/about/history.cfm.

[13] *Alone We Cannot Touch the Fringes* [online]. Assemblies of God USA, Enrichment Journal, a journal for Pentecostal ministry [cited 24 December 2004]. Available from www.ag.org/enrichmentjournal/199904/gs_01_bell.cfm.

[14] *April 2, 1914, Pulling Together, Assemblies of God* [online]. Christian History Institute [cited 24 December 2004]. Available from www.gospelcom.net/chi/DAILYF/2001/04/daily-04-02-2001.shtml.

The vehicle in which J. S. and Hattie traveled the country – and their home – was the Gospel Car, a panel truck with hard rubber tires, chain drive, and an air-cooled two-cycle engine that would overheat after traveling only twenty miles. [15] With this vehicle, J. S. found the Lord had provided him "with the means to carry the Gospel away from the railroads." [16] Upon arrival in a town, front-page newspaper articles often announced the presence of "J. S. McConnell, a flamboyant evangelist, the great miracle preacher." Such pronouncements were indicative of an era when newspapers carried more society items and, as John recalled, "paid more attention to churches." J. S. preached in a tent or a tabernacle where he spread the Word of the Lord. With the aid of his booming centurion voice, powerful revivals and inexplicable miracles, J. S. converted many to the Way of the Lord. [17]

Into this roving religious environment, John Saunders McConnell, Jr., the eldest of six Scotch-Irish children, was born in Davis City, Iowa, on 22 March 1915. His parents moved from there when he was only a few months old, and his siblings Grace (1918), Hope (1920), Evan (1923), Ruth (1925), and Paul (1928) were born in various locations along the West Coast. [18] John was proud to proclaim he and his siblings were seventh-generation Americans.

The path for J. S. McConnell, traveling evangelist, and his wife and family was rife with challenges. Their physical path consisted, literally, of dirt or mud, with ruts that often ruined ill-fated rubber tires. Their spiritual path led them among the blessed and the unloving, into great revelations and personal danger. Their financial path was marked by scarcity and thrift, dependent upon the power of the preacher's message and the generosity of those who heard it. Hattie's life was filled with cooking and laundry, washed and hung to dry in whatever location might present itself. And their home was filled with prayer, every morning and every night. "Dad would always pray very enthusiastically, then he had us children pray," John remembered.

One night, prior to a revival in San Diego, J. S. held a service with his family in their home. Such a prayer meeting was the norm, of course, but the

---

[15] John McConnell, interview by author, Denver, Colorado, August 2004.

[16] J. S. McConnell, "Sowing the Seed," letter to Stone Church, Chicago, printed in *The Latter Rain Evangel* November 1911.

[17] John McConnell, interview by author, Denver, Colorado, August 2004.

[18] J. S. McConnell, song book (1939).

prayer intent was unusual. "We've got to really pray tonight," J. S. told his family. "We've got to meet a bill of $115.50." Hattie looked at her husband; that amount was more than double the offerings at recent services. "Let's pray that God will provide that amount at tonight's offering," J. S. intoned. His voice was fervent, as always, for J. S. believed prayers were answered if they were specific, spoken with faith and a belief in God, and for a good purpose.

After the service, young John anxiously watched people leave the church. He watched them drop offerings into the collection box in the vestibule, and he noted that his father, unlike other preachers, did not pass a collection plate. Instead, J. S. believed people would donate from their hearts, giving offerings while leaving the church, if they had been inspired by the Holy Spirit and not due to influence by friends and neighbors. When everyone had left, John ran to the box and, as was his job, counted the offerings. The amount he counted – twice, to be sure – was exactly $115.50. "To the penny!" he exclaimed. [19]

J. S. had faith in divine intervention and divine healing. On 25 August 1911, he penned a letter to the Stone Church in Chicago where he had ministered for several months earlier that year. In the letter, which the church published in its newsletter, *The Latter Rain Evangel*, in November 1911, J. S. wrote of having traveled in the Gospel Car to Pierceville, Kansas, by way of Nebraska, Wyoming and Colorado. Of miracles, he described having "a slight accident to the machinery and in the morning it refused to run. After I had worked with it for about two hours, I came to the conclusion that I could do nothing. We got down on our knees and asked God to make it go. We got up and it started right off and didn't bother us any more." Of another incident, J. S. related, "I was driving up a steep hill: there had been a heavy rain that had washed large holes in the wagon tracks. In spite of my efforts, the wheels sank into these holes and, try as we would, we could not get the car out. Finally, we went to God and asked Him to get it out, and as I got upon the seat and started the machine, it moved right off."

The letter contained a description of "a miracle of healing" that involved his nephew Victor Mountain. "My little nephew, who is traveling with me, fell off the car and bent his arm between the elbow and wrist, almost double.

---

[19] John McConnell, interview by author, Denver, Colorado, August 2004.

When I picked him up I thought it was broken, but it bent the arm in a L shape. The pain was so intense that he could hardly stand it, and the first thing we did was ask God to take away the pain, and it wasn't fifteen minutes until he was sound asleep. Then we asked God to straighten the arm out and heal it, and when we arose from our knees it was almost straight but God did not straighten it perfectly then, for if He had, the people would not have believed the boy was badly hurt, but he went to the meeting that evening, and from that time, the arm has not hurt him, and is now perfectly straight. He wrote a letter with it two days ago, and he is a living witness to the loving kindness and goodness of God." [20]

In light of such miracles, conversions among the faithful became commonplace, but a series of events in Walla Walla, Washington, caused J. S. to pray and preach for conversion of his enemies as well as his own physical salvation.

Entering the town, J. S. prayed, first, for a place to preach. He found the Lord's answer in an empty lot, which he took "in the name of God," in the center of town. Upon locating the owner and obtaining permission, J. S. erected the large tent he carried for revivals. Later, the owner, who believed in the fiery Irishman's ministry, offered to sell the property at a low price of $1,500.

J. S. declined. While offerings were abundant, the cost of the lot was beyond his means. Nevertheless, he was moved to pray that God would provide the money, and he fashioned that prayer into his sermons from which congregants spread the word beyond Walla Walla. Soon thereafter, J. S. received a telephone call from a man in Oregon who told him, "It's the strangest thing, but I had a dream last night that the Lord told me to give you $1,500." To which, J. S. replied, "That's great. You better do it." With that donation, J. S. bought the property and, with the aid of his congregation, built a tabernacle.

One night, a man came forward, asking to speak with J. S. alone. With hesitant voice, the man, who had served time in jail, thanked J. S. for the conversion he experienced that night. Then he confessed to being part of corruption within Walla Walla city government, a corruption that included

---

[20] J. S. McConnell, "Sowing the Seed," letter to Stone Church, Chicago, printed in *The Latter Rain Evangel* November 1911.

the mayor. Angered, J. S. began to preach that Hell's Gate was not the little town, so named, 150 miles to the west on the Columbia River. "Hell's Gate is right here in Walla Walla," J. S. declared, "and the mayor is leading his constituents through it." Adding fire and brimstone, J. S. stormed, "Hell is down there," pointing at the ground, "at the center of the Earth where science tells us there is molten fire and that is where the mayor belongs. He is doing the Devil's work and hindering the work of God."

Young John McConnell, who was only seven or eight at the time, recalled one night, after such a sermon, "a mob of men, maybe thirty" came into the church, knocked his mother to the ground, grabbed J. S. and forcibly took him from the tabernacle. One carried a rope with a hangman's noose.

In the car, bouncing along dark country roads, J. S. preached. He could not – would not – remain quiet, exhorting the men for their crimes and calling upon the Lord for deliverance. Suddenly, one car in the caravan of several hit something in the road and tipped over. Then, a tire on the car in which J. S. was a prisoner blew out, causing the man sitting next to him to bang his head against the car's interior.

Outside the car and restrained by two others, J. S. continued to preach until finally one of his captors said, "I'm sorry, preacher. I don't know what to say, but I think maybe we're doing the wrong thing. If you wait, we'll take you back to town." Feeling his arms free, J. S. said, "No. I'll walk." On the way back, he met people from his congregation who had heard what had happened and had come after him. Undeterred, J. S. continued to preach against the mayor at subsequent services. [21]

Fifty years later, in the early 1970s, John McConnell would experience physical danger under similar circumstances. Walking near New York City's Central Park on his way from the United Nations to a church on the other side of the park, John accepted a ride with two young men in a car adorned with peace sign decals. Once inside the car, John found himself face to face with the dark barrel of a revolver and a demand for his money. John responded, "I'm dumbfounded. You have peace signs on your car, and you don't look to me like robbers."

As he spoke, John reached out and took the barrel of the gun in his hand. As though moved by a higher power, he rotated his hand, and the

[21] John McConnell, interview by author, Denver, Colorado, August 2004.

barrel separated from the chamber, hilt and trigger. Both he and the would-be robbers looked at it, amazed. John said, "You see. The Lord doesn't want you to do a thing like this."

With that, John opened the car door and resumed his way across the park. He heard footsteps behind him. The driver, running, said, "Man, I'm sorry for what I did. But would you please give me back the barrel?" Later, John admitted that, logically, he should not have done so, but, moved again by some higher force, perhaps the memory of what he believed was God's role in his father's similar incident, he did. [22]

Hattie McConnell would say the words and actions of her husband and her son, as well as the outcomes of their situations, were the work of God, a divine manifestation of faith and prayer, a tribute to which she penned in song: "Oh, the faith that works by love / will move mountains when we pray. / Oh, the faith that works by love / will turn darkness into day."

Throughout his life, John McConnell carried that lyric and its melody high in his consciousness. Similarly, in his octogenarian years, he took his father's song book in hand and, even though it contained no musical notations, he easily recalled the melodies and recorded many of its 200 hymns, which J. S. and Hattie had composed or compiled nearly a century earlier. At his mother's 100th birthday party, John and Hattie sang some of her favorite hymns – in harmony. [23]

In doing so, they reveled in memories from those years of travel when music and ministry commingled into extraordinary events. Those reveries included recollections of J. S. being a banjo and trombone player, young John learning trombone, guitar and banjo, and his sister Grace's talented voice. "Dad put us all to work at revival meetings," John remembered. "We had a quartet made up of my father and mother, my sister and myself. Grace's voice was unusually good, and she knew how to put feeling into her singing."

Later on, Grace sang at large churches in New York City where she was featured in her father's evangelism and on national radio programs. She also sang and preached sermons in churches and theaters around the country. "I remember that we rented a theater on the western side of Colorado, my

---

[22] Ibid.

[23] Ibid. John and Hattie McConnell, personal audio tape.

sister and me," John recalled with rising humor that broke into laughter with the punch line. "Grace was preaching a sermon about the devil, and she had given her sermon a very clever title. My name was on the marquee, too – underneath the title – so the way it read, people thought she was going to appear with the devil, John McConnell." [24]

In September 1929, J. S. slowly motored another peculiar vehicle, a successor to the Gospel Car, through Manhattan, New York. This vehicle, which John dubbed simply "our house car," was a panel van, custom made on a Pierce Arrow chassis by its previous owner, a wealthy Los Angeles businessman who took it on expeditions into Mexico. John recalled, "The man liked what Dad was doing, and I believe he let Dad have it for a few hundred dollars." Its interior living quarters included a stove, an ice box and convertible bunk beds for J. S., Hattie and their six children. J. S. would preach from the top of this vehicle when he couldn't find a church or an empty lot for his revival tent. [25]

A low railing, like a luggage rack, circled the top of the bus, and strapped to the railing was a rowboat that the family carried, but seldom floated, to catch fish in lakes and streams beside which they camped. Riding atop the row boat, there in Manhattan, were the Tindley Seven, a Negro gospel group that included, among other singers, a son of Charles Albert Tindley. The elder Tindley was a former slave who taught himself to read and write at age 17 [26] and was renowned as "the father of gospel music." [27] One of Tindley's early compositions, "I'll Overcome Some Day," which he wrote in 1900, [28] later became "We Shall Overcome," an anthem of the American Civil Rights Movement in the 1950s and '60s.

At the time of the McConnell-Tindley entry into New York City, the senior Tindley was pastor of the Bainbridge Street Methodist Episcopal

---

[24] John McConnell, interview by author, Denver, Colorado, August 2004.

[25] Ibid.

[26] *Charles Albert Tindley, 1851-1933* [online]. The Cyber Hymnal [cited 23 November 2004]. Available from www.cyberhymnal.org/bio/t/i/tindley_ca.htm.

[27] *History of Tindley Temple United Methodist Church* [online]. General Board of Global Ministries, The United Methodist Church [cited 23 November 2004]. Available from www.gbgm-umc.org/Tindley/history.htm.

[28] *We Shall Overcome* [online]. Kansas State University, Department of English [cited 23 November 2004]. Available from www.ksu.edu/english/nelp/american.studies.s98/we.shall.overcome.html.

Church in Philadelphia, Pennsylvania, a position he assumed in 1902 after having served as the church's janitor. The church was later named Calvary Methodist Episcopal Church, then East Calvary Methodist Episcopal Church, and finally Tindley Temple United Methodist Church, [29] one of the largest churches in the City of Brotherly Love and Sisterly Affection.

Riding with the Tindley Seven atop the bus was John McConnell. A photograph in a newspaper, *The Home News,* showed him, a boy of 14, wearing coveralls and holding a fishing pole. [30] He had attached a string to the pole with a clothespin at the end. Leaflets clipped in the clothespin promoted prayer meetings on Coney Island, where J. S. started God's Power House, a storefront church on Surf Avenue near Lower New York Bay; and at Cornell Memorial Methodist Church, a large facility on East 76th Street that filled to capacity to hear J. S. preach and the Tindley Seven sing.

John recalled that pedestrians flocked around the bus as it coursed slowly through the city. People on the street removed the leaflets as quickly as John could reattach another. "We stopped traffic," he said. "The police had to come and open a way for us to get out of there." [31] The crowd's curiosity was also instilled by the Rev. Lincoln H. Caswell, the tall, thin, fiery pastor at Cornell, who dressed like and impersonated Abraham Lincoln. [32]

While J. S. McConnell, "the walking Bible," possessed power and zeal to convert others, he encouraged his son to think for himself. "That was one thing I appreciated," John said of his father. "He said to me, 'I want you to listen to what I say. I want you to think about it. But when it comes to your worship and what you believe in, you decide what's best.'"

Following his father's advice, which he described as "very helpful later on," John adopted an independent attitude that became an essential element of his character. Although he was a very religious man, John was never misled by church orthodoxy. And even though J.S. and Hattie were steeped in the Assemblies of God, John saw spiritual beauty in all the world's faiths. He

[29] *History of Tindley Temple United Methodist Church* [online] General Board of Global Ministries, The United Methodist Church [cited 23 November 2004]. Available from www.gbgm-umc.org/Tindley/history.htm.

[30] "Southern Spiritual Singers Tour the Bronx Atop Bus to Advertise Religious Meeting," *The Home News*, 26 September 1929.

[31] John McConnell, interview by author, Denver, Colorado, August 2004.

[32] "Southern Spiritual Singers Tour the Bronx Atop Bus to Advertise Religious Meeting," *The Home News*, 26 September 1929, sec. The Home News.

was particularly fond of St. Francis of Assisi, and the Franciscan religious order would later become strong supporters of John's work for social and environmental justice.

Thus setting himself aside from prescribed canons, John found spiritual guidance in his daily devotion to prayer. "I base my faith on early experience, insight and healing," he said. "I spend at least an hour a day in silent meditation and prayer because I know there must be a creator. I can't imagine a creation without a creator, and this creator must have wisdom far beyond anything we know on Earth. What we've discovered on Earth is that the greatest wisdom is the wisdom of real love, of creative altruism. I shared my father's view that there must be a God who wanted creatures who could love Him. But God realized that, in order for their love to be true, they had to have free will. That meant they could love Him or turn away. But knowing this, God also knew He could win their love, and they would end up being in His image and capable of love." [33]

[33] John McConnell, interview by author, Denver, Colorado, August 2004.

2

Care of Earth
(1939 to present)

Come together where you agree while leaving room for your differences.
– John McConnell, numerous occasions

In addition to the influence of his father and mother, John McConnell found a message of faith on a scrap of paper lying on an isolated dirt path in San Diego when he was a lad of ten. Moved by curiosity, he picked up the paper, unfolded it, and found it contained a poem:

> Lord, give me the strength of the pioneer
> and the faith of his hearty soul.
> Provide me with courage to persevere.
> Make me fight until I reach my goal.
> Let others indulge in a sheltered life
> where they curse when their luck goes bad.
> But fit me for battle with storm and strife.
> Give me brawn like my fathers had.
> I want to be known as a man who wins,
> as a fellow with nerve and pluck,
> who finishes everything he begins,
> and as one who can whip his luck. [34]

[34] Ibid.

Immediately, John associated this message with his paternal grandparents, T. W. and Belle, who had been born in Arkansas in 1855 and 1858, married in Kansas in 1876, and then joined other pioneers who crossed the country, from St. Louis to Oregon, in a covered wagon. [35] "We were born of pioneer stock," J. S. often told his children. "Finding that poem," John said, "further stamped my father's message on me." [36]

In the 1930s, the nation was embroiled in the Great Depression, topsoil from the Great Plains was being blown eastward – all the way to Washington, D.C. – leaving in its wake the Dust Bowl. And Americans, in general, were either standing in, or striving to get out of, bread lines.

In 1939, near the end of that dark period of U.S. history, John McConnell met Albertus Schnucker, a plastics chemist, at a lecture in Los Angeles. "I had heard about a preacher, Joe Jeffers, who was proclaiming the Jews were not the chosen people of God, but it was the English, the Anglo-Saxons," John recalled. "He claimed the Israelites left the Holy Land and settled in the British Isles and the Stone of David, the stone David used when he was made king back in Israel, was found there in England. I went because I was curious."

But, while dismissing Jeffers' presentation as "filled with all kinds of mysteries and contradictions," the event did bring him into contact with Schnucker. [37] Soon after they met, Schnucker changed his name to Albert Nobell, employing an extra "l" at the end, as John stated, out of respect for Alfred Bernhard Nobel, the Swedish engineer, manufacturer and philanthropist who, in 1901, had established the Nobel Prize for outstanding achievement in physics, chemistry, medicine or physiology, literature, and the promotion of peace. Albert Nobell's daughter Marleen said her father dreamed of winning the Nobel Prize for chemistry.

Having brought his knowledge as well as his young wife Margaret and their newborn child Dorothy from New Jersey, Nobell founded one of the first plastics facilities on the west coast. John McConnell became vice-president and business manager for Nobell Resins Company, located in Azusa, California, near Los Angeles. There, Nobell worked with phenolic resins and

---

[35] J. S. McConnell, song book (1939).

[36] John McConnell, interview by author, Denver, Colorado, August 2004.

[37] Ibid.

dyes to create plastics in color, rather than black, which is characteristic of the synthetic material. Later in his career, Nobell would apply his knowledge to impregnating pine slabs with dyes to simulate the color of precious redwood, which, at that time, was being harvested for pencils. [38]

Nobell developed a thin thermosetting plastic, which he dyed the color of human skin, that attracted interest in Hollywood. "Nobell came up with a plastic you could spray on a person's face to get a mask," John McConnell recalled. "So when they [movie producers] wanted a mask of a movie star, they would take our plastic, spray it on a person's face to get their features. That was state of the art back in those days." [39]

Technological innovations were also occurring within other branches of industry, which furthered a shift from an agrarian to an urban-centered manufacturing society. Prior to the first decades of John's life, the nation had employed ecologically beneficial practices that featured readily available agricultural resources. In the early 1900s, George Washington Carver initiated the use of peanuts, soybeans, pecans and sweet potatoes for hundreds of food and mechanical applications. [40] In the 1890s, Rudolf Diesel invented the diesel engine, which ran on peanut oil and vegetable oil. [41] In the mid-1800s, American pioneers employed the process of transesterification to make soap from vegetable oil. [42] And people throughout world history, including North American colonialists who legally mandated its growth, valued hemp as being necessary for sustainability. [43]

Adding to the plant's multiplicity, auto pioneer Henry Ford made cars with body panels composed primarily of undentable hemp fiber. [44] In addition, Ford built a plant to convert hemp seed into an ethanol biomass that produced high-grade diesel fuel, engine oil and machine lubricant, a

---

[38] Marleen Nobell, telephone interview by author, 3 January 2005.

[39] John McConnell, interview by author, Denver, Colorado, August 2004.

[40] Mary Bellis. *George Washington Carver* [online]. The New York Times Company [cited 26 December 2004] Available from inventors.about.com/library/weekly/aa041897.htm.

[41] *Straight Vegetable Oil* [online]. BE Bioenergy [cited 7 November 2005]. Available from www.bebioenergy.com/straight_vegetable_oil.htm.

[42] *A History of Biodiesel/Biofuels* [online]. Yokaya Biofuels [cited 7 November 2005]. Available from www.ybiofuels.org/bio_fuels/history_biofuels.html.

[43] Ibid.

[44] *Oil, Plastics, and Car Parts* [online]. biomassive.org [cited 7 November 2005]. Available from biomassive.org/g2012/hemp/paper.html.

product he first used in his Model Ts in 1908 and advocated throughout the 1930s. [45] Hemp fiber was also a viable source of pulp for paper, so much so that, in 1938, *Popular Mechanics* magazine cited government estimates that "10,000 acres devoted to hemp will produce as much paper as 40,000 acres of average pulp land." [46] These figures were made possible, in part, by George Schlichten's invention of the hemp decorticator, which he patented in 1919, for mechanically stripping hemp fiber in much the same manner that Eli Whitney's cotton gin mechanically removed cotton fiber from the cotton plant. [47]

Even though *Mechanical Engineering* magazine, in February 1938, touted hemp as "the most profitable and desirable crop that can be grown," [48] the hemp industry met its demise when engine manufacturers modified Diesel's engine so it ran only on residual, low-grade fossil fuel offered at low prices by the petroleum industry. The campaign against hemp was abetted by wood pulp and newspaper magnate William Randolph Hearst and major investors in the oil industry, such as the DuPonts, the Rockefellers and U.S. secretary of the treasury Andrew Mellon. Hearst's newspapers ran articles that called hemp by its Mexican-Spanish name, marihuana, thus obscuring the distinction between high-fiber varieties with industrial applications and related varieties with psychoactive components used for medicinal and recreational purposes. [49] This campaign, viewed by some historians as "yellow journalism," [50] created a popular fear, rooted in racism, that led to the Marihuana Tax Act of 1937. [51]

The Act exacted a stiff, if not "cruel and unusual," punishment of up to five years imprisonment and a $2,000 fine, or both, to anyone, including

---

[45] *A History of Biodiesel/Biofuels* [online]. Yokaya Biofuels [cited 7 November 2005]. Available from www.ybiofuels.org/bio_fuels/history_biofuels.html.

[46] *Paper Production* [online]. biomassive.org [cited 7 November 2005]. Available from biomassive.org/g2012/hemp/paper.html.

[47] *The Billion Dollar Crop* [online]. biomassive.org [cited 7 November 2005]. Available from biomassive.org/g2012/hemp/billiondollar.html.

[48] Ibid.

[49] *A History of Biodiesel/Biofuels* [online]. Yokaya Biofuels [cited 7 November 2005]. Available from www.ybiofuels.org/bio_fuels/history_biofuels.html.

[50] *Rudolf Diesel: 1858-1913* [online]. Hempcar Transamerica [cited 7 November 2005]. Available from www.hempcar.org/diesel.shtml.

[51] *A History of Biodiesel/Biofuels* [online]. Yokaya Biofuels [cited 7 November 2005]. Available from www.ybiofuels.org/bio_fuels/history_biofuels.html.

doctors and veterinarians, who failed to pay a $1.00, or in some cases $3.00, per year licensing fee to plant, cultivate, harvest, compound, buy, sell, import, transfer, possess, prescribe or give away marihuana. [52] The legislation, in effect, killed one of the country's principle annual cash crops.

John McConnell, who witnessed so much of the country's beauty and bounty as a young man, was keenly aware of environmental ravages caused by great economic and environmental calamities of the 1930s, the Great Depression and the Dust Bowl. Searching for different ways to make plastic, he and Nobell turned their attention to another food source – walnuts. [53]

The Franciscan Fathers, for whom John was developing a strong spiritual interest, had brought the English walnut from Spain to California in the early 1800s. [54] By the mid-1930s, the volume of product grown in California was a staggering 50 million pounds, much of which was shelled and exported to foreign markets. [55] In addition, the California crop was experiencing a dramatic horticultural venue shift – from southern California northward to the Central Valley, [56] sixty miles east of San Francisco, which offered a milder climate, deep fertile soils, [57] improved irrigation, better pest control methods and, the big draw, even higher yields. [58]

John and Nobell noted nut meat was not the only product being harvested from walnuts. Its wood was being used for airplane propellers [59] on the most successful aircraft of the era: Beech of the 1930s, WACOs of the 1920s and '30s, and Curtiss and Dayton Wright airplanes before that. [60] Husks were being used for an insecticide in the 1930s, and had been

---

52 *The Marihuana Tax Act of 1937*, 75th Cong., 1937, Public 238.

53 John McConnell, interview by author, Denver, Colorado, August 2004.

54 *Walnuts in California* [online]. California Walnut Designs [cited 28 November 2004]. Available from www.ca-walnutdesigns.com/history.htm.

55 *Walnut Growers Market 50 Million Pounds* [online]. U.S. Department of Agriculture [cited 28 November 2004]. Available from www.rurdev.usda.gov/rbs/pub/jan99/1930s.html.

56 Agriculture Online [cited 28 November 2004]. Available from www.agriculture.com/100years/feb_slideshow/images/February_Sacks.pdf.

57 Ibid.

58 *Walnuts in California* [online]. California Walnut Designs [cited 28 November 2004]. Available from www.ca-walnutdesigns.com/history.htm.

59 Jeff Ball. 2002. *The prized Black Walnut* [online]. American Forests [cited 29 November 2004]. Available from www.findarticles.com/p/articles/mi_m1016/is_2_108/ai_89023211.

60 *Historical Timeline* [online]. Hartzell Propeller Inc., [cited 29 November 2004].

converted into high-quality charcoal for gas mask filters during World War I. [61]

Inspired, John asked his partner, "Can we make plastic from walnut shells?" Through experimentation, they discovered they could. Unfortunately, marketing the product proved to be a greater challenge and the walnut-derived plastic did not meet with commercial success. [62]

The two entrepreneurs shared a common religious and philosophical belief, rooted in the *Bible*. They questioned and actively sought answers, an explorative endeavor that would help and haunt John throughout his life. [63]

John owned several copies of a 64-page tract, yellowed with age that his father wrote in the early 1940s after reading the work of Ivan Panin on Bible numerics. In *What's It All About?*, J. S. asked: "DO YOU KNOW ... Who you are – Why you are here – Where you are going?" As he had done with his children, J. S. asked readers: "DO YOU THINK FOR YOURSELF?" And he admonished, "Repent now. He is coming again as King of Kings to Judge the world." [64]

"I remember Dad was preaching at a theatre in Los Angeles when we got the news of [the Japanese attack on] Pearl Harbor," John said. "I was at the back of the theatre and heard the cry of 'Extra.' I went out and got a paper and took it up to my father in the middle of his sermon. He had been preaching that the United States was about to receive a terrible blow because of its sins. He read the headlines to the audience and said, 'What I was saying has begun to happen.'" *What's It All About?* was in print at that time. [65]

Displaying similar fervor, Albert Nobell founded the Nobell Research Foundation, an organization through which he devoted energy to the study of Bible numerics. Nobell penned an "Endorsement," comparable to a foreword in modern literature, for a book called *Astounding New Discoveries*, copyrighted by lecturer and world traveler Karl Sabiers in 1948. In his endorsement, Nobell wrote, "The strange phenomenon disclosed in the following pages deserves the time and consideration of laymen, theologians,

---

Available from www.hartzellprop.com/history/history_timeline.htm.

[61] Jeff Ball. 2002. *The prized Black Walnut* [online]. American Forests [cited 29 November 2004]. Available from www.findarticles.com/p/articles/mi_m1016/is_2_108/ai_89023211.

[62] John McConnell, interview by author, Denver, Colorado, August 2004.

[63] Ibid.

[64] J. S. McConnell. *What's It All About?* (1940s).

[65] John McConnell, interview by author, Denver, Colorado, August 2004.

and scientists. Its universal importance merits wide attention." [66] Sabiers claimed his work was a "scientific demonstration of the divine inspiration of the *Bible* ... the indisputable proof you've been wanting." [67]

The effect of such compelling language – from his father, from his business partner, and from the books he read – profoundly influenced John McConnell, and he often quoted humanitarian and medical doctor Albert Schweitzer, whom he described as "a Christian who kept exploring questions of faith." [68]

John found courage, even audacity, in Schweitzer's words: "Once man begins to think about the mystery of his life and the links connecting him with the life that fills the world, he cannot but accept, for his own life and all other life that surrounds him, the principle of Reverence for Life. He will act according to this principle of the ethical affirmation of life in everything he does. His life will become in every respect more difficult than if he lived for himself, but at the same time it will be richer, more beautiful, and happier. It will become, instead of mere living, a genuine experience of life." [69]

As though assuming prophesy in Schweitzer's words, John McConnell's life was one of genuine experiences fraught with financial difficulty and spiritual wealth. As he aged into his 80s, John expressed his frustration at understanding so little. "I have been on a long quest to find what life is all about, and the more I learn, the greater the mystery," he said.

Likewise, John developed an enigmatic view of his beliefs. Like Schweitzer, he envisioned his way of thinking was right for all. "We would have a better future ... we could turn the world right side up ... if we could get attention and connect people who have a similar vision," he often stated. At the same time, he honored religious and philosophical disagreement, often stating, "People should come together where they agree while leaving room for their differences." [70]

---

[66] Albert Nobell, foreword in *Astounding New Discoveries* by Karl Sabiers (Los Angeles, CA, USA: Christian Books of the World, 1948). [cited 30 November 2004]. Available online at home.mindspring.com/~apostle2/karl.htm.

[67] Karl Sabiers, *Astounding New Discoveries* (Los Angeles, CA, USA: Christian Books of the World, 1948). [cited 30 November 2004]. Available online at christianbeliefs.org/articles/biblenumerics.html.

[68] John McConnell, interview by author, Denver, Colorado, August 2004.

[69] Albert Schweitzer, *Out of My Life and Thought*, Epilogue. [cited 8 December 2004]. Available online at www1.chapman.edu/schweitzer/sch.reading3.html.

[70] John McConnell, interview by author, Denver, Colorado, August 2004.

Thus fueled by his faith, his philosophical link with the great thinkers of his time, and his personal and professional bond with Albert Nobell, John McConnell firmly believed in the environmental value of Nobell's products. He was, too often, dismayed at the businesses' lack of operating capital.

Early in their professional acquaintance, John was staying at Nobell's home in Tujunga, California, a Los Angeles suburb, and saw the scientist was converting his garage into a chemical research laboratory. John said, "My gosh, you've got to have something better than this." At John's encouragement, the two men prayed for financial assistance. Upon concluding the prayer, John read in a newspaper article that George Pepperdine, a Christian businessman who started the Western Auto Supply Company and, in 1937, founded Pepperdine College in Los Angeles, had formed a foundation and was giving away money.

That day, a Sunday, John looked up Pepperdine's business address, which was on Wilshire Boulevard. Reminding himself it was hard to see powerful, wealthy people, he drove there anyway. Looking through the front window, he saw someone inside, so he tapped on the pane. A man opened the door, and John said, "I just wonder if I could contact George Pepperdine." The man replied, "I'm George Pepperdine."

The two men talked and found they shared a strong connection on religion and peace. "He was a member of the Church of Christ," John recalled, "and he sympathized with my pacifism. He funded our laboratory. Initially, I believe it was $5,000 that he invested." With additional funding, Pepperdine became what John referred to as "a silent partner who demonstrated his support by his generous contributions." [71]

Unfortunately, Pepperdine's financial support for the plastics lab evaporated a decade later, in the early 1950s, and Nobell, who was fiscally overextended, declared bankruptcy. Forfeiting his manufacturing plant as well as residences in San Dimos, California, and the Mojave Desert, Nobell moved his wife and eight children to primitive ranchland in central California where they lived in tents for more than a year. Fortunately, with research knowledge he carried in his head, Nobell reestablished himself as a chemical consultant for large corporations. [72]

---

[71] Ibid.

[72] Marleen Nobell, telephone interview by author, 3 January 2005.

By that time, John McConnell had experienced his own misfortunes due to World War II, the Korean War and the military draft. But during George Pepperdine's early involvement with Nobell, the philanthropist took an interest in John's education, which had been both varied and minimal, at least by formal standards. John had attended schools in Florida, British Columbia, New York, California and other places during his elementary years. His high school education had consisted of only one year, in Oakland, California, in 1931, during which he played trombone in the school band and worked at a library.

In spite of John's sundry preparatory education, he attended Pepperdine College for one semester. He credits his acceptance to both George Pepperdine and Hugh Tiner, who was the college's second president at the time of John's enrollment. Tiner had been supervisor of Los Angeles County Schools, one of the youngest men in the nation to hold such a position. In addition, he ministered at the Sichel Street Church of Christ in Los Angeles and originated a Sunday morning radio program, "Take Time to Be Holy." His enthusiastic ministry motivated Pepperdine to hire him as the college's founding dean. As president, beginning just two years later in 1939, Tiner awarded scholarships freely. He took John into his home as a temporary resident and enjoyed his competition at tennis.

John was an avid reader who consumed classic literature and poetry plus history, science and philosophy. A Boy Scout, he read all the books by American naturalist Earnest Thompson Seton, who was instrumental in founding the Boy Scouts and wrote the *Boy Scout Handbook*.[73]

In 1929, *The Indianapolis (Indiana) News* ran a photograph of 14-year-old John pulling his youngest brother Paul, then a baby, in a wooden wagon the older sibling had made. The photograph was taken at the Indianapolis Central Library where, according to a detailed caption, "John reads while the baby sleeps." The caption added that J. S. was preaching at the Gospel Tabernacle, behind which the McConnell family lived in their "specially-fitted automobile," and John, "traveling as he does all the time, has to depend on the libraries to help him keep up with his school work."[74]

Throughout his life, John gained much knowledge through personal

[73] John McConnell, interview by author, Denver, Colorado, August 2004.

[74] "All Around Town," *The Indianapolis News*, 1929.

contact with scientists, lecturers, educators and philosophers. In later years, John's bookshelf was crowded with nonfiction volumes, many of them signed by authors such as Robert Muller, Norman Cousins, Herbert W. Armstrong, C. V. Narasimhan, Glenn Clark, Helen Smith Shoemaker, Solomon Huber, Montague Ullman, Garry Davis, the Rt. Rev. Bishop James A. Pike, and former Alaska governor Walker J. Hickel. [75]

John used knowledge from various sources, as well as his drive and imagination, to marry science and technology with environmental preservation. In the early 1980s, for example, he interacted with Ridgway Banks who developed and constructed an electric engine that employed, as its power source, Nitinol, an alloy of nickel and titanium that produced energy under the influence of alternating hot and cold water, and not petroleum fuel.

Described as a "shape-memory" metal, Nitinol was first discovered by accident at the United States Naval Ordnance Laboratory in 1958. Nitinol was regarded as "a scientific curiosity" [76] until 1973 when Banks discovered Nitinol's "magical properties." Banks was a backyard inventor and amateur musician who worked as a technician at the Lawrence Berkeley Laboratory in Berkeley, California. Philosophically comparing the distinct, yet harmonious, compatibilities between malleable nickel and durable titanium with the converging melodies of a fugue, Banks saw Nitinol as a way to make a practical steam engine that would run on solar power, so he designed and built the first working model of his Nitinol Heat Engine. [77]

Nitinol was later tested by McDonnell Douglas Research and Development Center in Huntington Beach, California, as well as by private and government researchers working in conjunction with the U.S. Department of Defense, the U.S. Department of Energy, the U.S. Navy, the National Aeronautic and Space Administration (NASA), The National Science Foundation, General Motors Corporation, and The Goodyear Tire & Rubber Company. [78] The alloy became the subject of articles in science magazines and the *Whole Earth Catalog*. It was the topic of a two-day Nitinol Heat Engine Conference in Silver Spring, Maryland, sponsored by the U.S.

[75] John McConnell, interview by author, Denver, Colorado, August 2004.
[76] Kevin Sanders, *Getting Ready for Nitinol.*
[77] Ridgway Banks, telephone interview by author, 24 January 2005.
[78] Kevin Sanders, *Getting Ready for Nitinol.*

Naval Surface Weapons Center and the U.S. Department of Energy, in late September 1978. [79]

Nitinol promotional literature explained, "If you bend the wire while it is cold (in ice water), it will remain bent until it is heated (in hot water), and then it will forcibly resume its original straight shape. ... The property of shape memory is due to a solid-state phase change ... a switch from one crystal structure to another as the temperature increases or decreases." [80] A lengthy, detailed report by Kevin Sanders, who was science editor for the fledgling Cable Network News (CNN) and who would later become the master of ceremonies at United Nations Earth Day celebrations, forecast, "There is talk of a Nitinol economy." [81]

Impressed, John McConnell brought Nitinol engines to the attention of the United Nations Development Programme (UNDP) in 1981, and on 13 November of that year, the UNDP responded with enthusiasm its desire "... to explore its potential for service to the needs of developing countries." [82] Five weeks later, on 21 December, the Earth Society Foundation, which John had founded in 1976, submitted to the UNDP a proposal to create a Nitinol Information Center that would "acquire, develop, and disseminate information about Nitinol and Nitinol engines." [83]

The technology didn't advance as Sanders had predicted, however. "Too small" was the key message from the Navy's 1978 conference on Nitinol, at which, as Sanders' report stated, "Several ingenious and promising prototype devices were displayed. All were relatively low-output machines, the maximum being in the tens of watts range." But Sanders hinted there might have been a hidden, larger side of the story when he quoted Nitinol investigators who stated, "Operating engines of larger power output could be considered proprietary because of the tremendous commercial potential of Nitinol engines. Design and performance information exchange under

---

79 David M. Goldstein and Leo J. McNamara, ed. *Proceedings of the NITINOL Heat Engine Conference*, 26-27 September 1978, Silver Spring, Maryland.

80 *Nitinol* literature.

81 Kevin Sanders, *Getting Ready for Nitinol.*

82 Bradford Morse, United Nations Development Programme, letter to John McConnell, 13 November 1981.

83 John McConnell, Earth Society Foundation, "Proposal for Nitinol Information Center," 21 December 1981.

these circumstances understandably would be restricted." [84]

Such profit-induced restriction of beneficial information appalled John McConnell who adhered to a philosophy – consistent with his definition of justice – that ideas and inventions, even natural resources, should be shared freely. "The way our legal structures are," he said, "it's the person who has the most money and the best attorney who has control of what's written in copyright laws. I think that's terrible. Some of the best philosophers I've met said they like to be credited for what they said, but they don't claim it as their property. It's available to anybody, free. Anybody can have it. Anybody can use it. Anybody can print it." [85]

These words carried the tone of a missionary admonishing a greedy society that didn't comprehend how a life of conviction toward mutually beneficial goals would lead to rewards far greater than transitory financial gains. But John did follow the path of sharing. He, like so many agricultural and mechanical tinkerers in the early 1900s, generally chose to eschew patent and copyright claims that could have brought wealth. Rather, he aligned with the philosophy found in the epitaph on the grave of George Washington Carver, who saw his discoveries as gifts from God, "He could have added fortune to fame, but caring for neither, he found happiness and honor in being helpful to the world." [86]

---

[84] Kevin Sanders, *Getting Ready for Nitinol.*

[85] John McConnell, interview by author, Denver, Colorado, August 2004.

[86] Mary Bellis. *George Washington Carver* [online]. The New York Times Company [cited 26 December 2004] Available from inventors.about.com/library/weekly/aa041897.htm.

3

Passion for Peace

(1939 to present)

A preacher should not have to take up arms and fight. His praying and preaching will do more good than his fighting.
– John McConnell, "On Pacifism," 25 May 1967

On 1 September 1939, the same year John McConnell met Albert Nobell, Germany attacked Poland. England and France retaliated with a declaration of war against Germany two days later. And people in the United States watched as President Franklin Delano Roosevelt declared neutrality on 5 September. [87]

These events perplexed John McConnell as did conflict that had emerged within his family. J. S. and Hattie had recently separated when she chose a permanent home in Oakland, California, over further travels with her husband. But J. S. continued to evangelize, preaching from pulpits and on streets throughout the country, "Christians cannot kill, even in a war."

"My father was preaching in Washington, D.C. during World War II," John recalled, "and he used to carry all of his notes and his *Bible* in a leather case. Walking near the White House, guards stopped him and wanted to

[87] Steve Schoenherr. *World War II Timeline 1917-45: Poland 1939* [online]. Steve Schoenherr [cited 4 December 2004]. Available from history.acusd.edu/gen/WW2Timeline/Prelude11.html.

know what he had, and he said, 'Oh, that's my sword. The Sword of the Spirit. The Word of God.' My father believed, as it says in the *Bible*, the power of love is greater than the power of swords."

At thc samc time, Hattie, in California, chose to help the war effort. She took a civilian job at U.S. Naval Station Treasure Island, [88] a man-made island in San Francisco Bay, originally intended for a city park and civilian airport that became a military base on 1 April 1941. While the naval station's main purpose was to receive, train and dispatch service personnel, [89] Hattie's responsibility was to receive and dispatch secret strategic military messages. Discord developed between siblings also, as John's younger brother Evan joined the U.S. Air Force and, later, became a pilot for General Dwight David Eisenhower.

"I was totally against the war," John said. "I'm a peacemaker, and part of the reason was my father, who was, without question, the greatest influence in my life." But affected by his mother, John "wanted to be a loyal American," and he "felt guilty" because, by being a pacifist, he wasn't risking his life. "I really prayed about this," John said. Eventually, he decided to enter the Merchant Marine, seeing that as a way to help the country. He hoped – even intended – to "only go on merchant vessels that didn't carry military equipment." [90]

When John entered the Merchant Marine in the summer of 1942, the U.S. was embroiled in fighting in both Europe and the Pacific Ocean, a direct response to Japan's attack on Pearl Harbor seven months earlier. He shipped out of Los Angeles, California, aboard *Watertown* on 10 July 1942 and served on that vessel until 20 August 1942. He sailed aboard *Mangore*, a 4,000-ton vessel owned by Ore Steamship Corporation, from 2 September 1942 until 16 October 1942 and *Alcoa Banner*, a Hog Islander, from 20 April 1943 until his honorable discharge in New York City on 4 August 1943. [91] John was assigned as a wiper, an entry-level position in which he was responsible for maintaining cleanliness of engineering spaces below decks,

---

88 John McConnell, interview by author, Denver, Colorado, August 2004.

89 *Naval Air Station, Treasure Island* [online]. GlobalSecurity.org [cited 27 November 2004]. Available from www.globalsecurity.org/military/facility/treasure-island.htm.

90 John McConnell, interview by author, Denver, Colorado, August 2004.

91 *Certificate of Release or Discharge from Active Duty*, U.S. Coast Guard, Merchant Marine, John Saunders McConnell, Jr., 9 May 1989.

which he described as "a hot, energetic place to work."

Having been ordained a minister by his father, John held prayer services aboard the vessels. "There was one young man I prayed with who was terrified of what might happen. He wouldn't sleep below; he slept by the life rafts," John said. "Well, I discovered when I talked with him that he had been with his brother on a previous voyage and his brother had been shot when he was up in the rigging and his body had come down and crashed on the deck by his side." John also preached ashore in Rio de Janeiro, Brazil. "I attended a church there and spoke to the minister. He was interested in me, and had me speak. I might have had a translator," John recalled.

In spite of John's intentions to avoid conflict, battle found him. [92] In correspondence that accompanied John's Certificate of Service, which was not awarded to him or other Merchant Marine seamen until 1989, the U.S. Department of Transportation's Maritime Administration noted, "During World War II alone ... enemy attacks sank more than 700 U.S. flag merchant ships and claimed the lives of more than 6,000 civilian seafarers. ... U.S. merchant seamen died as a result of enemy attacks at a rate that proportionately exceeded all branches of our armed services, with the single exception of the United States Marine Corps." [93] Another letter, from the United States Coast Guard, posted 9 May 1989, quoted General Douglas MacArthur, "I hold no branch in higher esteem than the Merchant Marine Services." [94]

John recalled, "On one occasion, our convoy was attacked. The ship ahead of us was hit and went out of control and swung around and hit our bow. Fortunately, it was above the waterline so we didn't go down." Laughing amidst his recollection, John continued, "I had an impulse to jump onto the other ship. I could hear men hollering and I thought I could help them, but it occurred to me, 'If I make that leap, my life will be entirely different.' So I decided not to jump. Later, that ship was bombed and sank. The choices we make." [95]

As a result of his work belowdecks and attacks upon his convoys, John

---

[92] John McConnell, interview by author, Denver, Colorado, August 2004.

[93] Capt. Warren G. LeBack, Maritime Administrator, U.S. Department of Transportation, form letter to John McConnell, November 1989.

[94] Capt. F. J. Grady, U.S. Coast Guard, form letter to John McConnell, 9 May 1989.

[95] John McConnell, interview by author, Denver, Colorado, August 2004.

suffered a hearing loss and, what he called, "tinning in the ears" that plagued him greatly in later years. In his Veterans Application for Compensation or Pension, submitted on 2 August 1994, John wrote, "I am applying for whatever benefits I am entitled to receive ... as I am 79 years old and do not receive Social Security or have an income." [96] In reply, on 25 August 1994, the U.S. Department of Veterans Affairs denied his request for "nonservice-connected disability pension" because "your family income is $24,200.00 per year from your spouse earnings." [97] Anna's income records confirmed that amount of income, which was the most she ever earned, doing so only at the end of her professional career. [98]

Thinking his time aboard oceangoing merchant ships during World War II had fulfilled his wartime obligations, John returned to California where he met Mary Lou Clark in a Los Angeles restaurant. Their brief romance began with swim dates in Long Beach and evolved quickly into marriage in 1944. Mary Lou was 19, and John, ten years her senior, described her as "a beautiful girl, very talented, with a wonderful voice and wholly in support of my thinking."

At the same time, Uncle Sam discovered John was no longer in the Merchant Marine and drafted him into the U.S. Army. "I refused as a conscientious objector and because I was a minister. I held services in the Merchant Marine and in California churches while working with Albert Nobell," John said. But even if the draft board were willing to listen to his ministerial claim, John acknowledged they apparently didn't like his direct evangelistic admonishment. "I said to them, 'There are Christian missionaries in Japan, and the Japanese government is calling for more Christian missionaries. If we would do the things that promote peace, we wouldn't have wars.' That was a terrible mistake. Doing the right thing is not always the best thing. They got angry, stopped the deferment and drafted me."

In basic training in Texas, John found himself with an M1 carbine in his hands at the base rifle range. "I had to lie on the ground and shoot at an image of a person and try to drill him in the heart. And when I looked at it, I suddenly saw I was killing Jesus. And in the *Bible*, Jesus said, 'Inasmuch as ye

[96] John McConnell, U.S. Department of Veterans Affairs and *Veterans Application for Compensation or Pension* form, 2 August 1994.

[97] U.S. Department of Veterans Affairs, letter to John McConnell, 25 August 1994.

[98] Anna McConnell, manuscript review with author, Denver, Colorado, October 2005.

have done it unto one of these, the least of my brethren, ye did it unto me.' [99] I absolutely refused to go on." John laid his weapon on the ground, got up and walked off the rifle range.

For that, he was put into a stockade. "Most of the people there had been late coming back from leave," John said of his fellow prisoners. "Every spare moment was spent in having us march to keep us from causing trouble. We marched back and forth hundreds of times."

On one occasion, late in the evening, the men were told to take a break. John entered a barracks in the stockade, went to a second-floor window and began to shout at the guards, "The things you are making these men do are wrong! These men need to get home, need to be released, need to visit their families instead of going through this torture you're putting them through."

John's sermon was cut short. "Of course, I was causing a little unrest, you know," John said in retrospect with a mischievous twinkle in his eye. "The guard took me away and put me in solitary confinement in what they called "The Black Box." I had an iron bed and absolutely nothing else, but bare ground and the bed and the door. One of the guards was sympathetic and brought me a New Testament."

During incarceration, John refused to eat and managed to live on water, prayer and song. "The thing that sustained me lying there through the night, in the darkness, in this black hole was the words from a hymn written by a woman who had also been in prison, 'Blessed, beloved of my soul. I am here alone with thee. And my prison is a haven since thou sharest it with me.'" [100]

After being taken from "The Black Box," during which time his brown hair turned prematurely white, [101] John was given an office assignment during which he overheard a sergeant say, "McConnell's file [seeking military discharge] is going under the pile and won't come up again until after the war." Soon thereafter, John found a means to exit the compound and be absent without leave. "Mary Lou and I had a car, and the first thing I did was change out of my uniform so I wouldn't be picked up," John remembered. "We drove without any problem from Texas to Florida, and there I bought a

---

[99] *Bible*, Matthew 25:45.

[100] John McConnell, interview by author, Denver, Colorado, August 2004.

[101] Anna McConnell, manuscript review with author, Denver, Colorado, October 2005.

sailboat, a 38-foot yawl that I christened *The Christian*. Mary Lou's mother gave us the money. She knew I was going to have more trouble because of my pacifist views."

Embarking early in the morning in late January 1945, John and Mary Lou snuck out of Tampa Harbor and set sail southward. Near Cuba, they encountered pirates who were, fortunately, in a smaller sailboat that could not overtake John and Mary Lou's faster craft. The couple turned west toward Central America. [102] John related their voyage in a missionary letter to a church in the U.S., which, in its April 1945 newsletter, *Fellowship News*, published, "We experienced, in succession, a calm, engine trouble, and then a storm that broke our boom, ripped some of our sail and blew us several days we knew not where." [103]

With the boat's instrumentation damaged from the storm, John and Mary Lou relied on *The United States Coast Pilot*, a nautical book published by the National Oceanographic and Aeronautic Administration (NOAA) that provided channel descriptions, anchorages, tides and water levels. Relying upon a copy of *The Raft Book*, published by Harold Gatty, which was often put in lifeboats aboard commercial vessels, the couple gained their bearing from the stars.

With repaired sails and lashing on the spliced boom, they sailed slowly, and after two weeks, arrived at Roatan, the largest of three major and several minor islands, known collectively as the Bay Islands, off the coast of British Honduras. "I went into the first little harbor, a beautiful place, but along the shore there was only one house, and it was a ruin of an old fort from the time of the Spaniards," John remembered.

They sailed to another good anchorage at Oak Ridge, a relatively long inlet on Roatan's southern side. Speaking of the islanders, John recalled, "They weren't accustomed in war time to having many visitors, so they were delighted to see us and treated us royally." [104] His written account at the time elaborated, "The people of the village (about 1500 pop.) have received us with open arms. There has been a steady stream of children paddling out to our boat with gifts from the neighboring homes. In the past few days, we

---

102 John McConnell, interview by author, Denver, Colorado, August 2004.

103 John McConnell, letter to *Fellowship News*, April 1945.

104 John McConnell, interview by author, Denver, Colorado, August 2004.

have received over ten different kinds of cake, as well as eggs, bread, sweet potatoes, plantains, three kinds of bananas, green and ripe cocoanuts – of which we are both very fond – grapefruit, limes, candy, etc." [105]

Of John and Mary Lou's ministry on the island, John wrote to the *Fellowship News* congregation that he was introduced as "Reverend Miracle." He explained, "God must have sent us to this isolated community, as we found they had a nice church and a fair Sunday School, but no minister. We are preaching at the little church and I believe a revival is on the way." [106] Since the Bay Islands were once British territory, John said, "They spoke Old English. Instead of 'he asked me,' they would say 'he oxed me.'" [107] And he journaled, "By Divine Providence, we were able to get busy for the Lord as soon as we arrived." [108]

With the use of a dinghy, John and Mary Lou rowed into inland channels to where more people lived. "We had great spiritual experiences there. One woman had been laid up in bed with some kind of injury. We prayed with her, and I came away realizing we had not given to her but she had given to us. She was so radiant, so wonderful." In neighboring Guatemala, they encountered ancient Indians begging amid the background of an enigma, thatched huts with dirt floors that seemed to be built around beautiful thick mahogany tables. [109]

Mary Lou, using the pseudonym "Gale," wrote her account of the journey, which *The Rudder* magazine published in July 1946. In an article titled "The Mate Speaks," "Gale" told wives and girlfriends of sailors she was 20 and had "never set foot aboard a sailboat until after my 19th birthday." She recounted lessons learned during the sixteen-day passage to British Honduras, including, "If your husband has ever been at sea, you will spend the greater part of your leisure time aboard, so you might as well like it." She advised practical clothing, a short, functional hair style, and "a keen interest in sailing the boat and lack of self pity" as the best remedy for seasickness. "Forget the movies you have seen about yachting," she wrote. "For you, life afloat consists of more realistic scenery and cast. And no audience. You will

---

[105] John McConnell, letter to *Fellowship News*, April 1945.

[106] Ibid.

[107] John McConnell, interview by author, Denver, Colorado, August 2004.

[108] John McConnell, letter to *Fellowship News*, April 1945.

[109] John McConnell, interview by author, Denver, Colorado, August 2004.

find fishing less romantic and more slimy ... but more fun." [110]

Shortly after John and Mary Lou's arrival in Central America, agents from the U.S. Federal Bureau of Investigation (FBI) in La Ceiba, British Honduras, interrogated the couple. A report, dated 28 February 1945, stated John and Mary Lou had "no authority for trip, no passports, have photostatic copies of birth certificates and documents of boat registry. ... Did not attempt contact Consulate or other American authorities. ... yacht well stocked food supplies, gasoline, clothes. ... John McConnell had no selective service card, no marriage certificate, claims commission ordain minister International Fundamental Christian Association Incorporated, Washington, D.C. In no hurry to leave McConnell preaching singing in church (sic)." [111]

FBI director John Edgar Hoover's reply a month later identified John Saunders McConnell as "Fugitive; Deserter ... who is presently absent without leave from the United States Army." The telegram instructed, "Inasmuch as no formal request has been received from the War Department for the Bureau's assistance in locating and apprehending this subject, this information is being forwarded to you so that you may take whatever action you may desire." [112]

In another telegram on 30 April, Hoover instructed local agents to "make a preliminary investigation regarding the status and activities of the above subjects in Honduras." [113] Further communiqués throughout the summer concluded, "McConnell is still in the Bay Islands and occupies himself by preaching and maintaining himself by the collections he makes as a minister of the Gospel." [114]

Then, after six months of surveillance, Hoover sent a final telegram, instructing, "In view of the fact that this matter is being followed by both the Naval Attaché and the Vice Consul at La Cieba, and that no charges have been made that the subjects are engaged in subversive activities, no further investigative action need be taken by your office." [115]

---

[110] Mary Lou (Clark) McConnell, pseudonym "Gale," "The Mate Speaks," *The Rudder*, vol. 62, No. 7, July 1946: 42.

[111] [Agent] WSB, FBI telegram, 28 February 1945.

[112] John Edgar Hoover, FBI telegram, 31 March 1945.

[113] John Edgar Hoover, FBI telegram, 30 April 1945.

[114] [Agent] L.A., FBI telegram, 9 August 1945.

[115] John Edgar Hoover, FBI telegram, 24 August 1945.

Then another person, yet to be born, entered the couple's idyllic lives and altered their plans. "Mary Lou was pregnant and she wanted to have the child back in the States," John recalled. "I sold my boat. I only got $1,500 or some small amount." John and Mary Lou then flew home without difficulty. Their daughter, Constance Blyth McConnell, was born in Youngstown, Ohio, Mary Lou's hometown, on 23 December 1946.

From Ohio, the young couple and their infant traveled to California to visit John's mother. "I came home to get some things but I, kind of, snuck in because I didn't want the Army to know where I was," John remembered. Hattie fed her son a good meal then suggested he stay the night and rest. She and Evan, who was appalled at his brother for being a pacifist, insisted that John let the authorities pick him up. John refused, saying, "If my dad were here, he would totally support me."

John was arrested, four years later, for unintentionally writing a check with insufficient funds. By that time, Mary Lou had given birth to the couple's second child, Cary, in Santa Cruz, California, on 19 January 1949. "I was struggling financially," John said. "All my life at critical points, I lacked money. I misjudged what I had in the bank, and the person I wrote the check to reported it to the police."

With the Army claiming indebtedness to military service and faced with the prospect of fighting in the growing Korean conflict, John again claimed pacifism as a conscientious objector and minister. [116] As a result, he was given a psychiatric examination by clinical psychologist Wilson Van Dusen, who recalled John's case as being "most unusual." Of John's responses to Rorschach cards, Van Dusen, who was a contracted civilian intern in his mid-20s, eight years younger than John, said, "He saw things no one had ever seen, but they were there! ... He gave a number of unusual responses, which suggested he was very bright."

Nevertheless, Van Dusen diagnosed John as "unfit for the army" and recommended a psychiatric discharge. "He was questioning everything. That's why he didn't fit in," Van Dusen explained. "It was boot training. What do you do? You obey orders. You just take all the guff they hand out and you do it, that's all. Well, he couldn't do that. He was too brilliant for

---

[116] John McConnell, interview by author, Denver, Colorado, August 2004.

the Army." [117]

John's difficulties with the military affected Mary Lou's health, requiring psychiatric care. "I will never forget the powerful sorrow it was," John recalled. "I went to see her at the hospital. She was in a straightjacket. In bed. Screaming. The double tragedy was we had a daughter and a son who were staying with my mother."

After John's eventual release from the military and Mary Lou's discharge from the hospital, the couple and their children lived in several places in California, including Los Angeles and San Diego. There, John had a music store in which he sold wire recorders, a state-of-the-art technology for capturing sound on an electronic device. John's customers included movie stars Lauren Bacall and Humphrey Bogart, whom John met while swimming off the coast of Catalina. [118]

Wilson Van Dusen was also a customer. The psychiatrist, who had recently married, recalled, "John came into my house, selling this wire recorder. He could talk a thing up quite well, so I bought the wire recorder. All of our good music was on wire for awhile." [119]

By January 1954, the McConnell family moved to Oregon where John took a job as a traveling salesman for the American School, promoting high school correspondence courses for nontraditional students. [120] Mary Lou divorced John [121] within the year, on 27 September 1954, leaving the children with him. In a statement apropos to both the family of his youth and the family of his marriage, John said, "We were a close family when the children were smaller. When we got older, why, everyone went different ways." [122]

While the end of his marriage was a sad time in John's life, he found strength in his pacifism. In the early 1960s, John had an opportunity to meet and speak with General Eisenhower, who had become U.S. President in 1952 primarily for his military prowess. Through the rest of John's life, a photograph

---

117 Wilson Van Dusen, telephone interview by author, 24 December 2004.

118 John McConnell, interview by author, Denver, Colorado, August 2004.

119 Wilson Van Dusen, telephone interview by author, 24 December 2004.

120 John McConnell, American School letters to prospective students, January 1954.

121 John and Anna McConnell, manuscript review with author, Denver, Colorado, January 2006.

122 John McConnell, interview by author, Denver, Colorado, August 2004.

of the two men shaking hands was among John's proudest possessions. "I was totally against the war, which he, of course, led successfully," John said. "Nevertheless, when I met him and spoke my mind, he said, 'John, I agree with you. I think there was a better way.'" [123]

But while John would later make significant public contributions for peace in his professional life, perhaps the most telling sign of John's desire to generate good will came in October 1970 when he wrote a letter on behalf of his son, who was a conscientious objector to the Vietnam War. In that letter to the chairman of Cary's local draft board, John wrote, "In World War II, I had undergone a terrible confusing struggle involving my conscience, country, ideals and beliefs that led to a deep conviction that any individual who gives himself to works of peace with the same fervor that others give to works of war will contribute far more to ending war and resolving differences. ... I must confess that after long years of ceaseless effort for peace, it is a terrible blow to see my son faced with the same senseless dilemma I faced 25 years ago. ... I can assure you that Cary is one of the most honest young men I know. ... His service in a civilian, nonprofit agency will contribute far more to the future of his country and the world than any service he could render in the army." [124] Apparently the Army agreed, and Cary was deferred as a conscientious objector to military combat. [125]

John's assistance to Cary may have been inspired by love and forgiveness Hattie exhibited to J. S. While his parents had traveled and ministered together when young, they later separated, divorced, remarried and separated again. During the final separation, J. S. lived alone in a mountain cabin where he died, ostensibly, from brain damage after falling off the cabin's roof. [126] In June 1967, three years before John composed the letter to Cary's draft board and within a year after J. S. died, Hattie penned a poem in memory of her husband in which she recalled their wedding day, their growing ministry, his questioning of his faith, and his search for a greater connection with God. [127] She concluded with her belief: "He died alone with no one near, /

---

123 Ibid.

124 John McConnell, letter to Cary McConnell's draft board, California, October 1970.

125 John McConnell, interview by author, Denver, Colorado, August 2004.

126 Ibid.

127 Hattie McConnell, "In Memory Of My Dear Husband, John S. McConnell," 7

but I am sure his God was there."

A week after Hattie died on 21 August 1992, John dictated his thoughts about his mother and father: "It's a good thing to change our mind. … It's good to have our heart fixed … If our hearts are fixed, through the grace of God, then we grow on the grace of God and we come to the final day with the recognition that we have prevailed." [128]

June 1967.

[128] John McConnell, interview by author, Denver, Colorado, August 2004.

4

Star of Hope

(1957 to present)

I, a citizen of this planet, dedicate my friendship and knowledge to work for peace among men. I will aid the efforts that heal, build and unite mankind.
– John McConnell, "Star of Hope Pledge,"
September 1958

Observing the international situation, however, John McConnell saw the world had not been fixed. Yes, the United Nations, a world organization committed to international cooperation, had been chartered by China, France, the Soviet Union, the United Kingdom and the United States in San Francisco on 26 June 1945. [129] Yes, U.S. Lieutenant General William K. Harrison and Korean Lieutenant General Nam Il had signed a treaty that ended the Korean War on 27 July 1953. [130] But the Cold War, a conflict of ideology, propaganda and nuclear armament between the United States, the banner carrier of democracy, and the communistic Union of Soviet Socialist Republics, had begun. In addition, the U.S. House Committee on

[129] "Basic Facts About the United Nations 2000," Sales No. E.00.1.21., quoted in *About the United Nations/History* [online]. United Nations [cited 4 December 2004]. Available from www.un.org/aboutun/history.htm.

[130] *July 27, 1953: Korean War cease fire signed* [online]. Life in Korea [cited 4 December 2004]. Available from www.lifeinkorea.com/cgi-bin/calendar/kwshowevent.cfm?EventID=39.

Un-American Activities was scouring the nation for communists, [131] Joseph Stalin was ruling Russia with an iron fist, [132] and British Prime Minister Winston Churchill declared, "An iron curtain has descended across the Continent" of Europe. [133]

Amidst this international friction, John moved from Oregon to North Carolina in 1956, taking Connie and Cary with him, in search of what he called "a fresh start." [134] There, in Bakersville, population less than 500 and ten miles southeast of where the meandering Appalachian Mountains' crest creates the border with Tennessee, John and the children found a home in Celo, an intentional community for pacifists founded in 1937. [135] And within Celo, John met Erling and Louise Toness.

Erling was unhappy working for a newspaper in Spruce Pine, North Carolina, and wanted to start his own paper. With resolve, the threesome established two weekly papers, *The Toe Valley View* and, later, the *Avery County News*, which served 2,400 readers in Avery, Mitchell and Yancey counties. John and Erling were co-publishers, and Louise was editor. [136] The motto under the nameplates for both publications, which carried a daily price of five cents and an annual subscription rate of $2.00, proclaimed, "An Independent Newspaper Serving the Toe River Valley." [137]

John, Erling and Louise exercised their independence by positing their opinion on significant issues. One story involved a criminal investigation about which John wrote, "The story my paper carried was about the gross injustices of the local court refusing to bring [a prominent person's] son to trial. Following this, I was threatened and an employee of our paper was attacked and had to go to the hospital." Undeterred, John sent copies of

---

[131] *House Committee on Un-American Activities* [online]. Encyclopedia Britannica online [cited 4 December 2004]. Available from www.britannica.com/ebi/article-9277495.

[132] *The Cold War* [online]. Nuclear Age Peace Foundation [cited 4 December 2004]. Available from www.nuclearfiles.org/hicoldwar/.

[133] Winston S. Churchill, "Sinews of Peace" aka "Iron Curtain Speech," Westminster College, Fulton, Missouri, 5 March 1946.

[134] John McConnell, interview by author, Denver, Colorado, August 2005.

[135] George L. Hicks, *Experimental Americans: Celo and Utopian Community in the Twentieth Century* (University of Illinois Press, 2001), summarized online at www.press.uillinois.edu/f01/hicks.html.

[136] John McConnell, interview by author, Denver, Colorado, August 2005.

[137] *The Toe Valley View* and *Avery County News* nameplates.

his editorials and articles to other newspapers, and the case gained national attention when Hugh Sidey and Paul Schutzer, a reporter and a photographer for *LIFE magazine*, came to Bakersville to write a story they titled "Trouble in Toe Valley." "They followed me around for several days, interviewing people and taking pictures," John wrote of that event. [138]

Within months, on 4 October 1957, the feast of St. Francis, Russia launched Sputnik 1, a forty pound sphere with a simple transmitter. That event marked the Dawn of the Space Age, and, immediately, the Space Race became the rage of worldwide conversation.

Many Americans, conditioned by nationalism during World War II, saw Sputnik as a defeat for the U.S. space program. *The Voice-Journal* of South Milwaukee, Wisconsin, described the event as "... awesome and frightening ... that the secrets of space might first fall to evil men bent on world – and space – control." [139] Other newspapers, fueled with fervor, viewed Sputnik as a wake-up call and urged American scientists and space engineers to push harder. [140] *The Jewell County Record* in Mankato, Kansas, editorialized, "[Sputnik was] the greatest piece of psychological propaganda ever released. It set up a chain reaction of fear and doom." [141]

These sentiments of a perceived "technology gap" between the world's two super powers echoed even louder when Russia launched its second satellite, Sputnik 2, a 250-pound capsule with a live dog on board, less than a month later, on 3 November 1957. [142] After that event, *The Baltimore (Maryland) News-Post* editorialized, "The Russians are using them [Sputniks] as a major threat of things to come in their drive to become the Godless and ruthless masters of the world." [143]

But a few Americans, including John McConnell, saw Sputnik as a global

---

138 John McConnell, notes regarding *LIFE magazine* photographs, 15 March 2002.

139 "Make Explorer a Star of Hope," *The (South Milwaukee, Wisconsin) Voice-Journal*, 6 February 1958, Vol. 66, No. 6, p. 2.

140 Various newspapers in John McConnell Document Group (#212), Swarthmore College Peace Collection.

141 *The Jewell County Record*, Mankato, Kansas.

142 Anatoly Zak. 1999. *The True Story of Laika the Dog* [online]. Space.com [cited 7 December 2004]. Available from www.space.com/news/laika_anniversary_991103.html.

143 "Send Up Peace Star" editorial, *The Baltimore (Maryland) News-Post*, 14 November 1957.

accomplishment, worthy of praise from all world citizens. North Carolina senator Sam Ervin agreed with this minority sentiment, and *The Toe Valley View* quoted him as saying, "It would have been better to congratulate Russia on her achievement instead of trying to belittle it." [144]

On 31 October 1957, John McConnell wrote and published an editorial, "Make Our Satellite A Symbol Of Hope!" In it, John urged U.S. space officials to launch "some symbol of peace" that would instill in people of all nations a desire to "work together for some great goal they share ... peace and understanding ... peace and unity ... peace and world cooperation." [145]

"Star of Hope" editorial, *The Toe Valley View,* 31 October 1957

Make Our Satellite A Symbol Of Hope!

Usually in these editorial columns we stick pretty closely to local matters. But some issues arising outside our own locality become so universal in importance that they are "local" for everyone in the world. Of course we are referring now to earth satellites and man's venture into the conquest of Space.

What was science fiction only yesterday has become visible – audible – fact today. "After a lifetime of some 250,000 years on earth ... man has conquered earth gravity and stands poised on the era of universal exploration," writes Norman Cousins in a penetrating editorial in *The Saturday Review* for Oct. 19, called "Sense and Satellites."

But, he points out, the event brings "no universal feeling of release or jubilation," overcast as it is by the chill of a cold war and the threat of extinction by intercontinental missiles utilizing the same principles used in launching the satellite. The answer, Cousins says, is "not to conjure up more effective ways of destroying the world." (How trivial is the whole argument of who or what is to blame for the Russians getting ahead of us in the armed missiles race – when we consider that the race itself can lead only to destruction!) "The principal need," insists *The Saturday Review* editor, "is to tap our intelligence and moral imagination to the fullest in creating a working design for a better tomorrow

---

[144] Sam Ervin, *The Toe Valley View*, 14 November 1957.

[145] John McConnell, "Make Our Satellite A Symbol Of Hope!" editorial, *The Toe Valley View*, 31 October 1957.

in which all the world's people can share. ... A great idea looking towards the development of a world community will circle the globe more rapidly than the fastest satellite. It will give us access to the majority of the world's peoples – on whom security really depends. It will also help to make life bearable on this planet before we take off for other ones."

Now is the moment when "Peace On Earth" might have its best opportunity for realization. When men work together for some great goal they share, the forces that make for peace and understanding have the best chance to operate. And a greater goal could scarcely be dreamed of than the exploration of the Universe, in man's eternal search to find and understand his place in the Universe.

What will be the effect upon the world when our own satellite is launched? Will it turn the world toward peace and unity, or away? We need some symbol of peace, to give the world a promise that conquest of space will be for good and not for evil. To create such a symbol would require no new discoveries.

The means are already at hand to make the appearance of our satellite as startling an event as the appearance of Sputnik, but startling in a different way. Could not the small satellite to be launched in December according to present plans appear as a brightly shining Star of Hope?

The mechanics of the thing should not be too difficult. The body of the satellite could be covered with some highly reflective material such as aluminum foil. More difficult would be the task of convincing the peoples of the earth that this was not just a propaganda device. Indeed, we would need to make sure ourselves, as a nation, that it was not! The symbol would need to be accompanied by sincere words and convincing deeds in the direction of peace and world cooperation.

It is true that certain segments of humanity do not believe in the Event symbolized by the star of Christmas. But there is no religion or no nation on earth (considering people, not governments) that does not respond with hope and longing to the angel's song of Peace on Earth, Good Will to Men.

Seeing his idea in print stirred John's evangelical nature. Encouraged by his recent success at gaining widespread attention with *LIFE magazine*, he sent a copy of the editorial to the *Asheville (North Carolina) Citizen*, a daily paper, which also published it. [146] The newswire services United Press, the forerunner of United Press International (UPI), and Associated Press (AP) picked up John's editorial and sent it to newspapers and radio stations across the country. Within a week, it appeared in four other North Carolina papers, *The Charlotte News*, which invited John to write a weekly supplement, [147] *The Charlotte Observer*, *The Raleigh News and Observer*, and *The Morganton News-Herald* as well as *The Washington (D.C.) Star* and many other major urban dailies. [148] On television, still in its fledgling decade, the National Broadcasting Company (NBC) presented John's idea on its program *Three Star Extra* – "Your Newspaper on the Air" – on 13 November. [149]

Letters of support confirmed John's belief, "If you can get what you're trying to do on the front page of a paper or on television, it gets attention." [150] Fueled by that principle, John and volunteer assistant Peter Hill wrote personal letters, promoting the Star of Hope concept, to each of the nation's 5,000 editors of weekly newspapers [151] and to key people in universities, labor unions, church organizations and government. [152]

John contacted S. Fred Singer, who was director of the Center for Atmospheric and Space Physics at the University of Maryland. [153] Singer had received praise from President Dwight Eisenhower for his work in satellite research, [154] including Operation Farside, a mission that, on 28 October 1957, rocketed a balloon-shaped exploratory scientific payload 4,000 miles into space. Although that rocket flew perpendicular to the Earth's surface, the operation was named by an Air Force general who hoped to expand the

---

[146] John McConnell, interview by author, Denver, Colorado, August 2004.

[147] Thomas L. Robinson, *The Charlotte News*, letter to John McConnell, 2 November 1957.

[148] John McConnell, interview by author, Denver, Colorado, August 2004.

[149] Joseph R. Bergey, letter to John McConnell, 25 November 1957.

[150] John McConnell, interview by author, Denver, Colorado, August 2004.

[151] Ibid.

[152] Peter Hill, numerous letters.

[153] *S. Fred Singer, Ph.D.* [online]. The Science & Environmental Policy Project [cited 24 September 2005]. Available from www.sepp.org/bios/singer/biosfs.html.

[154] "President Lauds Physicist Singer," *The Washington Post*, 4 February 1958.

project so a rocket would circle the moon and take photographs of the lunar orb's far side. [155]

Of a satellite visible from Earth, Singer said, "At the beginning of the Space Race, it would be possible to see a satellite if it were large enough and reflected enough sunlight. But because of the size of rockets at that time, payloads were limited, and they couldn't launch a satellite that weighed more than 100 pounds. That would mean launching something like a balloon with a diameter of 100 feet or so and a very thin skin of metalized plastic or Mylar." [156]

Recalling his initial discussion with this pioneer in rocket satellite technology, John remembered, "Singer asked me to come to Washington, so I did. He was speaking – I believe it was that evening – for a big meeting about space. Instead of using his prepared speech, he talked about my proposal."[157]

"John latched onto the idea that this satellite could become a symbol of world peace, and he wanted to launch it at Christmas time," Singer said. [158]

The next day, 14 November 1957, *The Washington (D.C.) Post and Times Herald* reported that Singer, in his speech before the Rotary Club of Washington, D.C., had encouraged the U.S. government to send "a harmless, uninstrumented sphere into a globe circling orbit." Calling the satellite "The Christmas Star," Singer said the U.S. satellite "would help offset the propaganda advantage Russia has gained with its two Sputniks." The article mentioned John McConnell as the inspiration for Singer's remarks. [159]

Two weeks later, on 28 November, the *New York Herald Tribune* gave Singer editorial space in which he defined Sputnik as "a metal ball devoid of any spiritual significance, indeed of little scientific significance." Posing an alternative philosophy, which he headlined "A Statement of Conscience," Singer asked the United States to launch a Star of Hope satellite to "inaugurate the program, which will surely lead to man's mastery of the solar system in a spiritual and moral way." [160]

---

155 S. Fred Singer, telephone interview with author, 27 December 2005.

156 Ibid.

157 John McConnell, interview by author, Denver, Colorado, August 2004.

158 S. Fred Singer, telephone interview with author, 27 December 2005.

159 Erling Toness, *The Toe Valley View*, 21 November 1957.

160 S. Fred Singer, "A Statement of Conscience," *New York Herald Tribune*, 28

To foster cooperation between the world's space leaders, Singer wrote a 12-page report, dated 18 November 1957 and titled "A Reply to Sputnik," in which he advocated "a meeting of the minds between East and West so that man's further exploration of space, including a manned landing on the moon, can be done as a joint international effort." [161]

The Toe Valley View reported on John McConnell's interaction with Singer under the headline "'Peace Satellite' Idea Meets Favorable Response." In the article, Erling Toness reported John McConnell was in Washington, D. C., "discussing with government officials and others a proposal that the United States launch its first satellite as a highly reflective object to symbolize the Star of Bethlehem." The article added, "Before leaving for Washington, McConnell talked with U.S. senator Sam Ervin and U.S. congressman Charles R. Jonas about the idea of a peace satellite." The paper reported that both North Carolina legislators responded "with much encouragement." Specifically, Ervin wrote that the Star of Hope proposal would "afford the U.S. an unprecedented opportunity to dramatize the conviction of this country that the fundamental hunger of all mankind is for peace." [162]

The Star of Hope message officially reached the White House via correspondence from Ervin and his North Carolina colleague senator W. Kerr Scott. In his letter, Ervin told President Eisenhower, "It seems there is much wisdom in Mr. McConnell's suggestion, and I hope you can take public notice of the same and endorse it." [163] Scott concurred, citing John's idea as "a candid and vigorous good will crusade, a progressive and positive action on the part of the United States." [164] A reply from an aide to the President promised, "Mr. McConnell's suggestion will have earnest attention." [165]

John, himself, wrote to President Eisenhower. Noting, "The greatest power on earth is the spiritual and moral force of good will in action," John asked the President to "call upon individuals, families, and communities all over the country to bring into being all the compassion and kindness of which they are capable so the 'Star of Hope' could be a symbol of what

---

November 1957.

161 S. Fred Singer, "A Reply to Sputnik," report, 18 November 1957.

162 Erling Toness, *The Toe Valley View*, 14 November 1957.

163 Sam Ervin, letter to Dwight Eisenhower, 25 November 1957.

164 W. Kerr Scott, letter to Dwight Eisenhower, 25 November 1957.

165 *The Toe Valley View*, 12 December 12 1957.

people the world over seek – peace on earth, good will to men." [166]

"Star of Hope" newspaper headlines, November and December 1957

Dr. Singer Backs Plan for Lighted Yule Satellite – *Washington (D.C.) Star* (front page), 13 November 1957

Send Up Peace Star – *The Baltimore (Maryland) News-Post*, 14 November 1957

U. M. Scientist Suggests U.S. Raise Glowing 'Moon' – *The (Baltimore, Maryland) Sun*, 14 November 1957

Glow-in-the-Dark Satellite Proposed To Shine Over Earth at Christmas Time – *San Bernardino (California) Sun*, 14 November 1957

We Applaud Carolinian's 'Star of Hope' Idea – *Johnson City (Tennessee) Press*, 15 November 1957

Missiles or Stars For Outer Space? – Malvina Lindsay, *The Washington (D.C.) Post*, editorial, 7 December 1957

Hitch Your Wagon to a Star – Walter Lippmann, *New York Herald Tribune*, editorial

Yule Satellite Hailed – *Oklahoma City (Oklahoma) Times*

Throughout the rest of November and December, John's idea gathered momentum. He was a guest on *The Today Show*, hosted by Dave Garroway, and appeared on NBC's *The Arlene Frances Show* on Thanksgiving Day. Resulting letters and post cards indicated support for the Star of Hope. [167] A retired solder from Illinois sent a song, "Peace Beyond Victory," that he had composed after D-Day in 1945. [168] A viewer from New York wrote, "More than a million Americans may be sufficiently interested – or could be aroused – to give a dollar or more to such an opportune, constructive cause." [169] Another from Texas sent a check for $5.00 made out to "Christmas Satellite Fund." [170]

John personally received letters of encouragement from Glenn Harding, executive director of Koinonia Foundation; Pitirim Sorokin, director of

[166] John McConnell, letter to Dwight Eisenhower, 12 December 1957.

[167] Viewers letters. Also, Nancy Coulter, NBC Audience Relations, letter to John McConnell, 2 December 1957.

[168] Frank A. Braje, Hollywood, Illinois, letter to John McConnell, 26 December 1957.

[169] Joseph R. Bergey, New York, New York, letter to Fred Singer, 25 November 1957.

[170] Robert W. Geis, Texas, undeposited check, 21 November 1957.

Harvard University Research Center for Creative Altruism; and Clarence Cranford, president of American Baptist Convention. Others, including Eugene Exman, president of Harper & Brothers, a New York publishing company, sent copies of correspondence they had sent to President Eisenhower and to Fred Singer advocating the Star of Hope idea. [171]

Star of Hope statements

I am delighted to see how encouraging the response to Star of Hope has been. – Mrs. Eleanor Roosevelt

Made to look like a star… it would dramatically carry, not a sinister 'beep' but a light of hope. – Eugene Exman, editor, Religious Books, Harper & Brothers

The idea is wonderful. And we'll learn a lot more from a satellite that glows than from the other ones. – Francis J. Heyden, S.J., director, Georgetown University Observatory, Washington, D.C.

A Star of Hope like this could go far toward ending the international missile-satellite race. – Robert U. Brown, editor, *Editor and Publisher Journal*

Wishing you every success in your venture to launch the Star of Hope. – Billy and Ruth Graham

I have read your article with keen interest and appreciation. We share the conviction that the fraternal resources of the world community have not begun to be exploited. – Norman Cousins, editor, *The Saturday Review*

Will do anything we can to help. – Erwin D. Canham, editor, *The Christian Science Monitor*

John received a reply from the U.S. Naval Research Laboratory, which President Eisenhower had directed, in September 1955, to place at least one scientific satellite in orbit during the International Geophysical Year (1 July 1957 to 31 December 1958). [172] In a letter dated 3 December 1957, Raymond H. Wilson, Jr. of the Theory and Analysis Branch of Project

[171] Eugene Exman, Harper & Brothers, to Dwight Eisenhower, copy to John McConnell, 18 December 1957.

[172] Steve Garber and Roger Launius. *A Brief History of NASA* [online]. National Aeronautics and Space Administration [cited 9 December 2004]. Available from www.hq.nasa.gov/office/pao/History/factsheet.htm.

Vanguard, thanked Peter Hill for "explaining your very laudable proposals" and acknowledged, "Many of us connected with Project Vanguard have put much thought and effort during the past few months toward arranging for brighter satellites for all to see." [173]

According to a Star of Hope fact sheet, "One of America's leading space scientists [told John McConnell], 'If you can get public support for the Star of Hope, we scientists will put up a star that will outshine Venus.'" In similar fashion, Singer submitted a proposal to the National Academy of Sciences for a luminous satellite, visible to the naked eye, that would "serve geodetic purposes and be useful to all nations." [174]

While Christmas came and went with neither comment nor commitment from the White House, many others picked up the torch, sometimes giving credit to John McConnell and sometimes not. On 14 January 1958, the *New York World-Telegram and Sun* carried a United Press article in which Raymond Loewy, one of America's foremost industrial designers, stated, "It is most important for America to associate with our first launching the idea of spiritual values – instead of looking like a threat, to make it a peaceful gesture toward mankind." [175] Two weeks later, on 29 January 1958, Texas senator Lyndon B. Johnson read the article, which did not mention John McConnell but did employ the phrase "star of good will," into the U.S. Congressional Record. [176]

Two days later, at 10:55 p.m. EST on 31 January 1958, the United States launched its first satellite, Explorer 1, an event through which, according to the *New York Herald Tribune*, "the United States of America regained its national pride." [177] The satellite carried neither a light-reflecting surface nor a high-powered light. Disappointed but not daunted, John McConnell pressed on.

Recalling the assistance he had received from Californians George Pepperdine and others during World War II and also recalling San Francisco, named after St. Francis, as the birthplace of the United Nations, John, with

---

[173] Raymond H. Wilson, Jr., Project Vanguard, letter to Peter Hill, 3 December 1957.

[174] San Francisco Star of Hope Committee, "Fact Sheet on the Star of Hope."

[175] H. D. Quigg, United Press, "Loewy Has Designs On 1st U.S. Sputnik," *New York World-Telegram and Sun*, 14 January 1958.

[176] *Congressional Record, Appendix*, 85th Cong. 2nd sess., 29 January 1958.

[177] "Now, Voyager!" *New York Herald Tribune*, 2 February 1958, sec 2, p. 4.

Connie and Cary in tow, moved from the Blue Ridge Mountains to the City by the Bay in the summer of 1958. It was, in John's mind, the perfect place to launch a global Star of Hope organization. An article in the *San Francisco (California) Chronicle,* which covered twenty column inches and included John's photograph, announced his arrival. The article stated, "John's simple, sincere plan [for world peace] just might work, because it's based on the almost universal characteristic of friendship ... [which] is everywhere but hasn't been organized, as the forces of hostility have been." [178] By the time the article was published on 1 August 1958, John had already approached San Francisco mayor George Christopher who suggested a core of leading citizens to serve as a board of directors for the San Francisco Star of Hope Committee. The members included a radio columnist, clergy, and directors of world and social service organizations, United Nations agencies, and a planetarium.

Members of the San Francisco Star of Hope Committee [179]

President: the Rev. Francis Geddes, Minister, Fellowship Church of All Peoples, San Francisco. Secretary-Treasurer: Mr. Trevor Thomas, Executive Director, Friends' Committee on Legislation, San Francisco. Members: Mr. George Bunton, Director, Morrison Planetarium, San Francisco; Mr. Fred Burrous, Public Relations Director, American Red Cross, Golden Gate Chapter; Dr. Norman L. Conard, Minister, Glide Memorial Methodist Church, San Francisco, and President, Northern California Council of Churches; Mrs. David Harrison, Executive Director, American Association for the United Nations, San Francisco Chapter; Miss Ann Holden, Radio Columnist, San Francisco; Mrs. William Lister Rogers, Board of Directors, World Affairs Council, San Francisco, and former president of the San Francisco Council of Churches; The Rt. Rev. Bishop James A. Pike; Rabbi Saul White, Congregation Beth Sholom, San Francisco; Miss Phyllis H. Brinks; Miss Ethel Cotton; Mrs. George Culler; Mrs. Charles

[178] Mary Frazer, "World Peace Satellite: S. F. Chosen for Launching," *San Francisco Chronicle*, 1 August 1958.

[179] San Francisco Star of Hope Committee, "Fact Sheet on the Star of Hope;" "By-Laws for Star of Hope, Inc.," 10 September 1959; "Board of Directors, Star of Hope, Inc.," 1 October 1959.

Gillenwater; Kamini K. Gupta; Miss Wanda Ramey; Benjamin Swig; and Mrs. Vernon B. Winiker.

A month later, in September, John attended a large scientific conference, Atoms for Peace, in Geneva, Switzerland. In a telegram, dated 13 September 1958, four days after the conference began, John reported to the committee, "I arrived very late ... with less than twenty dollars and was completely confused by the strange languages, the endless corridors of the UN Palace, the impossibility of finding the right people and getting things done among 6,000 delegates – most of whom were just as confused as myself." [180]

The committee had provided John with airfare but no money for accommodations, so in that Swiss city, which he described as a wonderful place to visit with a nice climate, John slept on a park bench for two nights before getting a room. [181]

In spite of those shortcomings, and armed with audacity, he persuaded thirty leading scientists from as many countries to sign his Star of Hope Declaration, a statement against global fear, hunger, illiteracy, poverty and barriers. Signers agreed to a personal pledge, "I, a citizen of this planet, dedicate my friendship and knowledge to work for peace among men. I will aid the efforts that heal, build and unite mankind."

Among the original signers were professor Francis Perrin of France, the president of the conference; K. S. Krishnan of India; A. P. Alexandrov of the USSR; professor I. E. Oliphant of Australia; and Hideki Yukawa of Japan. People who signed the Star of Hope Declaration after the Geneva conference included Albert Dussoix, the mayor of Geneva; Morris Fishbein of the American Medical Association; Arthur Larson, special assistant to President Eisenhower; Raymond Deonna, president of the Geneva Grand Parliament; and Denis De Rougemont, president of the European Cultural Centre. [182]

The Star of Hope Committee's fact sheet reported professor Charles Burky, advisor to the European Council of Communities, "was confident their 50,000 member towns in Europe would join the Star of Hope campaign

---

[180] John McConnell, telegram to San Francisco Star of Hope Committee, 13 September 1958.

[181] John McConnell, interview by author, Denver, Colorado, August 2004.

[182] John McConnell, "Star of Hope Declaration," 1958.

when it got underway." [183]

An article in the *Geneva (Switzerland) Diplomat* on 1 October 1958, reported, "There are no political or religious overtones in his idea. It is not anti-anything including communism. It is only FOR friendship ... inherent in almost everyone." John averred that, by being in Geneva, he was putting into action advice spoken by President Eisenhower two years earlier, "All people [who] want peace ... [should] get together and leap governments." "That is exactly what I am doing," John told the reporter, who concluded the article with an editorial comment, "Good Luck to the citizen of this planet, John McConnell!" [184]

In a telegram to the committee in San Francisco, John told of voluminous scientific papers available "on up-to-date information about atomic energy" and the "spirit of fraternity" at the conference. One scientist told him, "Among scientists there is no 'East and West.'" John wrote about the "slow laborious job getting these [Star of Hope] signatures from delegates who were all very busy." He added, "I had to track them down, get them at an opportune time, and usually talk to them for an hour and a half in order to give them the whole story of what was involved." He said, "I was up till one o'clock in the morning three nights in a row with the top Russian scientists at their hotel before I finally got one of their three top men to sign. For a time it was very discouraging, for I felt the document would not be valid as an expression of international support without the signature of a leading Russian scientist." [185]

Later, John related the unaccomplished conclusion of his mission. "Dr. [Glenn T.] Seaborg was there. He was chancellor of the University of California [at Berkeley] and came representing the United States. He said, 'John, this [Star of Hope Declaration] is a great idea. If you could get the Soviet delegate to sign it, then I'll sign it.'" John's initial attempts to get close to Soviet delegate A. P. Alexandrov were blocked by security guards. "They pushed me away," he said, "then on the last day, I saw Alexandrov sitting alone. I had a copy that had been translated into Russian for me (John also had a copy in French), and I went to him, let him read it, and asked him to

[183] San Francisco Star of Hope Committee, "Fact Sheet on the Star of Hope."

[184] "Grow Up or Blow Up", *Geneva (Switzerland) Diplomat*, 1 October 1958.

[185] John McConnell, telegram to San Francisco Star of Hope Committee, 13 September 1958.

endorse it. He said he would be glad to, so he put his signature on it. I was very excited, and I ran to get Seaborg, but he had left the conference early." Then, with a tone of resignation, John concluded, "A couple of years later, when I met Seaborg again, I told him this. He said, 'Oh, John, bring it to me. I'll be glad to sign it.' Well, I didn't have it with me and it wouldn't have meant anything then." [186]

Less than a month after the Atoms for Peace Conference, the U.S. government created the National Aeronautics and Space Administration (NASA). Going into operation on 1 October 1958, NASA enrolled, under one agency, the earlier National Advisory Committee for Aeronautics, its 8,000 employees, an annual budget of $100 million, three major research laboratories, and two test facilities. Other organizations that soon came under the NASA umbrella included the space science group at the Naval Research Laboratory, the NASA Jet Propulsion Laboratory, and the Army Ballistic Missile Agency where Wernher Von Braun's engineers were developing rockets. [187]

Back in San Francisco, the Star of Hope Committee was buoyed by John's efforts at the Atoms for Peace Conference. Committee member Fred Burrous commented on John's courage. "If he wanted to try and do something, he created the vehicle and got organized to get it done. He's one of those guys who seemed to work miracles," Burrous said. [188]

One such miracle was an encounter with Von Braun that allowed for a lengthy philosophical conversation. John, who had attended a conference of the American Rocket Society, later called American Institute of Aeronautics and Astronautics, had flown to Dallas, Texas, to hear an address by the noted rocket engineer. Afterwards, he was thwarted in an attempt at one-on-one conversation by a throng of people who swarmed around Von Braun. But boarding the airplane back to San Francisco, John was surprised to see his ticket seated him next to the famous scientist – "the work of the Holy Spirit," John called it – and the two men engaged in conversation. "We talked about the mystery of space and how the United States and other countries could

---

[186] John McConnell, interview by author, Denver, Colorado, August 2004.

[187] Steve Garber and Roger Launius. *A Brief History of NASA* [online]. National Aeronautics and Space Administration [cited 9 December 2004]. Available from www.hq.nasa.gov/office/pao/History/factsheet.htm.

[188] Fred Burrous, telephone interview by author, 31 December 2004.

take steps and have policies and actions that would bring harmony in the world. That's what I always keep coming back to. How can we have mutual trust and cooperation? How can we promote justice and peace?" Upon descent, the airplane emerged from a cloud cover, and John, thinking about his conversation with Von Braun, wondered, "What planet is this? Earth or somewhere in space?" [189]

Earth it was, of course, and that is where John and his contemporaries continued to work for those issues of trust and cooperation, justice and peace. The Star of Hope Committee incorporated into an official nonprofit entity, recognized by the State of California, on 26 May 1959, as "an international program to further the peaceful uses of outer space so they may serve the needs of all humanity and at the same time inspire world-wide cooperation in other fields of human endeavor." [190]

The corporation's bylaws, signed on 10 September 1959, stated the organization intended to fulfill its purpose "by encouraging the launching of a visible satellite to symbolize world friendship." Consistent with John's original objective, which he had editorialized in North Carolina, the bylaws declared this satellite would "be a civilian rather than a military satellite and [be] launched through the participation of the world scientific fraternity" and it would "have scientific as well as psychological value that would benefit people of all countries [and] serve international understanding." In addition, the Star of Hope satellite would carry microfilmed signatures of all who would sign the pledge at the bottom of the Star of Hope Declaration, [191] hopefully as many as 100 million names on a two-ounce strip of film. [192]

By means of newspaper promotions and other efforts by McKinney Associates, a contracted public relations firm, [193] the Star of Hope Committee of San Francisco obtained hundreds of signatures in the latter part of 1959. But this was short of their goal of 10,000 signatures in Oakland alone. [194]

---

[189] John McConnell, interview by author, Denver, Colorado, August 2004.

[190] *Exemption Application* (form 1023), U.S. Treasury Department, 6 October 1959.

[191] "By-Laws for Star of Hope, Inc.," 10 September 1959.

[192] David Perlman, "'Star of Hope' in the Sky? S. F. Drive for 'Peace Satellite,'" *San Francisco Chronicle.*

[193] McKinney Associates, letter to San Francisco Star of Hope Committee, 13 August 1959.

[194] San Francisco Star of Hope, Inc., board of directors, memo to Organizational Committee.

Likewise, contributions did not match either expectations or expenses. Fred Burrous recalled in later years, "It was just one of those things that never panned out. We did not have the means to make it go." [195]

On 3 February 1960, Star of Hope president Francis Geddes wrote to the board, "We have had difficulty building a suitable organizational structure as a vehicle for the [Star of Hope] idea. ... We face some rather crucial decisions about our future course of action." The letter stated contributions had been very small and the corporation was over $500 in debt in spite of the fact that John had been working as executive director without salary "on faith from week to week." Geddes posed a concern, "Mr. McConnell has often worked independently of board policy and direction." And he asked, "What should be the lines of administration and authority between the board and Mr. McConnell?" [196]

Answers came seven days later at a meeting, to which John was not invited so members could speak freely in his absence. The board decided, "The position of executive director be vacated [and] all honoraria and fees that Mr. McConnell receives while speaking for the Star of Hope be applied to his back salary." Future contributions were to be allocated equally between further salary compensation and current obligations. Perhaps signaling burnout, the board expressed their sentiment, "Fresh and original thought was needed, and additional people were needed to carry forward the next step of the Star of Hope project." [197]

Even without official support, John persisted. In a letter to the board shortly after their decision, he encouraged them to retain the corporation's legal status even if most of the members resigned and the entity was not active. [198] In 1961, John appeared on KABC Radio in Los Angeles and encouraged listeners who "will work for world peace" to submit their signatures for a future Star of Hope satellite. [199] He wrote letters to newly elected President John F. Kennedy [200] and to the European Space Research Organization. [201]

---

195 Fred Burrous, interview by author, 31 December 2004.

196 Francis Geddes, letter to Star of Hope, Inc., board of directors, 3 February 1960.

197 Minutes, Star of Hope, Inc., board of directors meeting, 10 February 1960.

198 John McConnell, letter to Star of Hope, Inc., board of directors.

199 John McConnell, "Radio Broadcast Christmas Day ... KABC," transcript, 1961.

200 John McConnell, letter to John F. Kennedy.

201 John McConnell, letter to European Space Research Organization.

In each circumstance, he spoke on behalf of the Star of Hope Committee, urging that satellites be launched as symbols of global peace.

Amidst these activities, John saw the need for fiscal security. He, therefore, contacted Erling and Louise Toness, who were still in North Carolina, and encouraged them to join him in another newspaper venture in California. In the spring of 1960, the trio established *The Mountain View* in the community of Mountain View, located in Silicon Valley, forty miles south of San Francisco. The benefits of owning and operating such a weekly were not new to John. "The town of Mt. View, 32,000 population, composed of a suitable cross section of business and industry and located next to Lockheed and Moffett Field and major missile centers, would be an ideal place to begin," he wrote in a memo to the Star of Hope Committee nearly a year earlier, on 11 May 1959. "We would control the local newspaper and be very close to people who direct the affairs of Mt. View." [202]

On 19 April 1961, John published an editorial, titled "Astronauts for Peace," in which he congratulated Yuri Gagarin for being the first man to complete a space orbit of earth. [203] John sent a copy to Norman Cousins, editor of *The Saturday Review*, who promised "to find ways of commenting on it editorially." [204] But more significantly, John's comment, "There has been increasing cooperation in scientific efforts divorced from the cold war ... and meaningful cooperation in space exploration would be another great step forward," seemed to predict a swing toward international mutuality in space. In fact, the U.S. adopted that approach less than one year later, albeit motivated more by economics than by peace. [205]

"Astronauts for Peace" editorial, *The Mountain View*, 19 April 1961

We wish to congratulate Mr. Yuri Gagarin, the first man to complete a space orbit of the earth. His achievement represents an important turning point in history as man begins to explore the unknown reaches of space. This high goal by its very nature

---

202 John McConnell, memo to Star of Hope Committee, 11 May 1959.

203 John McConnell, "Astronauts for Peace" editorial, *The Mountain View*, 19 April 1961.

204 Norman Cousins, letter to John McConnell, 8 May 1961.

205 John McConnell, "Astronauts for Peace" editorial, *The Mountain View*, 19 April 1961.

should be undertaken through cooperation on a world-wide scale. In this way, billions of dollars could be saved in unnecessary duplication. At the same time, dramatically converting the missiles of atomic destruction into vehicles for man's greatest exploration would be an effective step toward peace.

Premier [Nikita] Khrushchev has stated that their astronaut completed his trip in the service of all mankind. However, more effective collaboration is needed if the fears of atomic destruction are to be changed into hope for the future.

There has been increasing cooperation in scientific efforts divorced from the cold war. Leaders in all countries have praised the achievements of the International Geophysical Year, the Atoms for Peace Program and research cooperation in the Antarctic. It is felt by many that these and other cooperative efforts have brought communication and understanding which may lead to more peaceful attitudes in dealing with the serious political and ideological differences that exist.

Meaningful cooperation in space exploration would be another great step forward. It would be childish for us to be held back from pushing for such cooperation by a fear of seeming fearful. It would be a sign of maturity as a nation to push for cooperation because it is right and in the interest of all mankind – regardless of how the box score in the missiles race may stand at any particular moment!

We would like to suggest that in the service of man and in the interest of peace, both President Kennedy and Premier Khrushchev encourage actual collaboration in space by sending two astronauts, one American and one Russian, in a joint venture of exploration. It would be hoped that these astronauts would not only be equipped with scientific and technical ability, but also with deep human understanding. Should these men stay in orbit for several days or weeks, they could broadcast not only their new perspective of the physical properties of our planet, but a fresh and inspiring perspective of its inhabitants as well.

Certain basic concepts and hopes shared by all humanitarians could be reflected in the messages from these space pioneers. The idea is that we must explore every possibility for sincere

> global cooperation and make determined efforts to succeed in this in spite of our grave differences. That with new faith, friendship and love, we can create a new world of freedom and order – without the threat of war.
> Our new pioneers will see earth as a unit, hurtling through the vast regions of space in search of its destiny. Their new vantage point will also reveal the common destiny and essential unity of the world of flesh and spirit that lies below.
> Their message will be filled with wonder and hope.

The initial U.S. step toward joint space endeavors came after the successful space flight of Colonel John Glenn in Friendship 7 on 20 February 1962. On 6 March, Eugene M. Zuckert, secretary of the U.S. Air Force, addressed the Los Angeles Chamber of Commerce and stated, "There is a glimmer of hope that space may be a challenge great enough to initiate cooperation between the two great power blocs of the world ... to establish a broad international base for peaceful exploitation of space. ... Certainly space exploration is so costly, and there is so much to be done, that collaboration would be useful." [206]

Zuckert's predictions became a reality only six weeks later. On 27 April, the day after crippled U.S. moon probe Ranger 4 crashed into the lunar surface, [207] United Press reported, "America launched a new era of space-age collaboration yesterday by joining Great Britain in orbiting the world's first international satellite and helping Japan with a separate experiment." The space mission with the United Kingdom involved a three-stage, U.S.-made Delta rocket that was launched from Cape Canaveral, Florida, and carried an international satellite known as UK-1. [208]

Also on that date, *The New York Times* reported another U.S. step toward space collaboration in an article headlined "'Flasher' Satellite for All Nations." The lead paragraph read, "The United States will invite all nations today to join in the most extensive international space project so far – the use of a flashing-light satellite to determine the shape of the earth." The article continued, "At an international symposium on the geodetic uses of

[206] U.S. Department of Defense, news release, 6 March 1962.

[207] Associated Press, "Crippled Ranger-4 Crashes Into Moon," 26 April 1962.

[208] United Press, "First Joint Satellite In Orbit," 26 April 1962.

satellites, the U.S. will reveal once-secret details of a satellite that the Defense Department plans to launch soon." [209]

This satellite proved to be a source of several ironies for John. First, the satellite was to be visible from Earth as well as a cooperative venture, as John envisioned the Star of Hope would be. Plus, the satellite's name was ANNA, an acronym to represent Army, Navy, NASA, and Air Force. [210] And Anna was the name of the woman John would come to marry in 1967. [211]

These cooperative space ventures were precursors for later U.S. missions with the former Union of Soviet Socialist Republics, the most notable of which was the Mir Space Station, the first element of which Russian space engineers launched on 20 February 1986. [212] By then, the mood of America had completely changed from the time of Sputnik. Noting that Earthlings around the globe were watching television broadcasts of cosmonauts and astronauts working shoulder to shoulder in the weightlessness of space, John rekindled his Star of Hope program, which he had diminished to a pilot light in the early 1960s. "The information explosion of the last 20 years has made the people of our planet aware of Earth's resources and possibilities. ... The Earth Society Foundation will proceed with plans to see a visible satellite launched in the next five or six years," he wrote on 18 November 1986. [213]

Only a few days later, on the opposite side of the globe in New Delhi, India, Russian Secretary Mikhail Gorbachev proposed an international "Star Peace" program. "It is our profound conviction that space, this common property of mankind, should be exclusively peaceful and that what we need is Star Peace, not Star Wars," Gorbachev told the Indian Parliament. [214] Upon seeing an account of the Russian Secretary's remarks in the 28 November 1986 *San Francisco Chronicle*, John wondered if a packet of Star of Hope information he had mailed to Gorbachev, President Ronald Reagan, Pope John Paul II and the United Nations a year earlier [215] had,

---

209 "'Flasher' Satellite for All Nations," *The New York Times*, 26 April 1962.

210 Ibid.

211 John McConnell, interview by author, Denver, Colorado, August 2004.

212 *MIR Station* [online]. National Aeronautic and Space Administration [cited 25 December 2005] Available from liftoff.msfc.nasa.gov/rsa/mir.html.

213 John McConnell, "Star of Hope Program and Satellite," 18 November 1986.

214 Associated Press, "Gorbachev Proposes 'Star Peace' Program," *San Francisco Chronicle*, 28 November 1986.

215 John McConnell, "Star of Hope Space Program" information packet, 18 June 1985.

somehow, influenced the Russian's presentation. John, himself influenced by Gorbachev, added the words "Peace Star" to the headline of his documents about the Star of Hope program. [216]

With the aid of his friend and associate Kevin Sanders, John further defined specifications for the Star of Hope satellite as a "module … in low Earth orbit (80-90 miles). [With a] solar-cell powered signal light, the beacon would pulse at the rate of a new-born child's heartbeat, [217] … and will be seen every night in every continent." [218] Borrowing newswire text about the Star of Hope from the late 1950s, John envisioned, "A child [looking up to the night sky and] asking his father, 'What is that star?' And the father answering, 'Do not be afraid. That is the Star of Hope launched by men who believe in freedom.'"[219]

But with modern technology of the day in mind, John proposed a laser disk – and not his earlier idea of microfilm – with "millions of signatures of people young and old who have signed a simple statement that they will work for peace and the care of Earth" would be placed in the satellite. [220] He suggested that data from this laser disk be housed at the United Nations so visitors who had signed the Star of Hope Pledge could access it and obtain a souvenir copy. [221]

Unfortunately, benevolence and idealism required money. Sander's proposal included a civilian satellite price estimate of $600,000 to launch and another $400,000 a year for administration, service and operations. And there, in that state of inertia, John's idea sat for another decade until, in the summer of 1996, at the age of 81, John contacted NASA about the feasibility of launching a satellite. A reply from Stuart Jordan, the agency's senior staff scientist, complimented John's idea as one that would "contribute to international understanding … among young people who are most likely to become tomorrow's international leaders." Jordan offered, "If you secure financial backing, [our agency can] provide names of people who might be

---

[216] John McConnell, "Star of Hope Program and Satellite," 18 November 1986.

[217] Kevin Sanders, "Proposal for an Orbiting Information and Communications Satellite for World Peace and Development."

[218] John McConnell, "Star of Hope: Formula for World Peace."

[219] *The Jefferson County Democrat*, 5 February 1958, et al.

[220] John McConnell, "Star of Hope: Formula for World Peace."

[221] John McConnell, interview by author, Denver, Colorado, August 2004.

able to arrange for implementation of the Star of Hope concept." [222]

Looking four years into the future, John saw the upcoming millennium as the perfect time to finally bring his idea to the launch pad. Cosmonaut Anatoly Berezovoi, who spent what was then a record seven months in space aboard space station Salyut 7 in 1982, confirmed John's enthusiasm when the two men met at the Earth Day ceremony at the United Nations in 1998. "He told me I was far ahead of my time in regard to space cooperation," John recalled. [223]

But, just as Christmas 1957 passed without the launch of a Yule satellite to bring "peace on earth and good will to men," the transition from 1999 to 2000 passed with greater public concern about crashing computers due to the "Y2K" phenomenon than solutions for global conflict, much less the creation of celestial symbols for peace.

---

222 Stuart Jordan, National Aeronautic and Space Administration, letter to John McConnell, 1996.

223 John McConnell, manuscript review with author, October 2005.

5

Meals for Millions

(1961 to 1963)

Since the means of preventing hunger and malnutrition are now at hand, we hereby resolve that, with our words and money, we will support the efforts of Meals for Millions to rid the world of hunger.
–John McConnell, "Freedom from Hunger Proclamation," 24 June 1962

Beginning in 1961, while still in the newspaper business and still heavily promoting his Star of Hope idea, John McConnell invested nearly two years with a program called Meals for Millions, "a non-profit foundation dedicated to the relief and prevention of starvation." [224] John learned of Meals for Millions when dining at Clifton's Cafeteria in Los Angeles. John recalled that Clifford E. Clinton, who combined his first and last names to moniker his eatery, "was a wonderful Christian who had a big restaurant, and in the basement, you could go there and get a meal for five cents if you were up against it." [225]

Clinton's philosophy of never turning away a hungry customer stemmed from his youth as a missionaries' son in China where he had witnessed

224 Meals for Millions letterhead.
225 John McConnell, interview by author, Denver, Colorado, August 2004.

starvation. [226] In 1945, at a time when his seven Los Angeles restaurants were serving 25,000 meals a day, [227] Clinton and his wife Nelda Patterson visited Henry Borsook, a prominent research biochemist at the California Institute of Technology. Clinton told Borsook he wanted a high-protein food product that would provide one-third of a day's full nutrition in a two-ounce serving, not offend any religious dietary law, not drain supplies of food to which people were accustomed, could be shipped in bulk, have a long shelf life, require no refrigeration, could be served hot or cold, and would cost less than five cents a meal. To that end, Borsook hired a skilled French cook, Soulange Berczeller, who developed a product of low fat soy grits plus dehydrated vegetables and spices. [228] Later recipes would include seed oil from native crops that had previously been used only for animal food and fertilizer. [229]

With this food supplement product, which he named "Multi-Purpose-Food" (MPF) because it could be added to rice, noodles or other indigenous foods, Clinton established the Meals for Millions Foundation, a nonprofit unendowed California corporation, in 1946. [230] *Reader's Digest* published an article about Meals for Millions titled "How We Can Feed Europe's Hungry," [231] and General Mills agreed to manufacture MPF on a massive scale. [232]

By the early 1960s, Meals for Millions had already provided over 70 million "3¢ meals" to starving and malnourished children and adults in 125 countries. Meals for Millions staff did not actually serve, or even deliver, the meals but turned them over, free of charge, to organizations involved with missionaries, doctors and others who operated soup kitchens, hospitals or clinics. In addition, program volunteers were helping people in India,

---

[226] Linda Burum. *Clifton's Brookdale Cafeteria* [online]. LA weekly [cited 12 December 2004]. Available from www.laweekly.com/ink/99/34/dining-burum4.php.

[227] *Clifford E. Clinton* [online]. California Community Foundation [cited 12 December 2004]. Available from www.calfund.org/3/unsung_heroes_3.2.4.2.php.

[228] William Shurtleff and Akiko Aoyagi. 2004. *The Meals for Millions Foundation and Multi-Purpose Food: Work with Soyfoods* [online]. The Soy Daily [cited 12 December 2004]. Available from www.thesoydaily.com/SFC/MFM78.asp.

[229] *Program and Purpose of the Meals for Millions Foundation*, May 20, 1959.

[230] Althya Youngman, *Fact Sheet on Hong Kong Refugee Week.*

[231] "How We Can Feed Europe's Hungry," *Reader's Digest* (September 1945), referenced in *How Freedom from Hunger Began* [online]. Freedom from Hunger [cited 12 December 2004]. Available from www.mealsformillions.org.

[232] *How Freedom from Hunger Began* [online]. Freedom from Hunger [cited 12 December 2004]. Available from www.mealsformillions.org.

Japan, Korea, Brazil and Mexico produce high-protein food from untapped resources in their countries. [233]

These activities paralleled the People-to-People Program launched by President Dwight Eisenhower in September 1956, which was designed to promote contacts and activities among individuals around the world to further international understanding and friendship. Eisenhower's initiative was not governmental, but private, in nature, and the President asked economic, social and cultural leaders to organize committees that would develop thousands of methods for international people-to-people interaction. [234]

Adopting this concept, the Meals for Millions campaign used the term "People-to-People" in their promotional materials. [235] For their efforts, the organization won the prestigious Freedoms Foundation Awards in 1956 through 1960. Campaign literature quoted praise from medical missionaries Albert Schweitzer, who sat on the Meals for Millions board of counsellors and advisors, and Tom Dooley, founder of Medical International Cooperation Organization, who referred to Multi-Purpose-Food as "Dooley's third hand." [236]

After learning this information through conversation with Clinton and others involved with the program in Los Angeles, John McConnell decided to leave the newspaper business and devote his time to Star of Hope and Meals for Millions. "Our [*The Mountain View* newspaper's] attention had gotten away from local news," John said in later years. "I was gallivanting all over the world, doing nothing with our newspaper except sending material back to Erling." [237] A week before Christmas 1961, John sent a letter of disassociation from *The Mountain View* to Carlton E. Byrne, who had invested several thousand dollars in the business during its startup period and with whom John had a limited partnership. [238] The responsibility for publishing then fell solely into the hands of Erling and Louise.

John started a Meals for Millions chapter in San Francisco where he

---

[233] William Shurtleff and Akiko Aoyagi. 2004. The Meals for Millions Foundation and Multi-Purpose Food : Work with Soyfoods [online]. The Soy Daily [cited 12 December 2004]. Available from www.thesoydaily.com/SFC/MFM78.asp.

[234] People-to-People, "What is the People-to-People Program?" brochure, page 1, circa 1956.

[235] Meals for Millions newsletters, early 1960s.

[236] Meals for Millions, "Food for Freedom" flyer.

[237] John McConnell, interview by author, Denver, Colorado, August 2004.

[238] John McConnell letter to Carlton Byrne, 17 December 1961.

secured the free use of an abandoned office on a major street in Chinatown. He recalled, "The chapter was focused on getting food to refugees fleeing from Communist China to Hong Kong. We had a big sign out front that read 'Share a Meal.'" [239] John became program coordinator, and Althya Clark Youngman, who had founded Artists Embassy International in 1951 "to further peace and understanding through the universal language of the arts," [240] was public relations and program director.

At Youngman's request, John, who seemed to surge with ideas, wrote a letter in June 1962 to Clifford Clinton in which he suggested that restaurants add 3 cents to every meal of one dollar or more, then donate that money to Meals for Millions. A poster in the restaurants would indicate their participation in the "Share a Meal" campaign. [241]

Within the same month, John wrote a "Freedom from Hunger Proclamation," which was a variation on the restaurant theme, applied to homes and families. In his five-point paper, John encouraged people to place a "share-bank" on their dining room table into which they would deposit three cents, preferably a nickel, every time they sat down to eat. Incorporating his principles with practicality, John explained: "1. In this new technological age of plenty, every family everywhere has a right to basic nutritious food, regardless of whether they have money to buy it. 2. Food must no longer be a pawn in ideological conflicts, political maneuvers or economic competition. 3. We reject the idea that denying a man food can influence him for good. Hunger is a bad advisor. 4. Problems of trade imbalance in other countries must not take precedence over feeding a hungry world. 5. As long as there are hungry people, food surpluses must be used. We urge our farmers, our industries, our government and the United Nations to make the global war on hunger a first objective and a common cause of all peoples." [242]

This idea took off. The front page of the Fall 1962 Meals for Millions newsletter displayed a photograph of President Eisenhower, John McConnell and Jimmie Tom, a second grade student at a San Francisco Chinatown elementary school. In the photo, Eisenhower is placing his donation into

---

[239] John McConnell, interview by author, Denver, Colorado, August 2004.

[240] *Monument for a New Millennium* [online]. Artists Embassy International [cited 12 December 2004]. Available from www.artistsembassy.org/monument.htm.

[241] John McConnell, letter to Clifford E. Clinton, 3 June 1962.

[242] John McConnell, "Freedom from Hunger Proclamation," June 24, 1962.

Tom's "share-bank," one of ten thousand small customized milk cartons donated by five California dairy companies. The photograph's caption read: "School children take them [share-banks], drop in 3¢ every time they wish to invite a hungry unseen guest to dinner." [243]

At about the same time, California governor Edmund G. "Jerry" Brown and San Francisco mayor George Christopher declared the week of 10-17 October 1962 to be Hong Kong Refugee Week. In his decree, Brown stated, "The people of California have watched with concern during the past few months as many thousands of refugees have streamed across the border from Communist China into Hong Kong. Their concern for the welfare of these people has been heightened by the fact that the greatest percentage of these refugees must be turned back by the officials of Hong Kong who cannot provide food, clothing and shelter for the hapless refugees." [244]

Known as the "Rice Bowl" campaign, Hong Kong Refugee Week coincided with Chinese Independence Day and began with a large parade, featuring a colorful dragon usually reserved for the Chinese New Year. The fundraising goal for the week was $100,000, which would provide 400,000 pounds of Multi-Purpose-Food from which 3.2 million 2-ounce, 3¢ meals could be obtained. [245]

For their endeavor, the Meals for Millions group in San Francisco received acclaim in *Chinese World*, "America's Only Bi-Lingual Chinese-English Daily Newspaper." A front-page article in the 9 March 1963 issue proclaimed that the campaign raised $30,000. Although short of the goal, this amount of money allowed the Citizens Committee for Hong Kong Refugees, chaired by James H. Loo, to ship thousands of pounds of food supplement to Hong Kong in each of several upcoming months. [246]

But amidst these public accomplishments, strife was brewing beneath the surface. In late 1962, John advocated a fundraising idea that involved a company called International Holiday, Inc., a producer of "membership books." For each $25.00 book sold, $9.25 would go to the sponsoring organization, typically service clubs, and another $9.25 would go to a charity.

---

243 Meals for Millions newsletter, Fall 1962.

244 Edmund G. Brown, Hong Kong Refugee Week statement.

245 Meals for Millions, "Rice Bowl Drive for Hong Kong Refugees" news release.

246 *Meals for Millions Chairman Praises Work of Chinatown Citizen Committee*, Chinese World, San Francisco, 9 March 1963.

Meals for Millions was among the suggested recipients, as was CARE, Inc., ACCION International, Church World Service, Catholic Relief Services, The Albert Schweitzer Fellowship, and the Thomas A. Dooley Foundation. [247]

At first, this idea met with approval from the Meals for Millions parent organization in Los Angeles, including executive director Florence Rose. Then, John conceived elevating their status from that of a potential recipient to sponsor, and thus earning $18.50 per copy sold. Fred Burrous, who had become director of public relations for the Golden Gate Chapter of the American Red Cross in San Francisco and acting chairman of the California Council of Meals for Millions, wrote to Rose that the idea had been "tested on several hard-headed businessmen who were enthusiastic about the plan." [248] But this endeavor extended beyond the bounds of Meals for Millions protocol, and Rose responded, "Meals for Millions just cannot take a major role in becoming a salesman for a ticket-selling program." [249]

Another idea met a similar fate two months later when John, at the request of Youngman and Burrous, sent an enthusiastic letter to Rose, suggesting that Meals for Millions in San Francisco could benefit by sponsoring the world premier of a Japanese-produced Technicolor movie called *Buddha*. [250] Rose replied that Meals for Millions should "get maximum mileage from the tools we now have." [251]

Such directives, plus John McConnell's autonomous nature proved to be too much for both parties. On 29 May 1963, Rose sent a letter to Fred Burrous, Claude Lindquist, Althya Youngman, John McConnell and Sylvia Scott that announced reorganization of the San Francisco office. That letter placed control back in the hands of the Los Angeles headquarters and put Lindquist, a professional fundraiser, in charge of the Bay Area operations. In the sentence defining John McConnell's responsibilities, Rose acknowledged, "John's special talents can be helpful in so many ways – but only if he is not doing a solo flight on projects he considers of prime importance regardless of how the rest of us feel about them." Suggesting, "Each member of the

[247] John McConnell, draft agreement between International Holidays, Inc., and Share Foundation.

[248] Fred Burrous, letter to Florence Rose, 26 February 1963.

[249] Florence Rose, letter to Fred Burrous, 27 February 1963.

[250] John McConnell, letter to Florence Rose, 26 April 1963.

[251] Florence Rose, letter to John McConnell, 29 April 1963.

team work in his or her sphere of competence," Rose cautioned, "We must resist the impulse to climb to the top of the flag pole every other week to inaugurate some new and over ambitious venture." [252]

While this last statement may, or may not, have been directed at John, the metaphor of climbing a flag pole to gain attention was indicative of his personality as a world visionary and his initiative for coming up with ways to help people – in this case, by providing 3¢ meals to millions of people.

[252] Florence Rose, memo to Fred Burrous, Claude Lindquist, Althya Youngman, John McConnell and Sylvia Scott, 29 May 1963.

6

Minute for Peace

(1963 to present)

> *Our planet … is a mysterious orb of mind and spirit, a world of hope and love – but, unfortunately, a world of clashing thoughts and feelings. … If our world is to survive and find its destiny, new ways of achieving harmony must be found.*
>
> – John McConnell, "Minute for Peace" speech to National Education Association, 29 June 1965

IN 1963, JOHN MCCONNELL expanded his thinking beyond the issue of world hunger and began to wonder about a link between prayer and the potential for world peace. He thought about his devotions, which he practiced for at least one hour each day. He thought of the "Prayer of Saint Francis," a copy of which he carried in his wallet and recited often, which begins: "Dear Lord, make me an instrument of your peace. Where there is hatred, let me sow love." He considered the medical phenomenon in which people who pray, or are prayed for, have a higher rate of recovery than those who don't believe in a higher power. He thought about "miraculous answers to prayer" he had seen as a boy, traveling the country with his parents. "There have been times of great spiritual awakenings," he reminded himself, "when people are awakened in their hearts and in their minds to true values, when more people pray and more people do the right thing." [253]

From these meditations, John developed an idea he hoped would inspire people to pray silently each day. He called his idea "Minute for Peace," believing that, if thousands of people would pray for peace and good will at a specific time each day, we "might help move the world." [254] He acknowledged that one minute of silent prayer, only 1/1440th of each day, would not immediately convert conflicted people, but he believed it "would have its effect and encourage people to go much further than that." [255]

"The Role of Prayer in My Life," 9 November 1965

Minute for Peace will become a High Court of Conscience – the conscience of the world. Instead of waiting for a "Golden Age" in some nebulous future, why not make it a reality now? The means are at hand. If we act vigorously now, by the turn of the century, we will see a world of prosperity, peace and beauty, far exceeding the wildest dreams of even a generation ago.

These are some of the practical possibilities. The springs of freedom and creativity will be released in the majority of individuals throughout the world, because the world's communications media will first of all inspire men everywhere with a new vision of the sovereignty of each. The ways and techniques of peace will take control and conduct man's conscience. Checked by his intellect, strengthened by faith, his intuition will give him new confidence, wisdom and a sense of his responsibility to the Kingdom of God, the Kingdom of Love. This will be aided by a daily "Minute for Peace" shared in unison around the world.

Let us not wait. Let us begin now to build the new world of tomorrow. Let us not think in the old terms of ideologies (Catholicism, Communism, Socialism, Capitalism). If we open the minds of men to good will and mutual trust, all social, economic and political ideas will be encouraged as experiments for progress. Openly pursued, checked by the new honest sources of evaluation, (aided by modern electronics) which mutual trust

---

[253] John McConnell, interview by author, Denver, Colorado, August 2004.

[254] John McConnell, "The Development of Earth Day, At Koinonia with John McConnell," 1971.

[255] John McConnell, interview by author, Denver, Colorado, August 2004.

> will provide, each system will gather value from the other. Competition in the pursuit of excellence will replace the competition which arises in the pursuit of greed or power. The Rule of Gold will be replaced by the Golden Rule as each man checks his conscience as well as his intellect, for evaluation.

Seeking broad attention, John took his idea to Jules Dundes, who was vice-president and general manager of radio station KCBS in San Francisco and president of the San Francisco Bay Area Broadcasting Association. The men met for lunch on 11 November 1963. "The reason I remember the date," John said, "is that Jules mentioned we were meeting on Armistice Day [later Veterans Day], the day that ended the First World War, and that London would … observe it with a special minute … [and] Big Ben would ring in St. Steven's Tower."

Dundes' comment proved to be a perfect segue for the message John wanted to deliver. He told Dundes about Minute for Peace, saying the event "could appeal to everybody … [by including] a thought for peace by some recognized world leader." He suggested they "give it feeling by ringing a bell" and have a good announcer intone, "Add your thought, your prayer, your commitment to work for world peace." Dundes liked the idea and invited John to his office for further discussion.

Eleven days later, on 22 November, President John F. Kennedy was assassinated, and the United States entered a thirty day Period of Mourning, which would conclude on 22 December, the winter solstice. John called Dundes and said, "Why don't we get the nation to end the Period of Mourning for President Kennedy with a Minute for Peace?" Dundes concurred.

John went to the KCBS studio to listen to recordings made by President Kennedy. Almost immediately, he found the statement he had hoped to find, spoken at the United Nations two years earlier on 25 September 1961. [256] "Never have the nations of the world had so much to lose or so much to gain," came Kennedy's famous New England accent from the audio tape. "Together we shall save our planet, or together we shall perish in its flames. Save it we can – and save it we must – and then shall we earn the eternal

---

[256] Ibid.

thanks of mankind and, as peacemakers, the eternal blessing of God." [257]

Audio engineers at KCBS produced copies of the tape and Dundes sent them to Bay Area Broadcasting Association member stations and other local media. Dundes' news release announced that KCBS would broadcast a Minute for Peace on Sunday, 22 December 1963, at 11:00 a.m. [258] which coincided with the approximate time of day President Kennedy had been shot a month earlier in Dallas, Texas. [259]

The *San Francisco Chronicle* publicized the event, news wire services picked it up, and the concept spread across the nation. Some radio and television stations broadcast an hour-long special about the deceased President leading up to their Minute for Peace.

"Minute for Peace" newspaper statements, 22 December 1963

At 11:00 a.m. today in the Bay Area, in response to proclamations by public officials and appeals by church leaders, a "Minute for Peace" will be observed in the late President's memory. – *Oakland (California) Tribune*

At the conclusion of the mourning period for the late and honored President John Fitzgerald Kennedy, there has been officially proclaimed a Minute for Peace. – *The Monitor (Archdiocese of San Francisco)*

Cleveland will observe a "Minute for Peace" in Public Square at the same hour as the President's death. – unidentified newspaper Cleveland, Ohio

Phoenix citizens were urged yesterday to observe the "International Moment for Peace" at noon today when the 30-day mourning period for the late President Kennedy officially ends. – unidentified newspaper, Phoenix, Arizona

San Franciscans will join at 11 a.m. today with all Americans – with nearly the whole world, really – in prayerful observance of a "Minute for Peace" ... for the late President John F. Kennedy. – *San Francisco (California) Examiner*

---

[257] John F. Kennedy, Address before the General Assembly of the United Nations, 25 September 1961.

[258] San Francisco Chamber of Commerce, news release, 20 December 1963.

[259] President John Fitzgerald Kennedy was shot at 12:30 p.m. Central Standard Time in Dallas, Texas.

Churches and synagogues became involved. Rabbi Alvin Fine, an outspoken advocate for civil and human rights and, later, a charter member of San Francisco's Human Rights Commission, helped organize a Minute for Peace Committee within the San Francisco chapter of the national People-to-People Program. [260] Catholic Archbishop Joseph T. McGucken asked pastors of the 134 churches in the Archdiocese of San Francisco to ring their church bells for one minute at 11:00 a.m. and recite the "Prayer of Saint Francis" in all churches that celebrate an 11:00 Sunday Mass. [261] The Rev. Jacob M. Bellig, pastor of the Oakland Neighborhood Church, said all members of his congregation would join hands in a prayer for world peace. [262] And the Rt. Rev. James A. Pike, bishop of the Episcopal Diocese of California, wrote, "By pausing to observe the Minute for Peace, mankind throughout the Christian world has the opportunity to join with his neighbors of every conviction in a brief but significant interval of common dedication to the principles of eternal truth and love." [263]

Another cleric took Minute for Peace into the political arena at the Republican National Convention, held at San Francisco's Cow Palace in July 1964. There, the Rev. John G. Geranios, Presbyter of the Greek Orthodox Archdiocese of North and South America and Dean of the Greek Orthodox Archdiocese of Northern California, stated in his benediction, "The City of San Francisco, birthplace of the United Nations and a city dedicated to peace, has initiated global observance of a daily simultaneous Minute for Peace. Let us unite our thoughts and prayers as we seek the understanding and good will that will bring peace in our own hearts, peace with our neighbors, and peace throughout the world." [264]

California governor Jerry Brown honored John McConnell with a telegram in December 1963 that read: "I think this [Minute for Peace] would be a fitting memorial to President Kennedy and I have sent your suggestion on to Washington. I personally intend to devote a part of my day on December 22 in prayer for President Kennedy and for world peace." [265]

---

[260] Minute for Peace Committee, "People-to-People Program."

[261] John McConnell, news release, 17 December 1963.

[262] San Francisco Chamber of Commerce, news release, 20 December 1963.

[263] Bishop James A. Pike, letter 28 December 1963.

[264] John G. Geranios, news release, 16 July 1964.

[265] San Francisco Chamber of Commerce, news release, 20 December 1963.

President Lyndon B. Johnson also received word of these San Francisco events from Harry A. Lee, president of the San Francisco Chamber of Commerce, who sought White House participation. [266]

These telegrams motivated John to draft a suggestion for President Johnson's Christmas speech to the United Nations. John's communiqué to the President read, in part: "The history of man has a long record of almost continuous war. … However there are those who see in the ancient message of Christmas … a promise that peace will come to men of good will. … All over the world people are now joining in a daily Minute for Peace, stopping for at least a minute to seriously think about peace or to pray for peace, conscious of a link in mind and spirit with the whole family of man." [267]

The City of San Francisco decided to take the Minute for Peace idea east to the New York World's Fair in 1964 and 1965. Peter Tamaras, a member of the city's board of supervisors who strongly believed in John, presented to his peers an idea that the city erect an exhibit consisting of a ten-foot globe, circled by a three-foot plastic satellite that would trace a beam of light across the globe's surface; each revolution would take one minute and would, therefore, represent one Minute for Peace. [268]

The cost for design and construction was estimated at $25,000 to $50,000 plus another $40,000 to $50,000 for space rental, equipment and operation for each of the fair's two-year run. [269] The board of supervisors granted their unanimous support for the idea but did not approve funding, [270] presumably because of massive sewer and street light replacement projects, the bond issues for which were to appear on an upcoming ballot on 2 June. [271] Instead, the board issued a proclamation, signed by mayor John F. Shelley on 11 June 1964, that endorsed the exhibit as "one which has undeniable merit as a humanitarian concept." The proclamation authorized the mayor "to appoint a Citizens Committee whose objective shall be the raising of

---

266 Ibid.

267 John McConnell, telegram to Lyndon B. Johnson, December 1963.

268 Editorial, *(San Francisco) News Call Bulletin.*

269 Minute for Peace, "Proposal for San Francisco Exhibit at the New York World's Fair."

270 Editorial, *(San Francisco) News Call Bulletin.*

271 "And lighting bonds … top level support," a partial newspaper article with a partial headline.

sufficient funds from the public." [272]

John McConnell, naturally, was on this committee, using his power of persuasion to promote the project through newspapers, electronic media and public speaking engagements. One fundraising idea, estimated to cover the entire cost of the exhibit and pavilion rental, was the sale of 150,000 Global Peace Clocks, called UNICLOK, with a rotating outer ring that would show designated Minute of Peace times around the world. These were to be miniature replicas of a large ten-foot UNICLOK that would be part of the San Francisco exhibit.

In addition, John visualized a Minute for Peace Scroll that would be signed by visitors at the World's Fair. He hoped as many as one million people would inscribe their names as "members of the family of man who have determined to deepen their own understanding and to encourage understanding in others that will lead to world peace." The scroll, John proposed, would be placed on permanent display in the rotunda of the San Francisco City Hall after the World's Fair. He suggested it then be copied onto microfilm and, reaching back to his Star of Hope concept, "be placed in a visible satellite to circle the earth."

In his proposal to the San Francisco Board of Supervisors, John wrote, "Minute for Peace offers a new approach. Its purpose is not to convert, but to inspire. Not to teach new dogmas, but to make dynamic the neglected beliefs and commitments common to all men of good will." [273]

However, in spite of the city's good intentions and John's hard work, insufficient preparation time prevailed and the Minute for Peace exhibit did not make an appearance at the World's Fair in 1964. When it did arrive in 1965, it was less spectacular but, perhaps, more effective because it was associated, not with San Francisco, but with the United Nations in a stylistic pavilion vacated by the Government of Sierra Leone. [274]

This change in venue resulted from John's attendance at the International Convocation on Pacem in Terris in New York City in February 1965. There, world leaders considered mechanisms to obtain world peace in the context of

---

[272] San Francisco, *Resolution No. 293-64.*

[273] Minute for Peace, "Proposal for San Francisco Exhibit at the New York World's Fair."

[274] Minute for Peace, "International Exhibit on the United Nations at the New York World's Fair 1965 featuring Minute for Peace."

Pope John XXIII's April 1963 encyclical of the same name. The convocation coincided with a resolution by the United Nations General Assembly that 1965 was to be an International Co-operation Year. [275]

At the conference, psychiatrist and educator Jerome Frank spoke in favor of Minute for Peace as one practical step toward the conference goals. As a consequence, John and Althya Youngman, who had also come from San Francisco to advance Minute for Peace, received an invitation to the home of Paul G. Hoffman, director of the United Nations Special Fund. Offering an entrée into the UN, Hoffman suggested that John and Youngman meet with Earl Osborn of the Institute for International Order (later the World Policy Institute), an educational organization focusing on global affairs, and Hilary Barratt-Brown, director of the World Federation of United Nations Associations. [276]

"Again my faith was challenged," John wrote in November 1966 in *Faith at Work*, a New York magazine that stemmed from the work and writings of Episcopal priest the Rev. Sam Shoemaker, co-founder of Alcoholics Anonymous. "If the [Minute for Peace] movement was to gain widest acceptance, no one less than Secretary-General U Thant would suffice to produce the first of a series of broadcast messages. I was told such a thing was impossible. A dozen reasons of policy and precedent were cited." [277]

However, John trusted his faith, coupled with his initiative, his value of international symbolism, and his innate skill to communicate his vision into credible concepts for people who operated at high levels of global influence. [278] As Hoffman had suggested, John contacted Osborn and Barratt-Brown, who were receptive. He also called the Secretary-General's assistant C. V. Narasimhan, who, as John recalled, "seemed anxious to help." [279] Narasimhan said he would take the idea to U Thant because Minute for Peace was an official project of the City of San Francisco and the Secretary-General was to go there in June for the twentieth anniversary of the signing of the United Nations Charter. Narasimhan instructed John to contact Robert Gros,

---

[275] United Nations, "Plans for Observance of 'International Co-operation Year' in 1965" news release, 21 December 1964.

[276] John McConnell, memo, 7 March 1965.

[277] John McConnell, *Faith at Work*, November 1966.

[278] Tom Dowd, telephone interview by author, 8 November 2005.

[279] John McConnell, interview by author, Denver, Colorado, August 2004.

chairman of the UN anniversary program in San Francisco to enlist his participation with the request.

"My heart leaped for joy," John wrote in *Faith at Work*, "for Robert Gros was a cherished friend of long standing and one of the staunch supporters of Minute for Peace." With the ease of a phone call, John secured Gros' endorsement. [280]

The result was a moving speech by U Thant at the UN anniversary ceremony at the Cow Palace on 26 June 1965. "We live in a world of noise," the Secretary-General said, "yet our conscience is called the still, small voice. As Dag Hammarskjöld once pointed out, 'We all have within us a center of stillness surrounded by silence.' Unless we heed our own conscience, we shall continue to be attracted by what is loud and garish, and lose our sense of values. If there is no peace in the world today, it is because there is no peace in the minds of men. It is important, therefore, that all of us should determine to set aside some time each day to commune with ourselves, to talk with our own still, small voices, to devote even one minute for thoughts of peace and good will." [281]

U Thant's message, which he had also pre-recorded four days earlier, was played over the public address system at the World's Fair simultaneously with his live appearance on the West Coast. [282] The speech subsequently reached the world via United Nations radio, major U.S. news networks, networks in other countries, and international shortwave. [283]

Prior to this major UN event, San Francisco mayor John F. Shelley proclaimed 26 June 1965 as Minute for Peace Day, urging city citizens "to observe a Minute for Peace at 12 noon on that day, and at 12 noon on each succeeding day in 1965." [284] Likewise, in New York, John McConnell addressed a convention of the National Education Association on 29 June, telling them Minute for Peace was a "new way for achieving harmony." [285]

John noted arduous realities of his stint in New York. "Since there is no

---

280 John McConnell, *Faith at Work*, November 1966.

281 Brother Mandus, "Minute for Peace History," *Power Lines Magazine*, May-June 1967, p. 33, posted online at www.earthsite.org/Minute2004.htm.

282 John McConnell, "Minute for Peace Report," 1965.

283 John McConnell, *Faith at Work*, November 1966.

284 *Minute for Peace* proclamation, San Francisco mayor John F. Shelley, 12 May 1965.

285 John McConnell, speech to National Education Association, 29 June 1965.

staff here to work on the urgent problem of fundraising for the [World's Fair] exhibit, Mrs. Youngman and I have been drafted." To that end, John and Youngman relied on, what he referred to as, his "many appropriate contacts" and her "extremely important connections and valuable experience in this field." [286]

The Minute for Peace exhibit opened on 17 May 1965, a month before U Thant's speech. John's and Youngman's labors continued until the World's Fair closed on 17 October 1965. The exhibit, as originally envisioned, was not built, even though John had secured design and construction assistance from Raymond Loewy, [287] the celebrated industrial designer whose comments advocating a "star of good will" had been read into the U.S. Congressional Record by senator Lyndon B. Johnson in January 1958. Likewise, pledges or contributions from the United Nations, the Government of Sierra Leone, the Institute for International Order, the Center for Democratic Studies, ITT Corporation, IBM World Trade Corporation, Studio Press of San Francisco, a New York restaurant associated with the UN cookbook, and interested individuals, including members of San Francisco's Minute for Peace Committee, went unused. [288]

Instead, the exhibit consisted primarily of a Minute for Peace book, which was signed by over 50,000 visitors from seventy-two countries. [289] John, while encouraged, was not satisfied with this. Reaching beyond the fairgrounds, he found recorded peace statements by Pope Paul VI and Mahatma Gandhi and added these to U Thant's message. He secured current statements from world ambassadors by toting "a heavy Uher reel-to-reel tape recorder" around the United Nations Headquarters. [290]

Radio Corporation of America (RCA), the official media network at the World's Fair, provided technical personnel and facilities to combine peace-oriented visuals with these audio recordings [291] then telecast them three times a day on over 200 closed-circuit color television sets at the fair. [292] Soft drink

[286] John McConnell, memo, 7 March 1965.
[287] Ibid.
[288] Multiple Minute for Peace documents, 1965.
[289] Hilary G. Barratt-Brown, letter to John McConnell, 24 November 1965.
[290] John McConnell, interview by author, Denver, Colorado, August 2004.
[291] John McConnell, memo, 7 March 1965.
[292] John McConnell, "Minute for Peace, Broadcast plans and commitments," 6 June 1965.

company Coca-Cola played their carillon to gain attendees' attention before and after each telecast. [293]

Commercial networks Columbia Broadcasting System (CBS) and National Broadcasting Company (NBC) transmitted Minute for Peace messages throughout the U.S. [294] while people in Europe and Africa heard them via NASA and the International Telecommunication Union, the UN's oldest specialized agency, which, coincidentally, celebrated its 100th anniversary on the same day the Minute for Peace exhibit opened. [295] In addition, Radio New York Worldwide, the International Education Broadcasting Corporation of the Mormon Church, operating under the call letters WRUL, sent the messages via shortwave around the globe. [296]

As John observed the RCA telecasts, he noted the enigma of "ambassadors from warring countries saying the same thing about peace." [297] These words, signals that most people want peace, inspired John to further his campaign for global accord. In later months, he used the original few statements by U Thant, Gandhi and Pope Paul VI as models for more Minute for Peace messages, about 100 words in length, [298] by globally respected people such as Paul G. Hoffman, author and anthropologist Margaret Mead, author and psychiatrist Erich Fromm, Britain's Lord Caradon, Chief S. O. Adebo of Nigeria, G. P. Malalasekera of Ceylon, M. Rafik Asha of Syria, and ambassadors Francisco Cuevas Cancino of Mexico, Mohamed Awad El-Kony of the United Arab Republic, Michael Comay of Israel, and Adlai Stevenson of the United States. [299] John asked people on New York Streets to make statements of peace, [300] and the United Nations International Children's

---

[293] John McConnell, "Minute for Peace Report," 1965.

[294] John McConnell, "Minute for Peace, Broadcast plans and commitments," 6 June 1965.

[295] Communicorp, "United Nations Exhibition to open at World's Fair in the Sierra Leone Pavilion on May 17," news release.

[296] John McConnell, interview by author, Denver, Colorado, August 2004.

[297] Ibid.

[298] Donald E. Mullen, "Minute for Peace: One Man's Dream," United Press International, 9 October 1966.

[299] John P. Shanley, "Prominent World Figures to be heard as WOR commences Minute for Peace June 26," WOR Radio news release, 24 June 1966. "'Minute for Peace' Gathers Momentum Around the World," *The Sun-Reporter*, 9 July 1966. *Faith at Work*, November 1966.

[300] Donald E. Mullen, "Minute for Peace: One Man's Dream," United Press

Emergency Fund (UNICEF) distributed comments by children from the United Nations International School (UNIS). [301]

In his Minute for Peace broadcast, Alex Quaison-Sackey of Ghana, the nineteenth president of the UN General Assembly, stated, "The desire for peace is not enough. We must work hard to remove the root causes that create friction between nation and nation, between man and man. We should devote a minute a day to silence, in which to examine ourselves and find out if, in fact, in our individual lives, we accept every man, whether he be yellow, white, or black, as part of the human race. Only when there is a moral conscience can we hope to achieve effective peace." [302] Seeking to attract attention from as many people as possible, John arranged for these messages to be aired on WOR Radio, one of New York City's flagship broadcasting facilities. [303]

Seeing himself now in the midst of major spokespersons for world peace, John McConnell felt fully alive, inspired and invigorated. The United Nations was the place to be. So, in late 1965, John moved to New York City and took residence at the New York Theological Seminary. He initially obtained desk space across from Grand Central Station at 415 Lexington Avenue, then established a Minute for Peace office at 777 United Nations Plaza in a large office building known as the UN Church Center, directly across First Avenue from UN Headquarters at New York. [304] An article by author and columnist Cleveland Amory in *The Saturday Review* in January 1966 identified John as "a man with no previous connection with any organized peace movement" at the time he launched Minute for Peace. [305]

That statement may have been true in late 1963, but by early 1966, it demonstrated how far John McConnell had come in a little over two years. Walking the UN corridors, John could hear his mother's prayer song: "Oh, the faith that works by love / will move mountains when we pray. / Oh, the faith that works by love / will turn darkness into day," resonating in his mind.

International, 9 October 1966.

301 John McConnell, interview by author, Denver, Colorado, August 2004.

302 Alex Quaison-Sackey, Minute for Peace news release, 19 September 1965.

303 John P. Shanley, "Prominent World Figures to be heard as WOR commences Minute for Peace June 26," WOR Radio news release, 24 June 1966.

304 John McConnell, interview by author, Denver, Colorado, August 2004.

305 Cleveland Amory, "First of the Month" column, *Saturday Review*, 8 January 1966.

For, in New York, he not only had connections, he had a plan "to create a worldwide network of mind and spirit fostering good will and peace."

His plan recommended that people "invite two or more friends to observe Minute for Peace. Exchange thoughts with them on methods and techniques for achieving peace – personal, family, global. Each of these partners will, in turn, get two others." [306]

Then John applied exponential mathematics – "two, raised to the thirty-third power" – and saw the potential for world peace in as few as thirty-three days. Describing his "33 Campaign," John said, "By each person enlisting two friends who care for each other and for world peace, in 33 days, everyone on the planet will be participating in a great network, held together by the substance of good will, to build a climate for peace." [307]

Later, John modified the plan to thirty-three weeks, then thirty-three months as he realized his fellow humans were not adopting his peace plan as swiftly as he desired. He offered this advice, "If you feel insecure, choose close friends for peace matters. If you feel secure, choose an adversary and be a bridge of understanding." [308]

Regardless of the time required for implementation, thirty-three days or thirty-three months, John's idea was innovative because of its expansiveness. While it would be easy for a preacher to convince those already baptized or initiated, John hoped people would reach out and convert friends who might have reasons to favor war and conflict. This hope embodied one of his common themes, spoken many times in various ways throughout his life, that people should "come together where they agree to cooperate for peace in different ways."

The transformation of John's concept into practical reality paralleled changing social paradigms that resulted in massive marches associated with the Civil Rights Movement of the 1950s and 1960s and resounding protests, especially on college campuses, against the Vietnam War in the 1960s and 1970s. Expanding on the sentiment of U.S. author and Unitarian clergyman, Edward Everett Hale, who lived most of his life in the 1800s, John created Minute for Peace brochures that iterated, in verse:

---

[306] John McConnell, "Peace Plan."

[307] "'Minute for Peace' Gathers Momentum Around the World," *The Sun-Reporter*, 9 July 1966.

[308] John McConnell, "Meanings of Peace," meditations, 5 June 1966.

I am only one – I cannot do very much, but what I CAN do, I will do.
I will tell my neighbor what I am doing, and soon he will do what he CAN do.
Neighbors will tell neighbors until millions of neighbors are doing what they CAN do.
We are each only one, but there are a lot of us and we CAN change the world! [309] [310]

"Meanings of Peace," 5 June 1966

The inner glow in each individual can be increased by connecting it with the glow in all the other people of the world. This can be aided by Minute for Peace, which provides a conscious link with the glow of good will in every man. Awareness of this common bond of spirit, which encompasses the wordless meaning of being at the heart of all great humanitarian teaching, religious and non-religious, will provide a global glow of good will and mutual trust.

In this way the dark barriers of fear and greed will be pierced by the rays of faith and love. This will bring a new climate where the peace builders can lead in creating a new world of freedom, order, beauty, meaning and joy. This "inner glow" refers to the feeling of wonder, awe, gratitude, worship, which is experienced by most everyone at some time. The most numerous examples of it are found in poets, artists, musicians, scientists (sometimes at the moment of discovery), religious mystics, gifted teachers, some political zealots, and most everyone truly in love. It is found most in new mothers and little children. It goes by many names, but none truly defines it. Love, Joy, turned on, salvation, Holy Spirit, serenity, etc.

As a New Yorker and a world citizen, John threw himself wholeheartedly into his campaign for peace. One example occurred regarding a conflict

---

[309] John McConnell, "Power for Peace."

[310] Edward Everett Hale (1822-1909): "I am only one, but still I am one. I cannot do everything, but still I can do something; and because I cannot do everything, I will not refuse to do something I can do."

between India and Pakistan over the Himalayan land of Kashmir in 1965. John and Althya Youngman had hosted a meeting at the United Nations Church Center for a special program of music to honor Mahatma Gandhi. Because Gandhi was revered by people throughout that part of the world, they invited delegates from the UN missions of both India and Pakistan.

"I had a record on which Gandhi spoke," John recalled, "and the playing of this record was followed by a long period of silent prayer, which ended in the delegates spontaneously singing 'Ramdhun,' Gandhi's favorite tune." The event was, to John, a sign the Lord had answered a prayer. "I had gone to a store that sold records and found the exact message from Gandhi that I had hoped to find. The man I bought it from said, 'It's interesting that you should ask for that because I just obtained this recording, and prior to that, I didn't know it existed.'" [311]

Because of that event to honor Gandhi, John and Youngman felt emotionally close to people of both India and Pakistan. Writing in *Faith at Work*, John recounted in great detail his experience of praying at the United Nations for a peaceful resolution to the conflict: "On the night [in September 1965] that the Security Council met to call for a ceasefire, we entered the council chamber and remained there until the ceasefire was secured after three in the morning. The room was charged with tension as India and Pakistan delegates maneuvered for advantage. Angry words were hurled from one side of the table to the other. I looked around and realized that less than 20 observers were watching this most important meeting. I wondered how many of them were praying, as we were, for those who held the power of decision.

"Now it was after midnight. The men below us faced a crisis that could easily escalate into widespread warfare and multiply by a thousand times the deadly carnage that had already taken place. I was deep in intercessory prayer, striving to bring into that room the consciousness of the presence of God. I prayed that wisdom would be given our [U.S.] Ambassador [Arthur Joseph] Goldberg, who was chairman, as well as Lord Caradon and Soviet Ambassador [Nikolai] Federenko in their efforts toward reconciliation – that they would hear the still, small voice.

"I do not know how much our prayers contributed to the success of the

[311] John McConnell, manuscript review with author, October 2005.

meeting that night. I do know that Ambassador Goldberg surpassed himself in handling it, that Ambassador Federenko spoke words of understanding and conciliation, that the violence of the disputants was gradually tempered, and that a reluctant but welcome ceasefire was finally obtained. I shall never forget the experience and the conviction it strengthened in me that great power is released whenever people agree in prayer." [312]

John's recounting of the possible role of prayer during this critical UN debate was consistent with U Thant's belief, "Meditation is a process that cleanses the mind of impurities. It cultivates such qualities as concentration, awareness, intelligence and tranquility, leading finally to the attainment of the highest wisdom." [313]

As though mystically uplifted through prayer, the Minute for Peace concept gained more momentum at several ceremonies, especially one in which Secretary-General U Thant, as well as children from the UN International School, rang the Peace Bell at the United Nations on 4 October 1966, the feast of St. Francis. That date marked the first anniversary of an historic visit to the UN by Pope Paul VI.

The Peace Bell, also known as the Japanese Peace Bell or the Children's Peace Bell, had been the idea of Chiyoji Nakagawa, former mayor of Uwajima, Shikoku, Japan. Nakagawa's country cast the bell on United Nations Day, 24 October 1952, as a symbol of everlasting peace and presented it to the UN on 8 June 1954, even though the Pacific island nation had not yet gained admission to the world body. Metal in the bell, which was a little over three feet tall, two feet wide and weighed 256 pounds, consisted of coins, collected by children, from delegates of the UN's Member States who attended the 13th General Conference of the United Nations Association in Paris, France, in 1951. Inscribed inside the bell, in Japanese, are the words: "Long live absolute world peace."

The Peace Bell was erected in a landscaped area, known as the Japanese Peace Garden, next to the Secretariat Building. It was housed in a Japanese-style structure, made of cypress, that resembled a Shinto shrine. The base was

---

312 John McConnell, *Faith at Work*, November 1966.

313 U Thant, quoted in *The Spiritual Work of the United Nations and the Liberation of Humanity* [online]. Aquarian Age Community [cited 12 February 2005]. Available from www.aquaac.org/un/medmtgs.html.

donated by Israel. [314] Even though a beautiful symbol of peace, located in a prominent site in the United Nation's main courtyard, it was never used. In fact, in 1966, prior to the 4 October ceremony, *The Christian Science Monitor*, described the bell as "the mellow, green-stained Japanese temple bell that hundreds of thousands of visitors to the UN Headquarters see but never hear." [315]

The historical bell-ringing ceremony was John McConnell's idea. It came about, in part, because of a letter from Chief S. O. Adebo, Nigeria's permanent UN representative, to U Thant on 19 September 1966. In his letter, Adebo wrote that John's inspiration to ring the Peace Bell was "a suggestion which appears to be deserving of consideration." The Nigerian ambassador elaborated, "Mr. McConnell feels that the ringing ceremony would encourage people all over the world to pause and reflect for one minute how peace might be attained through their own personal thoughts and actions and that this would create renewed interest in your own often-expressed thought that 'Peace begins in the minds of men.'" [316]

The Christian Science Monitor credited John McConnell as the originator of the Minute for Peace ceremony, reporting, "[The bell] will toll at the hands of a select group of children from the UN International School" with the objective "to encourage people around the world to pause and reflect for a minute on ways in which they can help keep peace." [317] The seven children who rang the bell were from Ghana, Hungary, Jamaica, Libya, Pakistan, Panama and the United States. [318]

Elsewhere, six foreign exchange students from as many countries were among 400 people who participated in a United Nations Festival in Titusville, Pennsylvania, where tapes of the UN International School children ringing the Peace Bell were played. [319] Students at Woodstock Country School in South Woodstock, Vermont, originated a petition for peace that they sent to

---

314 *Japanese Peace Bell – Gift of People of Japan to United Nations* [online]. Japan-101 [cited 12 February 2005]. Available from www.japan-101.com/history/japanese_peace_bell.htm.

315 "How and why ...," *The Christian Science Monitor*, 27 September 1966.

316 S. O. Adebo, letter to U Thant, 19 September 1966.

317 "How and why ...," *The Christian Science Monitor*, 27 September 1966.

318 United Nations Press Services, "Note to Correspondents," 4 October 1966.

319 "400 Present at Festival Held in City Rec Center," *The Titusville(Pennsylvania) Herald*, October 1966.

the United Nations. [320] Children from Sanchez School in the San Francisco Unified School District, representing at least six different nationalities, considered activities that bring personal tranquility: reading stories about peace, dancing, singing lullabies, living at home, helping mothers, playing with friends, talking peace. [321]

The city council in Fairfax, California, agreed to blow the fire department whistle "at noon hereafter to signal residents to take 'a minute for peace.'" [322] San Francisco hosted several Minute for Peace events; one of them involved children at the St. Francis Day Home ringing a replica of the UN Peace Bell. [323] And other communities participated in various ways.

However, some city councils, such as officials in San Anselmo, California, chose not to demonstrate an outward sign of peace lest it, as one councilman posed, "strengthen the resistance of the people we're fighting over there [in Southeast Asia]." [324]

Pope Paul VI included a Minute for Peace in his 1966 Christmas message, saying, "Peace must live and reign in men's consciousness." [325] The Pope delivered his statement at 1900 Greenwich Mean Time (5:00 p.m. in Rome, 1:00 p.m. in Dallas, and 11:00 a.m. in San Francisco) on 21 December, marking, to the minute, the origination of the first Minute for Peace broadcasts. The incentive for the Pope to honor Minute for Peace stemmed from John McConnell's initiative to present the Minute for Peace idea to the Vatican's delegate to the United Nations and the papal secretary of state. [326]

A front page article in the *San Francisco (California) Progress* attributed such successes to John, noting that, in three years, Minute for Peace had "become a simple, daily ritual for many people in many countries." The paper quoted John as saying, "These are people of all religions and of no

---

[320] "Petition for Peace" letter, Woodstock Country School.

[321] "What Is Peace? Ideas from the children of Sanchez School in San Francisco," 15 June 1967.

[322] "Whistle to Signal Minute for Peace," *S.R. Independent Journal*, 23 August 1966.

[323] Photograph and caption, *Chinese World*, 8 October 1966.

[324] Stephen Cook, "Peace Siren Stilled: Hub Council Cool to Idea Unless China Does Too," *S. R. Independent-Journal*, 24 July 966.

[325] Pope Paul VI, "Minute Messages from taped Minute for Peace broadcasts."

[326] John McConnell, "Minute for Peace Report."

religion, of practically every color and political persuasion." [327]

In late 1966, as part of its fiftieth anniversary, Lions International, the world's largest service club with a membership of 850,000 in 140 countries, adopted Minute for Peace. The Lions' initiative began with a $50,000 essay contest for young people of the world to write on the theme "Peace is Attainable." The contest was judged by former U.S. President Dwight Eisenhower, former President of Costa Rica Jose Figueres, Prince Bernhard of the Netherlands, president of the University of the Philippines General Carlos Romulo, U.S. secretary of state Dean Rusk, and professor Hideki Yukawa of Kyoto University, Japan. [328]

John McConnell recognized the opportunity inherent in this contest and contacted members of the San Francisco Lions Club, suggesting Lions include a Minute for Peace as part of their meeting agenda. The San Franciscans, particularly Moreland M. Smith, who later became chairman of the Lions Minute for Peace Committee, liked the idea and took it to the officers of their Multiple District Four, which included California and Nevada. On 21 January 1967, delegates at the District Four convention unanimously adopted [329] a resolution "that a period of silent prayer known as 'A Minute for Peace' be considered as a regular part of every Lions Club meeting [and that Lions] contribute to a growing awareness of the need to set aside some time each day to commune with ourselves, to talk with our own still, small voice, to devote one minute for thoughts of peace and good will." [330]

The district delegates sent their Minute for Peace resolution to the officers and directors of Lions International "with the earnest plea that 'A Minute for Peace' be seriously considered as an ongoing program for Lions and Lions Clubs everywhere." [331] Then in July, Lions International, at their global Golden Anniversary Convention in Chicago, Illinois, adopted the Minute for Peace program and recommended its use to all 22,000 clubs.

---

[327] "Minute for Peace observance," *San Francisco (California)Progress,* 21 December 1966.

[328] "Lions International: Peace Is Attainable" article, Public Relations Board, Inc., newsletter, Vol. 13, Nos. 2-3, November-December 1966.

[329] "Lions Salute to International Understanding" convention program, 28 October 1967.

[330] Lions International District 4, "Minute for Peace Resolution," 21 January 1967.

[331] Ibid.

[332] Three months later, Lions International president Jorge Bird of Puerto Rico spoke at a Lions banquet in San Francisco. His speech, titled "Salute to International Understanding," included a silent Minute for Peace. [333]

Minute for Peace momentum continued as John seemed to straddle the country, organizing activities from his footholds in New York and San Francisco. Others lit complementary torches. Muriel H. Alstrom of Fairfax, California, and founder of Creative Thinking Inc., became director of Bay Area Minute for Peace and asked city councils throughout Marin County to pass Minute for Peace resolutions to be marked by the sounding of city bells and fire sirens. [334] Florence Seymour of Sausalito, California, took an extended trip to Europe as an emissary for Minute for Peace. [335] New York insurance agent Solomon Huber sponsored a fundraising luncheon, stating in his invitation, "I met a man, a self-less man, John McConnell, and the course of my life has changed. I find I have become a crusader for a new idea developed by him, called Minute for Peace, and I love it. I am dedicated to a campaign that may mean the difference between survival and total annihilation." [336]

The International Cooperation Center established a corporate fundraising campaign aimed at the industrial sector, [337] and the World Wide Broadcasting Foundation in New York donated money for Minute for Peace announcements. [338] The actions and sentiments of these, and others, were summarized in the words of Harold S. Miner, president of CARE, Inc., who wrote to John in July 1965, "Prayer is the most powerful force in the world, and it is becoming more and more imperative that this force be harnessed to the cause of peace while we still have a planet on which we can survive." [339]

Likewise, several of the twenty-five notable persons at Huber's luncheon contributed short speeches, all of which were action oriented, on behalf of the Minute for Peace concept. Ralf Brent, president of Radio New York Worldwide, stated, "The more we talk about it [peace] and the more we

---

332 Jorge Bird, memo, 28 October 1967.

333 Minute for Peace International Committee, "Minute for Peace Plan," 1967.

334 "Whistle to Signal Minute for Peace," *S.R. Independent Journal*, 23 August 1966.

335 "Sausalitan Plans Travel for Peace," *S.R. Independent Journal*, 5 July 1966.

336 Solomon Huber, fundraising letter, 15 September 1965.

337 Larry Bogart, International Cooperation Center, letter to members, June 1965.

338 Walter S. Lemmon, letter to John McConnell, 12 July 1965.

339 Harold S. Miner, president, CARE, Inc., to John McConnell, 28 July 1965.

hear about it, more and more into our consciousness Minute for Peace will drive the idea." Norman Ober, director of program and publicity for CBS Radio, spoke of his desire that the National Advertising Review Council grant their "approval for Minute for Peace, which would enable the networks to broadcast these messages coast to coast." Margaret Mead, with whom John would later forge a momentous professional alliance, concluded, "This [Minute for Peace] plan is a device to create a climate of opinion. … If it really goes and goes well, it will create the conditions within which it is easier for people to do other things." [340]

Minute for Peace also spread to other nations. Articles appeared in major Japanese newspapers. [341] Brother Mandus, an ecumenical religious leader, author and lecturer from Blackpool, England, spoke on the benefit of Minute for Peace. [342] People from Belgium, South Africa and Malaysia sent letters of inquiry and support. A leper from India wrote, "Maybe if people stopped thinking so much about war, they could devote more time and effort to help us, lepers, who seem to still exist in spite of atom bombs and space crafts." [343]

Paradoxically, in the late 1960s, at a time when a collective spiritual peace consciousness was needed most, people in the U.S. and its allied countries seemed to think more about the conflict in Vietnam, which continued to escalate, than about creating peace. Television played a role by bringing horrific images of the war into the nation's living rooms via news broadcasts, especially at the time of the evening meal, which heightened people's awareness of war. Even people of good will became ill at ease, and therefore not at peace, within their hearts.

On 20 October 1967, John penned an essay, "Counterforce," that addressed the enigma of the conscious mind that wants peace but continues to think of war, especially when confronted with images of war. "The evildoers are not the ones preventing peace," he wrote. "Our problem is the confusion and indifference in men of good will. They need an idea, a symbol, an experience that all can share. Minute for Peace can provide this; it can bring a consciousness that will unite, inspire and mobilize a compassionate

340 "Comments at Minute for Peace luncheon," Gotham Hotel, 25 August 1965.

341 "Minute for Peace" newsletter, December 1966.

342 Ibid.

343 Ibid.

will for peace." [344]

"Counterforce," 20 October 1967

> The evildoers are not the ones preventing peace. Our problem is the confusion and indifference in men of good will. They need an idea, a symbol, an experience – that all can share. Minute for Peace can provide this; it can bring a consciousness that will unite, inspire and mobilize a compassionate will for peace.
>
> If people of good will on both sides of this conflict (and this can include President Johnson and Ho Chi Minh) will together take a tiny step each day toward peace, the growing unity will soon provide an irresistible counterforce to war.
>
> This can best begin with a silent "minute" observed together (people on both sides agreeing they will participate); with each person in his own way turning his thoughts and feelings to love and peace.
>
> As this is seriously done, more and more individuals will be aware of its great importance and conscious of each other's good will. Words and deeds of peace will then pursue one another through the barriers of prejudice, fear and greed that separate men.
>
> Then the voices of compassion and justice will become words of thunder that cannot be ignored. Those on either side who cling to the methods of war will stand exposed – without reason, without excuse, without sympathy – and without help.

Yet, showing his humanness, John, himself, contributed to this enigma by using doomsday language, such as "the present grave global crisis" and "global holocaust," in letters and essays that also contained messages of hope. [345] However, most of his writing contained clear vision that helped him define peace, an elusive commodity that others, from delegates to the United Nations to anti-Vietnam War demonstrators in American streets, said they wanted.

"Peace is not the cessation of war, which is a period of waiting for other wars," he journaled on 10 June 1966. "Peace is not negation. Peace

---

344 John McConnell, "Counterforce" essay, 20 October 1967.

345 John McConnell, "A New Approach to Solving the Present Grave Global Crisis," 29 May 1967.

is obedience to the law of life. By obedience to the law of mathematics, we acquire instant powers. By obedience to the law of harmony, we acquire music. By obedience to the law of form, we acquire beauty. What's new is the awareness of the human mind and its overwhelming, possibly infinite potential![346] There is power for peace in thoughts of good will."[347]

In an interview with United Press International correspondent Donald E. Mullen in October 1966, John added a nuance about the levels of peaceful thinking. "We must make the important decision between thinking *about peace* and thinking deeply and seriously *about ways of turning the world toward peace*," John told the reporter.[348]

John's creative mind flowed freely at this time and his essays were rich with spiritual awakening and literary metaphor. Yet, on the practical front, he and his associates wrote copy for radio and TV spots and promotional literature. From these, he developed the concept of broadcasting "Earth Minutes," which would differ from Minute for Peace announcements in that they would be "minutes without words, using scenes and sounds that convey a common commitment to harmony with neighbor and nature, views of nature's wonders: children, birds, whales, wind, sea." Through this creative process, John formulated and congealed the phrase, "peace, justice and the care of Earth," that would define his mission in life.[349]

Peace, justice and the care of Earth – the life mission of John McConnell

In 1968, John drafted an eight-year "tactics" document for a "World Peace Blitz" that would envelop the Minute for Peace movement as well as his earlier Star of Hope idea. This tactics document contained two new initiatives, "World Peace Week" for the days of Christmas through New Years, and a Council of World Cities and Towns. In the latter, John envisioned "every town as a town for humanity" with peace proponents growing into a grassroots peace army that would come together for a World Conference on

---

346 John McConnell, journal, 10 June 1966.
347 John McConnell, "The Role of Prayer in my Life," essay.
348 Donald E. Mullen, "Minute for Peace: One Man's Dream," United Press International, 9 October 1966.
349 John McConnell, "Earth Minutes."

Peace in 1975. [350]

He encouraged people to become "Earthbuilders," employing a three-part plan with spiritual, physical and communication components as "the key to personal and global peace." The spiritual component, he suggested, was to be a private Minute for Peace, through which people would "begin each day with a consciousness of God in a silent minute of meditation or prayer, then throughout the day, as you are able, turn your thoughts to the awareness of God's love and of loving people. Your inner voice will then guide you in works of joy and peace." He named the physical component "Planetary Inheritance" through which people would find their "mission to help build the Earth in harmony with nature, tithing time and money to actions that will improve the environment and/or help the poor find their inheritance in the Earth." The communication component invited individuals and groups to "share your experience with your friends ... [and] be a link in a dynamic global network that is building a new Earth." [351]

In many ways, John was aligned with positive thinking advocates Tessie Durlack and Norman Vincent Peale and with Carl Jung's concept of the collective unconscious. He carried a card in his wallet that reminded him to "Expect a Miracle." And he expressed his optimism, albeit in minimalistic monetary terms, in a letter to his friend Althya Youngman on 13 June 1967, "If I had $100.00 a week for a few weeks, it could make the difference between war and peace." The letter described John's daily financial condition, which was meager if not literally from hand to mouth, "Your check gave me a new spurt of energy. I was dreading another day without bus fare or breakfast (I always manage to get lunch) when the letter came with your $7.65. Thanks a million." [352]

Telling Youngman about "terrific" TV spots he had viewed for Minute for Peace, John realized he needed an organization through which he could manifest his vision. To that end, Solomon Huber and Ralf Brent presented a plan to convert the Minute for Peace campaign into a non-profit, tax-exempt foundation. [353]

In 1966, John drafted a proposal for a Minute for Peace board of

---

[350] John McConnell, "World Peace Blitz," 1968.

[351] John McConnell, "The Key to personal and global peace."

[352] John McConnell, letter to Althya Youngman, 13 June 1967.

[353] "Minute for Peace meeting minutes," 28 February 1968.

directors, which would consist of twenty-five international persons, and a small annual budget of $62,600 to pay the salaries for himself as director as well as wages for an administrative director and executive secretary plus office expenses and a promotional campaign. He drafted similar budgets for 1967, 1968 and 1969, the latter of which itemized total projected annual expenses of $125,000, which allowed less for personnel salaries but included a $75,000 film documentary project plus substantial expenses for radio and TV spots, printing and publishing.

The 1969 budget appeared in a multi-page Minute for Peace plan in which John proposed a United Nations resolution that would ask the world body to formally designate 1900 Greenwich Mean Time (GMT) as the world's official Minute for Peace. In other documents throughout the late 1960s, John suggested people around the world recognize three times, each eight hours apart – 0300, 1100 and 1900 hours GMT – "to offer a moment in the waking hours of everyone." [354] His Minute for Peace plan proposed that the United States initiate a global 33 Campaign, beginning on 22 November, the anniversary of John F. Kennedy's assassination.

Yet in spite of these good intentions, John continued to be a man rich with vision while poor with practicality regarding the role of money in society. Like his contemporary, Peace Pilgrim, who forsook money to walk more than 25,000 miles in North America on a personal pilgrimage for peace, he continued to operate, for the most part, alone, freely giving away most of his intellectual property.

Correspondent Mullen, in his UPI interview, wrote of the Minute for Peace operations, "It's not a formal movement at all. It has no board of directors or members, dues paying or otherwise. It's McConnell's baby, and it survives on occasional foundation grants and individual offerings. Its appeal has brought him support from the City of San Francisco, the Secretary-General of the United Nations, and influence, time, money, offices, duplicating machines, recording tape and hundreds of other boosts toward synchronizing world hope." Indeed, Mullen's report was verified by his observance of the scene where the interview occurred, "in a borrowed

---

[354] Donald E. Mullen, "Minute for Peace: One Man's Dream," United Press International, 9 October 1966.

office at the top of the Chrysler Building." [355]

Congruently, in his plan for 1969, John noted Minute for Peace had, to date, been "limited and experimental," subsisting in its first five years on only two grants totaling $7,000 from the World Wide Broadcasting Foundation, a $6,000 grant from the Institute for International Order, and approximately $3,000 from friends who believed in Minute for Peace. John, not a person endowed with wealth, took no salary and had no other job. He slept in his office, reasoning "no one was using it at night, why leave it empty?" [356] He seemed to exist on love for his cause and the belief, as he wrote in his plan, "There is now enough experience, preparation and material that a great Minute for Peace campaign could be launched in 1969." [357]

Offering another point of view, Brother Mandus described John, who was then in his early 50s, as a "simple, humble dreamer with a gentle voice, kindly face and shy smile [whose] blue eyes glowed with enthusiasm as he talked … inspired and invincible … enlightened by the love he radiates. … I frankly marveled how this quiet soul has won his way into the confidence and friendship of world leaders and delegates in the United Nations and established radio broadcasts of Minute for Peace over networks in many countries." Then Mandus offered his own answer, "Of course, he is a man of prayer." [358]

Similarly, Mullen described John as "not a religious fanatic or a picket-waving peace demonstrator," but as having "a shock of grey hair [that] tops a ruddy face with mild blue eyes and a smile that's shy and disarming. [He's a] soft tootling pied piper who really believes that, as a species, man is peace loving, [and his] soft voice belies the fact that he has almost single-handedly brought the Minute for Peace movement to the edge of a global experiment." [359]

While John's softspokenness contrasted his father's booming voice, the image of John in a borrowed office parallels the life of J. S. and Hattie, eking their way across the country on the power of the preacher's word and the message of his ministry. Certainly, John was influenced by his upbringing

355 Ibid.

356 Hans Janitschek, telephone interview by author, 25 February 2005.

357 John McConnell, "Minute for Peace Plan."

358 Brother Mandus, "The Children's Peace Bell."

359 Donald E. Mullen, "Minute for Peace: One Man's Dream," United Press International, 9 October 1966.

and its inherent independence, nomadicity and monetary scarcity as well as his early and intimate association with nature. But, unlike his father, who, with his sermons and published tracts, attempted to direct people's thoughts and actions, John expressed more liberalism, allowing his followers to interpret his messages in ways applicable to them.

His policy memo, drafted in the mid-1960s, advised that Minute for Peace should be "dynamic, but neutral" in order to "provide freedom in extending the movement." John noted, "[Minute for Peace] has obtained support from [political] right and left without leaning either way. ... Participation is spreading without Minute for Peace taking on the label of any particular organization." And, just as a preacher would direct a congregation to spread the word through action, John wrote, "I feel it is important that Minute for Peace be extended through existing organizations as an idea that they implement in their own way." Thus, as he so often did, John willingly gave up potential control of his idea, offering it as a philosophical and spiritual resource to his fellow human beings. [360]

In another essay, titled "Each Man's Conscience," written for Independence Day, John called for "a new declaration ... [with] a greater moral authority ... [and] a new sense of individual responsibility ... for the final answers to life's perplexing problems and for the decisions they require." [361]

"Each Man's Conscience"

> To achieve in our nation and throughout the world a freedom and justice ordained in the American Declaration of Independence, a new declaration is needed – a Declaration of Each Man's Conscience.
>
> If each man recognized his conscience as a greater moral authority than any nation, despotism would soon die and there would be a new birth of peaceful freedom throughout the world. A new sense of individual responsibility would grow as each man saw his importance in society. The quest for knowledge would continue and increase, but every man would search his own conscience for the final answers to life's perplexing problems and for the decisions they require.

---

[360] John McConnell, "On Keeping Minute for Peace Dynamic but Neutral," memo.

[361] John McConnell, "Each Man's Conscience," 4 July (year not given).

> While men would still make mistakes, the results of having each person listen to his own still, small voice would result in a great swing toward attitudes and actions conducive to world peace. Modern communications can promote a daily Minute for Peace, during which people in all countries will turn to their own conscience for thoughts on peace and good will. This new connection in thought and purpose across national boundaries will soon bring the needed climate for understanding and accord and the moral pressure on world leaders to choose the ways of peace.

In another document, "Minute for Peace Will Only Speak for Accord," which he drafted as verse, John poeticized, "Let unity be the mainspring and controversy the balance wheel. The work of Minute for Peace is to wind the mainspring of agreement and accord with words of peace, with headlines for happenings that inspire good will and cooperation." [362]

"Minute for Peace Will Only Speak for Accord"

In controversy,
Minute for Peace will seek and praise the words and actions
that express sincere accord.
Minute for Peace
recognizes the need
to express conflicting opinions
in a free society;
but
Minute for Peace
sees its role as a constant reminder of the good
of accord and cooperation –
essentials for peaceful progress.
Minute for Peace
endorses the idea of a continuing search
to provide the widest possible freedom of voice and action
by individuals, groups and nations;
but
maintains that this should be equaled

[362] John McConnell, "Minute for Peace Will Only Speak for Accord," poem.

by a counterforce,
seeking and affirming unity and cooperation.
At the same time,
Minute for Peace messages will avoid empty clichés and
sentimental phrases
that bring a pseudo-agreement,
void of thought or understanding.
In order to achieve peaceful progress,
the major energy of society,
in money, talk and time
should be directed to areas of agreement and cooperation.
Let unity be the mainspring
and controversy the balance wheel.
The work of Minute for Peace
is to wind the mainspring of agreement and accord with
words of peace,
with headlines for happenings
that inspire good will and cooperation.

In the 1970s and 1980s, John set Minute for Peace aside, at least officially, as he turned his attention to other ideas and endeavors. But, like Star of Hope, the concept never left his consciousness, and he began to promote it again in the 1990s after he had reached the age of 75, during the Persian Gulf War. He wrote letters, news releases and copy for public service announcements, asking people to pause and pray on global, American and Christian holidays: the spring equinox, Independence Day, 22 November, 22 December, and Christmas Eve. He spoke to civic service clubs, church congregations and schools. He made requests to individual cities, states and to U.S. presidents and secretaries-general of the United Nations, asking them to "take the lead in moving the world toward peace." [363] Some of these people and governmental units responded, among them the Franciscans who offered an endorsement in 1991. [364] And events, such as the transcendental meditations that effectively offset crime in Washington, D.C. in June and July 1993, proved that prayerful meditation does generate positive human

[363] John McConnell, interview by author, Denver, Colorado, August 2004.
[364] Brother Thomas Grady, OSF, fax to John McConnell, 9 January 1991.

energy that can aid society. [365]

In the first decade of the third millennium, John stated, "If we had major media and maybe one web site get the ball rolling with creative altruism and love, then we might see Minute for Peace contagiously spread all over the world. We could get down to the local level with people who believe in nonviolence and the power of peace. Then our celebrations wouldn't be of governments or presidents or corporations or institutions but celebrations of the amazing web of life that we have on our planet." [366]

---

[365] *Effects of Group Practice of the Transcendental Meditation Program on Preventing Violent Crime in Washington, DC: Results of the National Demonstration Project, June-July 1993* [online]. Institute of Science, Technology and Public Policy [cited 16 July 2005]. Available from www.istpp.org/crime_prevention/.

[366] John McConnell, interview by author, Denver, Colorado, August 2004.

7

Anna, John Paul, and Christa Marie

(1965 to present)

John is a visionary and we need visionaries on Planet Earth to point the way to a better future.
– Anna McConnell, 25 July 2005

WHEN JOHN MCCONNELL MOVED from the Bay Area to New York in 1965, he traveled alone, leaving his children, Connie and Cary, then 18 and 16, to live with their grandparents, J. S. and Hattie, in Oakland. But while in New York, enmeshed in Minute for Peace, John met the woman who would become his second wife. [367]

Anna Marie Zacharias weighed only three pounds, ten ounces when she was born prematurely on 11 February 1931 in New York City. Her father Ferdinand was born in 1905 in Peterkau, a German village in the country then known as Russia-Poland. When he was 5, the Zacharias family emigrated to Canada, then to New York City seven years later. Anna's mother, Hannah Anna Bertha Richter, was born in Nordhausen, Germany, in 1908. Her family came to New York City in 1913, a year before the First World War erupted in central Europe. Ferdinand and Hannah met at a New Year's Eve party in 1927 and married the following October. The couple raised Anna and her younger brother Paul, her only sibling, in Westport and Bridgeport,

[367] Unless otherwise footnoted, all information in this chapter originated from: Anna and John McConnell, interview by author, Denver, Colorado, August 2004; Anna McConnell, telephone interview by author, 25 July 2005; Anna McConnell, e-mails to author, August 2005; Anna and John McConnell, manuscript reviews with author, Denver, Colorado, October 2005 and January 2006.

Connecticut, where Anna attended Zion Lutheran Elementary School and Bridgeport Central High School, graduating in 1949.

Her mother's side of the family was blessed with professional opera singers, and Anna's childhood passion was to follow their lead. She started with tap dance lessons, and her first performance was for her school's Christmas program. She was in "kindiegarten," as she pronounced it. "I remember coming out on the stage to this day," she recalled nearly seventy years later, "and looking at that audience and thinking, 'Wow! This is what I want to do.'"

Anna's grandparents on her father's side of the family had moved from a farm in New Jersey and taken jobs as caretakers for an apartment house in Bronx, New York. When visiting, Anna and Paul slept on the floor. "I remember lying awake, listening to the noise of the city," she said, "and shortly after that, I heard 'Rhapsody in Blue.' It was like the city noises I heard at Grandma and Grandpa's." Lured by George and Ira Gershwin's music, she took piano lessons. Voice training came a little later, when she was 14, along with her intention to become an opera singer.

"I took every music course offered in high school and college," she recalled. In addition, starting as a high school sophomore, Anna received private lessons from a voice teacher at the Brooklyn Conservatory of Music. Her once-a-week commute included a round-trip train ride from Bridgeport to New York City's Grand Central Station then another across the Brooklyn Bridge. When she arrived back in Bridgeport at 9:00 p.m., her father would meet her at the station for a welcome car ride home. In the summer prior to her junior year, Anna enrolled in voice and sight singing courses at The Julliard School, to which she traveled daily by commuter train and bus.

While obtaining her Bachelor of Arts degree in music from the University of Bridgeport, counselors and family encouraged Anna to take education courses, but she resisted and, upon graduation in 1953, she had taken only one. Nevertheless, her first professional job, after two short stints as an office worker for an insurance company and a utility company, was as assistant teacher for Immaculate Conception Day Care in Brooklyn, New York. "I went to New York City for my singing," Anna said, "and took the day care job to earn my bread and butter." The job, working with children four and five years of age, was easily attained, Anna recalled. "Even though my degree was not in education, New York City was looking desperately for teachers and would hire anyone who had a degree."

Anna remained in that position for only one school year. "It was awful," she remembered. "All of those kids were without a father, raised by single mothers. My upbringing was that I didn't speak unless I was spoken to, but those kids were all over. I was able to control them, but I would go home at night and I would cry over those poor children."

When June came, Anna returned to her parents' home in Bridgeport, having decided to leave education forever. But, during the summer, she received a phone call from Mrs. Watts, the teacher she assisted at Immaculate Conception, who asked to speak to Anna's mother. That conversation resulted in Mrs. Watts and her husband coming to the Zacharias' home for a picnic, but, as soon became evident, food was not the primary reason for socializing. During the meal, Mrs. Watts turned to Anna and said, "You really have to go back to teaching because that's where you belong." Anna reluctantly agreed, saying, "The only reason I'm doing this is to pay rent and have some food."

But instead of returning to Immaculate Conception, she took a job as a substitute day care teacher for one month. Then, she became an assistant teacher at Colony House Children's Day Care, also in Brooklyn, working with three-year-olds. She was there for two years, until December 1956, during which time she received "a call from the Lord" to immerse herself even further in education.

"I was reading *The New York Times* and watching the children sleep when a voice came to me," Anna recalled, "and the voice said, 'Go into Lutheran school teaching." Anna replied, "No, thank you, Lord." The next day, the voice spoke to her again, and Anna protested, "Lord, you know I don't want to teach." Then, Anna recalled, the Lord admonished her with these words, "I'm not coming back again." Contemplating the nature of the voice, "inaudible" and "coming *at* me, not from *within* me," Anna accepted the calling and took a job as kindergarten teacher at St. John's Lutheran School in Glendale, Queens, New York. Working there from September 1957 through June 1963, she taught kindergarten, first grade and third grade and discovered the joy of "teaching the little ones reading and writing."

Anna began undergraduate studies in early childhood education from Hunter College in New York, then took masters degree courses from New

York University and Concordia Teacher's College in River Forest, Illinois, completing her studies, sans a degree in education although she had adequate credits, in 1964.

In July 1963, Anna reopened St. Mark's Lutheran School, which had been built in the 1890s then closed since 1932. There, she was the kindergarten teacher and principal from 1963 through 1967. Her pupils were Brooklyn's inner-city children, whom the school accepted regardless of religious denomination. In June 1968, she took time off to raise her own children, then returned to St. Mark's in August 1975. Through June 1979, she shared principal duties with Mary Nordeen, wife of St. Mark's pastor, who Anna described as "a whiz at curriculum."

Throughout the decade from 1953 to 1963, Anna continued to sing, first in a professional choir at St. Bartholomew's Episcopal Church in New York City, then in the chorus of Jerome Hines' opera, *I Am the Way*. While Hines' troupe performed primarily at the Salvation Army on 14th Street in Manhattan, Hines, who played the part of Jesus Christ, took the show on the road to churches and colleges in New York State and New Jersey. Throughout this time, Anna found energy to both perform and teach. "I would stay up all night from doing the show and traveling and go in to St. John's and teach, then I would go home and go to bed," she recalled with a laugh steeped in accomplishment.

Many of St. Mark's students lived in government-subsidized housing units known as "The Projects." Therefore, the school's curriculum guidelines were impacted by the U.S. government's Title IX requirements for education, and Anna was responsible for taking some children and their parents to a nearby public school for counseling. These appointments were in the evening, causing Anna to arrive late for prayer meetings at St. Mark's that she liked to attend. At one of these prayer meetings, she met John McConnell. "He had come a couple of times," Anna recalled, "and each time with the same woman who I thought was his wife."

Three days after finally being introduced to John, Anna was sitting at the piano in the kindergarten room while her students sang. As before, she heard the Lord's voice say to her, "John McConnell is going to be your husband." Flabbergasted, Anna thought, careful not to blurt, "Lord, he's too old!" In her mind, she quickly calculated that he appeared to be around 50 while she was only 34. Then she silently protested, "And he's married!"

In actuality, John's companion at the prayer meetings was Althya Youngman, who had come to New York to help him promote the Minute for Peace campaign at the World's Fair and the United Nations.

John and Youngman had attended the prayer meetings at the suggestion of Pastor Richard Neuhaus, the minister at nearby St. John's Lutheran Church in Brooklyn, who encouraged them to connect with Pastor Ervin Prange, the minister at St. Mark's, who, as Anna recalled, "had received the gift of tongues." Prange had invited John to speak about Minute for Peace at the prayer meetings.

In spite of her initial protestations, Anna found John attractive. As they became friends, she became particularly fond of his gentleness and his love of music. For their first social encounter alone, Anna invited John to her apartment for dinner. "I had bought a Steinway upright for $350 by paying $5.00 a month, because I was only earning $100 or $125 a month at that point," she said. "He sat down and, for three hours, he sang and played gospel songs."

During that evening, Anna told John about the Lord's message that they would marry. "He didn't believe it," she said. But neither did he run away. Instead, he told her about his first marriage and his episodes with the military. And she chose not to run away either.

Their courtship, which Anna called "wonderful," did not consist of "dates," per se, but rather "socializing with people of common interests." Anna explained, "We would talk after the prayer meetings, and I had dinners periodically in my apartment for the pastor and his wife and other friends. I hosted a prayer group of women, and I invited John." In return, John took Anna to the United Nations and to social dinners, including one at the home of Margaret Mead.

Two years after their initial meeting, Anna and John married on Christmas Day 1967 at St. Mark's Church. He was 52. She was 36. The ceremony occurred during the regular morning service. Afterward, the people and clergy of St. Mark's gave the newlyweds a coffee-and-Danish reception, which friends documented with snapshot photographs. From there, the wedding party and Pastor and Mrs. Prange accompanied the bride and groom to a Christmas dinner at the home of Else and Jerry Salvio, Anna's aunt and her husband, in Westport, Connecticut. The additional guests swelled the number in attendance to over fifty people. For Anna's mother and brother, the day was a mixture of joy and sorrow, for Anna's father, Ferdinand, had died from a sudden and massive stroke only six months earlier. In his stead, Anna's brother Paul gladly accepted the privilege of escorting her to the altar. Neither John's parents nor any of his siblings were able to attend. J. S. had died in October 1966, fourteen months prior to the wedding, and Hattie McConnell chose not to make the trip from California.

When Anna became pregnant with the couple's first child, they decided to call their baby John Paul, which, to Anna was a tribute to her husband, her brother, and John's youngest sibling. The baby was born premature, as Anna had been, on 28 June 1968. "He was beautiful, just beautiful," Anna remembered. But while the infant appeared to be "a perfect child," further examination indicated he had Downs Syndrome.

Anna and John's initial response was to solicit prayers from friends. Then, they heard of a noted physician at Children's National Medical Center in Washington, D.C., who, as John recalled, "was doing miraculous things with mongoloid children." Setting his work on Minute for Peace aside and entrusting their apartment to friends, Anna and John went to the nation's capital where their prayers continued but now for two reasons, the health of their child and sufficient money to find a place to live.

Their prayers for the latter request were answered by a couple they met in the hospital. This couple, whose child also had Downs Syndrome, gave the McConnells a house, rent free, while John Paul received treatment. In a letter written 24 October 1968, John described the house and grounds as "a beautiful 40-acre country estate with our own lake, a large double house (1/2 of it is a 170-year-old log cabin) on a beautiful knoll with a 200-year-old oak tree." Anna added that the "double house" consisted of "two Revolutionary War cabins, with a partition." She recalled that she and John didn't have money for electric heat so they warmed the cabin, including the loft where they slept, with a wood stove.

While quaint and historic, the gift came with a complication. The house was in Falmouth, Virginia, more than fifty miles from the hospital. John and Anna, who relied on public transportation in New York, now found themselves in need of a car. So, again, they "prayed and prayed and prayed," after which, John recalled, "I felt the miraculous grace of God helping us through these difficulties."

In that same letter of 24 October, John described in detail the miracles of money and transportation that came their way: "I spent a day in Washington trying to find something cheap. At six o'clock in the evening I called Anna to tell her, 'no luck.' We prayed [over the phone] that I would find something and immediately I felt I had 'connected.' The next phone call I made was to a man who worked at the State Dept and had advertised a 1961 Volvo for '$100.00 or less.' The moment I heard his voice I knew we were getting the car. But it didn't sound like it [at first]. He said he had just taken the car out and it was much worse than he thought. It had a terrible shimmy. The generator didn't work and carburetor was leaking bad. He thought he would junk it for $35.00. I told him I just wanted transportation and I knew a little about cars and I would like to see it. I finally persuaded him to let me come over and look at it. The motor sounded pretty loose, but not too bad. I told him I would give him $35.00, but only had $10.00 with me. I'd give him that as a deposit and pay the rest the next day. (I didn't tell him I'd just found the $10.00.) When we got to the notary public to sign the papers, he said, 'How much money did you say you had with you?' I told him. He said, 'Well, you'll need some money for gas. You can have the car for $7.50!' On the way home in my new car (driving slowly because of the shimmy), I stopped at a market to get some groceries. Thinking of what I wanted to get, I said to myself, 'My, I wish I had another dollar.' Within 10 seconds, I found a dollar bill on the floor! The next morning I switched tires and the shimmy disappeared. Tightened the fan belt, and the generator was okay. Spent $4.00 on getting the carburetor fixed. Washed and waxed and we had a beautiful car that has taken us over 3,000 miles with no trouble. Doesn't even use oil." [368]

Anna prayed after John's phone call from D.C., "Lord, don't let him buy that car on credit. We can't afford it. Don't let him buy it on credit, Lord." When she saw him drive home in the car, she was dismayed, but when she heard John's story of the transaction, her supplication turned to gratitude, "Thank you, Lord." Of her husband's ability to repair the car, she was not surprised; rather she well appreciated his mechanical ability. After the Volvo

---

[368] John McConnell, letter to Charles (surname unknown), 24 October 1968.

broke down on a Pennsylvania highway many months later, a minister from Virginia who had visited John and Anna in Falmouth, gave John and Anna a Volkswagen Beetle that they drove for two-and-a-half years until it was stolen in Brooklyn.

While their son received treatment, John wrote to friends of the miracle of John Paul, who "has been surrounded by love and prayer of many great souls. ... We are so grateful for our good fortune that I don't want to complain about anything." [369] John was, himself, a source of love for his son. "I was not able to nurse him because he was premature and mongoloid," Anna said, "so John would sit on our bed and put the nipple of the bottle in and out of his mouth so he would suck it; that was an accomplishment for John Paul. John enjoyed feeding him, and John would sit and talk with him every night for an hour or more, right from the time he was born."

John Paul continued to have problems, however. In April 1969, Anna wrote to a friend, "John Paul is delightful, even though we're still battling the convulsions. We have them down to one a day now and had one-a-half days without them last week. We know the Lord will give the victory. All we need is patience." She also wrote of John Paul's "good signs," his desire to crawl and improved movement of his legs and arms. [370]

Unfortunately, the child died while still an infant, at age 14 months, from a virus that infected his heart and thyroid. The family was visiting John's mother, Hattie, in Oakland, California, at the time, and Anna was in her first term of pregnancy with their second child Christa Marie. "I was sad, of course," Anna stated. "I cried, but I was also grateful that I was pregnant with Christa. I remember my mother, when we called her, said, 'Anna, don't be too sad. You and John would have had a hard time bringing John Paul up.'"

John wrote in his journal, "The love-light in his eyes told more of heaven than any words can speak." To his son, John pledged, "In my remaining years, the things I do will prove how much I learned from you." Next to this handwritten notation, John drew a circle, representing the Earth, surrounded by three Ws on the left and three Es on the right. Thus, by employing the letters of WE, Inc., the organization he founded in March 1969 while John

---

369 Ibid.

370 Anna McConnell, letter to Dorothy Rust, 29 April 1969.

Paul was still alive, John expressed his "WOE"-fulness, while in the same gesture, he emphasized the "WE"-ness of family. [371] Because of this love for his son, John felt in his heart a greater desire to successfully promote his Earth Day initiative, which he announced at a large United Nations conference in San Francisco only fifteen days after John Paul's death.

On 4 April 1970, less than three weeks after the initial Earth Day celebrations, John and Anna flew from California to the east coast. The couple planned to stay two weeks with her mother so Anna could rest, but bleeding, ostensibly from a tear in her placenta, caused them to return to Brooklyn immediately. Driving their Volkswagen Beetle, John took Anna directly to her doctor's office who ordered her to bed for the remaining six weeks of pregnancy. But Christa, like her mother and brother, did not go full term and was born three weeks premature in New York City on 5 May 1970. Christa's doctor and parents recognized her as a healthy child with bright eyes that shone as a precursor to exceptional intelligence. John was 55 and Anna 39.

A month after Christa's birth, John and Anna received a visit from Wilson Van Dusen, the psychologist who analyzed John when he was in the Army and who, later, wrote a grant request to the Ford Foundation in an attempt to fund John's Minute for Peace endeavors. [372] Van Dusen paid $50.00 to get John's Beetle out of a police impoundment because John had parked illegally. The psychiatrist, who had become quite wealthy and famous, expressed his dismay about John's pauperish lifestyle. "He was a gifted person," Van Dusen analyzed, "but what use was it? His wife supported the family." [373]

In contrast, Anna, who knew her profession as a parochial school teacher and her marriage to John were callings from God, considered Van Dusen's visit "marvelous." She recalled, "He said to me, 'Now, Anna, you know that losing a child is not the worst thing in the world and there's many women who do.' That brought me back to when I was in high school, studying Shakespeare, and there's a sonnet that says, 'There's nothing new in the world, everybody had gone through,' and I've always believed that." [374]

---

[371] John McConnell, journal, September-October 1969.

[372] Wilson Van Dusen, letter to Ford Foundation, 1971. Also, William H. Nims, The Ford Foundation, letter to Wilson Van Dusen, 8 July 1971.

[373] Wilson Van Dusen, telephone interview by author, 24 December 2004.

[374] William Shakespeare, Sonnet 59: "If there be nothing new, but that which is / Hath

Anna disagreed with Van Dusen's assessment of their financial situation. "John completely had to take care of his phone and other things for the office. My finances took care of the house things – rent, food and electric," Anna explained. "We, more or less, kept it that way all those years. It didn't bother me. My job was the way, to me, that the Lord was giving us the money we needed."

Regardless of their financial circumstances, Anna enjoyed the travel inherent with John's mission. In 1973, for example, the McConnells, including Christa and Anna's mother, traveled to Geneva, Switzerland, for a United Nations conference on the environment. While there, they stayed on the estate and in an apartment owned by Bernard Masset, the husband of Ellen (nee Bella) Masset, who was Anna's closest friend from third grade through college. "Ellen's father was a minister who moved his family to Geneva while he worked in Czechoslovakia," Anna explained. "When we were in our late teens and starting college, she came back to Bridgeport and stayed with us." Anna fondly recalled that when she and Ellen met again in Geneva, "After all those years, we both yelled, 'You haven't changed!'" During the day, Anna and her mother took Christa to a park where the toddler played with other children and Anna practiced the French language she had studied in high school and college.

During the years of 1968 to 1975, when Anna took a sabbatical from teaching in order to raise their children, she helped John by typing letters and filing papers. Living in their modest five-room apartment, which they rented from St. Mark's, she sang to her favorite audience who listened from a playpen. Anna recalled one day Christa, who was then 9 months of age, "hiked herself up, holding on to the wooden playpen, and began to sing the first few measures of Mary Had a Little Lamb." The youngster began to pick out tunes on Anna's piano when she was 3 or 4. For Christa's precocious talent, Anna thanked the genes of both her mother and husband. And for Christa's excellence in school and love of books, Anna thanked John for reading to their child every night.

When Anna returned to St. Mark's as both principal and teacher, she did so to give her daughter a Christian education, which the McConnells could

---

been before, how are our brains beguiled, / Which, labouring for invention, bear amiss / The second burden of a former child!"

not afford on John's income that, for example, was approximately $2,000 in 1971. Christa, who was Anna's pupil in kindergarten that first year, benefited from tuition-free schooling, paid by St. Mark's Lutheran Church throughout her elementary years. In addition, John and Anna paid only a modest sum for her education at Martin Luther High School in Maspeth, Queens, New York.

Anna found her first year back in the classroom to be as tough as her initial orientation in 1953, mainly because, twenty-one years later, she also had household and family responsibilities. One night, she said to John, "You and I are going to save to buy a small dishwasher because I can't do the dishes if I'm cooking and then I have schoolwork to do after that." John's reply was, "I'm your dishwasher."

By assuming that domestic role, which he performed for the next forty years, John was repaying Anna for having helped with his professional appearance. While tall and handsome, John generally didn't travel with more than one suit, one shirt, and one pair of shoes. Yet, he was resourceful. "I discovered if I washed the shirt and then rinsed it out and stuck it on the wall of the shower, it would come out looking ironed," John bantered. Anna, while loving, was not amused. After their wedding, Anna insisted that John travel with more than the clothes on his back. John took her assistance gracefully while acknowledging, "I was more concerned about what I have to say than how I look."

Throughout the remainder of her professional career, which ended with her retirement in 1996, Anna was either the principal or a teacher of elementary grades at St. Mark's Lutheran School, Brooklyn, New York; St. John's Lutheran School, Glendale, Queens, New York; and Our Savior Lutheran School, Rego Park, Queens, New York. Her annual income rose to $21,000 during her final year, an amount for which she expressed her appreciation to the Lord and to the congregation. After leaving the Jerome Hines opera in 1963, Anna's singing venue became her home and classroom. Her preference was classical music, which complemented John's and Christa's love of praise music.

In 1990, the McConnells moved from Brooklyn to Queens. Then, in June 2002, they moved to a senior housing complex, operated by three churches, in Denver, Colorado, to be near Christa and her husband Garin

Paul Mason.

Garin and Christa had met at a Lutheran youth activity in Queens in 1985 when she was 15 and he was 16. Garin's father and mother, the Rev. Dennis and Chris Mason, were Denver residents working as missionaries to Africa at the time, and Garin had come to the East Coast to stay with his aunt Judy and her husband, the Rev. Donald Miles, who was pastor at John and Anna's church, St. John's Lutheran, in Glendale, Queens.

Christa attended Oral Roberts University in Tulsa, Oklahoma, from 1987 until 1990 then worked an assortment of jobs before a series of circumstances, blended with prayer and a recommendation from Pastor Miles, took her to a secretarial position at St. John's Lutheran Church in Denver. Garin, who had neither seen nor heard from Christa in more than a decade, also worked at the church. They recognized each other immediately and "remembered each other quite fondly," as Christa recalled. She, hesitant to date, declined his invitations, until, she said, "God showed me Garin was to be my beloved husband." They married six months later, in November 2000.

Christa continued to enjoy music, which she considered to be a gift of God, and, therefore, utilized her talent to help people spiritually. In 2005, she completed her first compact disc, "Simply Psalms – Blessed Is the Man," for which she sang and played piano. [375]

Christa gave birth to two children, Hannah Rose and Bethany Anne, in October 2002 and November 2003. Much to Anna's delight, she cared for her two grandchildren two or three days a week. John enjoyed his life near the grandchildren, too, filling each day with essay writing, phone calls, e-mails and occasional toddler care, while being careful not to step on small toys.

From the time of her retirement to when the McConnell's moved from Queens, Anna organized John's voluminous files of papers, photographs and audio tapes that dated from 1957 through the present time. Together, they donated these to the Swarthmore College Peace Collection on the campus of Swarthmore College, a Quaker liberal arts school in Swarthmore, Pennsylvania. There, the materials, which numbered in the tens of thousands, occupied more than thirty-five linear feet of shelf space.

[375] Christa McConnell, e-mails to author, 9 and 11 August 2005.

Throughout their lives together, Anna questioned John only a few times. "When he was launching Earth Day," she recalled, "we were walking in San Francisco, and I said, 'You've just gotten Minute for Peace going. Why go into the environment?' I couldn't connect the two things. But John said to me, 'Getting everyone to work together for the care of Earth is a means for peace.' Then I understood and that was the end of that."

Equally high in her memory was initial advice she received from Pastor Prange. "I can remember my minister brought John in by himself for a talk before we were married. Then he brought me in by myself and said to me, 'Anna, if you're marrying John to change him, forget it. Get out of your engagement because you'll never change him.' And I've stuck to that. I don't think I ever wanted to change John."

Of their financial situation, she was matter of fact. "When I went into Lutheran school teaching, I knew I would never earn the money of a public school teacher. But when we do the work of the Lord, we're not going to have the money of the world." Among her blessings, Anna counted "the love of the Lord, our love for each other, and the love for our daughter and John's children and our grandchildren."

Anna admitted she and John had disagreements, but placed greater value on their deeper, richer common goals. Approaching their fortieth year of marriage, Anna reflected on wisdom she read after their move to Denver: "If a wife works with her husband for the first five to seven years of their marriage, instead of going off on her own, that marriage will, no doubt, last longer." Anna then reflected on the first years of her marriage, through August 1975, when she was unemployed yet working and traveling with John and caring for their children. She recalled the significant people and events of that time: John Paul and Christa, parents and pastors, Minute for Peace and WE, Inc., the Earth Flag and Earth Day in San Francisco and New York, typing and filing, cooking and cleaning. "I just automatically did what needed to be done," she said, "and the Lord has supplied everything we should have."

8

Earth Flag

(1969 to present)

Since all the nations have flags, and the UN has a flag, and states and businesses have flags, maybe there ought to be a flag that's just for people.
– John McConnell, Earth Flag advertisement, *Whole Earth Catalog*, 1971

Encouraged by acceptance of his Star of Hope idea by the public and scientists, John McConnell looked upon the developing U.S. and Russian space programs as a means to promote global consciousness of the vast ecological infrastructure of planet Earth. With awe and wonder, he, like most people who had access to television, watched a decade of space flights: Yuri Gagarin, the first Earthian in space in April 1961, followed by astronaut Alan Shepard less than a month later; cosmonaut Guerman Titov, the first person to fly in space for more than 24 hours; John Glenn, the first American to orbit the globe; Virgil Grissom and John Young, the first American two-person crew; several simultaneous flights and in-space rendezvous by cosmonauts in the mid-1960s; and Apollo 7 astronauts who were the first to transmit live television coverage of crew activities. [376]

He continued to believe in benefits to be reaped if space scientists from the U.S. and the USSR would work together, and he searched for some symbol that would bring the space superpowers, and other world leaders,

---

[376] Robert A. Braeunig, *Manned Space Flights* [online]. Rocket & Space Technology [cited 26 February 2005]. Available from www.braeunig.us/space/manned.htm.

to a state of cooperation in space. Then, when *LIFE Magazine* printed the first photo of Earth taken from outer space on its cover on 10 January 1969, John's idea gelled. He knew the symbol he would create – a likeness of Earth on a flag. To Anna, John exclaimed, "That's it! That's what I've been looking for!" [377]

Margaret Mead confirmed the popular belief that that image of Earth, taken from an Apollo 8 spaceship, was "the most sobering photograph ever made. Our lovely, lonely planet afloat in a vast black sea of space. So beautiful yet so tragically fragile. So dependent on so many people in all countries." Espousing what she called, "the One Earth view," Mead added, when Earth is seen from space, "There are no boundary lines except those made by water and mountains: no zones of influence, political satellites, international blocs, only people who live in lands, on land, that they cherish." [378]

In actuality, even though people were moved by the full-color images of Earth taken from space, John's original Earth Flag was a simplistic, two-color rendition. And while the original photo on *LIFE* showed only a partial orb, John commissioned an artist to create a complete circle, then color it with light blue and white to represent clouds and oceans but, purposefully, no continents. He had this design silkscreened on a field of midnight blue. John called the Earth Flag, "A flag for all the people of Earth … an appropriate symbol of man's unity and destiny. It represents his nest in the stars, the environment for his spiritual and material development." [379]

In retrospect, any one of millions of people could have created the Earth Flag, and, later, others would emulate the flag and even alter the design and corrupt John's copyright, but, as was the case with making plastics from walnut shells during the Great Depression and initiating the Star of Hope campaign amidst the Cold War, John McConnell was the first, a visionary who saw global opportunity where others did not.

In the years since the first Earth Flags were made, thousands of people purchased them. Most of John's early customers lived in the United States or Canada, but orders also came from as far away as Australia. [380] The National

---

[377] Anna McConnell, "A Brief History of the Earth Flag, Earth Day, Earth Society," 16 November 1998.

[378] Margaret Mead, "One Earth View," 1977-78.

[379] John McConnell, "Earth Flag Company," 1970.

[380] Ian Robertson, North Sydney, Australia, aerogramme to John McConnell, 28

Science Foundation flew the Earth Flag at their Amundsen-Scott South Pole Station during their missions there in 1982 and 1983. [381] An international expedition of seven paratroopers from Australia, Canada, Holland, Ukraine, South Africa, and the United States airdropped onto the North Pole with an Earth Flag carried by Russian cosmonaut Anatoly Berezovoi in April 2000. [382] In 1998, the flag orbited the globe aboard the Mir Space Station. [383]

When news shows reported the upcoming Apollo 11 mission in the summer of 1969 would place an astronaut on the moon's surface, John sent a telegram to President Richard Nixon on 4 July, requesting that astronaut Neil Armstrong have an Earth Flag in his hand when he stepped from the lunar module. This, however, was not to be, for the U.S. Congress prohibited astronauts from carrying anything but the Stars and Stripes. In an interview with United Press International, John stated, "A world flag should be exempt from Congressional proscription because the banner has no national legality." [384]

Eugene Carson Blake, general secretary of the World Council of Churches, conveyed a similar belief when he told a reporter from the National Broadcasting Company, "I would have liked it better if the United Nations flag had been planted on the moon." [385] An editorial in *The New York Times* three weeks after Armstrong's moonwalk offered a related sentiment, noting the accomplishments of the U.S. astronauts "were hailed in Moscow as well as in Washington, in Cairo as well as in Jerusalem, in New Delhi and Karachi, in East Berlin and West Berlin, ... [which] makes it particularly unfortunate that the formal celebration planned [exclusively in the U.S. with a brief appearance at the UN on 13 August 1969] has such a narrow, nationalistic cast." [386] Similarly, a woman from Staten Island, New York, who

---

February 1973.

[381] W. R. Seelig, National Science Foundation, letter to John McConnell, 17 December 1982.

[382] *North Pole, April 15, 2000* [online]. WOW Zone [cited 26 February 2005]. Available from www.wowzone.com/npole.htm.

[383] Anatoly Berezovoi, fax to John McConnell, 20 March 1998. Photo at *Earth Flag aboard the Mir Space Station, March 1998* [online]. WOW Zone [cited 26 February 2005]. Available from www.wowzone.com/mir.htm.

[384] (given name unknown) Danner, "With Apollo," United Press International, 10 July 1969.

[385] Eugene Carson Blake, "Eugene Blake comments on U.S. nationalism and lunar landing," 7 August 1969.

[386] "Homage to the Astronauts," editorial by *The New York Times*, circa 7 August 1969.

bought an Earth Flag from John as a souvenir for her daughters during the New York ticker tape parade for the Apollo 11 astronauts, said she did so because she didn't like the nationalistic buttons that read "We Were First!" hawked by other vendors. [387]

Because nationalistic spirit in the U.S. prohibited the Earth Flag from debuting on lunar landscape, John unveiled his creation at Moon Watch in New York City's Central Park, held the night of 20 July 1969 when Armstrong landed on the lunar surface and took his "one giant leap for mankind." For Moon Watch, John commissioned American Banner Company of Brooklyn, New York, to silkscreen an eight-foot banner, [388] which he then handed to representatives of the National Council of Churches, who presented it as "the new vision of international unity."

John also ordered 500 12-inch by 18-inch rayon flags from American Flag & Banner Company of New Jersey. Because John placed this order a few days prior to Moon Watch, the flag supplier was able to ship only 231 of the 500 flags requested. [389] John and friends made their way through the crowd, selling and giving away flags. He also consigned 168 flags to Restaurant Associates, a consortium of various eateries, that sold seventy-two and returned the remainder. [390] The sale price was $2.00 each, which was divided equally with the consignee. With this fee plus American Flag & Banner's production cost of 75 cents each, John realized a profit of only 25 cents per flag. The total revenue from all flags sold was more than consumed by American Banner's silkscreen fee for the large flag of $86.50. [391]

While that net loss was disappointing, John was happy the flags were available at all. The two colors were reversed on the original silkscreen run of 500 flags, resulting in Earth images with blue clouds and white oceans.

Once that was corrected, John applied for a copyright and trademark rights for the design. The U.S. Copyright Office honored his application in February 1970. The Copyright Certificate, registered with the U.S. Patent

---

[387] Jane Kenamore, letter to World Equality, Inc., 13 August 1969. (Kenamore didn't have $1.00 to buy a flag, so John gave her one; she mailed the money and a thank you note to "the address [on] a pamphlet the man handed me.")

[388] American Banner Company, invoice, 10 August 1969.

[389] American Flag & Banner Company, invoice, 17 October 1969.

[390] Restaurant Associates, consignment receipt.

[391] American Banner Company, invoice, 10 August 1969.

Office, protected the design, identifying it as a "flag consisting of design on fabric." The copyright was for a period of twenty-eight years, starting from the date of the flag's "publication" on 20 July 1969 – the night of Moon Watch – with the option, according to statutes in effect at that time, to renew for another twenty-eight years. [392]

John's faith in the Earth Flag grew stronger the more he worked with it. He believed its purpose was "to encourage in young and old a new view of our beautiful planet as a home for all people, to inspire a new respect and concern for Earth's tender seedlings of life." [393] He printed flyers that reminded people "you are an Earth person; fly the Earth Flag" anytime, day or night, but especially on days that celebrated celestial events and commemorated conservationism: vernal equinox, Sea Day (22 May), summer solstice, Passenger Pigeon Day (1 September), [394] autumnal equinox, United Nations Day (24 October), Conservation Day (27 October), [395] and winter solstice.

Encouraged by an order for fifty Earth Flags from Stewart Brand, publisher of *Whole Earth Catalog*, followed by an order for another 100 two weeks later, in September 1969, John sought acceptancc by other distributors. However, F. W. Woolworth Company and Goldfarb Novelty Company told him his retail price was too high. A Goldfarb buyer said he would be interested if the wholesale price was 30 or 35 cents, which was less than half of John's production cost. [396]

Thinking like a minister who lacked ushers and must pass the collection plate himself, John took Earth Flag promotion into his own hands. He sold flags at the ticker tape parade for Apollo 11 astronauts Armstrong, Edwin "Buzz" Aldrin and Michael Collins in New York City on 13 August 1969. In the fall of 1969, he attended the International Industrial Conference in San Francisco where he met Taizo Ishizaka, a Tokyo attorney who was president of the Japan Association for the 1970 World Exposition; John proposed featuring the Earth Flag at the opening ceremonies of EXPO 70 in Osaka,

---

[392] *Certificate, Registration of a Claim to Copyright*, Register of Copyrights, United States of America, February 1970.

[393] John McConnell, "Earth Flag, a Flag for People of All Nations."

[394] The last passenger pigeon was shot on 1 September 1914.

[395] Conservation Day is the birthday of U.S. President Theodore Roosevelt, the father of conservation.

[396] John McConnell, "Distribution Prospects," handwritten list, August-September 1969.

Japan, an idea to which the Japan Association did not consent.

In the fall of 1969, John contracted the D'Arcy Advertising Company of San Francisco to generate promotional ideas. The agency's creative corps suggested the U.S. Postmaster General might develop a commemorative Earth Flag stamp, the International Film Festival might adopt the flag, and it could be prominently displayed at the World Series, Super Bowl and international soccer competitions. [397] While the ideas were good, John left them unattended, giving higher priority to fulfillment of his Earth Day idea.

In addition, while orders did come in, the flag's sale price was inadequate to cover costs associated with legal council, marketing consultation and order fulfillment, much less the time and effort needed to contact the groups and agencies that D'Arcy suggested. As early as October 1969, a bill from American Flag & Banner Company for more than $4,000 became overdue. [398] In addition, John and Anna had borrowed $400 from friends who believed in their cause, but Earth Flag revenue between its first appearance in June and the end of October 1969 was a little more than $250. [399]

While a few people and organizations wanted several flags and larger flags, most of the orders were for only one of the smallest size – at a price of $1.50 or $2.00. Many requests were handwritten, some on odd size note sheets and even scraps of paper. Often, the correspondence from the outside was simply a request for information: Are Earth Flags still available? What are the sizes? How much do they cost?

Anna, who was dealing with the emotional loss of her first child and the birth of her second, dutifully replied to each potential customer. And when supplies ran out, she sent a note that flags would ship later. All of these communiqués required time, attention, typing and postage. To deposit payments, Anna endorsed checks. Orders for larger flags, which sold for $12.00 without fringe and $35.00 with fringe, often came with a request to send an invoice, another secretarial task.

Mailing an order didn't necessarily conclude communication with a

---

397 Walter E. Terry, D'Arcy Advertising Company, letter to John McConnell, 10 October 1969.

398 American Flag & Banner Company, invoice, 11 December 1969.

399 John McConnell, "Earth Flag bills as of October 20, 1969," typed list, 20 October 1969.

customer. At first, John and Anna mailed flags wrapped only in heavy paper. But the wooden flag poles often broke in transit, sometimes tearing the cloth. Some customers replied unhappily, demanding a replacement.

To each customer, Anna was a lady, especially to the children who placed orders, and her letters to them carried the proper salutations of "Miss" and "Master." To people whose religious leanings she knew, she would close with "The blessings of the Lord be with you," "Yours in Christ," or simply "In His Love" or "In Him." [400] Even to Jane Kenamore, the woman from Staten Island, a stranger, who bought the Earth Flag at the Apollo 11 ticker tape parade and paid for it later, via mail, Anna replied with a personal note, "We are very happy to hear that you thought the flag a worthwhile souvenir for your daughters. We hope that they will appreciate this reminder of a beginning of a new age." [401]

Sprinkled into the midst of this melee came encouraging news. An ad in the 1971 *Whole Earth Catalog* brought hundreds of queries and orders with checks. A research editor for entertainment personality Dinah Shore wrote, requesting to have the Earth Flag on the television personality's new daily women's service program on NBC. [402] A photograph showing the Earth Flag hanging in the office of James H. Meyer, chancellor at the University of California at Davis, appeared in the university's *California Aggie* newspaper.

A greeting card company in San Francisco purchased 100 flags for resale. Requests for retail quantities came from other stores in Arkansas, Wisconsin and Washington State. A marketer of preschool products who sent catalogs through the mail to more than 500,000 families expressed interest; unfortunately this letter came to John and Anna's apartment in Brooklyn shortly after Christa's birth and went unanswered until after the catalog was printed. [403] A letter from *Harper's Bazaar* magazine, asking to "see what it looks like," also went unanswered. [404] In many instances, the letter writers assumed they were addressing a catalog company or a wholesale distributor with multiple products and full-time staff, not a wedded pair of

---

[400] Earth Flag, various orders, requests and replies.

[401] Anna McConnell, letter to Jane Kenamore, 19 August 1969.

[402] Kevin S. Hartigan, Jaffee-Stivers Productions, letter to WE, Inc., 4 August 1970.

[403] Sara B. Stein, Weiner Communications Systems, Inc., letter to WE, Inc., 29 June 1970.

[404] Barbaralee Diamonstein, *Harper's Bazaar*, letter to WE, Inc., 16 April 1970.

Earth visionaries with one product and many ideas, working out of their home.

Yet, with unfailing faith, John found encouragement in orders from notable organizations such as the International Society for the Protection of Animals, [405] the Temple of Understanding, [406] the Appalachian Mountain Club in New Hampshire, [407] a lodge in Maine, [408] and *The New Yorker* magazine, [409] to which John delivered flags in person. A soldier at Fort Monmouth, New Jersey, ordered a 3-foot by 5-foot Earth Flag, and a free spirit in Texas wrote to order a second flag after taking his first on a car trip across the country, flying it "on campsite flag poles, car antennas and mainly my backpack." [410]

While these letters buoyed their spirits, John faced the financial realities of his "business." Bills from Paramount Flag Co. of San Francisco, a firm John contracted to make flags while on the West Coast in the fall of 1969, became overdue, and while John did make payments, the outstanding balance in December 1971, two years after the initial order, was in excess of $1,500. [411]

John didn't let these debts overcome him, choosing instead to revel in the excitement of opportunity and possibility. In a letter to Melvin Shikora of Eder Manufacturing, a flag maker in Milwaukee, Wisconsin, on 22 January 1971, John wrote, "Things are going well, but an awful lot is happening fast. Meetings with the UN, City, etc. about Earth Day on March 21. We will have ringing of the Peace Bell at the United Nations, a great celebration at the [South Street] Seaport Museum with oceanographic and other vessels flying the Earth Flag, and it now looks like TV coverage will include a 12 hour special on Earth Day!" John included a check for $50.00 to cover partial expenses to date, adding by way of explanation, "We are managing at the present with practically no funds, but I have a brilliant volunteer (formerly with the Peace Corps) [412] who has a funding request in the works with HEW

405 International Society for the Protection of Animals, order, 26 December 1972.
406 Judy Hollester, Temple of Understanding, order.
407 Benjamin R. Sears, Jr., Appalachian Mountain Club, order, 29 July 1972.
408 Sprucewold Lodge, order, 12 May 1972.
409 *The New Yorker*, order, 21 April 1970.
410 Bruce Gray, Argyle, Texas, letter to John McConnell.
411 Paramount Flag Co., invoices, 1970-1972.
412 The volunteer was Tom Dowd, who later became president of the Earth Society

and some individuals. We hope to have some money in about two weeks."

John promised to "forward to you all the money owing on flags as they are sold," while also stating, "We … are planning a real pitch for Earth Flag contributions during Earth Week. We expect 25,000 people a day at the Seaport Museum." Then, in closing, he asked for more flags, "At least another 2,000 small flags and another 300-500 large flags available for that occasion," along with "the best arrangement you can make on extending credit." [413] But, even with these good intentions, John found himself with excessive debt to Eder – nearly $5,000, of which he paid $1,000 by November 1972 – and Eder found itself with extra flags it refused to ship. [414]

In June 1975, John spoke with Nelson A. Rockefeller, who was then Vice-President of the United States, about the Earth Flag being part of the next joint U.S.-Soviet space mission, and John's confirmation letter to the Vice-President indicated Rockefeller liked the idea. [415] Three weeks later, senator Mark Hatfield of Oregon, who had become a strong supporter of John's ideas, reported he had followed up with Rockefeller and the Vice-President had agreed to approach NASA about the subject. However, the vision did not materialize when Rockefeller telephoned Hatfield's office a few days later, stating, as Hatfield wrote in a letter to John, "He [Rockefeller] was withdrawing support for the project." Soon thereafter, a NASA official called Hatfield to say that agency had refused the senator's request. [416] The Earth Flag did not make its first appearance in space until Russian cosmonauts Talgat Musabaev and Nikolai Budarin took it aboard the Mir Space Station and had their photograph taken with it on Earth Day in 1998.

In January 1977, after having devoted the majority of his time to WE, Inc., and Earth Day and having started the Earth Society Foundation, John renewed his interest in Earth Flags, and he placed an order for more flags with the Valley Forge Flag Company, Inc., of New York. He enclosed a check for $250 with the order as a deposit on 100 3-foot by 5-foot flags and 2,000

Foundation.

[413] John McConnell, letter to Melvin Shikora, Eder Manufacturing Co., 22 January 1971.

[414] Eder Manufacturing Co., invoice, 1 November 1972, and letter to John McConnell, 7 November 1972.

[415] John McConnell, letter to Nelson Rockefeller, 23 June 1975.

[416] Mark Hatfield, letter to John McConnell, 15 July 1975.

12-inch by 18-inch flags. The total cost of the order was nearly $3,500, of which $250 was still due eight months later. [417]

A similar situation developed with Canadiana Textile Screen Prints Limited of Mississauga, Ontario. In August 1981, John paid the company $296 to create one large sample flag. Two months later, in October, he placed an order for 176 3-foot by 5-foot flags and 1,500 12-inch by 18-inch flags with or without grommets and with or without staffs. By the time John was able to make his next payment of $500 in June 1982, he had accrued over $1,000 in finance charges. [418] In his letter that accompanied that payment, John thanked W. E. Milton, president of Canadiana, "for your patience and your confidence in me." John also reported that Earth Flags were on display at the United Nations, that he was working on greater promotions, and that he expected "a rapid increase in orders in the next few months." On a personal note, John wrote, "I hope to soon get my head above water. We have survived doctor bills and the loss of my wife's job. (We know how to stretch beans and rice when the going's rough!)" [419] In spite of John's promise to "pay you in full before Christmas," the balance due was over $10,000, including $1,000 in interest, when Canadiana turned the account over to a collection agency the following summer. [420]

While these numbers told the financial aspect of this story, the greater message lay in words John expressed in a handwritten letter to Milton on 3 August 1982. He began with an apology for "my irritation" during a previous phone call. Then, he vaulted into a lengthy explosion of frustration: "I've given 20 years of full time service as a patriot of Earth in a desperate struggle to help save its life from extinction – most of the time with no compensation and no independent income to support my efforts. I've experienced some success but mostly failure. This past year has been fraught with many difficulties – family, health, unfulfilled commitments by organizations and individuals, but especially in the failure with the Earth Flag." John wrote, "[The Earth Flag] is overpriced for the general public." He complained about the forty percent discount required by retailers and noted an irony that Canadiana

---

417 Valley Forge Flag Company, Inc., invoices, March and September 1977.

418 Canadiana Textile Screen Prints Limited, invoice, 31 May 1982.

419 John McConnell, letter to W. E. Milton, Canadiana Textile Screen Prints, Ltd., 24 June 1982.

420 Credit Control Systems, letter to John McConnell, 26 July 1982.

would be "taking a 20% cut by turning the bill over to a collection agency." Then, logically or illogically, John stated, "Had you offered this [discount] to us, we would have quickly sold the flags." John did enclose a check for $500 with his letter and promised to "try to get a friend to advance what is needed, pay you in full – and save the excessive interest charges." [421]

This emotional outburst came six months after John had delivered a speech about the history of the Earth Flag at a gathering of The Flag Research Center, a member of the International Federation of Vexillological Associations, in the spring of 1982. John concluded that speech with emotional discourse regarding the Earth Flag's worth. "Flags have been used for centuries to communicate and encourage values and loyalties, but national flags have been divisive. While many depict sun, moon and stars, none depict our home planet. Not one has a symbol or representation of the Earth to which all are indebted for their very existence."

He concluded his remarks with words he spoke at an Earth Flag ceremony in New York City in 1978: "We raise the Earth Flag to encourage and inspire love of Earth. We raise the Earth Flag to enlist and unite young and old in courageous action for our planet's protection – for cautious nurture of its life and care of its resources in every acre and neighborhood. We raise the Earth Flag as a promise to all who work to help our planet that they and their children will obtain a fair stake in Earth and its future, with equitable access to its beauty and bounty. We raise the Earth Flag with a firm conviction that together we can save our planet." [422]

John knew, of course, speeches were not enough to motivate a majority to purchase and display the Earth Flag. Eventual success would depend on a full-fledged marketing campaign. In February 1973, he entered into an unsuccessful licensing agreement with Acme Agitprop, Ltd., a New York marketing corporation, to which he granted exclusive distributor and sales agent rights of the Earth Flag in the United States and non-exclusive rights for the rest of the world for one year. [423]

Then, in October 1987, John considered a detailed proposal by John

---

[421] John McConnell, letter to W. E. Milton, Canadiana Textile Screen Prints, Ltd., 3 August 1982.

[422] John McConnell, "History of the Earth Flag," speech.

[423] "License Agreement," between John McConnell, WE, Inc., and Ernest Lendler, Acme Agitprop, Ltd., 19 February 1973.

Sanbonmatsu, a young writer and media specialist with a recent degree from Hampshire College in Amherst, Massachusetts. Among Sanbonmatsu's suggestions was the creation of a company whose specific purpose would be to market Earth Flags. John chose not to act on this proposal. [424]

However, a year later, John did sign a licensing agreement with Ed Brennan, president of Earth Flag Corporation, an entity established to market Earth Flags, as Sanbonmatsu had proposed. The agreement gave Earth Flag Corporation "exclusive worldwide rights to sell this item" and asserted that Earth Flag Corporation would require start-up capital of $125,000 for initial production and advertising, which Brennan was to acquire from private sources and repay over the next fourteen months along with eighteen percent interest. In addition, Brennan was to pay the Earth Society Foundation a royalty of seven-and-a-half percent of sales. These terms were based on projections that 40,000 flags could be sold in the first year-and-a-half. [425]

But even with full-time promotion, Earth Flag Corporation experienced a loss of more than $135,000 over the next four years, through May 1993. During that time, the company paid a royalty to the Earth Society Foundation, but John was deeply troubled that loans from individuals, like board member Frances Stevens Reese, who had contributed $5,000, remained unpaid. [426] "I got the wrong impression of Brennan," John stated. "He was involved with New Jersey public schools, and I trusted him." [427]

Even more troubling was the personal and professional damage John incurred when Brennan applied for his own copyright to the Earth Flag. When John heard of this from a third-party, he confronted Brennan, who said he had applied for the revised copyright based on a change in reproduction process, from silkscreen to lithograph. [428] This was a partial truth. The application Brennan signed and submitted to the U.S. Patent Office in April 1990 referenced John's earlier patent registration by number and class, but it also stated Brennan's intent to "replace earth image of original Earth Flag

[424] John Sanbonmatsu, "Earth Flag, A Preliminary Proposal," 26 October 1987.

[425] "Licensing Agreement between The Earth Society Foundation & The Earth Flag Corporation," 28 October 1988.

[426] Edward L. Brennan, "Promissory Note," to Mrs. Willis L. Reese, 8 December 1988.

[427] John McConnell, manuscript review with author, Denver, Colorado, October 2005.

[428] John McConnell, interview by author, Denver, Colorado, August 2004.

with a reproduction of another Apollo photograph," thus altering the design, which was the point Brennan did not disclose to John. [429]

In early 1994, Austrian-born UN consultant Hans Janitschek, who was then president of the Earth Society Foundation, and Brennan came to an agreement through which Brennan was to pay a partial royalty to the Earth Society Foundation during the first six months of that year. [430] John McConnell, speaking with advice from legal counsel, requested Brennan to withdraw his copyright request, which Brennan did not do. Janitschek encouraged John to sue Brennan, but John deferred to his Christian upbringing, which had taught him "not to sue anybody for anything." [431]

In 1995, Brennan borrowed money from two investment bankers who advanced a few thousand dollars each to Earth Flag Corporation. These bankers also introduced Brennan to Hank Waxman, a respected environmentalist and president of Metropolitan Mining Co., a New York City recycling firm noted for social responsibility, specifically for employing prison inmates. Waxman had won Ernst & Young's Entrepreneur of the Year Award in New York in the Processing Manufacturing category in 1991.

Waxman's job was to monitor the financial operations within Earth Flag Corporation. When Waxman reported apparent fiscal improprieties, Brennan disappeared and the investment bankers cut their losses and walked away from the Earth Flag business. Shortly thereafter, Waxman answered a telephone call on the company's toll free phone line from someone who wanted to buy an Earth Flag. "I decided to ship them a flag," Waxman recalled, "and that put me into the Earth Flag business." [432]

Waxman met with John, and on 1 January 1996, John agreed to allocate to Waxman's new company, Earth Flag, Ltd., all rights to market the Earth Flag. In return, Waxman agreed to pay John a generous $1,000 a month for minor consultation services, to be provided at John's discretion from his home, pertaining to the Earth Flag, Earth Day and the Earth Trustee program. [433] While Waxman paid that amount in 1996, he, like others before him,

---

[429] *Certificate of Copyright Registration,* VA 388-412, 28 March 1990.

[430] Edward L. Brennan and Hans Janitschek, letter of agreement.

[431] John McConnell, manuscript review with author, Denver, Colorado, October 2005.

[432] Hank Waxman, telephone interview by author, 7 November 2005.

[433] Hank Waxman and John McConnell, "Business Consultant Agreement," 1 January

found the venture to be unprofitable, and, even though he continued to sell Earth Flags in various sizes on a limited basis, he paid John for consultation services only during the first year of their agreement.

The Earth Flags Waxman sold bore the popular full-color lithograph image initiated by Brennan and not John's silkscreen design. Because Waxman had acquired marketing rights for the original illustration from John in 1995 and purchased the copyright for the photograph version from Brennan a year later, his promotional material bore the imprint, "The Authentic Earth Flag."

Ironically, both Earth Flag designs, have entered the public domain – the original through John's failure to renew his copyright and the latter through a judicial decision in 2001. In that ruling, federal judge Shira Scheindlin of the New York South District Court observed that photographs taken by NASA, a government agency, are automatically in the public domain. Scheindlin further ruled that putting a NASA image of Earth on a blue piece of cloth lacked sufficient creative merit to have been granted a copyright in the first place, and she dismissed the case. Waxman, who had attempted to legally protect the design from manufacturers who promoted their product on eBay, an Internet commerce web site, said, "Now anybody in the world can make and sell Earth Flags." [434]

While most flags were of lower price and lesser quality, the flags Waxman sold were the only ones made of recycled material, spun and woven polyester that provided the feel of original, heavier cotton cloth.

In early 1996, in an attempt to promote the historical integrity of the Earth Flag, Waxman wrote a letter to Jeffrey Stine, curator of Engineering and Environmental History at the Smithsonian Institution's National Museum of American History, encouraging Stine to create a John McConnell Earth Flag exhibit to which both Waxman and John have donated materials. "A possible [Earth Flag] exhibit in your museum ... would be incomplete if it didn't revolve around John McConnell ... [who] is a noncommercial visionary," Waxman wrote to Stine. [435]

Waxman also discovered that the Earth Flag retained a high level of

1996.

[434] Hank Waxman, telephone interview by author, 7 November 2005.

[435] Hank Waxman, letter to Jeffrey Stine, Smithsonian Institution, 21 February 1996.

appreciation among many of the world's people, especially those committed to global oneness. When terrorists crashed commercial airplanes into the World Trade Center in New York City on 11 September 2001, world sympathy was high for the United States, and U.S. citizens expressed nationalistic zeal by flying the Stars and Strips. That was also a time when many new companies began to manufacture Earth Flags, and sales soared as a large percentage of Americans chose to express their link with the rest of Earth's people. [436]

And while Earth Flags remained not as commonly known as John had hoped, people who owned them cherished them. Even more treasured were the original 500 Earth Flags with the reverse color scheme. John and Anna have retained a few. Another was at the Smithsonian. The others, wherever located, have become collectors' items.

---

[436] Diane Brook, "Earth Flags, too, flying off store shelves," *Seattle Times*, 25 September 2001.

J. S and Hattie McConnell stand next to their Gospel Car near the Waco Bridge, Waco, Texas, 1912.
John and Anna McConnell

J. S. and Hattie McConnell are among 300 preachers and laypersons who participated in a Pentecostal revival conference that was the organizational meeting of the Assemblies of God in Hot Springs, Arkansas, in 1914. The meeting was held at the Hot Springs Opera House (photo inset).
Flower Pentecostal Heritage Center

Spiritual Singers tour the Bronx to advertise religious meetings. The Tindley Seven and John McConnell (holding fishing pole) atop the vehicle; J.S. McConnell standing on the hood; the Rev. Lincoln E. Caswell (dressed as Abraham Lincoln) near running board; and the Rev. Joseph H. Braun leaning on front fender.
Caption is as it appeared in The Home News, *26 September 1929*

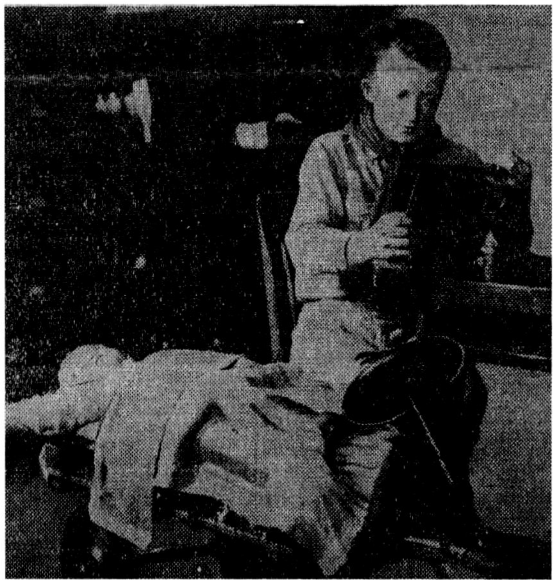

An article in ***The Indianapolis News*** shows John McConnell, a fourteen-year-old Boy Scout, caring for his baby brother Paul while reading a book at the Indianapolis library.
The Indianapolis News, *courtesy of* The Indianapolis Star

The McConnell family: Hattie, Hope, Ruth, John (tallest in back), Evan, Paul, Grace and J. S., circa 1930.
John and Anna McConnell

HEAR IT! FEEL IT! SEE IT!

The Greatest LOVE STORY Ever Told

As only the "Fiery Irishman" can tell it

Evangelist J. S. McCONNELL

will begin a series of Inspirational Preaching at the

PORTLAND ROSE TABERNACLE

East 13th & Sandy Blvd.

For 3 weeks beginning Sun., June 2, 1935

Mr. Mc CONNELL, former converted infidel, and recently from New York City, comes to Portland for the first time.

Hear the Unique Messages that converted fifty-two infidels and brought an entire town to accept Christ as their Savior.

Mr. McConnell begins a series of ten sermons on the "Greatest Love Story Ever Told" unfolding God's plan from Creation to Eternity and proving God's love in all the mysteries and plan of life in a unique and convincing way that is a challenge to the skeptic and an inspiration to the Christian. It will answer dozens of questions you have puzzled about.

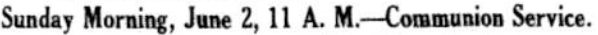

Sunday Morning, June 2, 11 A. M.—Communion Service.

Sunday Afternoon at 3 P. M.—"THE POWER OF GOD IN ONE WORD."

Sunday Night—"IS GOD PLAYING A GAME OF LOVE WITH THE DEVIL?" Why are we here? Why is the devil? Why is sin, suffering and battle in life.

Monday, June 3—"IS GOD SELFISH IN DESIRING OUR LOVE AND OBEDIENCE?" Why should we give to God? Does He need anything? Should a creature sacrifice to a Creator? Has God a right to demand our service and worship?

Tuesday, June 4—"DID GOD PUT MAN UNDER BONDAGE TO LAW?" Are we free moral agents? If so, why do we have to obey rules and regulations? Is God Lording it over His creatures? Is He a tyrant, robbing us of good things?

Wednesday, June 5—"CAN A LOVING GOD PUNISH HIS CREATURES?" Is God vindictive? Does he enjoy seeing us suffer? Why does God allow wars, famines, earthquakes and plagues? Did God command Israel to kill innocent children?

Thursday, June 6—"DID A LOVING GOD CREATE HELL?" Is man responsible for his sinful nature? We did not choose our parents, country, nature, training, environments, are we responsible for sin? Is there a hell? Where is it? Can a just God put anyone there? Facts prove he has and will.

Friday, June 7—"IS GOD RULING THIS WORLD?" If so, why are there different governments, laws, races, rich and poor, wasteful and starving. Why do the wicked prosper? Why is there so much injustice? Does God take children from loving parents? Why is life so short? What is it all about?

Saturday, June 8—"THE CHARACTER OF GOD'S LOVE." One glimpse of the adorable, unchangeable love of God will make you love Him. Don't miss this.

(Over)

A flyer, promoting the ministry of evangelist J. S. McConnell, identifies the preacher as "the Fiery Irishman," 1935.
John and Anna McConnell

John McConnell poses in his finest business attire in the hills overlooking Tujunga, California, 1940.
John and Anna McConnell

John McConnell stands amid the scenery of the Toe Valley, North Carolina. McConnell was featured in ***LIFE Magazine*** for his newspaper's editorial position of a controversial local murder trial in Bakersville, North Carolina, in 1957.
LIFE Magazine, *Paul Schutzer*

STAR OF HOPE

FRIENDSHIP : A FORCE FOR WORLD PEACE.

Today, every man can join in the task of building foundations for world peace. We, as members of one human family, can show our determination to be friends in spite of our political, religious and racial differences. New ways for cooperation and peaceful progress will be found. The dismal fear of global suicide will be replaced by hope for tomorrow's golden age.

COOPERATION : INTERNATIONAL GEOPHYSICAL YEAR

The I. G. Y. is a symbol of cooperation among scientists of all countries. Through their combined efforts the knowledge of earth and space has been significantly increased and promises many benefits to mankind.

This cooperation can be utilized to provide a dramatic symbol of our unity with the whole family of man.

A SYMBOL TO RALLY HOPE

In order to aid the will for peace the people of every country are invited to sign the Star of Hope Declaration. To dramatize their determination to be friends and to eliminate the conditions that cause war, the Declaration and signatures will be microfilmed and presented to the Secretary General of the International Geophysical Year with the request that they be placed in a satellite that will shine as a brightly visible Star of Hope, launched in joint effort by all the peoples of the world through the International Geophysical Year Committees.

STAR OF HOPE DECLARATION

I, a citizen of this planet, dedicate my friendship and knowledge to work for peace among all men. I will aid the efforts that heal, build and unite mankind.

Add my name to the Star of Hope :

Name	Address
K. S. Krishnan Sept. 9, 1958	National Physical Laboratory New Delhi (INDIA)
Hideki Yukawa Sept. 10, 1958	Kyoto, Japan
F. Perrin 12 Septembre 1958	Paris, France
E. Ole Rasmussen 12 Sept. 1958.	Copenhagen, Denmark
P. Savić, Jugoslavia 12-IX-58	Younis Sabet Egypt
[illegible]	(USSR)
[illegible]	Australia.
E. T. S. Walton,	Ireland.
[illegible]	Argentina.
	Mairie de la Ville de Genève (Suisse)

Star of Hope Committee, San Francisco, U.S.A.

Star of Hope Declaration, 1958.
John and Anna McConnell

General Eisenhower places a donation for Hong Kong refugees in the "share-bank" of Jimmie Tom, a second grader at Commodore Stockton School, Chinatown. Standing behind Tom is John McConnell, the coordinator for the Citizens Committee for Hong Kong Refugees. Ten thousand of these small milk carton share-banks were donated by five dairies. School children take them home, drop in 3¢ every time they wish to invite a hungry unseen guest to dinner.
Caption as it appeared in the Meals for Millions newsletter, Fall 1962. (Even though identified as "General Eisenhower," he was also a former U.S. President, from 1953 to 1961.)
Skelton Photography, San Francisco; Freedom from Hunger, formerly Meals for Millions.

Former President Dwight David Eisenhower and John McConnell share a handshake and conversation at the Fairmont Hotel in San Francisco during which both men expressed their preferences for peace, 1962.
Skelton Photography, San Francisco

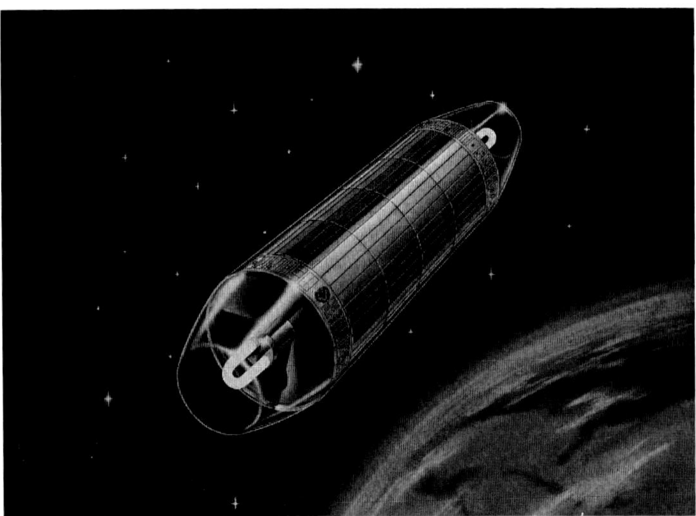

Industrial designer Raymond Loewy created an artist's rendering of a potential design for the Star of Hope satellite in 1958. Loewy's explanatory overlay (not shown) reads: "Paved in solar batteries that would recharge interior chemical batteries during sunlight hours, this satellite, as a symbol of our 'geo-spiritual' intent, would be visible to the naked eye at night as a second magnitude star. Loewy suggests the cost could be subscribed by the children of the U.S. donating a penny each. All known religious symbols, flags of all nations, and the United Nations shield would be inscribed on the star or contained inside on microfilm so that each individual might identify himself with the orbiting satellite."
Raymond Loewy Associates

Seven children of the United Nations International School, dressed in costumes of their countries, ring the Peace Bell on 4 October 1966 to mark the first anniversary of an historic visit to New York by Catholic pontiff, His Holiness Pope Paul VI.
United Nations, YN/PAS

Anna and John McConnell stand before the altar at St. Mark's Lutheran Church after their marriage on Christmas Day 1967.
John and Anna McConnell

Christa, Anna, John and Hattie McConnell pose outside Anna's and John's Brooklyn apartment, 1974.
John and Anna McConnell

Artist's rendering of the proposed Minute for Peace exhibit at the New York World's Fair, 1964 and 1965. Explanatory text attached to the rendering states: "The 1965 MINUTE FOR PEACE exhibit will publicize International Co-operation Year and help celebrate the Twentieth Anniversary of the signing of the United Nations Charter in San Francisco. It will also highlight the Fair's theme 'Peace through Understanding.'" A description of the display reads: "A revolving model of earth; model satellite above, emitting sharp beam of light which traces MINUTE FOR PEACE pathway across the Earth."
Swarthmore College Peace Collection

Moreland M. Smith, chairman of the Lions Minute for Peace Committee, and Lions International president Harry J. Aslan hold the Lions' Minute for Peace International scrapbook, 1967.
Swarthmore College Peace Collection

A "flag for the whole earth" designed by John McConnell, a globally minded Brooklyn man, will fly over the city's Central Park moon watch during the Apollo 11 landing on the moon. It is an 8-foot banner of royal blue with a silk-screen representation of the earth as seen by astronauts in space. Arthur Norman Liberte made the flag under a grant from the National Council of Churches. This photo shows John holding the flag with his wife, Anna Marie.
Caption is as it appeared in New York Daily News, *11 July 1969*

Film actress Gloria Swanson and John McConnell display an Earth Flag aboard an aircraft carrier in New York Harbor on 4 July 1978 as part of the United States Bicentennial celebration.
Swarthmore College Peace Collection

The Earth Flag flies under the United States' national flag at the Amundsen-Scott South Pole Station, 1983.
***National Science** Foundation/ U.S. Antarctic Program*

Russian cosmonauts Talgat Musabaev and Nikolai Budarin pose with an Earth Flag aboard the Mir Space Station, March 1998.
John and Anna McConnell

Paratroopers from six nations, including cosmonaut Anatoly Berezovoi, display the Earth Flag they carried on their drop to the North Pole in 2000.
John and Anna McConnell

9

World Equality
(1969 to 1973)

This planet belongs to us – all of us. We have spiritual and material rights and responsibilities during our journey here.
– John McConnell, WE, Inc., definition

Seeing the need for an organization to further promote their efforts, John and Anna McConnell incorporated WE, Inc., – an acronym for "World Equality" – in the District of Columbia on 28 February 1969. [437] Intending to expand upon success with Minute for Peace, John saw WE, Inc., as "a worldwide institution of peace to replace the institutions of war." He believed the organization would represent "a new world view that appeals to all men of good will regardless of religion, ideology, race or culture ... [and] clearly show what is required of any individual who would do his part in building world peace." He produced a brochure that capitalized on the WE name: "This planet belongs to us – all of us! 'WE' can make Earth a beautiful home for all mankind."

Once again ahead of his time, John's brochure transformed his long-held philosophy of "come together where we agree while leaving room for our differences" into the phrase "unity in diversity," which would become organizational buzzwords years later. He saw WE, Inc., as "a fresh statement, a new world view that will recognize the universal values and unite men in care for one another ... even though they follow different paths in pursuing

[437] *WE, Inc. Articles of Incorporation*, 28 February 1969.

them." WE, Inc., he said, "is an effort to bridge the barriers ... with a down-to-earth followup that will provide maximum communication and cooperation."

He observed, "People ... want a better world, but their institutions for achieving this are out of joint with each other. Viewed on a lateral plane, the situation is a hopeless maze." So he called on people to "take a new look at our world. Not laterally, trying to see through the barriers of prejudice and semantics, but vertically with an astronaut's view." He noted, "Whether in communist or capitalist countries, whether in Hindu temples or Christian churches, most people want the same things ... to learn ... to grow ... love ... security. And regardless of their culture or ideology, there is a broad base of values that are common to most people – courage, justice, equity, self-determination, freedom – to name a few."

He drew upon the Minute for Peace concept and established a WE, Inc., goal "to quicken the conscience of every man through meditation, ... inspire communication on the same mental wave length through shared goals and common experience, ... [and] create a democracy of spirit."

And he described the organization's operating procedures as "democratic and open" with a "unique communications system," specifically, a "communications card" to record and disseminate information and through which members could express opinions to the board and cast ballots. He saw applications for such a card, beyond WE, Inc., as "an important democratic aid to legislators." From his perspective as an octogenarian in the twenty-first century, more than thirty years later, John acknowledged such communication cards were never invented, per se, but the concept did become the basis of e-mail communications, especially to lawmakers, via the Internet.

Starting small in his Brooklyn apartment, John predicted "independent WE branches" would spring up in other parts of the United States and in other countries where they would have "the greatest possible appeal to all organizations and to all people of good will."

John hoped existing organizations would become WE, Inc., affiliates for a cost of $15.00 per year. Individual life memberships were only $10.00 with a proviso, "Those who cannot afford this all at once may pay $1.00 a month for ten months." In the spirit of the 33 Campaign, his WE, Inc., brochure copy suggested, "Each member obtain at least two other members." In turn, John promised, "A member will receive a $5.00 credit for each new member he obtains – payable to any nonprofit project he believes will contribute effectively to world peace." [438]

Members usually wrote checks for more than $10.00, showing that John's growing number of followers recognized the nobility of his idea as well as the impracticality of his intended fiscal redistribution. As Hans Janitschek commented later, "John was a great man, but I didn't see him as a chief executive." [439] And while John promised his backers that WE, Inc., would become self sufficient, he also acknowledged, "I am very poor at raising funds." [440]

He considered the life of St. Francis, who took a vow of poverty, and wondered "if some inner feeling [within himself] ... was causing a conflict with money-making pursuits." [441] But looking beyond money, John found confidence to continue his endeavors in scripture. On 15 October 1969, he journaled the *Bible* verse, "My meat is to do the will of Him who sent me and to finish His work." [442]

To that end, John penned an essay, called "Peaceful Progress," in which he wrote, "If change is going to be in the direction of progress, then we must use the peaceful methods of change. The will to build must replace the will to destroy." Of protest and violence, he added, "It is possible to protest without malice and personal condemnation, and thereby minimize violence. But every ounce of effort in the protest must be followed by ten stronger efforts to take advantage of the gains in a peaceful way; to constantly build something better wherever anything is torn down." And on pacifism, he concluded, "The new way was not to force change, but to inspire change; not to protest evil, but to praise good; not to speak so much of injustice, but of new examples of justice; not the destruction of the old house, the old system (which is inevitable), but the building of a new and beautiful home.

---

[438] John McConnell, *WE* brochure, 1968.

[439] Hans Janitschek, interview by author, New York, New York, 8 June 2004.

[440] John McConnell, letter to Irving Laucks, Center for Studies of Democratic Institutions, 15 October 1968.

[441] John McConnell, journal, September-October 1969, 15 October 1969.

[442] *Bible*, John 4:34.

Then it will be easy to move out of the old house, to leave the old ways." [443] With these words, John recommitted himself to spreading God's message of peace, regardless of financial results.

The organization's first meeting was at the apartment home of Helen Putnam on East 51st Street, New York, on 6 March 1969. Seven people attended, including John and Anna who drove from their temporary home in Falmouth. This was the first of many such meetings, evangelical in nature, that John and Anna hosted either in their apartment or in the homes of others.

Cecil Thomas became the first WE, Inc., member, contributing $10.00. Other founding members included Robert Beussee of WOR Radio-TV; Melvin R. Goode, American Broadcasting Company's (ABC) correspondent to the United Nations; Trevor Hoy of Berkeley Center for Human Interaction; Harold Oram who organized a conference of scientists, including Albert Einstein, on the dangers of atomic weapons in 1958; Ralf Brent; Solomon Huber; Brother Mandus; Althya Youngman; and Frank O. Braynard who, later, joined John in three other endeavors, Earth Society in 1973, Sea Citizens in 1974, and Earth Society Foundation in 1976. Braynard also organized Operation Sail 1976 for which a fleet of tall ships from around the world sailed into New York Harbor for the U.S. Bicentennial.

In the fall of 1969, John journaled, "A new world is being born. Real peace is coming. New towns. Education with ecstasy. And music, art, dancing with love and joy. ... Building instead of bitching. Improving – not just the quantity of goods but the quality of life. And most of all, no more killing! How soon will it come? As soon as more energy is going into works of peace than into works of war. How soon will it come? As soon as other people start doing their part. Too bad I have to wait for them! Or is it possible they are waiting for me?" He continued with thoughts about the true identity of "The Other Man" for whom he was waiting. "Other people are to blame for war and for violence, greed and hate. The other man is the problem. And when will we have peace? When each one sees that, at least in part, he is the 'other man.'" [444]

At the same time, John used his journal to chastise "the Gods of

[443] John McConnell, "Peaceful Progress," essay, 1968.

[444] John McConnell, journal, September-October 1969, 15 October 1969.

Force, the Gods of Military Might" and "the Priests of the Pentagon." He admonished, "Real peace comes not by works of war, but by works of peace," and he urged, "Change in our strategy from bombing the Earth for Peace to building the Earth for peace." Appealing to "the God of Compassion and Moral Right," he suggested, "An appropriate test of His power ... could be obtained in One Hour of Peace."

Specifically, he averred that the U.S. could employ the money spent in "one hour of saturation bombing in Vietnam [and] offer this full amount to N[orth] V[ietnam] with the provision that it be distributed equally to each and every homeless citizen." During that symbolic "Silent Hour of Peace, a time of soul searching," he hoped all U.S. citizens would attend churches or synagogues, radio and television would be silenced at the President's behest, and all but emergency traffic would be stopped. John concluded, "We have spent billions to make bombs work for peace and they have failed. Why not spend a billion dollars to make prayer work?" [445]

Wilson Van Dusen, who paid $20.00 to become a WE, Inc., member, was a frequent observer of John's activities during this period. Of John's idea for worldwide, or even nationwide, prayer, the psychiatrist noted with cynicism, "If we ever get all people on the earth praying together, all problems will have already ended." [446]

On the practical side, Wilson advocated John's cause to James Milne, a procurer of funding for humanitarian projects; Charles E. Watson, president of People-to-People Foundation; and George L. Killion of Metro-Goldwyn-Mayer movie studio, who had been on the Meals for Millions board of directors of the Citizens Committee for Hong Kong Refugee Week in San Francisco. All of these potential benefactors expressed interest and praise for John's work but chose not to offer financial backing. Telling John, "Your single-handed work provides a good background for a grant – Earth Day, flags, U Thant, etc.," [447] Van Dusen submitted a grant request to the Ford Foundation, which returned a polite rejection within a week. In these letters to potential benefactors, the psychiatrist noted that the visionary was achieving "his successes while living on an annual income near $1,000 per

---

[445] Ibid.

[446] Wilson Van Dusen, letter to John McConnell, 7 August 1972.

[447] Wilson Van Dusen, letter to John McConnell, 7 May 1970.

year, now with a wife and child." [448]

At the same time, in personal correspondence to John and Anna, Van Dusen offered a continuum of fiscal observations. On one hand, he suggested John try welfare, justifying it as "the government's way of supporting peace efforts." On the other hand, he compared John's freedom – "you pretty much are always doing what you want to do" – with his more affluent, but mostly vacation-less, lifestyle. "I feel like a poor man and admire your wealth," Van Dusen wrote to John. [449]

Louie Hilford of Consultants to Business & Industry, Inc., (CBI), in San Francisco, offered a more objective observation. In his assessment of the organization's by-laws, he wrote, on the plus side, "WE, Inc., has the idea … that peace and ecology are necessary if man is to survive; has the timing … in the era of ecological glamour and priority; [and] has the product … the Earth Flag." But on the minus side, "WE, Inc., does not have the vehicle, the organizational structure; … does not have the staff, … an experienced administrator; [and] does not have the identity … an office address, telephone, letterhead, business cards and on-going flow of correspondence and publicity." CBI then proposed "to maximize the possibilities and to resolve the deficiencies" by providing John with desk space, materials and secretarial services for a fee of $15.00 per hour or $300, later $400, per month, whichever was greater. [450]

But John found the suggested restrictions contrary to his lifestyle. Instead, he preferred to preach the gospel of peace from any venue. And, for the moment, that venue was San Francisco where John had many long-standing contacts. There, working out of his mother's home, John launched WE, Inc.'s first major endeavor – Earth Day.

---

448 Wilson Van Dusen, letter to Charles E. Wilson, 19 June 1970.

449 Wilson Van Dusen, letter to John McConnell, 1970.

450 Louie Hilford, "A Proposal for John McConnell of WE, Inc.", 28 January 1970.

10
The Origin of Earth Day
(1968 to 1970)

Nature's Day. A day of drama, dreams and dedication to the restoration, renewal and improvement of Earth's natural beauty and bounty.
– John McConnell, "Celebrate Earth Day," 20 March 1991

With his passion to preach for world peace, John McConnell prayed for "the possibility of a new world view, new structures and systems that would get everybody around the world working together, each in his own way, peacefully building a new earth … in harmony with nature." Mentally, John reviewed his accomplishments with Star of Hope, Meals for Millions, Minute for Peace and the Earth Flag. He considered the movie treatment, called "Stowaway on a Satellite," that he had written in 1957 in which he conceived a "would-be astronaut" – emblematic of himself – who snuck aboard a test space vessel then, after launch and revealing his dire situation to an enthralled world, transmitted back to Earth a message of universal hope and peace. With these recollections, John realized that, for many years, he had been "concerned about symbols that would … encourage global unity." [451]

He prayed for inspiration for another symbol – an event, a pageant, a special day – that would help people gain "a sense of the mysterious wonder of life." [452] He imagined a holiday that would remind people of "Earth's

[451] John McConnell, "The Development of Earth Day," speech at Koinonia, 1971.
[452] Ibid.

beautiful systems of balance that humanity has partially upset and must restore," [453] a global holiday that would help people "get connected with others who are learning more about the earth." [454] A day for all people of the entire earth. An earth day.

Earth Day. John liked the name. Succinct, catchy and meaningful, it was also unique. Through his knowledge and extensive contacts at the United Nations, John was certain no one, neither within the environmental movement nor advocates of any other cause, had ever used the name "Earth Day" before. [455]

Anna recalled that John coined the Earth Day name in 1968. [456] Then, in August 1969, when she, John and John Paul traveled by train from New York City to Oakland, California, to visit Hattie, John worked diligently on the Earth Day plan, sketching ideas for community activities that would help "turn the course of human action from Earth Kill to Earth Care" [457] by means of "a day to celebrate our global unity and destiny." [458]

While John wished he could introduce Earth Day in New York at the United Nations where he had enjoyed camaraderie at the highest levels, including with Secretary-General U Thant, he took great delight in sharing the idea with Californians. He formulated plans to launch Earth Day in the city where the UN Charter had been signed in 1945, and he honed the Earth Day resolution for that venue, the City of San Francisco.

When the McConnell family arrived on the West Coast, a date for Earth Day was the only detail lacking from John's resolution. At the first opportunity, he met with Peter Tamaras, who, by then, had been a member of the San Francisco Board of Supervisors for eight years. Impressed, Tamaras said he would present the resolution to the board and to mayor Joseph Alioto, but he told John to come up with a date first.

When to have Earth Day? That question haunted John. He considered

---

[453] John McConnell, "Earth Day Proposal to the City of San Francisco," 3 October 1969.

[454] John McConnell, "The Development of Earth Day," speech at Koinonia, 1971.

[455] John McConnell, "Earth Day Proposal to the City of San Francisco," 3 October 1969.

[456] Anna McConnell, "The Beginning of Earth Day," 1989 or 1990.

[457] Ibid.

[458] John McConnell, "Earth Day Proposal to the City of San Francisco," 3 October 1969.

4 October, the feast of St. Francis, which is also the date Russia launched the first Sputnik. He thought about 20 July, the day Neil Armstrong stepped on the moon. No, both of those dates bore nationalistic imagery. And while the feast of St. Francis would appeal to Christians, it would have little significance to other religions of the world. [459] Not satisfied with any date that came to mind, John prayed for guidance. "Lord, when should Earth Day be?"

Then, in his mother's home, he happened upon a book about Stonehenge that discussed the Druids' ability to pinpoint geo-celestial holidays by sighting the rising sun and moon over key stones within the sarsen circle. Already familiar with the solstices and the equinoxes, he read their descriptions again. Suddenly, like a flash, the word "equinox" jumped off the page at him. "It came so strong and so clear, and I knew that was the perfect day for Earth Day," he later wrote. [460]

John was sitting in the living room of his mother's home when he received that inspiration. He called to Anna, who was in the kitchen, washing dishes, and announced to her, "Anna! Anna! I know when Earth Day will be. It will be on the vernal equinox when night and day are equal. The whole Earth will be in balance." [461] At that moment, the husband and wife team felt a slight tremor as a minor earthquake quivered throughout the Bay Area, [462] an indication in their minds that God – through the Earth – was confirming John's decision. [463]

For John and Anna, that spiritual indicator was sufficient, yet John sought further confirmation, of the academic variety, that would help others understand Earth Day's global significance. He learned that festivals and celebrations on the equinox existed within Persian, Mayan and early Chinese civilizations. Prior to the Gregorian Calendar, Europeans honored the spring equinox as the first day of the year. And people in many Muslim countries still celebrated their new year on the equinox. In addition, the Christian holy days of Easter and the Annunciation were determined by the first full moon in spring.

Linguistically, John toyed with the word "equinox" – Latin for "equal

---

459 John McConnell, "The Development of Earth Day," speech at Koinonia, 1971.

460 Ibid.

461 Anna McConnell, "The Beginning of Earth Day," 1989 or 1990.

462 John McConnell, journal, 1 October 1969.

463 John and Anna McConnell, interview by author, Denver, Colorado, August 2004.

night" – and considered the physical phenomenon of global rotation and geomagnetism. The vernal equinox was one of two days each year when the Earth was in perfect equipoise, when daytime and nighttime were equal in both the Northern and Southern hemispheres, when the sun rose or set at the two magnetic poles, when people on the Equator did not cast a shadow. The equinoxes, either of them, representing spring's anticipation and autumn's serenity, would be perfect for a global holiday.

But springtime, when dormant plants and hibernating animals re-emerged, when wintering people came out of their homes to celebrate sunshine, was more appealing than autumn with its characteristic of maturity and quiescence. Looking at a globe, he noted the planet's largest land masses were, and most of the population lived in, the Northern Hemisphere.

Yes, Earth Day on the vernal equinox possessed the key quality of universality – a global holiday determined by the tipping of the Earth itself, a geo-celestial event that occurred simultaneously around the globe at local time, either on March 20 or 21, depending on each location's position relative to the International Date Line. "Celebrating Earth Day on the equinox will bring a unique universal awareness of our planet and its human family," John told Anna. [464]

Two days later, on 3 October 1969, John told Peter Tamaras about the date – Saturday, 21 March 1970 – and the city supervisor put John's resolution draft on the board's agenda.

John then wondered how to get the United Nations and U Thant involved. Fortunately, the U.S. National Commission for UNESCO [465] had announced its 13th National Conference for the St. Francis Hotel in San Francisco on 23-25 November. That was his opportunity.

The registration list for the conference read like a Who's Who of dignitaries, scientists, educators, business people, politicians and representatives of labor unions, major corporations, media, environmental and civic associations, and private citizens. The participants, who numbered more than 400, included: San Francisco mayor Joseph Alioto; television personality Arthur Godfrey who, in 1970, would be appointed to a new State Council of Environmental Advisors in New York; anthropologist

---

[464] John McConnell, "The Authentic Date for Earth Day."

[465] United Nations Educational, Scientific and Cultural Organization (UNESCO)

Margaret Mead, curator of the American Museum of Natural History in New York; U.S. congressman Paul N. McCloskey of California; biologist and educator Barry Commoner; professors and administrators from Notre Dame University, University of Wisconsin, Florida State University, University of California at Berkeley, University of California at Davis, Stanford University, New York University, and North Carolina State University; executives, directors or members of Sierra Club, The Nature Conservancy, National Wildlife Federation, The National Audubon Society, National Congress of Parents and Teachers, National Educational Television, National Education Association, Planned Parenthood Association, AFL-CIO, Pacific Telephone Company, Pacific Gas & Electric, Dow Chemical, U.S. Catholic Conference, American National Red Cross, League of Women Voters, Girl Scouts of America, The Izaak Walton League, Ford Foundation, U.S. Department of State, U.S. Army Corps of Engineers, U.S. Forest Service; and people from the United Nations. [466]

John attended the conference and promoted Earth Day. [467] Cynthia Wayburn, one of the youth leaders on the Earth Day Committee and whose father had been president of the Sierra Club through most of the 1960s, presented the idea and showed the Earth Flag at the conference's closing luncheon. Many people expressed support for the idea to both Wayburn and John. [468]

Immediately after Wayburn's speech, two young men approached John and introduced themselves as aides to senator Gaylord Nelson, who had been a strong environmental advocate throughout his political career, starting in the Wisconsin State Senate in 1948 and continuing through his governorship of Wisconsin in 1958 and his election to the U.S. Senate in 1962. The young men spoke of "Environmental Teach-Ins" the senator and his political aides and student volunteers were organizing to be held on college campuses that spring. They told John the teach-ins would be patterned after anti-Vietnam

[466] "Attendance List, 13th National Conference of the United States National Commission for UNESCO," San Francisco, California, 23-25 November 1969. (23 pages)

[467] "Addendum I" to "Attendance List, 13th National Conference of the United States National Commission for UNESCO," San Francisco, California, 23-25 November 1969. (6 pages; John McConnell's name is on page 4.)

[468] John McConnell, "Earth Day Proposal to the City of San Francisco," 3 October 1969.

War protests that had become popular among college students. However, the Environmental Teach-In, the senator's people said, would focus on waging war against pollution. They mentioned the date for the teach-ins – April 22, 1970 – and they invited John to join their campaign. [469]

John recognized the date. April 22 was the original date of Arbor Day, founded in Nebraska in 1872 by J. Sterling Morton, a connection that offered an environmental tradition and, thus, validity for the senator's efforts. He quickly analyzed the intended audience: United States college students. He considered the methodology to be used: protest. He weighed these factors with Earth Day's broader purpose of "peace, justice and the care of Earth." He considered Earth Day's greater audience, which would be all people on the planet, and Earth Day's celebratory approach to "global unity and destiny." [470] He responded with hope that the Environmental Teach-In would be a success, but as for redirecting his efforts toward that event and that date, he replied, "Absolutely not! The global history and symbolism of having Earth Day on the equinox are too great." [471]

Throughout that fall and winter, John received encouragement for Earth Day from numerous and various sources. His friend and colleague S. Fred Singer offered encouragement. [472] Huey D. Johnson, who later became secretary of the California Resources Agency under governor Jerry Brown and founder and president of the Resource Renewal Institute in San Francisco, wrote to John, "I've read with interest your plan to celebrate Earth Day on March 21. At a time when the public is at last expressing concern for the source of all life – the earth and its complex environment – it is particularly fitting that you undertake this project. The activities planned for the day sound interesting and I look forward to attending. I am sure you can count on the support of conservationists for this positive celebration." [473]

On 3 February 1970, the San Francisco Board of Supervisors passed the resolution, making it the first governmental proclamation for Earth Day.

---

[469] John McConnell, interview by author, Denver, Colorado, August 2004.

[470] John McConnell, "Earth Day Proposal to the City of San Francisco," 3 October 1969.

[471] John McConnell, interview by author, Denver, Colorado, August 2004.

[472] John McConnell, letter to S. Fred Singer, 16 January 1970.

[473] Huey D. Johnson, letter to John McConnell, 3 February 1970.

Mayor Alioto signed the proclamation on 11 February, [474] which happened to be Anna's 39th birthday.

Spurred by leadership from the mayor and supervisors, San Francisco responded. KRON-TV, the city's NBC affiliate, broadcast a half-hour color special that extolled the beauties of the world. [475] The Golden Gate chapter of the American Red Cross raised the Earth Flag over Union Square and distributed seedlings to be planted by school children. [476] The Junior Chamber of Commerce urged activities and legislation that would diminish pollution and encourage environmental preservation. [477]

At the University of California at Davis, (UC, Davis) students and faculty converted the campus into a stage for drama and exhibits with ecological themes such as "Street of Spring," "Street of Recycling," "Street of Crafts," and "Street of Nature." [478] The event, held 15 March to 22 March 1970, was dubbed "Whole Earth Week, an Aquarian Festival of Life," and pop artist Peter Max designed a poster exclusively for the festival. [479] In Berkeley, Tom Glase of the Ecology Center designed another poster that John and Anna referred to as "the first Earth Day poster." [480]

The festival at UC, Davis, germinated with a speech that John delivered on the campus in October 1969. [481] This was augmented by a lecture by Sri Swami Satchidananda during Christmas break at the Unitarian Church in San Francisco. The student newspaper, *The California Aggie*, reported, "After the famous Indian spiritual teacher had finished his message, he introduced a gentleman named John McConnell, describing him as a person of whom, 'Every time I see him, he is talking of Peace.'" [482]

The newspaper depicted John as "a silver haired senatorial figure with a space-age view of planetary unity" who revealed his plan for Earth Day at the UNESCO conference. A representative from UC, Davis, brought John's idea back to the college where according to the paper, it "landed ...

474 *Earth Day Proclamation*, City of San Francisco, California, 11 February 1970.
475 "KRON-TV Presents Spring Rites Color Special," news release, 12 March 1970.
476 Golden Gate Chapter, The American National Red Cross, news release, 1970.
477 "Earth Day International and Earth Society Foundation," fact sheet.
478 Ibid.
479 *The California* Aggie, 4 March 1970.
480 "Earth Day 1970 helpers."
481 John McConnell, letter to Gaylord Nelson, 11 October 1989.
482 "History Behind Earth Week," *The California* Aggie, 4 March 1970.

in a manner resembling a nuclear reaction" and exploded into "a spiritual festival dedicated to re-attuning the people of Davis to closer contact with their environment and uniting people in the realization of themselves as Earthians, as the virtual children of Mother Earth." [483]

Satchidananda led formal discussion groups during the week, as did Catholic priests, Jewish rabbis and leaders of other religious denominations. [484] Evening lectures covered topics such as astrology, spirituality, theosophy, yoga, Zen, macrobiotics, optimism and international understanding. Over 400 students who took classes from Art History professor Jose Arguelles made outdoor exhibits that served as their final exam projects. Engineering students constructed a "Global Village," using an assemblage of three geodesic domes, an architectural style advocated by Buckminster Fuller. And the aromas of natural foods permeated the campus quad, which was the site of a keynote address by Satchidananda. [485]

A student editorial proclaimed the event, even though held during exam week, was an "opportunity to give us respite from our exaggerated differences, to celebrate, to emphasize the harmony of all people, to put joy and fun above worry and sorrow – if only for a week." The paper's editorial page also promoted an all-day ecology fair to be held at Lincoln Junior High School in Sacramento. [486] Correspondence from the Whole Earth Brotherhood within the Associated Students at the University of California, Davis, reported to John, "Along with more 'traditional' skill or knowledge oriented classes, we're now putting together action groups, such as World Game and the Frontiers of Science Fellowship, ... free school groups, and ... we'll begin to center all this activity around a group called WE! Peace!" [487]

John McConnell was ecstatic at the enthusiastic response to his Earth Day idea both at the university and in San Francisco. Anna wrote to a friend that he had been "working day and night" for Earth Day activities in various California locations. [488] He was a featured speaker at UC, Davis on the night

---

483 Ibid.

484 John McConnell, "The Development of Earth Day," speech at Koinonia, 1971.

485 "History Behind Earth Week," *The California Aggie*, 4 March 1970.

486 "Join the Celebration of Whole Earth Week," *The California Aggie*, 11 March 1970.

487 Chuck Sweet, letter to John McConnell.

488 Anna McConnell, letter to Marcia Hopkins, San Jose, California, 16 March 1970.

of 18 March, [489] an event to which Anna accompanied him in spite of having been ill with morning sickness on previous days. [490] And on Earth Day, John enjoyed the company of San Francisco mayor Alioto as they visited several events. [491]

In Berkeley, California, mayor Wallace Johnson signed a proclamation that reminded the city's residents "of our common destiny ... [and] the present danger we human beings have caused to our environment on this planet." The Berkeley proclamation recognized the Earth Flag and Earth Day as "the date of the year when ... all inhabitants ... have the hope of constant renewal," and, therefore, urged citizens "to do something significant to the preservation and renewal of our precious Earth." [492]

New Yorkers, many of them friends of John and Anna, celebrated the first Earth Day with "a celebration of Earth, its people and a call for the protection of both" at a rally, followed by an "anti-nuke benefit party." The event featured musicians, speakers and the creation of an urban garden. [493]

Enthusiasm for Earth Day spread to the nation's capital thanks to California congressman Charles Teague who introduced a bill to the House of Representatives to declare Earth Day a national day of reflection on which people would focus on earth's preservation. [494] On 3 February 1970, senator George Murphy of California wrote to John that he had presented the idea to President Richard Nixon. [495] Within a week, Murphy received a White House memo that acknowledged receipt of Murphy's letter with a promise it would "reach the appropriate office for consideration." [496] John followed Murphy's communiqué with a letter to President Nixon asking him to designate "a national Earth Day on March 21." [497]

Two months later, when Pete Seeger heard of John's request to the White

---

489 Anna McConnell, letter to Jim Christian, Lynchburg, Virginia, 17 March 1970.

490 Anna McConnell, letter to Marcia Hopkins, San Jose, California, 16 March 1970.

491 John McConnell, interview by author, Denver, Colorado, August 2004.

492 *Earth Day in Berkeley Proclamation*, City of Berkeley, California, 17 March 1970.

493 "Earth Day, a celebration of Earth, its people and a call for the protection of both," poster, 21 March 1970.

494 "Earth Day International and Earth Society Foundation," historical fact sheet.

495 George Murphy, letter to John McConnell, 3 February 1970.

496 Kenneth E. Belieu, deputy assistant to the president, letter to George Murphy, 5 February 1970.

497 John McConnell, letter to George Murphy, 8 February 1970.

House, the folk singer and environmental activist cautioned, "I'm not sure I'd want to get President Nixon behind the campaign. There is a real danger that the whole movement to clean up the environment could be co-opted by the very people mainly responsible for making things such a mess." [498]

[498] Pete Seeger, letter to John McConnell, 5 April 1970.

11

The Battle over Earth Day

(1970 to present)

The Vernal Equinox is a distinct annual astronomical occurrence in our Solar System. It is a special moment that affects nature on a grand scale, an event that predates Mankind and one that will last for as long as the Earth spins on its axis.
– John McConnell, "What Is Earth Day?" 20 March 1974

ON SUNDAY, 18 JANUARY 1970, John and Anna McConnell were getting ready for the birth of their second child and preparing for the first Earth Day when John received a phone call from his attorney Tony Roisman in the nation's capital. Roisman stated, "I thought Earth Day was going to be on the spring equinox." John replied, "It is." To which the attorney returned, "Well, *The Washington Post* and *The New York Times* just ran full-page ads announcing Earth Day on April 22." John was incensed. "What? We can't have *two* Earth Days. Why, Christmas wouldn't be the same if we celebrated it all year long. The same with your birthday." [499]

Over the next two days, John attempted to telephone Gaylord Nelson, who, Roisman said, was mentioned in the ad. The legislator did not return the phone calls, but John did speak with Denis Hayes, who had dropped out of Harvard Law School to become the student coordinator on the national staff of the Environmental Teach-In, Inc., a nonprofit entity that Nelson

[499] John McConnell, interview by author, Denver, Colorado, August 2004.

established in the fall of 1969 to promote the April 22 Environmental Teach-In. Hayes told John he didn't know who had suggested the Earth Day name. [500]

In a letter to John on the same day, 20 January 1970, Hayes wrote, "We learned through our law firm that you were out on deck with Earth Day only after we had our ad placed in the N.Y. Times. No one in our deliberations over the ad had been to the UNESCO conference, and we were simply unaware of your existence." The letter stated, "The nationwide environmental Teach-In on April 22 is coming to be known by a variety of names … E-Day, Environment Day, Ecology Day, End-of-the-World Day and Earth Day."

The letter also acknowledged John McConnell as the head of "a world peace organization" that had "announced some months ago in San Francisco that it wished to make March 21 Earth Day," stated "there is no connection between the two organizations," and concluded with wishes for the success of "the March 21 Earth Day" and an apology "for any confusion which has resulted from our common name."

Although written in the style of a news release, the letter was addressed to John and did not indicate any other person or organization to whom Hayes mailed or distributed this correspondence, other than a copy to Tony Roisman. [501] John noted he did not see Hayes' statement in any newspaper, while acknowledging the announcement would not be of significant magnitude to attract media attention. [502]

Upon receipt of the letter, John placed a small "x" next to Hayes' comment about no one in their deliberations having attended the UNESCO conference and noted in the margin, "Perhaps this was true, but two people who claimed to represent Denis spoke to me at the conference and urged me to change the date to April 22, which I refused to do. The March 21 equinox, which I had chosen for Earth Day, was nature's choice." [503] Similarly, in a letter to Roisman on 31 January, John wrote of the men who approached him, "One of them said that 'Earth Day' would be a good name for the

---

[500] Anna McConnell, "The Beginning of Earth Day," 1989 or 1990.

[501] Denis Hayes, letter to John McConnell, 20 January 1970.

[502] John McConnell, interview by author, Denver, Colorado, August 2004.

[503] John McConnell, handwritten notation in the margin of Denis Hayes letter to John McConnell, 20 January 1970.

Teach-In." [504]

In addition, a close associate of Gaylord Nelson, California senator Paul McCloskey, was listed among the UNESCO conference attendees. [505] McCloskey served on the board of directors, called the "Teach-In Committee," for the Environmental Teach-In, Inc., along with Nelson and Sidney Howe, president of The Conservation Foundation. McCloskey, a Republican, joined with Nelson, a Democrat, to give bipartisan support to the April 22 Environmental Teach-In. And all three men signed the Environmental Teach-In, Inc., Articles of Incorporation. [506]

The circumstances involving Tony Roisman, including the fact that Hayes sent him a copy of his 20 January letter, proved to be an enigma. As John's attorney, Roisman had donated his services to establish WE, Inc., in 1968, and he co-signed the WE, Inc., Articles of Incorporation in 1969. Those Articles listed Roisman's address in Washington, D.C. as the organization's official address. [507]

In January 1970, John sent two letters to Roisman. In the first, on 13 January, prior to Roisman's phone call about the April 22 Earth Day ads, John wrote familiarly about "a wonderful visit with a friend [presumably Wilson Van Dusen] I had not seen in 20 years," asked about an agreement Roisman was to have sent but which John had not received, and thanked him "for your great help." [508] In the second correspondence, a four-page handwritten letter on 31 January that bore the salutation "Dear Tony" and closed with "warm regards," John apologized for his irritation during the phone call that bore Roisman's disturbing news about the April 22 Earth Day ads. Employing friendly discourse, John acknowledged, "What happened was an eye opener. ... My reaction indicated I had somehow gotten my ego involved in the whole thing. ... [I hope] I'm far enough along on my spiritual journey to know the highest good comes from detachment – without ego satisfaction or disappointment – but always grateful for the Grace of God." The letter

504 John McConnell, letter to Tony Roisman, 31 January 1970.

505 "Attendance List, 13th National Conference of the United States National Commission for UNESCO," San Francisco, California, 23-25 November 1969. (23 pages)

506 *Articles of Incorporation of Environmental Teach-In, Inc. of the District of Columbia*, 19 November 1969.

507 *Articles of Incorporation of WE, Inc.*, 28 February 1969.

508 John McConnell, letter to Tony Roisman, 13 January 1970.

contained an offer to provide Earth Flags for the Environmental Teach-In, an Earth Day fact sheet for Roisman's edification, papers pertaining to a legal agreement for Roisman to review, and a promise to call the following Tuesday. [509]

Then, suddenly, Roisman resigned from the WE, Inc., board on 13 April 1970, nine days prior to the April 22 Environmental Teach-In. In sharp contrast to the casualness of John's correspondence, Roisman's letter of resignation formally stated, "As you know my membership was always pro forma and I have not had the time to actively participate. Of course, I will still be glad to consult with you when I can but feel that I should not be on the board of any organization unless I actively participate in it." [510]

Years later, Roisman acknowledged he was representing Gaylord Nelson and Denis Hayes at the time. He claimed to have had little association with John McConnell at any time during his life, although he did speak fondly of John, calling him "a delightful person concerned about the broadest issue of Earth Day." [511]

In regard to the phone call that John said came from Roisman on 18 January, the attorney offered a different recollection, stating, "John came to me because I represented the people who had been involved with the April 22 Earth Day. He was concerned about the use of the term Earth Day, and I made some effort to put people together." [512]

Anna described that statement as untrue. "We did not know he was involved in the Environmental Teach-In until later," she said, "and how could John have come to see him? We were in Oakland." [513] Her sentiment was supported by the timing and content of John's 31 January letter, which he posted from Oakland, in response to the April 22 Earth Day ads. Anna and John surmised, while Roisman was unique and important to them, they were probably one of many forgettable clients to him. Giving Roisman ample benefit of doubt, they presumed he inadvertently found himself in a conflict of interest situation that involved two organizations – WE, Inc., first, and

---

509 John McConnell, letter to Tony Roisman, 31 January 1970.

510 Tony Roisman, letter to John McConnell, 13 April 1970.

511 Tony Roisman, telephone interview by author, 14 July 2005.

512 Ibid.

513 Anna McConnell, manuscript review with author, Denver, Colorado, October 2005.

Environmental Teach-In, Inc., second – both of which were using the Earth Day name for similar events, and he chose to align with the politicos. Even if the McConnell's assumption was correct, they bore no grudges against Roisman and continued to hold him in high regard for earlier services he had performed for them. [514]

However, John's ongoing experiences with people associated with the Environmental Teach-In were far less reconciliatory. When John and Anna returned to New York City in early April 1970, John received an invitation to appear and be introduced at an Environmental Teach-In event in Manhattan. "John came home angry," Anna recalled, "because he was not given a chance to speak, as he had been invited to do." [515] Similarly, at a luncheon meeting, Denis Hayes told John the April 22 Environmental Teach-In was a one-time happening. When John replied the original Earth Day would continue as an annual celebration, Hayes promised he would join the vernal equinox Earth Day effort in 1971. [516] That promise went unfulfilled.

In fact, the April 22 Earth Day met with such resounding success in its first year, involving an estimated 20 million Americans [517] in 2,000 colleges and universities, 10,000 primary and secondary schools and hundreds of communities, [518] that it also continued as an annual event. And, with two Earth Days, John's words of potential confusion – like having two Christmases or two birthdays each year – proved prophetic.

This confusion not only originated because of the April 22 group but, at first, appeared to be stronger among Gaylord Nelson's people than anywhere else. *The New York Times* ad, while emblazoned with the "April 22 Earth Day" headline, also showed the sponsoring organization as "The Environmental Teach-In, Inc." Copy within the ad promoted both names: "Earth Day is a commitment to

---

[514] John and Anna McConnell, manuscript review with author, Denver, Colorado, October 2005.

[515] Anna McConnell, manuscript review with author, Denver, Colorado, October 2005.

[516] Anna McConnell, "The Beginning of Earth Day," 1989 or 1990.

[517] Jack Lewis, *The Spirit of the First Earth Day* [online]. U.S. Environmental Protection Agency [cited 18 June 2005]. Available from www.epa.gov/history/topics/earthday/01.htm.

[518] *Denis Hayes* [online]. AbsoluteAstronomy.com [cited 18 June 2005]. Available from www.absoluteastronomy.com/encyclopedia/D/De/Denis_Hayes.htm.

make life better" and "April 22 is the Environmental Teach-In." [519]

Other documents, less easily changeable, indicated Nelson's intention to use language other than "Earth Day." The Articles of Incorporation for Environmental Teach-In, Inc., registered in Washington, D.C., on 19 November 1969, mentioned "Environmental Teach-In" multiple times in the document's "purpose" article, but did not include any statement of, or relating to, "Earth Day." [520] The letter that Denis Hayes wrote to John McConnell on 20 January bore the words "Environmental Teach-In, Inc." in large block characters as its letterhead. [521] *The Environmental Handbook*, edited by Garrett de Bell and published as "A Ballantine/Friends of the Earth Book," according to its cover, was "prepared for the first national environmental teach-in – April 22, 1970." [522] And a newsletter published in early 1970 by the Student Conservation Association, an environmental organization started in 1955 to encourage young volunteers to perform natural resource conservation in federal parks, included an article that promoted "the Environmental Teach-In scheduled for April 22." [523]

Likewise, Nelson used the term "Teach-In" when he announced the concept at a groundbreaking speech in Seattle, Washington, in September 1969. He told reporters he got the idea while reading *Ramparts* magazine about anti-war teach-ins. [524] Nelson continued to use the Teach-In term in his public dialogue in 1970. Speaking at the University of Michigan in Ann Arbor, Michigan, in April 1970, he titled his address "Ann Arbor Teach-In," and his schedule for the week of 20 April through 24 April was headed "Teach-In Tour." That tour included events in Massachusetts, Indiana, Wisconsin, Colorado and California that were promoted as "Environmental Action Day," "Earth Day Rally," "Environmental Teach-In Kick-off Rally," "Environmental

---

[519] Environmental Teach-In, Inc., "April 22. Earth Day.," advertisement, *The New York Times*, 18 January 1970.

[520] *Articles of Incorporation of Environmental Teach-In, Inc. of the District of Columbia*, 19 November 1969.

[521] Denis Hayes, letter to John McConnell, 20 January 1970.

[522] Garrett de Bell, editor, *The Environmental Handbook*, 1970.

[523] "Environmental Teach-In Gains Support," *Long Island Press* (22 January 1970), quoted in *Conversational Conservation,* newsletter, Student Conservation Association, 1970.

[524] Jack Lewis, *The Spirit of the First Earth Day* [online]. U.S. Environmental Protection Agency [cited 18 June 2005]. Available from www.epa.gov/history/topics/earthday/01.htm.

Teach-In," "Environmental Teach-In," and "Environmental Teach-In." [525]

Even though Nelson, the event's originator, continued to use "Teach-In" in his speeches – "Whatever name was attached to it didn't matter one way or the other," he wrote in 1993 [526] – the "Earth Day" name adhered to April 22. Nelson later explained, "The press increasingly referred to it as Earth Day," [527] while conveniently ignoring that someone within his organization designed the ad with the "Earth Day" name and paid several thousand dollars to place the ad within the nation's major newspapers. Or, as Hans Janitschek later observed, "Privately, Nelson credited John for having founded Earth Day, but publicly, he let the lie continue." [528]

Resulting correspondence and conversation between John McConnell, Gaylord Nelson, and their associates in the early 1970s and in subsequent years ranged from complimentary and conciliatory to accusatory and disrespectful.

Earth Day communiqués from John McConnell, Gaylord Nelson and Denis Hayes

He [John McConnell] is a fine gentleman who has long dedicated his considerable talents and energy to the cause of peace and the protection of the environment. – Gaylord Nelson, letter to Hans Janitschek, 9 August 1993

We have always wished you the best in your efforts to promote environmental consciousness and world peace on the spring equinox. – Denis Hayes, e-mail to John McConnell, 1 March 1999

My concern is that our different Earth Days complement instead of conflict with each other. – John McConnell, e-mail to Denis Hayes, 17 March 1999

I argued with John McConnell over this date nonsense for months last time around. ... This time I don't intend to argue; frankly, the date of Earth Day '80 is not one of the 600 or 700 most important items in my life right now. So anyone else who writes about it will get a Xerox of this letter. And please tell John not to call me

---

525 Gaylord Nelson, letter to Hans Janitschek, 9 August 1993.

526 Ibid.

527 Ibid.

528 Hans Janitschek, interview with author, 15 August 2005.

about it. – Denis Hayes, letter to Earth Society board member Hannah Durlach Wasserman, 2 October 1979

I am writing to formally invite you for a meeting to discuss your plagiaristic use of my nomenclature, 'Earth Day,' in relation to your environmental observance on April 22. – John McConnell, letter to Denis Hayes, 13 April 1989

I must state, unequivocally, that in no way whatsoever have I been responsible for any injustice or injury of any kind to Mr. McConnell. – Gaylord Nelson, letter to Hans Janitschek, 9 August 1993

Whether harmonious or acrimonious, the back and forth rhetoric between the major parties, at best, only added to the Earth Day confusion.

In a typed five-page letter in August 1993, Gaylord Nelson wrote to Hans Janitschek that the suggestion for the Earth Day name "came from a friend of mine who had long been in the field of public relations and the same suggestion came from a New York advertising executive." [529] Nelson's public relations friend was probably Joe Floyd, who was traveling with Nelson in Florida during the fall of 1969. Floyd told John McConnell, during a phone conversation twenty years later, he "had seen an item in the papers about some kids in California who were planning an Earth Day … [and he] suggested 'Earth Day' would be [a] better [name] than 'Environmental Teach-In.'" [530] John then wrote of this conversation in a letter to Nelson, adding, "This may have been the students at the University of California at Davis who warmly supported my proposals when I spoke there in October [1969]." [531]

In an attempt at reconciliation, John invited Nelson to participate in the Earth Day ceremony at the United Nations in 1994. [532] The senator did not attend. Similarly, in the same year, New York State representative Edward Abramson, who was chairman of the Earth Day 1994 World Peace Essay Contest and a former chair of the Earth Day Committee, suggested a dinner to

---

529 Gaylord Nelson, letter to Hans Janitschek, 9 August 1993.

530 John McConnell, "Earth Day Controversy About Date," notes after phone conversation with Joe Floyd, 10 October 1989.

531 John McConnell, letter to Gaylord Nelson, 11 October 1989.

532 Ibid.

recognize both John McConnell and Gaylord Nelson along with other noted environmentalists, such as Ralph Nader. [533] The dinner did not occur.

Twice, in 1989 and 1993, John attempted to gain Nelson's agreement to a joint statement that would avoid confusion about the two Earth Days, by recognizing the spring equinox as Earth Day with its purpose of "peace, justice and the care of Earth," while equally recognizing April 22 as Earth Teach-In Day with its agenda of environmental awareness. Twice, the senator ignored the invitations.

Proposed joint Earth Day statement

(Drafted by John McConnell 11 October 1993; not acknowledged by Senator Nelson)

Two dates have been termed Earth Day. One, on April 22, which was initially intended as an Environmental Teach-In. The other, on March 20-21 (first day of Spring), was intended as a global holiday that would foster "peace, justice and the care of Earth." These events were both started independently in 1970.

While both events have benefited people and planet, we believe a singular Earth Day would avoid confusion and better serve the future. We agree on the advantage of calling the March equinox Earth Day – which is celebrated at the United Nations with the ringing of the Peace Bell at the moment Spring begins. This is the moment when light and darkness are equal on both hemispheres.

Any day that provides events to increase concern for the environment is to be commended. But to avoid confusion, we hope that in the future the March equinox will be designated Earth Day and April 22 as Earth Teach-In Day: its original name was Environmental Teach-In.

Senator Nelson joins in asking that bells ring all over the world when the United Nations Peace Bell rings at 3:28 p.m. EST on Earth Day, March 20, 1994.

By that time, Nelson was claiming full credit for Earth Day. In a speech at the University of Illinois in October 1990, Nelson recounted 1960s "turmoil

---

533 Earth Society Foundation, "Meeting Minutes," 23 September 1993.

on the college campuses over the Vietnam War" and "protests, called anti-war teach-ins." He recalled, "I read an article on teach-ins, and it suddenly occurred to me, why not have a nationwide teach-in on the environment? That was the origin of Earth Day." [534]

Even so, in the early 1970s, people of good intention, including the State of Maryland and its largest city Baltimore, proclaimed an "Earth Month" that began with the spring equinox and ended on April 22. [535] Others, including Margaret Mead, tried to link the two Earth Days with the United Nations' World Environment Day, celebrated on 5 June, to create a season of environmental awareness that would last throughout the spring. [536] Richard Register of World Community Events, Inc., and others in the Southern Hemisphere, enlisted the autumnal equinox, 22 or 23 September, as World Life Day to raise environmental awareness at that time of year, if not throughout the year. But the two men who started their similar, yet different, campaigns, John McConnell and Gaylord Nelson, failed to reach agreement that would have facilitated that, or any, level of cooperation. [537]

Indeed, when Fred Burrous suggested, in April 1990, that John meet with Denis Hayes, who had become international chairman for the twentieth anniversary of the April 22 Earth Day, Burrous reminded John of the dominance and popularity the April 22 group had attained. "Denis absolutely owns Earth Day lock, stock and barrel now," Burrous wrote. [538] In like manner, Hayes, himself, wrote to John on 1 May 1989, "History now views April 22 as the 'real' Earth Day. It is time you ended your futile, two-decade campaign against this historical reality."[539] A meeting involving John and Hayes did not occur.

It was no surprise that Nelson and Hayes would not readily give up their claim to the Earth Day name. While April 22 events were minimalistic in the early 1970s, the senator from Wisconsin and his protégé, who later earned his law degree at Stanford University, continued to apply pressure

---

534 Gaylord Nelson, "History of Earth Day," speech, Catalyst Conference, University of Illinois, 6 October 1990.

535 *Earth Month Proclamation*, City of Baltimore, Maryland.

536 Margaret Mead, memo to John McConnell, 2 April 1973.

537 Earl Arnett, "Earth Day attempts to make comeback," *The (Baltimore, Maryland) Sun*, 1 April 1974.

538 Fred Burrous, letter to John McConnell, 20 April 1990.

539 Denis Hayes, letter to John McConnell, 1 May 1989.

to replicate their first-year success. Their endeavors, along with efforts by John McConnell and his supporters to broaden awareness and support of the equinox Earth Day, added fuel to the fire of confusion that flared into the upper hierarchy of U.S. government.

At the executive level, President Richard Nixon endorsed April 22 in 1971 and 1972. President Gerald Ford proclaimed March 21 to be Earth Day in 1975. Then presidents Jimmy Carter and George H. W. Bush backed April 22 in 1977, 1980, and 1990. Irony entered the picture when John McConnell received, from the White House, an official copy of President Carter's 1980 proclamation, complete with a gold seal and blue ornate border on formal cream-colored stock. John's handwritten notation on the back revealed his belief that the document had been sent to him "by mistake."

Confusion reigned in similar fashion on Capitol Hill. In 1971, the United States House of Representatives passed a joint House/Senate resolution, introduced by Charles Teague of California, that designated "March 21, the vernal equinox, of each year as 'Earth Day.'" [540] Then, in 1973, the U.S. Senate passed another joint resolution, this one introduced by Gaylord Nelson, that made April 9 through April 15 Earth Week. [541] In 1975, the House passed still another joint resolution, introduced by Patricia Schroeder of Colorado, that designated March 21 of that year as Earth Day. [542] All three resolutions contained nearly identical language that the equinox Earth Day and the April Earth Week were "a day [or "a time"] to determine what further steps must be taken to continue the nationwide effort of education on environmental problems, and to review the commitment of each American to restoring and protecting the quality of the environment." [543]

Forty-five state governors and hundreds of mayors signed proclamations for one day or the other – most of them for April 22 – in the early 1970s. Governor Arch A. Moore, Jr., of West Virginia, for example, proclaimed 9-15 April 1973, to be Earth Week, in accordance with the U.S. Senate resolution. But, in July 1973, Moore wrote to his fellow governors of his desire they observe "the first day of spring as Earth Day" the following year, thus creating "one Earth Day celebration, which will include the former

[540] *H. J. Res. 406*, 92nd Congress, 1st sess., 25 February 1971.

[541] *S. J. Res. 2*, 93rd Congress, 1st sess., 4 January 1973.

[542] *H.J. 258*, 94th Congress, 1st sess., 18 March 1975.

[543] *H. J. Res. 406*. Also, *S. J. Res. 2*. Also, *H.J. 258*.

observances of Earth Week and World Environment Day." [544] Moore's hope did not become reality.

The New York Times, on 21 March 1973, quoted Margaret Mead as saying, "Some people were confused because another earth celebration, called Earth Week, had been set for April 9 through 15." [545] But that state of confusion, elevated to frustration, was best summarized in a letter from Michigan's governor William G. Milliken to Linwood Holton, the governor of Virginia, in which Milliken expressed his desire "for coordination and consistency in our observations of Earth Day. Just this year, for example, I was asked to declare three different dates as Earth Day or Earth Week by differing organizations." [546]

The confusion persisted for years both inside and outside the government. When John McConnell wrote to the U.S. Department of Energy, asking for financial support for the equinox Earth Day celebration in 1980, Victor P. Keay, director of Special Programs Division, Office of Public Affairs, replied the department was "working with the Environmental Protection Agency, as lead agency, on an inter-departmental federal effort to mark Earth Day on April 22, 1980, as proclaimed by President Carter." [547]

The 1992 Avon Products calendar and calendars in England listed March 20 as Earth Day. When publishing company Houghton Mifflin's School Division attempted to create a web page dedicated to the celebration of Earth Day in 1997, they discovered the disparate dates for the two Earth Days and sent an e-mail to John seeking clarification. [548] When McDonald's restaurants and *Nickelodeon Magazine* developed an Earth Day promotion campaign for Earth Week in April 1998, they printed posters that identified April 22 as Earth Day but listed the telephone number from John McConnell's Earth Day web site, which hundreds of children dialed. [549] In 2001, K. V. Sundaram of the Bhoovigyan Vikas Foundation initiated an Earth Day

---

[544] Arch Moore, letter to Linwood Hilton, governor of Virginia, 23 July 1973.

[545] David Bird, "Earth Day Hails Start of Spring," *The New York Times*, 21 March 1973.

[546] William G. Milliken, letter to Linwood Holton, 1973.

[547] Victor P. Keay, U.S. Department of Energy, letter to John McConnell, 19 February 1980.

[548] Marie E. Norris, Houghton Mifflin Company, e-mail to John McConnell, 15 April 1997.

[549] John McConnell, "President Clinton's Great Opportunity," essay 4 August 1998.

program in India on 21-23 April and, with John's knowledge, used a photo of the Earth Flag on the cover of the event's promotional booklet; Sundaram also read a statement by John during the event's opening ceremony, crediting him with being an inspiration. [550]

While Sundaram's juxtaposition of John with the April 22 Earth Day might appear to be a lack of loyalty, Sundaram was not alone. Swami Satchidananda, for example, who participated in the Whole Earth Week at the University of California at Davis, was also a prominent figure at the April 22 Earth Day celebration in New York's Union Square in 1970. [551] And, a year later, UC, Davis held its Whole Earth Week on 5-9 April to better conform to university schedules for spring break and final exams. [552] Even the City of San Francisco, where the equinox Earth Day began, observed citizen activities on both March 20 or 21 and around April 22. In addition to Earth Day, San Francisco has, in some years, honored 20 March as World Citizen Day. [553]

On 22 April 1995, the United Nations permitted another environmental group, other than the Earth Society Foundation, to plant a tree on UN property, [554] and the UN bookstore placed a book about Earth Day, written by Gaylord Nelson, on its shelves. [555] In 2004, John McConnell's new hometown of Denver, Colorado, conducted a four-day Earth Fair around April 22 and honored John as a keynote speaker at both the opening and closing ceremonies. [556]

By 1990, the twentieth anniversary of both Earth Days, John had voluntarily acquiesced to calling the vernal equinox "International Earth Day" to avoid confusion, and the April 22 group, with its political and promotional infrastructure firmly in place, had won the popularity race. Speaking at the University of Illinois in October 1990, Gaylord Nelson estimated that 200 million people in 141

---

550 Ravi Sundaram, e-mail to John McConnell, 25 April 2001.

551 Sri Swami Satchidananda. 1970. *Earth Day Message from Sri Swami Satchidananda* [online]. Integral Yoga Institute [cited 9 July 2005]. Available from www.iyiny.org/About_IYI/Founder/body_founder.html.

552 Chuck Sweet, letter to John McConnell, 27 December 1970.

553 *World Citizens Day Proclamation*, City of San Francisco, California, 26 February 1981.

554 Earth Society Foundation, "meeting minutes," 27 March 1995.

555 Earth Society Foundation, "meeting minutes," 12 June 1995.

556 Denver Earth Fair videotape, Denver, Colorado, municipal access television.

countries participated in celebrations on or near April 22 that year. [557]

Earth Society Foundation member and United Nations journalist Ann Charles expressed outrage at those claims. In April 1993, she wrote to other ESF members that she was irked by an article in *The Environmental Magazine* that prominently displayed the Earth Flag, featured Gaylord Nelson "talking about the first Earth Day," quoted environmental business consultant Bruce Anderson of Earth Day USA in a statement that Charles penned "sounds very much like Margaret Mead," and was "all about the other [April 22] Earth Day." Calling the article "disinformation or misinformation," she wrote, "It's time to set the record straight." [558]

Regardless of whether or not the claims by the April 22 group were exaggerated, the ceremony of the equinox Earth Day at the United Nations in 1990 typified the international flavor of the heritage that John McConnell initiated twenty years prior. New York mayor David Dinkins rang the Peace Bell at the moment of equipoise, 9:19 p.m. local time. Dinkins was accompanied by UN chief of protocol Ali Teymour and Cynthia Lennon, the former wife of The Beatles' John Lennon who was traveling the world to promote Lennon's love for the planet. Speakers included Jean-Claude Faby of the UN Environment Programme (UNEP), representing Secretary-General Javier Perez de Cuellar; Hans Janitschek, representing the UN Society of Writers and Artists; Ed Brennan, president of Earth Society Foundation; master of ceremonies Kevin Sanders; and John McConnell. The program featured a presentation of the Earth Trustee Environmental Award by Cynthia Lennon to Peter Bahouth of Greenpeace International. And the numerous musical and dance performers included the Limbora Slovak Dancers, the United Nations Singers, the UN International School Choir, folksinger Odetta, singers Stephen Chun-Tao Cheng and Paul James, accompanists Anthony Walker and Ed Bena, violinist Asako Urushihara, pianists David Boechner and Stan Free, and Scottish piper Duncan Robertson. [559]

This ceremony was one among thousands of celebrations that occurred, and continued to occur, around the planet on the equinox. The synchronicity of those events pleased John McConnell who reveled in rites of spring that

---

[557] Gaylord Nelson, "History of Earth Day," speech, Catalyst Conference, University of Illinois, 6 October 1990.

[558] Ann Charles, fax to Kurt Koenig, 30 April 1993.

[559] Earth Society Foundation, "Earth Day International," program, 1990.

embodied centuries-old traditions. Being a person who generally eschewed formal organization, he relied, instead, on "people who sincerely … are willing to work for peace to come together where they agree and do what they can to celebrate the amazing web of life that we have on our planet." [560]

Into the millennium, the catalysts for confusion continued their combat – to the extreme. John C. Munday, Jr., a professor of natural sciences at Regent University in Virginia Beach, Virginia, suggested three Earth Days: "Earth Day I" on the spring equinox, "Earth Day II" on April 22, and "Earth Day III" on 5 June (World Environment Day) as a means, so he hoped, of "resolving Earth Day confusion." [561]

In January 2001, Ervin Laszlo of the Club of Budapest offered John $500 to formally commingle Earth Day with his World Day of Planetary Consciousness, which was also celebrated on the spring equinox. Laszlo's offer stemmed from an event in October 1996 in which John flew to Budapest, Hungary, to "become one of the eminent signatories of The Manifesto on the Spirit of Planetary Consciousness," which Laszlo had authored. [562] On that trip, John met the Dalai Lama, who also signed the manifesto. But in 2001, John refused Laszlo's "contribution" after realizing it came "with strings attached." Instead, John chose to remain true to his universal vision for the equinox. "I did not try to use Earth Day to further my religious views," he said. "When we celebrated Earth Day at the United Nations, one year [1987] we had a delegate from the Soviet Union who was an atheist, a delegate from the U.S. who was a Presbyterian, and the head of the Muslim World League. They together rang the Peace Bell. … Earth Day should not be referred to as 'The World Day for Atheism,' 'World Day for Planetary Consciousness,' 'World Day for Christianity,' or 'World Day' for any religion or special interest." [563]

In contrast to these attempts to further Earth Day, regardless of its name and date, a conservative communications and research foundation, representing the U.S. military-industrial complex, offered a completely different opinion in March 1998. On its web site, The National Center for

---

[560] John McConnell, interview by author, Denver, Colorado, August 2004.

[561] John C. Munday, Jr., "Resolving Earth Day Confusion and Advancing Planetary Environmental Stewardship."

[562] Ervin Laszlo, e-mail to John McConnell, 18 October 1996.

[563] John McConnell, interview by author, Denver, Colorado, August 2004.

Public Policy Research posted an editorial that claimed the environment had improved sufficiently in thirty years and "the environmental movement is an outright obstacle to further environmental progress. ... Earth Day may be obsolete." [564]

Aging into his 90s, John McConnell still pined for greater acceptance for the spring equinox and for himself as founder of the original Earth Day. But both he and Gaylord Nelson recognized that their differences in philosophy – an enigmatic dichotomy that, somehow, created a distinction between ecological preservation versus world peace – would have made collaboration impossible, even in the early 1970s before April 22 established itself as an immovable tradition. As Nelson stated in his 1993 letter to Janitschek, "Mr. McConnell's proposal and mine had entirely different objectives. Mr. McConnell did not propose a major mass demonstration in behalf of the environment, but that was the central core of April 22. My specific purpose was political – its objective was to force the environment onto the National Agenda of major issues. It was a complete, indeed, an overwhelming success." [565]

In contrast, John believed the environmental movement, alone, was like a one-legged stool. He maintained the necessity of creating a climate of peace and justice as a prerequisite for ecological preservation. "War is the worst polluter," he stated succinctly. "Environmental efforts by themselves will leave us in ruins unless we stop war, unless we promote peace, and unless we have more economic justice." [566]

Even the venues in which Nelson and John operated supported their dissimilar philosophies. Nelson worked within the U.S. political arena to get the attention of his fellow citizens living in the planet's pollution-generating giant. John aligned himself with the United Nations, the world's major peace initiating entity.

The confusion over the two Earth Days also stemmed from the disparity of pragmatism versus idealism. In 1970, April 22 occurred on a Wednesday, the middle day of the week, when U.S. college students, for whom the Environmental Teach-In was designed, would most likely be on campus.

---

[564] Christopher Burger. April 2003. *Celebrate Earth Day by Taking Environmental Issues Seriously* [online]. The National Center for Public Policy Research [cited 12 July 2005]. Available from www.nationalcenter.org/NPA462.html.

[565] Gaylord Nelson, letter to Hans Janitschek, 9 August 1993.

[566] John McConnell, interview by author, Denver, Colorado, August 2004.

April 22 was approximately midway between the traditional spring break and final exams for most colleges. And it was late enough in the season that the weather would be moderate in northern states and spring rains would have disappeared. As Denis Hayes concluded, "Thinking as an organizer, these are not bad criteria." [567]

At the same time, the longevity of the equinox Earth Day ceremony at the United Nations as well as John McConnell's bevy of admirers verified his loftier ideals. "The concept of Earth Day," John wrote to Gaylord Nelson in October 1993, "was developed with the objective of providing a global holy day that would tap the best in the human heart and help people identify with the whole human family and its key role as caretakers of Earth." [568]

In their individual ways, both Gaylord Nelson and John McConnell were correct, and both men took the proper path for their individual purposes. The outstanding success of the April 22 Environmental Teach-In demonstrated the depth to which polluters had plundered the nation's resources as well as a strong previously unleashed desire by a multitude of concerned citizens to clean up their homeland. Nelson also played an important role in creation and passage of cornerstone environmental regulations in the United States: Clean Air Act (1970, amended 1977 and 1990), Clean Water Act (1972, amended 1977), Safe Drinking Water Act (1974), Resource Conservation and Recovery Act (1976), and Toxic Substances Control Act (1976). In addition, with the advent and growth of this environmental movement, the United States and Canada signed (1972), then renewed (1978), the Great Lakes Water Quality Agreement "to restore and maintain the chemical, physical and biological integrity of the Great Lakes Basin ecosystem," which holds the world's largest supply of fresh surface water.

Therefore, if fame and fortune were the measures of success, Gaylord Nelson and Denis Hayes were the clear winners, for the April 22 Environmental Teach-In heaped great environmental glory and, presumably, wealth on both men. Nelson served three terms in the U.S. Senate; when not re-elected in 1980, he moved on to become director of The Wilderness Society whose 250,000 members strove to protect and restore America's wilderness. In

---

[567] Denis Hayes, letter to Hannah Durlach Wasserman, Earth Society board member, 2 October 1979.

[568] John McConnell, letter to Gaylord Nelson, 11 October 1993.

1995, he received the Presidential Medal of Freedom for his environmental work. And when he died on 2 July 2005, obituaries consistently, perhaps unanimously, identified him as the founder of Earth Day.

Hayes became chairman of Earth Day Network, a group that coordinated April 22 Earth Day activities worldwide and presented itself as "a driving force steering environmental awareness around the world." He headed the federal Solar Energy Research Institute, was an adjunct professor of engineering at Stanford University, director of the Illinois State Energy Office, Senior Fellow at the Worldwatch Institute, and Visiting Scholar at the Smithsonian Institution. As an environmental attorney and author, Hayes received numerous awards, and was honored as an environmental hero by *Look* magazine and the National Audubon Society. He became president and chief executive officer of the Bullitt Foundation, a $100 million environmental philanthropy organization based in Seattle, Washington, his home state.

In contrast, Nelson's and Hayes' usurpation of the Earth Day name, whether through benign or malicious intent – and their intentions will probably never be confirmed by evidence any stronger than statements by the parties directly involved – has contributed to John and Anna McConnell living their senior years in relative obscurity, poor in money, yet unflinchingly rich in spirit and unyieldingly strong in determination to demonstrate, as John continued to say, "April 22 is *not* Earth Day."

12

Earth Day at the United Nations

(1970 to present)

> *Yes, Earth Day is only a symbol, but it is a powerful symbol that can serve to unite us globally. ... Ours is the first generation to inhabit this earth that will determine whether or not it will continue to sustain life.*
> – John McConnell, "Earth Day: The Evolution of an Idea," 1979

In retrospect, neither John McConnell nor Gaylord Nelson nor Denis Hayes were honest in their claims about Earth Day. At best, the attachment of the Earth Day name to April 22 by Nelson and Hayes was suspect. In turn, John made statements that stretched beyond reality. For example, John said, "Earth Day [on the equinox] in California [in 1970] triggered a much larger event in the rest of the nation in April." [569]

In fact, the April 22 Environmental Teach-In started independently of John's equinox Earth Day and became the big event at numerous locations in 1970, while the equinox Earth Day enjoyed pockets of acclaim in California, New York and various other locales. Noting communications she received regarding 1970 Earth Day events, Anna observed, "We have found that people we didn't know celebrated Earth Day on the equinox all over the country, including our [current] Denver mayor [John W.] Hickenlooper who was in college in Pennsylvania then." She surmised that news of John's idea traveled across the country as a result of having been "picked up by

[569] John McConnell, "Evolution of an Idea."

people at the UNESCO conference." [570]

Regardless of who celebrated on what date and irrespective of the confusion that resulted from having two distinct events with the same name, Earth Day and the Environmental Teach-In both proved instrumental in promoting ecological awareness and action. Both became traditions in their own right.

In July 1970, John attended the Whole Earth Fair and Aquarian Festival, a gathering atop Flagstaff Mountain west of Boulder, Colorado. There, he spoke to 300 students at a sunrise meditation service where he suggested they "help build the earth in harmony with nature [and donate] ten percent of their time and money to their mission." He distributed a flyer that promoted his Earthbuilder concept of spiritual, physical and communicative involvement. John described the event, at which Sri Swami Satchidananda also spoke, as "a strange but beautiful in-group thing; the first Fair I ever heard of where they limited promotion and tried to avoid publicity ... afraid ... there would be an influx of thousands of youth and difficulty with the city fathers who were already uptight." [571]

John left Colorado with great enthusiasm, writing to Wilson Van Dusen within the week, "Van, I've got so much wonderful material, contacts and rough plans. We can, and we must, bring together the people and plans that will provide an appropriate and effective campaign to build a new Earth." [572]

John took his enthusiasm to the United Nations. During the 1960s, John enjoyed the freedom to come and go with relative ease. He sometimes walked through security gates in conversation with Secretary-General U Thant, and, at times, with some audacity, waited in U Thant's office until the eminent leader of the world's greatest peace organization returned from lunch. [573]

With equal familiarity, John approached the Secretary-General with the idea of Earth Day at the UN. U Thant agreed and participated in the ceremony, held at 2:00 p.m. local time (not at the moment of equipoise,

---

[570] Anna McConnell, manuscript review with author, Denver, Colorado, October 2005.

[571] Associated Press, "300 at sunrise meditation atop mountain for earth," *Rocky Mountain News*, 27 July 1970.

[572] John McConnell, letter to Wilson Van Dusen, 30 July 1970.

[573] John Drysdale, interview by author, United Nations, 8 June 2004.

which was 1:38 in the morning), on Sunday, 21 March 1971, in the Japanese Peace Garden at UN Headquarters. The featured moment occurred when the Secretary-General rang the Peace Bell.

Incorporating the Peace Bell into the Earth Day ceremony was significant in that this bell had been rung officially only twice before – on the day it was installed on 8 June 1954 and again on 4 October 1966. This latter ringing was for a ceremony that marked the first anniversary of an historic visit to the UN by Pope Paul VI. The ringers at that time were seven children from the UN International School, and a letter from Nigerian ambassador S. O. Adebo to U Thant credited John McConnell as having been instrumental in initiating that event, too. [574] When the Secretary-General rang the Peace Bell for the Earth Day ceremony, its resonance was the only sound heard in the following two minutes of silent reflection. Thus, the ceremony also incorporated John's Minute for Peace, which U Thant practiced and promoted.

In his speech at the ceremony, the Secretary-General stated, "May there only be peaceful and cheerful Earth Days to come for our beautiful spaceship earth as it continues to spin and circle in frigid space with its warm and fragile cargo of animate life." [575] U Thant's statement appeared as the "Quotation of the Day" in *The New York Times*, and his speech was covered by newspapers in other countries, including Thailand and India.

In New York on Earth Day, bells rang at 2:00 p.m. at St. Patrick's Cathedral, and 2,000 people gathered in Central Park to watch the Earth Day Marathon, formerly called Cherry Tree Marathon, a favored warmup for the famous Boston Marathon, which occurred in April. [576]

In San Francisco, the Artists Embassy International Arts Gallery opened a month-long exhibit, "The Beauty of the Earth," and sponsored a concert by pianist Walter Ahlstedt of the Music and Arts Institute. San Francisco Park Superintendent Frank Foehr led an "Earth Stroll" in Golden Gate Park that featured a ground-breaking ceremony at the site of the Japanese Pond Garden and Moon Viewing Pavilion and the planting of a magnolia tree at the California Academy of Sciences. Participants for the "Earth Stroll"

---

574 S. O. Adebo, letter to U Thant, 19 September 1966.

575 "Earth Day International and Earth Society Foundation," fact sheet.

576 "Earth Day Marathon," *Runner's World*, March 1970.

included San Francisco supervisors Peter Tamaras, Dianne Feinstein and Terry Francois. [577] Activities in Los Angeles included a week-long ecology festival that included mayor Sam Yorty and one thousand others riding bicycles. [578]

With such events happening across the nation on 20 March 1971, Anna found herself totally caught up in the whirlwind of John's life. On 15 March, she took time to write to her friend Cinde Hay in Boulder, Colorado, "I fully expected to be living at the ranch come November, but it was only my daydreams, evidently. We put the fleece before the Lord and it wasn't answered in the way we were to go." Anna told her friend, "Christa is coming along fine. She's crawling all over the apartment." Then, she disclosed information that revealed John's ability to accomplish in spite of major obstacles, "I almost called your mother around Christmas and never got out to make the telephone call during that time. … We still don't have a phone." Anna signed the letter, "In Him, Mrs. John McConnell." [579]

Lacking phone service, John wrote letters to the presidents of Columbia Broadcasting System (CBS), American Broadcasting Company (ABC), MetroMedia Broadcasting and to Walter Cronkite, the famous evening news anchor on CBS. Quoting U Thant, John told the executives of the nation's major radio and television corporations that the Earth Day celebration at the UN was a "remarkable opportunity for TV and radio." He suggested that the media moguls produce and broadcast an Earth Hour program, which, as John envisioned, would contain neither dialogue nor advertisements but "only the sounds of nature with occasional reminders on the TV screen that this was … The Silent Hour for Peace." [580]

In addition, John's assistant within WE, Inc., Bob Rosensweet, contacted people associated with *The Tonight Show, Starring Johnny Carson*, seeking the celebrity's contribution to the success of Earth Day events. [581] WE, Inc, also purchased promotional advertisements for Earth Day that aired on

---

577 "How the City will mark 'Earth Day'", *San Francisco Progress*, 19 March 1971.
578 "Earth Day- NYC to LA," *San Francisco Chronicle*, 22 March 1971.
579 Anna McConnell, letter to Cinde Hay, 15 March 1971.
580 John McConnell, letters to Frank Stanton CBS, Leonard Goldenson ABC, Robert Bennett MetroMedia, Walter Cronkite CBS, 3 March through 1 April 1971.
581 Bob Rosensweet, letter to Craig Tennis of *The Tonight Show*, 3 March 1971.

WNEW Radio in the week prior to the equinox. [582] While the executives and producers of these media giants did not heed John's request, John did experience a fortuitous encounter that led to significant broadcast coverage on Earth Day 1972.

John had been given an office at 1440 Broadway near Bryant Park by someone who, John recalled, "liked what I was doing." A magazine involved with the New York Stock Exchange decided to run an article about the Earth Flag, and John needed a photograph. He walked to a different floor and encountered Al Korn, the program director of WOR Radio-TV, which had its broadcast facilities in the same building. Korn said he could help. While a WOR photographer worked on the image, John seized the opportunity to connect with the media. He intrigued Korn with his Earth Day idea, and Korn invited John to lunch.

Korn told John that, in order to meet federal government broadcast requirements, WOR needed to devote a certain amount of broadcast time to public service programs. Then, Korn proposed a twelve hour TV special on the equinox to coincide with the Earth Day celebration at the UN, and he asked John to participate as production advisor. John ecstatically agreed. [583]

The program, broadcast from 6:00 a.m. to 6:00 p.m. with no commercial announcements, drew major publicity and was seen on more than fifty television stations across the nation. [584] On-air participants included major environmental experts and entertainment celebrities.

Television personality Hugh Downs served as moderator. Downs, who had been a popular host of several NBC news, information and entertainment programs, including *The Today Show* from 1962 to 1971, led viewers through commentary from panelists who discussed the planet's environmental future, population growth, endangered wild life, pesticides, land use, suburbs, recycling, and air and water pollution.

A thirty-five minute segment was devoted to the Earth Day ceremony at the United Nations where the new Secretary-General, Kurt Waldheim, rang the Peace Bell at 2:00 p.m. after which UN delegates commented on environmental conditions in their respective countries. Even though the

---

582 WNEW Radio, invoice 31 March 1971.

583 John McConnell, interview by author, Denver, Colorado, August 2004.

584 Dan Lewis, "Ecology Marathon Set on TV Tuesday," newspaper article.

moment of equipoise was 7:22 a.m. local time and would have fit into the WOR broadcast schedule, John chose 2:00 p.m. for Waldheim to ring the Peace Bell because that was 1900 Greenwich Mean Time, the moment John hoped the UN would designate as the world's official Minute for Peace.

The twelve hour extravaganza concluded with a fifty minute discussion entitled "Where Do We Go From Here?" that featured Downs, President Richard Nixon's advisor on environmental affairs Russell Train, U.S. secretary of the interior Rogers Morton, secretary-general of the UN Stockholm Conference Maurice Strong, U.S. assistant secretary of state for environmental affairs Christian Herter, astronaut Wally Schirra, and U.S. Environmental Protection Agency administrator William Ruckelshaus. [585]

Touted in New York newspapers as "one of the most vital programs in television history" [586] and "a remarkable TV demonstration of public service," [587] the program, rife with ominous topics, also featured music by Pete Seeger, Odetta and Richie Havens. [588]

While the public was well aware of these celebrity names, Al Korn gave considerable behind-the-scenes credit to John for making the program happen. "We were always looking for a better idea for an event program," Korn said, "and when John walked in [looking for help with his photograph] and said who he was, he sounded interesting. We took his idea and his connections with the UN, and we embellished that. We had people from the Sierra Club, Friends of the Earth, and astronauts. Hugh Downs was in retirement, but I called him as a friend and he flew in to do this show. We got cooperation from the UN.

"And what we did – twelve hours of talk TV – was unheard of in those days. We had people who were so brilliant they had to bring down their conversation because TV reaches everyone. We did a heck of a job, but John was the leader of the pack. He was the key person to find somebody or suggest if we were doing things right or wrong. This was the first time that

---

585 WOR-TV, "E-Day '72, a monumental first," full-page newspaper advertisement, March 1972.

586 Phyllis Battelle, "Short Course on Ecology," newspaper opinion column, 21 March 1972.

587 John J. O'Connor, "Channel 9 Pays Earth Day a 12-Hour Tribute," *The New York Times*, 22 March 1972.

588 WOR-TV, "E-Day '72, a monumental first," promotional advertisement, March 1972.

any media company ever did anything to identify problems, and it was all through John. If he had not showed himself to me that day, this would not have taken place." [589]

The portentousness of the topics and intensity of discussion were reflective of environmentally concerned citizens throughout the country. The program was consistent with books being released at the time, such as *Limits to Growth*, that demonstrated the planet's finite resources could not support infinite exponential exploitation. [590] The messages concurred with published findings by the Union of Concerned Scientists, founded at the Massachusetts Institute of Technology in 1969 to protest the use of antiballistic missiles and nuclear power plants. [591] And the experts' commentary agreed with geologists and physicists who were gathering data that would show, a few years later, the rate of oil extraction and production was about to peak based on per capita of the world's population. [592]

Starting in 1973, Earth Day celebrations at the United Nations made a significant change. From that year on, the Peace Bell was rung precisely at the moment of equipoise with the schedule being determined by the tip of Earth, which meant some celebrations occurred in the middle of the night. Peace Bell ringers included UN officials, world leaders, children and celebrities, all of whom brought a distinct message and presence to the event.

John, the epitome of humbleness, did not ring the Peace Bell for an Earth Day ceremony in New York until 20 March 2004, two days prior to his 89th birthday. The time was 1:49 a.m., the crowd was sparse, and the event drew no media attention. But that moment, after-midnight on a chill New York morning, spoke volumes about John McConnell, a man of devout courage and inadequate acclaim. With eloquence, he stood before a small assemblage of admirers and chastised President George W. Bush for attacking Iraq exactly one year before, on Earth Day 2003, the day of the year John McConnell hoped would symbolize global peace and unity. John included a thundering statement, "We've got to kill our terrible addiction to

---

589 Al Korn, telephone interview by author, 20 January 2006.

590 Donella Meadows, Jorgen Randers, Dennis Meadows, and William W Behrens III, *Limits to Growth* (New York: Universe Books, 1972).

591 *History* [online]. Union of Concerned Scientists [cited 9 July 2005]. Available from www.ucsusa.org/ucs/about/page.cfm?pageID=767.

592 Dr. Albert Bartlett, "The Joseph Strategy," *Orion*, September/October 2003.

war. We ought to make friends, and not skeletons, of our enemies." [593]

But, of all the Earth Day ceremonies, the one in 1996 proved to be the most beautiful tribute to both John and Anna McConnell. After living with John's peculiar drive, financially supporting his efforts on her income as a parochial school teacher, and, at times, going without conveniences that most American spouses have come to expect, Anna gained the privilege of ringing the Peace Bell at the United Nations. John, her husband, was not present to witness the event; rather the honor of co-ringing the Peace Bell with Anna went to Hans Janitschek, who was then president of the Earth Society Foundation.

John's physical absence was to be expected. He was in Austria to ring a new Peace Bell at the UN Vienna International Centre. But John and Anna were connected on a higher plane, a plane that completely matched their spiritual intimacy and a plane that perfectly exemplified the concept of Earth Day. For, as Anna rang the Peace Bell in New York at 3:03 a.m. local time and John rang the Peace Bell in Vienna at 9:03 a.m. local time, both were ringing the respective bells at *exactly the same moment*, the moment Earth reached vernal equipoise.

While it could be said that, on a highly romantic or divinely synchronistic level, John and Anna would have it no other way, their plans for Earth Day were, indeed, quite different. "We had a good program of dignitaries coming even though the bell was to be rung at a weird hour in the morning," [594] Anna explained, "and John, before he left for Austria, had gotten a room for me on the top floor of the UN Plaza Hotel because he didn't want me traveling from Brooklyn in the middle of the night." Anna referred to her accommodations as "a celebrity room," and John added it was donated by the hotel. [595]

Lying awake in the early morning hours, Anna heard rain and wind howling outside her windows, and so she prayed that it would not interfere

---

[593] John McConnell, Earth Day speech, 20 March 2004.

[594] The 1996 Earth Day program, as planned, would have consisted of speeches by a representative of the Austrian Mission to the United Nations, Kurt Hupe of Rainforest Alliance, Robert Pollard of Information Habitat, and Joseph Reed, representing UN Secretary-General Boutros Boutros-Ghali as well as music by Paul Matthews and Linda Wetherill.

[595] Anna and John McConnell, manuscript review with author, Denver, Colorado, January 2006.

with the ceremony. "The Lord stopped the rain forty-five minutes before the ceremony was to begin," she reported. But a few minutes before that, the United Nations security department had called her and said the event was cancelled due to the severity of the weather.

Anna went to the United Nations anyway. There, she met Janitschek, Hank Waxman, Earth Society members Kevin Sanders, Mary Carlin, John Drysdale and others. Showing their security cards to a man Anna described as "one of our old, old guard friends who came to the gate," all but Waxman, who didn't have a card, were allowed to enter. Near the Peace Bell, the group found themselves devoid of dignitaries who had heeded the cancellation. "Mary told me to ring the bell," Anna said, "but I told her, 'I can't do that by myself.' Hans said he would ring the bell with me, so we did. There weren't steps to the bell at that time, and we had to scoot ourselves up onto the platform, but we rang it at just the right moment." [596]

When John heard about Anna ringing the Peace Bell, he was immensely pleased, calling it "one of the amazing coincidences in life." Anna's viewpoint was more down-to-earth. "I can't say it was a thrill. It was so spur of the moment. It was early in the morning and cold." [597]

Earth Day ceremonies at United Nations Headquarters at New York_
(date, time of equipoise, Peace Bell ringer and statement)

Friday, 20 March 1970
7:56 p.m. EST in New York City
3:56 p.m. PST in San Francisco
First Earth Day in San Francisco, New York and other cities

Sunday, 21 March 1971 (first time at United Nations)
Equipoise at 1:38 a.m.
UN ceremony at 2:00 p.m.
U Thant, United Nations Secretary-General
At long last, the concepts of Earth Day, of world patriotism, and of the family of

[596] Anna McConnell, manuscript review with author, Denver, Colorado, January 2006.
[597] Anna and John McConnell, manuscript review with author, Denver, Colorado, January 2006.

man have come into being. May there only be peaceful and cheerful Earth Days to come for our beautiful space-ship Earth.

Tuesday, 21 March 1972

Equipoise at 7:22 a.m.

UN ceremony at 2:00 p.m.

Kurt Waldheim, United Nations Secretary-General

Earth Day reminds us that fundamental issues such as peace, development, justice and the environment are joint responsibilities of the world community.

Tuesday, 20 March 1973

1:13 p.m.

C. V. Narasimhan, United Nations Chef de Cabinet

This day reminds us of the fundamental interdependence of man with man and of man with the life cycle on this planet upon which he so entirely depends for his very existence.

Wednesday, 20 March 1974

8:07 p.m.

Bradford Morse, United Nations Development Programme Administrator

This day serves as a powerful reminder to all of us of the need to preserve and to protect our environment and finite resources. We cannot forget our profound responsibility for the needs of generations yet unborn.

Friday, 21 March 1975

12:57 a.m.

Genichi Akatani, United Nations Under-Secretary-General

Earth Day serves as a reminder … that most of the great problems faced by mankind today are global problems transcending national boundaries and requiring global solutions.

Saturday 20 March 1976

6:50 a.m.

Robert J. Ryan, United Nations Assistant Secretary-General

The United Nations … not only bears a responsibility for the maintenance

of peace and security, but is also engaged in historic initiatives concerning the great economic and social issues of our time.

Sunday, 20 March 1977
12:43 p.m.
Margaret Mead, anthropologist, author and curator emeritus of the American Museum of Natural History
We have only one Earth and … all the people on this planet are one species.

Monday, 20 March 1978
6:34 p.m.
Margaret Mead
In developing Earth Day, we have tried to develop a symbol that all of us could share, a symbol that we all can reverberate to.

Wednesday, 21 March 1979
12:22 a.m.
Estafina Aldaba-Lim, United Nations Special Representative of the Secretary-General for the International Year of the Child
It is important that Earth Day be identified with children and with the worldwide effort for the improved care and protection of children on our Earth.

Friday, 20 March 1980
6:10 a.m.
Edward Gibson, astronaut
I could see from my spaceship … how really far away Earth is … how unique and how alone we are in being responsible for it.

Friday, 20 March 1981
12:03 p.m.
Arvid M. Pardo, Permanent Representative of Malta to the United Nations and "Father of the Law of the Sea Conference"
The Earth is a heritage common to us all which we must transmit substantially unimpaired to those who will follow.

Saturday, 20 March 1982

5:56 p.m.

Mrs. Rene Dubos, widow of Rene J. Dubos

Alone in space, alone in its life supporting systems, powered by inconceivable energies … is this planet not a precious home for all of us earthlings?

Sunday, 20 March 1983

11:59 p.m.

The Rev. Percival Brown, Pastor of Trinity Church, New York City

His Holiness Pope John Paul II … has asked me to convey to you and to all the participants in the Earth Day ceremony his best wishes for the success of Earth Day and all its objectives.

Tuesday, 20 March 1984

5:25 a.m.

Paul McRae, Member of the Canadian Parliament

Let the hopes and dangers that are with us in this 1984 celebration … promote an act of will whereby humanity dedicates itself to the removal of the immediate and longer-term threats to this planet Earth.

Wednesday, 20 March 1985

11:14 a.m.

Robert Muller, United Nations Assistant Secretary-General

Earth Day stands for… one Earth, and one humanity. This should be the vision of our future.

Thursday, 20 March 1986

5:03 p.m.

Robert Muller, United Nations Assistant Secretary-General

Friday, 20 March 1987

10:52 p.m.

Chester Norris, United States Ambassador to the United Nations

Valintin Karymov, Union of Soviet Socialist Republics Ambassador to the United Nations

Sheik Ali Mukhtar, Deputy Secretary-General of the Muslim World League
Norris: *Let history say that we, the guardians of Planet Earth, passed on to those that follow a better place to live than the one we inherited.*
Karymov: *At this special solemn moment of coming Spring, the Earth – Nature itself – reminds us of our most important duty of being the people on Earth ... [to] work and fight for our common future on this brilliant living planet.*
Mukhtar: *Recently certain local newspapers have published articles that, by innuendo, have attempted to link Islam with terrorism. This malicious defamation violates our sacred truth. It is also a disservice to the development of understanding and harmony.*

Sunday, 20 March 1988
4:39 a.m.
Edward Abramson, New York State Representative
The Rev. Umberto Mullare, director, and Francis McCullough, a resident, of the Cardinal Krol Center, a care facility for individuals with mental retardation near Philadelphia, Pennsylvania
Abramson: *This highly significant annual event is geared toward calling the world's attention to the overriding need for peace and ecological sanity.*
Mullare: *Peace must be in the minds and hearts of the people.*
McCullough: *This brings everybody together to show they want peace in the world.*

Monday, 20 March 1989
10:28 a.m.
Noel Brown, United Nations Environment Programme Director
The spirit of humanity's responsibility for the future of the Earth ... is a unique opportunity to begin in earnest the long and complex process of restoring the Earth's vitality, ecology and survival.

Tuesday, 20 March 1990
4:19 p.m.
David Dinkins, Mayor of New York City
The new enemy is not a foreign devil or an alien ideology. It is our own carelessness, our own wastefulness, our own apathy. The stakes are preserving

Earth for our children as a place where a miracle called spring will continue to take place every year.

Wednesday, 20 March 1991
10:02 p.m.
Antoine Blanca, United Nations Inter-Departmental Environment Committee (IDEC) Director General
The symbolic act of sounding a note for peace on the first day of Spring ... must bring with it a greater sense of harmony and coherence amongst all the people.

Friday, 20 March 1992
3:48 a.m.
Joseph Cicippio, former hostage in Lebanon for more than five years
Thomas Cicippio, Joseph's brother and family spokesperson
Joseph: *When I was in captivity, I was not privileged to read newspapers or listen to a radio. I had no knowledge of the outside world. But now I am part of a world ceremony because today people in so many cities around the world are ringing bells.*
Thomas: *To find a solution to Joes' plight, I sought information on how I could make a difference. ... Ceremonies such as this encourage all of us to ... reach out to each other in one voice, united in the ssame beliefs of love, peace and forgiveness.*

Saturday, 20 March 1993
9:41 a.m.
Rigoberta Menchu, Nobel Peace Prize Laureate
Earth is our mother. It's a fountain of our culture; it's a fountain of our life. It is the energy of life.

Sunday, 20 March 1994
3:28 p.m.
Daphne Tenne of Israel, child
Nasir Obeid of Palestine, child
Tenne: *Our Bible says, 'I will take away the stony heart out of your flesh and will give you a heart of flesh.' We, the children of Abraham, who have a heart of*

flesh, want to seek peace and pursue it together.
Obeid: *All the Arabic people wish for peace, and I wish no more fighting between the Arabs and the Israelis. I wish for the whole world to live in peace.*

Monday, 20 March 1995
9:14 p.m.
Edwina Sandys, artist with five sculptures at the UN and granddaughter of Sir Winston Churchill
Today, as we celebrate the 50th anniversary of the United Nations and the 25th anniversary of Earth Day, we can be proud that more and more people understand the meaning of world ecology.

Wednesday, 20 March 1996
3:03 a.m.
Anna McConnell, Board Member of the Earth Society Foundation and wife of John McConnell
Hans Janitschek, President of the Earth Society Foundation
Anna and Hans made brief impromptu statements that were not recorded. However, Australian ambassador Richard Butler rang the Peace Bell later in the day at an "echo" ceremony. At that time, Butler received the ESF Earth Trustee Environmental Award on behalf of 1995 Nobel Peace Prize Laureate, Sir Joseph Rotblatt, for his fifty years of effort to reverse the arms race.
Butler: *Joseph Rotblatt is one of the clearest and sanest voices against nuclear weapons … working for the simple idea that all of us, including distinguished scientists, are morally responsible for what we do.*

Thursday, 20 March 1997
8:55 a.m.
Razali Ismail, Malaysian Ambassador to the United Nations and United Nations General Assembly President
It is a beautiful thing to begin the day with rings of a bell and to commemorate events with lofty words, but celebration of life is not possible without freedom from nuclear domination.

Friday, 20 March 1998

2:55 p.m.

Gillian Sorensen, United Nations Under-Secretary-General for External Relations

As we gather at this moment of perfect, natural equipoise, the day brightens and reminds us that the cycle of seasons turns again and gives us hope. … In outer space the astronauts, too, are noting Earth Day. … From their perspective, there are no boundaries, no borders, except land and water.

Saturday 20 March 1999

8:46 p.m.

Lama Gangchen, Tibetan healer and teacher

Brother Ignacio Harding, Franciscan priest

Lama Gangchen: *Peace with the environment. Peace with Mother Earth elements. Peace with wind elements, water elements, sky elements, space elements. Peace with these world elements. Peace with everything. Everything with peace, please.*

Harding: *Brother Sun, Sister Moon and Stars, Brother Wind and Air, Sister Water, Brother Fire, Sister Earth are our Mother who feeds us in her strength and produces various fruits with colored flowers and herbs.*

Monday, 20 March 2000

2:35 a.m.

Gerhard Pfanzelter, Austrian Ambassador to the United Nations

The United Nations is the major international forum where all nations can exchange views and ideas and the only global 'green' network to enhance even further the sustainable development of nations so that life on this planet will be worthwhile even in centuries to come.

Tuesday, 20 March 2001

8:31 a.m.

Mary Catherine Bateson, writer, anthropologist and daughter of Margaret Mead

Planetary stewardship not only reminds us of what we all share, beyond our different creeds and cultures, but it is also a powerful symbol of balance. …

This is a reminder to balance the rhythms of striving and the rhythms of contemplation, the rhythms of growth and the rhythms of rest, for rest and recovery are necessary to every person and field and forest and even to the life of the oceans.

Wednesday, 20 March 2002
2:16 p.m.
Lisbet Palme, widow of Swedish Prime Minister Olof Palme
The protection of our environment… [and] peace are now the most important things for our future. The greatest destroyer of our environment is war and the terrible new development of environmental warfare, which threatens to destroy human environment for generations to come.

Thursday, 20 March 2003
8:00 p.m.
Pete Seeger, folksinger and political/environmental activist
(commenting on the performance that preceded him) *Friends, I cannot add anything to that magnificent artistry that we just witnessed. The children will carry on. The world will be saved because of artistry like that.*

Saturday 20 March 2004
1:49 a.m.
John McConnell, Chairman Emeritus of the Earth Society Foundation and Founder of Earth Day
We've got to kill our terrible addiction to war. We ought to make friends, and not skeletons, of our enemies.

Sunday, 20 March 2005
7:33 a.m.
Aye Aye Thant, President of the U Thant Institute and daughter of U Thant
United States Ambassador John McDonald, retired
New Zealand Ambassador Don MacKay
Nicaraguan Ambassador Eduardo J. Sevilla Somoza
MacKay: *At a time of war, we must keep our minds firmly focused on the*

need for peace, and the best route to achieve that … not only for the sake of humankind but also for the sake of our environment.

McDonald: *On November 10, 1980, the first U.N. decade on drinking water and sanitation was launched by a three-day session of the General Assembly. It was very successful. …But by 1990, the world began to forget about water as a critical issue.*

Somoza: *One aspect of our environment that connects us all and is vital to us all is water. … One of our challenges is getting smart about preserving our water.*

Thant: *As my father said on this day in 1971, "It is an important day to remind us that our small planet is perishable." … Sadly today, 34 years later, the rapid amazing progress in technology has brought new and greater threats. … To conclude with my father's hope and wishes: "May I express the hope that the wisdom of nations inspired by the vision of a world united around the human objectives of peace, justice and prosperity will soon enrich human life with a renewed respect for the earth's resources and reward us with a healthy, free and weapon-free environment." … Happy Earth Day!*

Earth Day ceremonies at United Nations Office at Vienna

In Vienna, the Earth Day ceremony is informal, and numerous people have rung the Peace Bell since it was installed in 1996. Franz Nahrada, who initiated and organized the ceremonies there, reported, "People from this small community gather around and are allowed to ring the Peace Bell if there is a deep feeling in their heart to do so. The atmosphere is always wholehearted and serious, but joyful and full of positive emotions." This festive mood has prevailed in the years since John McConnell and Kurt Waldheim were the first bell ringers. "Only in 2002, did we have the participation of high level representatives and politicians, but we still maintained the event's informal character," Nahrada added. Boris Znamensky, the protocol and NGO liaison officer at the UN Office at Vienna, addressed the attendees as a "group of friends with a positive vision" who are always welcome at Earth Day ceremonies. [598]

---

598 Franz Nahrada, e-mail to author, 21 February, 2006.

13

Earth Day Proclamation

(1970 to 2000)

Each signer of this People Proclamation will seek to help change Man's terrible course toward catastrophe.
– John McConnell, "Earth Day Proclamation," 21 June 1970

THE EARTH DAY PROCLAMATION became the singular document that would embody the entire vernal equinox Earth Day tradition. This Proclamation was not the resolution John McConnell drafted in late 1969 and which San Francisco's mayor Joseph Alioto signed in February 1970, but, rather, a beautiful document that John wrote, then calligraphed, "for the people of the Earth" on 21 June 1970. Anna recalled it was the one document he wrote completely, from beginning to end, without any editing and all in one session. [599]

In his qualifying "Whereas" paragraphs, John observed, "A new world view is emerging. Planet Earth is facing a grave crisis that only people of Earth can resolve." He enunciated, as a preacher might, "our shortsightedness … to make provisions for the poor, as well as the rich, to inherit the Earth." He noted the need for "world equality in economics as well as politics that would remove a basic cause of war."

[599] Anna McConnell, manuscript review with author, Denver, Colorado, October 2005.

Following the "world equality" mission of WE, Inc., John called upon individuals to "join with one another in building the Earth in harmony with nature" and for groups to "follow different methods and programs in Earthkeeping and Earthbuilding." He enlisted Earth Day as "a special time to draw people together in appreciation of their mutual home, Planet Earth." And he implored the proclamation's signers to resolve "to help change Man's terrible course toward catastrophe by searching for activities and projects to peacefully end the scourge of war, provide an opportunity for the children of the disinherited poor to obtain their rightful inheritance in the Earth, ... [and] redirect the energies of industry and society from progress through products to progress through harmony." [600]

Then, being true to his nature for individualistic action, John took his passion for persuasion on the road. He presented his Earth Day Proclamation to political leaders, social and entertainment celebrities, world diplomats and futurists. And he personally obtained the signatures and commitment of thirty-six men and women known throughout the world.

"Secretary-General Signs Earth Day Proclamation,"
United Nations press release

The Secretary-General, U Thant, signed today an Earth Day Proclamation for the celebration of Earth Day on 21 March 1971 – the vernal equinox, or first day of Spring in the Northern Hemisphere. [601]

John collected the initial signatures in the early 1970s from people he knew in New York and at the United Nations: New York City assemblyman Alexander B. Grannis, the first to sign; Luther Evans, director general of UNESCO; and Arvid M. Pardo, Malta's ambassador to the UN. John then extended himself to U.S. senators and known environmentalists Eugene McCarthy, Mike Gravel, Hugh Scott and Mark Hatfield. U Thant signed at the Earth Day ceremony in 1971. Soon thereafter came international scientists Y. Fukushima, Rene J. Dubos, Lubos Kohoutek and Buckminster Fuller. In the early 1990s, the growing cast of signatories included astronaut

600 John McConnell, "Earth Day Proclamation," 21 June 1970.
601 United Nations, "Press Release SG/1749," 26 February 1971.

Edwin "Buzz" Aldrin and cosmonaut Anatoly Berezovoi, entertainer John Denver, concert violinist Yehudi Menuhin, author Isaac Asimov, and heads of state Oscar Arias, Carlos Salinas, Yassir Arafat and Mikhail Gorbachev.

Canadian Prime Minister Brian Mulroney would have been another national leader to sign the Proclamation. In fact, he did in 1990, after meeting John at an April 22 environmental event in Ottawa. John, the guest of veteran member of Parliament Stan Darling, left the Proclamation with Mulroney to sign, but when he came back the next day, he saw the Prime Minister's distinctive looping strokes had been obliterated with whiteout correction fluid. Boss Howard, a Canadian journalist, reported in his "View from the Hill" column that Mulroney's office said, "There were no other heads of government on the document," [602] which was incorrect because the previous signatory was Oscar Arias, the president of Costa Rica. Audrey McLaughlin, leader of Canada's New Democratic Party, signed the Proclamation in the Prime Minister's stead.

Arias had signed the Proclamation in Washington, D.C., on the occasion of Mikhail Gorbachev receiving the Martin Luther King International Peace Award for his contribution to world peace and human rights. John and Hans Janitschek were among many notable persons at the event. A few others were India's minister of transportation George Fernandes, world champion pugilist Muhammad Ali, industrialist Armand Hammer, humanitarian Rabbi Arthur Schneider, former deputy secretary of state John C. Whitehead, and a person of highest honor, Coretta Scott King, the widow of the assassinated Civil Rights leader after whom the International Peace Award was named. [603]

John obtained the signature of Mexican President Carlos Salinas in Mexico City. "I was trying to get support from people around the world to make the Earth Day observance what it should be," John said. I was delighted when he signed it because some of the political leaders in Mexico were altruists and some were not. He was among the good." [604]

Yassir Arafat signed the Proclamation in early May 1996 while at the United Nations to meet with Secretary-General Boutros Boutros-Ghali of Egypt prior to taking part in an upcoming seminar on Palestine in Cairo. "I

---

602 Boss Howard, "Mulroney draws blank on Earth Day pledge," View from the Hill opinion column.

603 Hans Janitschek, journal 1990.

604 John McConnell, telephone interview by author, 13 February 2006.

had often written to Arafat," John recalled. "I told him I think it's ridiculous for Israel to claim Jerusalem when it was land that God gave to all His children. It should be recognized as the Holy City of Christians, Jews and Muslims." [605] Anna traveled to Jerusalem the following year with a church group. "The driver and the tour guide were Palestinian," she said, "and there were posters of Yassir Arafat all over. I told the guide that Arafat had signed my husband's proclamation, and he was very impressed." [606]

Mikhail Gorbachev was the final person to sign John's Proclamation. He did so in New York while attending the United Nations Millennium Summit in early September 2000. "I was delighted to see him in person," John said of the former Russian President. "I so admired the things he had done." When Gorbachev took the Earth Day Proclamation into his hands, he read it carefully, nodded and signed it. [607]

With Gorbachev's name in place, all thirty-six spaces available for signatures were filled. With that, John said simply, "It's finished now." [608]

"Earth Day Proclamation," 21 June 1970

By the people of Earth for the people of Earth

Whereas; A new world view is emerging; through the eyes of our Astronauts and Cosmonauts we now see our beautiful blue planet as a home for all people, and

Whereas; Planet Earth is facing a grave crisis which only the people of Earth can resolve, and the delicate balances of nature, essential for our survival, can only be saved through a global effort, involving all of us, and

Whereas; In our shortsightedness we have failed to make provisions for the poor, as well as the rich, to inherit the Earth, and our new enlightenment requires that the disinherited be given a just state in the Earth and its future – their enthusiastic cooperation is essential if we are to succeed in the great task of Earth renewal, and

Whereas; World equality in economics as well as politics would remove a basic cause of war, and neither Socialism, Communism

605 Ibid.

606 Anna McConnell, telephone interview by author, 13 February 2006.

607 John McConnell, telephone interview by author, 13 February 2006.

608 John McConnell, interview by author, Denver, Colorado, August 2004.

nor Capitalism in their present forms have realized the potentials of Man for a just society; nor educated Man in the ways of peace and creative love, and

Whereas; Through voluntary action individuals can join with one another in building the Earth in harmony with nature, and promote support thereof by private and government agencies, and

Whereas; Individuals and groups may follow different methods and programs in Earthkeeping and Earthbuilding, nevertheless by constant friendly communication with other groups and daily meditation on the meaning of peace and good will they will tend more and more to be creative, sensitive, experimental and flexible in resolving differences with others, and

Whereas; An international EARTH DAY each year can provide a special time to draw people together in appreciation of their mutual home, Planet Earth, and bring a global feeling of community through realization of our deepening desire for life, freedom and love, and our mutual dependence on each other,

Be it Therefore Resolved; That each signer of this People Proclamation will seek to help change Man's terrible course toward catastrophe by searching for activities and projects which in the best judgment of the individual signer will:

> peacefully end the scourge of war
>
> provide an opportunity for the children of the disinherited poor to obtain their rightful inheritance in the Earth
>
> redirect the energies of industry and society from progress through products to progress through harmony with Earth's natural systems for improving the quality of life

That each signer will (his own conscience being his judge) measure his commitment by how much time and money he gives to these purposes, and realizing the great urgency of the task, he will give freely of his time and money to activities and programs he believes will best further these Earth renewal purposes. (At least nine percent of the world's present income is going to activities that support war and spread pollution. Ten percent can tip the balance for healthy peaceful progress.)

Furthermore, each signer will support and observe EARTH DAY on March 21st 1971 (Vernal Equinox – when night and day are equal throughout the Earth) with reflection and actions that will encourage a new respect for Earth with its great potentials for fulfilling Man's highest dreams; and on this day will join at 1900* Universal Time in a global EARTH Hour – a silent hour for peace.
*Time changed to moment of the Equinox.

"Earth Day Proclamation" Signatories

Alexander B. Grannis, New York City assemblyman; Judith Hollister, Temple of Understanding; Luther Evans, director general of UNESCO; Estelle Feldman, chair of the Commission on Man and Environment of the 1970 World Youth Assembly; David R. Brower, founder of Friends of the Earth; Arvid M. Pardo, ambassador at the UN Mission of Malta; Margaret Mead, anthropologist; Eugene McCarthy, U.S. senator from Minnesota; John Gardner, president of Common Cause; Mike Gravel, U.S. senator from Alaska; Hugh Scott, U.S. senator from Pennsylvania; Edwin "Buzz" Aldrin, astronaut; S. O. Adebo, President of the UN General Assembly; U Thant, UN Secretary-General; Maurice Strong, UN Environment Programme; Y. Fukushima, environmental scientist; Rene J. Dubos, environmental scientist; Lubos Kohoutek, astronomer who discovered Comet Kohoutek; Buckminster Fuller, inventor, scientist and scholar; Mark Hatfield, U.S. senator from Oregon; John Denver, singer; Robert Muller, UN assistant secretary-general; Isaac Asimov, writer; Edward Abramson, New York State representative and Earth Day chairman 1990; Ali Teymour, UN assistant secretary-general; Anatoly Berezovoi, cosmonaut; Cynthia Lennon, artist and wife of Beatle John Lennon; Stan Lundine, New York lieutenant governor; David Dinkins, mayor of New York City; Oscar Arias, President of Costa Rica; Audrey McLaughlin, leader New Democratic Party, Canada; George Fernandes, minister of transportation in India; Carlos Salinas, President of Mexico: Yassir Arafat, President of Palestine; Yehudi Menuhin, concert violinist; Mikhail Gorbachev, President of the Soviet Union.

June 21, 1970

by the people of Earth
for the people of Earth

EARTH DAY PROCLAMATION

Whereas: A new world view is emerging; through the eyes of our Astronauts and Cosmonauts we now see our beautiful blue planet as a home for all people, and

Whereas: Planet Earth is facing a grave crisis which only the people of Earth can resolve, and the delicate balances of nature, essential for our survival, can only be saved through a global effort, involving all of us, and

Whereas: In our shortsightedness we have failed to make provisions for the poor, as well as the rich, to inherit the Earth, and our new enlightenment requires that the disinherited be given a just stake in the Earth and its future -- their enthusiastic cooperation is essential if we are to succeed in the great task of Earth renewal, and

Whereas: World equality in economics as well as politics would remove a basic cause of war, and neither Socialism, Communism nor Capitalism in their present forms have realized the potentials of Man for a just society; nor educated Man in the ways of peace and creative love, and

Whereas: Through voluntary action individuals can join with one another in building the Earth in harmony with nature, and promote support thereof by private and government agencies, and

Whereas: Individuals and groups may follow different methods and programs in Earthkeeping and Earthbuilding, nevertheless by constant friendly communication with other groups and daily meditation on the meaning of peace and good will they will tend more and more to be creative, sensitive, experimental, and flexible in resolving differences with others, and

Whereas: An international EARTH DAY each year can provide a special time to draw people together in appreciation of their mutual home, Planet Earth, and bring a global feeling of community through realization of our deepening desire for life, freedom and love, and our mutual dependence on each other,

Be it Therefore Resolved: That each signer of this People Proclamation will seek to help change Man's terrible course toward catastrophe by searching for activities and projects which in the best judgement of the individual signer will:

peacefully end the scourge of war

provide an opportunity for the children of the disinherited poor to obtain their rightful inheritance in the Earth

redirect the energies of industry and society from progress through products... to progress through harmony with Earth's natural systems for improving the quality of life

That each signer will (his own conscience being his judge) measure his commitment by how much time and money he gives to these purposes, and realizing the great urgency of the task, he will give freely of his time and money to activities and programs he believes will best further these Earth renewal purposes. (At least nine percent of the world's present income is going to activities that support war and spread pollution. Ten percent can tip the balance for healthy peaceful progress.)

Furthermore, each signer will support and observe EARTH DAY on March 21st, 1971 (Vernal Equinox -- when night and day are equal throughout the Earth) with reflection and actions that will encourage a new respect for Earth with its great potentials for fulfilling Man's highest dreams; and on this day will join at 1900* Universal Time in a global EARTH HOUR -- a silent hour for peace...

* Time changed to moment of the Equinox 1973.

John McConnell's Earth Day Proclamation

United Nations Under-Secretary-General Robert Muller displays the Earth Day Proclamation, written by John McConnell (right), and which Muller had just signed, 21 December 1989.
United Nations

Mayor Proclaims Earth Day

Krista Lynne Baumhoff, 5, and Mayor Joseph Alioto admire an Earth Flag in his office. Baumhoff had given the flag to Alioto in honor of him proclaiming March 21 as Earth Day.
San Francisco Examiner, *Seymour Snaer*

OFFICE OF THE MAYOR
SAN FRANCISCO

JOSEPH L. ALIOTO

Proclamation

As inhabitants of this Earth - Earthians, we need a day to celebrate our global unity and destiny.

The observance of EARTH DAY will alert concern and interest for our planet -- with its precious treasure of living things.

EARTH DAY is to remind each person of his right and the equal right of each person to the use of this global home and at the same time the equal responsibility of each person to preserve and improve the Earth and the quality of life thereon.

NOW, THEREFORE, I, Joseph L. Alioto, Mayor of the City and County of San Francisco, do hereby proclaim March 21st (Vernal Equinox) to be designated EARTH DAY -- a special day to remember Earth's tender seedlings of life and people; a day for planting trees and flowers; a day for cleaning streams and wooded glens; that on EARTH DAY the EARTH FLAG which portrays in its center our "Beautiful Blue Planet", be flown to encourage mutual respect for Earth and all its people.

On this day 1900 to 2000 Universal Time (11:00 a.m. to 12:00 noon PST) be designated EARTH HOUR - a Silent Hour For Peace; and do invite all citizens throughout the community to join in observing Earth Day and Earth Hour in every way they may deem appropriate.

IN WITNESS WHEREOF I have hereunto set my hand and caused the seal of the City and County of San Francisco to be affixed this eleventh day of February, nineteen hundred and seventy.

Joseph L. Alioto
Joseph L. Alioto
Mayor

San Francisco Earth Day Proclamation, 1970.

THE NEW YORK TIMES, SUNDAY, JANUARY 18, 1970

April 22. Earth Day.

**A disease has infected our country.
It has brought smog to Yosemite,
dumped garbage in the Hudson,
sprayed DDT in our food,
and left our cities in decay.
Its carrier is man.**

The weak are already dying. Trees by the Pacific. Fish in our streams and lakes. Birds and crops and sheep. And people.

On April 22 we start to reclaim the *environment we have wrecked.*

April 22 is the Environmental Teach-In, a day of environmental action.

Hundreds of communities and campuses across the country are already committed.

It is a phenomenon that grows as you read this.

Earth Day is a commitment to make life better, not just bigger and faster; To provide real rather than rhetorical solutions.

It is a day to re-examine the ethic of individual progress at mankind's expense.

It is a day to challenge the corporate and governmental leaders who promise change, but who short change the necessary programs.

It is a day for looking beyond tomorrow. April 22 seeks a future worth living.

April 22 seeks a future.

We are working seven days a week to help communities plan for April 22. We have come from Stanford, Harvard, Bucknell, Iowa, Missouri, New Mexico, Michigan and other campuses.

We are a non-profit, tax exempt, educational organization. Our job is to help groups and individuals to organize environmental programs to educate their communities.

Earth Day is being planned and organized at the local level. In each community people are deciding for themselves the issues upon which to focus, and the activities which are most appropriate.

We can help, but the initiative must come from each community. We have heard from hundreds of campuses and local communities in all fifty states. Dozens of conservation groups have offered to help. So have the scores of new-breed environmental organizations that are springing up every day.

A national day of environmental education was first proposed by Senator Gaylord Nelson. Later he and Congressman Paul McCloskey suggested April 22. The coordination has been passed on to us, and the idea now has a momentum of its own.

All this takes money. Money to pay our rent, our phones, our mailings, brochures, staff, advertisements.

No list of famous names accompanies this ad to support our plea, though many offered without our asking.

Big names don't save the environment. People do.

Help make April 22 burgeon.

For you. For us. For our children.

The Environmental Teach-In, Inc.
Room 200
2000 P Street, N. W.
Washington, D. C. 20036
I enclose $10, $20, $50, ____ dollars (tax deductible)
How can I help my community?
Name __________
Address __________

The Environmental Teach-In, Inc.
Room 200
2000 P Street, N. W.
Washington, D. C. 20036

National Staff: Denis Hayes, Coordinator; Linda Billings, Stephen Cotton, Andrew Garling, Bryce Hamilton, Sam Love, Barbara Reid, Arturo Sandoval, Philip Taubman

National Staff: Denis Hayes, Coordinator; Linda Billings, Stephen Cotton, Andrew Garling, Bryce Hamilton, Sam Love, Barbara Reid, Arturo Sandoval, Philip Taubman

An advertisement, placed by Environmental Teach-In, Inc. in *The New York Times* on 18 January 1970, promotes the other "Earth Day" on April 22. *Swarthmore College Peace Collection*

United Nations Secretary-General U Thant speaks at the Earth Day ceremony at the United Nations in 1971. The first Earth Day occurred in 1970, and the UN ceremonies began a year later.
United Nations, T. Chen

United Nations Secretary-General Kurt Waldheim rings the Peace Bell at the Earth Day ceremony at the UN in 1972.
United Nations

United Nations Chef de Cabinet C. V. Narasimhan enthusiastically rings the Peace Bell at the Earth Day ceremony at the United Nations in 1973.
United Nations, T. Chen

Genichi Akatani, the United Nations' Assistant Secretary-General for Public Information, rings the Peace Bell at the moment of vernal equinox, 1:57 a.m., as part of the Earth Day ceremony at UN Headquarters in 1975.
United Nations, Y. Nagata

Frank O. Braynard, director of Operation Sail 1976, displays the 1980 New York City Earth Day proclamation at the Earth Day ceremony at the United Nations. Other speakers included NASA scientist Stanley Freden, U.S. astronaut Edward Gibson, and UN Director and Deputy to the Assistant Secretary-General Robert Muller.
United Nations, Y. Nagata

The Rev. Percival Brown, Pastor of Trinity Church, New York City, rings the Peace Bell at the moment of equipoise in 1983.
United Nations

Mezzo-soprano Bettina Jonic sings a medley "Peace Today" as John McConnell and songwriter Ervin Drake look on. The ceremony, which began at 11:00 p.m., was preceded by a concert that included Jonic, pianist Michael Fardink, and the 60-piece Lansdowne Symphony Orchestra of Philadelphia, Pennsylvania, conducted by Jacques Voois.
United Nations

John McConnell joins Ed Abramson and Cynthia Lennon for Earth Day activities at the United Nations in 1990. Abramson, a New York State representative, was the Earth Day chair, and Lennon, the former wife Beatle John Lennon, was a co-recipient of the Earth Trustee Environmental Award that year.
Swarthmore College Peace Collection

Singer Eartha Kitt engages the crowd at the Earth Day ceremony at the United Nations in 1993. Honored for being selected, she told the audience, "I knew there must have been a reason my mother named me Eartha."
United Nations, E. Debebe

Nobel Peace Prize Laureate Rigoberta Menchu of Guatamala shares a greeting with a Tibetan monk at the Earth Day ceremony at the United Nations in 1993.
United Nations, E. Debebe

Nasir Obeid of Palestine, John McConnell, and Daphne Tenne of Israel pose with children at the Earth Day ceremony on 20 March 1994. Obeid and Tenne rang the Peace Bell and made statements about their desire for peace between Arabs and Israelis.

American folk singer Pete Seeger enjoys the honor of ringing the Peace Bell at the Earth Day ceremony in 2003. With him, is his wife Toshi.
Hans Janitschek

Aye Aye Thant, president of the U Thant Institute, rings the United Nations Peace Bell along with U.S. ambassador, retired, John McDonald, New Zealand ambassador Don MacKay and Nicaraguan ambassador Eduardo J. Sevilla Somoza on 20 March 2005. Ms. Thant's father, U Thant, rang the Peace Bell for the first Earth Day ceremony at the United Nations in 1971.
Robert M. Weir

Former United Nations Secretary-General Kurt Waldheim, John McConnell and Japanese ambassador Nobutoshi Akao pose with the United Nations Peace Bell in Vienna on 21 March 1996. That date marked the first Earth Day ceremony in Vienna; Waldheim, Akao and McConnell were the first persons to ring the Peace Bell.
Neue Kronen Zeitung (Austria)

Anna McConnell holds the Earth Day Proclamation immediately after it was signed by Russian cosmonaut Anatoly Berezovoi (right). Also in the photo are Steve Bloomberg, John McConnell, Hans Janitschek and Kristina Tomczak. Berezovoi and Tomzcak established the Earth Day ceremony as a national holiday in Russia where it has been celebrated since 1998.
John and Anna McConnell

To John McConnell
Best wisches!
NEW York 20.3.97. "EARTH DAY"

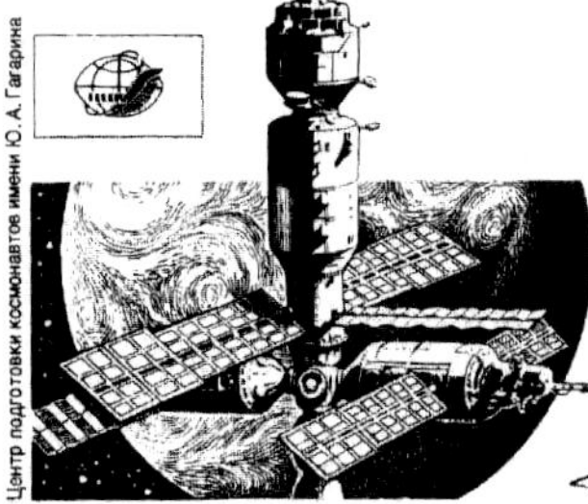

To Anna and John McConnell
Best wisches!
New York. 20.3.-97г
"EARTH DAY-97"

141160, Звёздный городок.Моск.обл. Россия.

Anatoly Berezovoy

14

Trustees of Earth

(1971 to present)

> *Let each person choose to be a Trustee of Planet Earth, each in their own way, seeking to think, choose and act in ways that will protect, preserve and increase Earth's natural bounty, ever seeking fair benefits for all Earth's people and for its creatures great and small.*
> – John McConnell, "Earth Trustee Challenge"

In the summer and fall of 1970, John McConnell set his concerns about two Earth Days aside and directed his creative energies toward a mechanism that would bring people of the world together for the common cause of ongoing environmental care, based on the prerequisites of peace and justice.

Over the next several months, John sought a phrase that would embody his ideal. He read books and attended lectures. He learned and decided, "The term 'Earth Steward' had been used by other environmentalists, and I wanted something better. A 'steward' is someone who manages somebody else's property, but our planet Earth is to be shared by all people, so that word didn't seem right." Then, the idea of "Earth Trustee" came to him.

"The first time he used Earth Trustee, we were visiting my mother outside Dallas," Anna recalled. "We were in a restaurant and Christa was still in a high chair. My mother and I were talking and John was doodling on the paper placemat. And he sketched out [the] 'Earth Trustee' [concept]. That was in December 1971."

John explained, "I liked 'Earth Trustee' because it had the word 'trust' in it, and I thought people would understand that." [609]

John then brought forth his Earth Trustee Agenda, which, interestingly, he did not attempt to present as a policy or doctrine through WE, Inc. Rather he believed the agenda's truth to be self evident, "a simple idea that can appeal to the most people on our planet and do the most good." [610] He was convinced Earth Trustees would inherently understand the *Bible* verse, "where there is no vision, the people perish," [611] but he added the positive corollary, "where there is vision, the people prosper," [612] Thus, he believed people would "focus on understanding and cooperation for a common goal to revive hope on our planet" [613] without the need for directives from formal organizations. Knowing, as he often said, "Actions good or bad begin in the mind," John believed the Earth Trustee idea "will change people's minds and fill the media and the world with solutions and hope for the future." [614]

To fulfill this goal, John adapted his belief in Minute for Peace, giving it a new appellation, "Earth Minutes," which were to be moments for silent meditation that would correspond with the broadcast of nature sounds on radio and nature scenes on television. [615]

He suggested that radio and television stations, universities and communities proclaim themselves to be "Earth Trustee Stations," "Earth Trustee Universities," and "Earth Trustee Cities," serving as way showers that would broadcast environmental messages, teach environmental classes, and adopt environmental civic programs. John advocated that these Earth Trustee entities announce and promote their activities, thus, providing both the momentum and mechanism through which the Earth Trustee Agenda would spread to institutions and communities around the world. In later years after the rise of the World Wide Web, John encouraged Earth Trustee and Earth Minute postings on the Internet, and wowzone.com, created by

---

[609] John and Anna McConnell, manuscript review with author, Denver, Colorado, October 2005.

[610] John McConnell, "My life mission is to see Earth Day and its Earth Trustee Formula for the future become a global reality."

[611] *Bible*, Proverbs 29:18.

[612] John McConnell, "An Earth Trustee Vision."

[613] John McConnell, "An Earth Day formula for the future."

[614] John McConnell, "Earth Trustee Purpose."

[615] John McConnell, "An Earth Day formula for the future."

Carmen Colombo to "Wish Only Well" (WOW) became the first Earth Trustee web site.

To individuals, John issued an Earth Trustee Challenge that he believed "contains the key elements that can invigorate reforms" in environmental, economic, social and spiritual arenas. [616] In addition, as he had done with his earlier endeavors, John approached the influential people of the world – Margaret Mead, Yassir Arafat, Oscar Arias, Chief S. O. Adebo and others – and encouraged them to be leading dignitaries in the Earth Trustee campaign.

Through these various institutions and individuals, John believed people could accomplish what he called "the over-arching goals of Earth Trusteeship ... [to] diminish conflict and bitter controversy and promote world peace." [617]

Offering a general guideline, he proposed a simple Earth Trustee Formula that consisted of: "1. An inner commitment – through prayer, meditation or reflection – to ... combine love of God, love of Neighbor and love of Earth. 2. Protect and nurture Earth's life and natural resources by ... buying, selling and giving [in ways] that diminish pollution and increase Earth's natural equilibrium and bounty. 3. Support efforts to provide the disinherited poor a stake in their planet [by means of] a secure homestead in city or country ... stabile money and fair credit." In addition, the Earth Trustee Formula recommended that people "join some group with a project for the care of Earth, tell your friends ... and invite them to do the same." [618]

The Earth Trustee Agenda became a common theme in John's life. Stopping planetary degradation was another of John's themes. He often wrote words that stated, in one way or another, "Our endangered planet is being carelessly and dangerously plundered." [619] Two documents, both of which contain these sentiments, showed the evolution of John's maturity from the early 1970s to his later authorship of more august essays.

While preparing for the first Earth Day celebration at the United Nations in 1971, John penned a short piece in which he advocated "a Global Controller [who would] provide the basis for global cost-benefit analysis in terms of economics, environmental and social values ... with a breakdown

[616] John McConnell, "It Is Our Planet," essay.
[617] Ibid.
[618] John McConnell, "Earth Trustee Formula."
[619] John McConnell, "Management of Planet Earth," 29 December 1970.

on waste or efficiency." [620]

Two decades later, his multi-page document, "Earth Trusteeship: Manual for Management of Planet Earth," started with a similar message: "We act as if Earth were not our Planet. No loyalty, no sense of responsibility, and, as a result, a diminished enjoyment and meaning in life." Then, in the following paragraph, John contrastingly put the emphasis for responsibility on individuals: "Earth is our home, our inheritance. ... With new vision, we can assume our rightful role as Earth Trustees, help Earth's rejuvenation and enjoy its natural bounty." [621]

John developed an "Earth Care Handbook," a fourteen page manual in which he detailed "Earth Care Criteria" to evaluate products for longevity, energy efficiency, pollution either during manufacturing or usage, and recyclability. His goal was to "avoid the garbage and glamorized junk that saturates our marketplace." He advocated energy efficient homes and communities designed to encourage local commerce and interaction. He wanted success stories to be carried on world media so solutions would be shared in order to "overcome problems of confusion and despair." He desperately desired to convince industry, "The business of business is not just to make money – but to meet human need." Above all, he saw the role of the human heart was to combine humankind's innate problem-solving skill with "creative altruism" to generate "right thinking and right action." [622]

People, of course, were to be the key. In 1971, John envisioned "Earth People," thinking and acting without a formal organization, would be "individuals who have embraced the new ecology world view and are re-evaluating their relationship with nature and one another as the only solution to the grave environmental crisis of our polluted planet." [623]

And by means of an "Earth People Presentation", which he delivered in various venues throughout the early 1970s, John observed that people in technically advanced societies consume an abnormal share of the planet's resources. He noted, "As a product-oriented society, we communicate the way we feel and think through the things we buy."

---

620 Ibid.

621 John McConnell, "Earth Trusteeship: Manual for Management of Planet Earth," 30 March 1992.

622 John McConnell, *Earth Care Handbook.*

623 John McConnell, "Earth People Proclamation," 1974.

Because of that observation and because he believed Earth People wanted solutions that "start at home," John turned to department stores, which he identified as "the crossroads of the community," as a "natural focal point for launching a nationwide Earth People effort." In a speech to the Associated Merchandising Corporation in November 1971, John advocated that department stores are "the most kinetic, facile, subtle and powerful person-to-person media we have," a feature through which "the department store can become the funnel for community environmental activity."

While acknowledging, "Earth People Centers were not designed as merchandising vehicles to make the most of the latest fad," John believed they would help stores "offer a real community service ... [that] will bring increased traffic." He asked store owners to realize their "participation requires a moral commitment ... beyond any material rewards" and to create "a plan for eradicating as much of their own pollution as possible through recycling ... and careful use of water and power."

A key feature of the Earth People Centers would have been two geodesic domes, designed by Buckminster Fuller and made of recycled cardboard. "A Dome of Doing" and "A Dome of Being" were to contain displays regarding how an individual could participate in environmental solutions and information on "the life that flows through all of us" as well as a self-scoring questionnaire to test a person's Ecology Quotient (EQ). John envisioned WE, Inc., would provide the graphic displays and presentation materials for the domes along with Earth People Action Kits and Earth Day Kits (buttons, bumper stickers, decals and Earth Flags) that department stores could buy and distribute. [624]

Unfortunately, the messages of John and other futuristic thinkers who were concerned about mass consumption were antithetical to greed-induced philosophies of too many store owners and the boards of directors of conglomerate superstores of subsequent decades. However, as many long-established, family-owned stores closed their doors in the late 1980s and early 1990s and as superstores grew to megalithic proportions with cluttered aisles of gaudy displays, more and more Americans began to rail against excessive consumerism as well as irresponsible corporate employment practices. Their crescendoing voices of the new millennium were, in effect, echoing the

---

[624] John McConnell, "Earth People Presentation."

message John McConnell espoused thirty years prior.

John's message to department store managers, "The healthy growth of our economy can come only through products and services that better the environment," [625] is the premise of socially responsible investment (SRI) strategies advocated by a few people who chose not to buy stock in munitions companies that supplied U.S. forces during the Vietnam War and institutions that had financially supported the apartheid government of South Africa.

In February 1972, *The Stock Market Magazine* published an article about John and "Earth People's new approach to equality." The article suggested socially responsible investing and advocated "the benefits of capital ownership be shared by requiring that, in all new issues of stock, a specified percent be given free to underprivileged families who excel in self-help improvement of their living quarters and neighborhood." In the article, John expressed his belief that such a requirement would "reduce welfare rolls and provide a new dignity and new incentives to the socially deprived." [626]

A decade or more after John espoused this idea, more people did turn to environmentally friendly, socially responsible investment. In fact, SRIs became recognized as a bona fide means to do good socially while doing well financially in the late 1980s, and their popularity continued to rise into the twenty-first century as financial forecasters reported, "While many companies had made money by polluting the environment, many more will make money by cleaning it up." [627]

With encouragement from Anna, through her involvement with school children, and with assistance from publicist Fred Burrous, John advanced an Earth Trustee program for young people, called Young Earth Trustees (Y.E.T.). Burrous proposed four programs, each customized for student age ranges. He wrote text and created illustrations, then conducted trial runs in schools north of San Francisco where he lived. And Burrous, who performed this work at his family's expense and without compensation, [628] envisioned

---

[625] John McConnell, "Earth People Centers, suggested statement by department stores."

[626] "Earth People Plan To Regenerate Our Planet," *The Stock Market Magazine*, February 1972.

[627] National Public Radio news report, circa 18 August 2005.

[628] Fred Burrous, memo to John McConnell, Hans Janitschek, Charles Donnelly and

giving away Y.E.T. materials "without restrictions ... to all interested parties seriously involved in environmental programs." [629] Burrous realized his wish, albeit indirectly, as more and more educators began to include environmental awareness activities, from a variety of sources, in their curricula.

But the greatest direct success for the Earth Trustee and the Young Earth Trustee programs occurred in 1994 via involvement with Gerry Coffey, an environmental activist who hosted a radio program in Decatur, Alabama, called *Coffey Break*. Coffey and John met fortuitously – John called it "by divine providence" – when she dialed, what she thought was the telephone number of Earth Day USA president Bruce Anderson, whom she had interviewed the year before. Through circumstances that defied logic, she reached John McConnell.

That conversation resulted in more phone calls and faxes through which Coffey learned the true origin of Earth Day on the vernal equinox. Coffey, impressed with John, made arrangements to interview him on the air in December 1993. "The charm, knowledge and insight Mr. McConnell demonstrated when responding to questions and comments from parents, teachers and school children was enlightening and inspiring," Coffey reported.

During the program, John told his radio audience he was searching for a community to become an "example of environmental excellence from which others could learn." Coffey asked, "What about Alabama?" while immediately realizing her state had often been described as the toxic waste dump of the nation. In typical McConnell graciousness, John replied, "Alabama is first in the index of States, first in space [in reference to Huntsville, Alabama, being the home of NASA and the U.S. Space & Rocket Center]. I see no reason why Alabama cannot be first in environmental excellence." [630]

The success of that interview led Coffey to propose a more elaborate program to be aired coast-to-coast on 14 January 1994 via Paul Gonzalez who hosted a national talk show on the People's Radio Network. [631] As the founder of Earth Day, John was Coffey's choice as the primary guest for the

---

Kurt Koenig, 1993.

[629] Fred Burrous, memo to John McConnell, 25 September 1993.

[630] Gerry Coffey, account of association with John McConnell, 1994.

[631] "Countdown to Earth Day at The Museum of Television & Radio," news release, The Museum of Television & Radio, 12 January 1994.

program. However, she also arranged for two other environmentalists to take part. One of them was Terry Anderson, an American journalist who had been held hostage in Beirut, Lebanon, for nearly seven years from March 1985 to December 1991. Anderson had recently been released and was much in the news. "Who could better appreciate the luxury of clean air, water and God's green Earth!" Coffey exclaimed in regard to the former hostage. The other guest was Paul Tracey, who, as a troubadour, traveled the world and starred in a Broadway play before devoting his talents to teaching children about earth care. He composed the "Y.E.T. Song" for Young Earth Trustees and had it recorded by students from Girls, Inc., a nationwide youth organization dedicated to inspiring girls. Then, for Earth Day in March of that year, Tracey performed the song at the Earth Day celebration at the United Nations [632] where a pictorial exhibit featured Alabama school children and the state's first lady Marsha Folsom.[633]

Communications technology linked John and Anderson, who were at the Museum of Television & Radio in New York City; Tracey, who was in Los Angeles, California; Gonzalez, who posed questions from a radio studio in Tampa, Florida; and Coffey, who broadcast the program from WAJF-AM in Decatur.

Thanks to contributions by Decatur environmentalist Jean Tune and Healthy Alternatives, Gerry and husband Ray Coffey's nonprofit organization, John then made a five-day trip from New York to Alabama in late January 1994. Appearing in-person with John on *Coffey Break* were Decatur mayor Bill Dukes and other community leaders.

John was thrilled by the interest generated for his Earth Trustee Agenda in Alabama, and while in Decatur, he tirelessly gave press conferences and spoke to civic clubs, libraries, schools and churches. John cherished the promise by the Rev. Rex Kibbler of First Christian Church to ring the church bell on the spring equinox and encourage neighboring pastors to do the same. [634]

The climax of John's tour was a town meeting at Decatur's Calhoun Community College where students, teachers, parents and activists met with

[632] Gerry Coffey, telephone interview by author, 9 January 2006.

[633] John McConnell, "Earth Day Founder's UN Address Highlights Alabama," 20 March 1994.

[634] Gerry Coffey, account of association with John McConnell, 1994.

leaders of major corporations – 3M, Novacor, Teledyne-Brown, Monsanto, Earthscope and Decatur Utilities [635] – and gained their commitments to "think globally and act locally to eliminate poverty and pollution, the seedbeds of crime and violence." [636] Everyone at that town meeting seemed to accept the premise stated in the agenda, "It takes an entire community to raise a child, an extended one to save the world." [637]

As a result of John McConnell's appearance in Alabama, mayor Dukes signed a proclamation that made Decatur the world's First Earth Trustee City, followed by Huntsville. Morgan County, where Decatur was located, became the First Earth Trustee County. Then, two years later on 20 April 1996, recently elected Alabama governor Fob James signed a proclamation, making Alabama an Earth Trustee State. [638]

Through these events, John earned Coffey's admiration for his persistence in spite of adversity. "Though Mr. McConnell's financial and material situation is meager, he still works endlessly via telephone, fax, snail mail or e-mail to recruit every man, woman, child, business and institution to become Earth Trustees," she wrote. [639] John summarized his tireless determination simply, "The Earth Trustee idea can change the human state of mind and continue the human adventure." [640]

[635] John McConnell, "Report to Earth Society Foundation," 2 February 1994.

[636] Gerry Coffey, account of association with John McConnell, 1994.

[637] "Campaign for Earth: Town Meeting for World's 'Common Ground,'" agenda, Decatur, Alabama, 28 January 1994.

[638] Gerry Coffey, telephone interview by author, 6 January 2006.

[639] Gerry Coffey, account of association with John McConnell, 1994.

[640] John McConnell, manuscript review with author, Denver, Colorado, October 2005.

15

Earth Society

(1973 to 1975)

> *[To] encourage people of all races, creeds, religions, nationalities and ideologies to become active participants in the preservation of the Earth's natural resources.*
> – John McConnell, "Earth Society Statement of Purpose," 1973

AT THE SAME TIME JOHN MCCONNELL was advocating his Earth Trustee Agenda, he continued to promote Earth Day, especially at the United Nations. These activities were consistent with a growing trend of national and international meetings to promote environmental awareness in the early 1970s.

In June 1972, the United Nations held its Conference on the Human Environment in Stockholm, Sweden. The event brought together nonprofit groups and individuals bent on citizen action. The delegates, many of whom spoke only their native languages, expressed concern about pollution, population growth, the relationship between humans and animals, natural resource conservation, preservation of soil, sea and sky, disease and famine, illiteracy, global conflict as a result of energy shortages, and the application of science and technology for the betterment of life. They sought ways to continue beneficial growth while avoiding destructive consequences. [641]

The conference led to creation of the United Nations Environment

[641] Maurice Strong, "Pressbook for World Environment Day," *United Nations* newspaper, 5 June 1974.

Programme (UNEP). Then, on 15 December 1972, the UN General Assembly passed a resolution that designated the date of the Stockholm conference, 5 June, as World Environment Day, intended "to deepen public awareness of the need to preserve and enhance the environment." [642]

The UNEP Governing Council held its first planning session the following summer, on 12-22 June, at the United Nations Office at Geneva, Switzerland. John McConnell attended as a delegate of WE, Inc., his expenses paid by colleague George Soerensen, who was chair of Educational Entertainment for Environment. [643]

At the conference, UNEP clarified its responsibilities and apportioned a one-year budget of $5.5 million in order to "move the work of UNEP from the phase of principles to that of concrete action." UNEP decided to recommend to the UN General Assembly that an Exposition on Human Settlements be held in Vancouver, British Columbia, Canada, in 1976. UNEP president Ingemund Bengtsson complimented UNEP for concentrating on priorities, and executive director Maurice Strong expressed gratitude that, after his earlier "feelings of gloom," the session ended on "a sound and constructive note." [644]

The UNEP conference contained a sub-conference of the World Assembly of non-governmental organizations (NGOs), which occurred on 15-17 June 1973. A report from the NGO World Assembly contained a stinging statement that provided a striking contrast between the detriments of a harsh human environment and the benefits of pleasant, productive surroundings. "The meeting took place in the New Conference Center of the United Nations under conditions of almost indescribable 'environmental' discomfort," the report stated on its first page. "This center ... has been so constructed as to deprive all conference rooms of any windows. ... The conference chambers are hermetically sealed and provided (apparently inefficiently) with total air-conditioning, thus ensuring a continuous and

---

642 United Nations Promotion and Public Services Division. *United Nations Conferences and Observances* [online]. United Nations [cited 4 August 2005]. Available from www.un.org/Overview/unconfs.html.

643 John McConnell, interview by author, Denver, Colorado, August 2004.

644 "Round-Up of the First Session of the Governing Council on the United Nations Environment Programme," press release, United Nations Environment Programme, Geneva, Switzerland, 23 June 1973.

wasteful use of increasingly expensive energy." The report further described "stale air and mental exhaustion," "temperatures resembling those of a Turkish bath," "brutal ugliness of colour and design," and "conference chairs that produce maximum physical discomfort" as among the reasons the delegates passed a unanimous resolution "condemning this particularly flagrant imposition of an unacceptable technological environment on the living needs of human beings." The report condemned the Conference Center as "typical of technologically arrogant, ugly and wasteful buildings that are being constructed around the world in the name of cost/benefit calculations ... [but lead to] longer term costs that are both economic and environmental." [645]

With such conditions inside the Conference Center, John McConnell called a meeting in Ariana Park on the lawn of the Palais des Nations. The Palais des Nations had been built in the 1930s as the home of the League of Nations, the world's first global peace entity, which was inaugurated in 1920. In 1966, twenty years after the League evolved into the United Nations, the Palais des Nations became the UN Office at Geneva. Ariana Park encompassed forty-five hectares, once owned by the Revilliod de Rive family and offered by the City of Geneva for UN use with a proviso that splendorous peacocks be allowed to roam freely. [646]

There, under a 100-year-old cedar tree, John and six others forged the Earth Society on 19 June 1973. He documented the occasion on a picture postcard [647] that featured the Palais des Nations fountain and the armillary Celestial Sphere, a thirteen-foot Art Deco orb of gilded constellations and silvered stars sculpted by Paul Manship as a "symbol of hope for the global community." [648]

This event began a process through which John and his followers eventually abandoned WE, Inc., in favor of the new organization. John explained this transference was necessary because, while WE, Inc., had mnemonic and acronymic flair, the name Earth Society served a more

---

[645] "Report on the NGO Assembly, June 15-17, 1973."

[646] *The Palais des Nations* [online]. The United Nations Office at Geneva [cited 17 February 2006]. Available from www.unog.ch/80256EE600581D0E/

[647] John McConnell, "Geneve – Le Palais des Nations," postcard, 19 June 1973.

[648] *The Sphere* [online]. Maecenas World Patrimony Foundation [cited 17 February 2006]. Available from www.celestialsphere.ch/

comprehensive purpose. "Our venture into space made us aware of the fact we were all one human family and have only one Earth. I thought we needed to use 'Earth' in our name. And 'Society' represents a group coming together for a benevolent purpose," John said. In addition, he recalled conversations with delegates from Korea and Russia who agreed the Earth Society name would help preserve the celebration of the society's primary endeavor, Earth Day. [649]

John's use of the phrase, "only one Earth," was consistent with the philosophy of Barbara Ward, a writer and speaker on economic affairs, and bacteriologist Rene J. Dubos who co-published a book in 1972 titled *Only One Earth: the care and maintenance of a small planet.* The book was commissioned by the United Nations Conference on the Human Environment and was funded principally by Columbia University's Albert Schweitzer Chair. The authors had the assistance of an international committee of corresponding consultants consisting of 152 individuals from fifty-eight countries. [650]

Maurice Strong wrote of the concept in 1974 in a communiqué to news editors and publishers that bore the letterhead, "Only One Earth, Une Seule Terre, Solo Una Tierra." In that correspondence, which served as a cover to a detailed media packet about environmental situations throughout the world, Strong posed the question, "What kind of world do we want?" Then, he suggested, "Global interdependence is both a reality and a necessity for surviving." He cited his belief, "Global solutions are possible," and he wrote, "Each person must take up the challenge individually and collectively ... [to] produce the kind of environment for human life on our planet to which we aspire." [651]

John, in his writing of that period, which he circulated at the UN, restated this societal challenge with an analogy: "As each cell in a human body receives, processes and circulates the nutrients that sustain life, so the human being exchanges the nutrients of consciousness that sustain the global body." John saw that the Earth Society, open to all "who wish to join in the

---

[649] John McConnell, interview by author, Denver, Colorado, August 2004.

[650] *Barbara Ward Jackson Papers on Only One Earth 1914-* [online]. Rare Book & Manuscript Library [cited 24 January 2006]. Available from www.columbia.edu/cu/lweb/eresources/archives/collections/html/4078935.html.

[651] Maurice F. Strong, "Only One Earth, Une Seule Terre, Solo Una Tierra," letter to media, June 1974.

task of caring for the Earth, offered a structure for expanding the conscious exchange essential to the growth of a global philosophy." [652]

"Earth Society: Potentials and Prospects," 24 September 1973

All over the world people are engaged in trying to understand and care for Earth and its life potentials.

THE NEW WORLD VIEW

An amazing transformation is occurring in Earth's governments, institutions and individuals. People are beginning to experience a new world view, a new whole way of relating to our planet and to one another. The Earth Society is a non-governmental program to aid this process.

EARTH IS ONE

The visit of Comet Kohoutek to our Solar System, like Sputnik, Apollo, and Sky Lab, reminds us that Earth is also a space voyager. It is our one and only Earth. We are all on it together.

HUMANKIND DEPENDENT ON NATURE AND EACH OTHER

Poets, mystics and philosophers have spoken through the centuries of how we are all one: one family, one community, all members one of another. It is only in the last few years that our mutual dependence and Interconnectedness has surfaced in the thinking and action of governments and institutions. More and more, we see the bonds that link man with man, and man with nature.

BIOLOGY PROVIDES EXAMPLES FOR SOCIAL EVOLUTION

Society as a whole is beginning to function as a human body with brain, blood, glands and nervous system. Today, we see the burgeoning of mutual assistance between all the major powers and joint action in United Nations agencies on pollution, population and poverty. In these and other institutions throughout the world, the critical problems of our environment, industries, social structures, and the needs of our personal body and spirit are being recorded, studied and debated with a new candor and humility.

HARMONY WITH NATURE

---

[652] John McConnell, Earth Society brochure.

Within Earth's institutions is a small but growing nucleus of individuals who are thinking globally and beginning to turn our society and technology toward the understanding and care of our Earth, its life and its people. They offer the hope that Man can successfully take the helm of planet Earth, understanding and adapting nature's ancient methods and systems, which through eons of evolution have increased Earth's life and beauty. These individuals are now acting as cells in a global organism.

THE INFINITE INDIVIDUAL

The individual cell in a human body receives, processes and returns nutrient products with the aid of nervous impulses from the brain. Each cell contains genes with a blueprint of the whole body, which assists in this task.

HUMANITY BECOMING AS ONE GLOBAL BEING

We see in our embryonic global social body the growth of similar systems for providing information, material and action, and "genes" to communicate the emerging Earth-view (ethics, criteria, guidelines) for improvement of Earth's life potentials.

UNIQUENESS AND UNIVERSALITY

Of course people have a much higher level of consciousness than cells and greater opportunity for mobility and creativity. And they can perceive and influence trends. Nevertheless, the analogy is useful. Through new links of communication and new bonds of feeling and awareness, now each person can uniquely affect the social and biological evolution of Earth's new global human organism.

ALL LIFE INTERCONNECTED

With our exploding population and ruthless technology we can quickly destroy the Earth, or by redirection slowly improve the delicate web of life that sustains us. Choosing and pursuing the latter is our urgent task.

The Earth Society will seek to aid this process.

16

In Search of Comet Kohoutek

(1973 and 1974)

Comets ... long tails are likened to the tresses on a ghostly head, and the name Comet derives from the Greek word Kome, meaning hair. They consist of frozen gases, methane, ammonia, carbon dioxide and ordinary ice sprinkled with a touch of meteoric dust. They have been said to be the nearest thing to nothing and still be something.
– Kohoutek Cruise invitation, December 1973

With the Earth Society, John McConnell created the organization through which he would contribute much to the overall paradigm shift from pollution to peace, social justice and environmental concern that began in the 1970s. An advocate for change, he exhibited considerable initiative in creating venues for his voice and the voices of others.

As Comet Kohoutek, the "Comet of the Century," captured media attention, John, with enthusiasm and audacity, went to work. Coordinating with the Hayden Planetarium, located within the American Museum of Natural History, and the South Street Seaport Museum, John organized two cruises to view the comet aboard the luxury passenger liner, *Queen Elizabeth 2*.

The first cruise on the 66,000 ton vessel, "the world's greatest ship," departed from New York Harbor on 9 December 1973 at 9:00 p.m., went east into the Atlantic Ocean away from city lights, then returned on 12 December. The second cruise lasted fifteen days, 5-19 January 1974, and included stops in Venezuela, the Caribbean, the Bahamas and Florida before returning to New York. [653] The timing of these cruises coincided with Comet Kohoutek's brightest appearance on 28 December and its nearest proximity to the Earth, 75 million miles, on 15 January. [654] During that time, the comet was 250 times brighter than the planet Venus as it streaked past Earth at 250,000 miles per hour. [655]

The cruise featured a spectacular array of programs, speakers and musical performers. Key among them was Lubos Kohoutek, the astronomer after whom the celestial body was named. Kohoutek first sighted the comet at Hamburg Observatory in Bergedorf, West Germany, on 7 March 1973 while photographing asteroids with a thirty-one inch telescope. [656] Entertainers included Burl Ives, who sang a new composition, "The Tail of the Comet Kohoutek," international pianist Deirdre O'Donahue, and composer and musical inventor Robert Mason, who performed on a recently debuted instrument called the synthesizer. [657]

"Comet Kohoutek Cruise Program," 9-12 December 1973

Speakers: Dr. Lubos Kohoutek; Dr. Henry Courten, astronomy professor at Dowling College and senior optical systems engineer at Grumman Aerospace Corporation; Robert Little, astrophotography instructor at American Museum-Hayden Planetarium, photographer and lecturer; Donald Albert, assistant professor of physics and astronomy at Adelphi University; Edward Mostowicz a member of the astronomy department at Dowling College; Dr. Kenneth L. Franklin, astronomer, television commentator on Apollo space flights, chairman of American Museum-Hayden Planetarium, and co-discoverer of Jovian radio emission; Thomas Lesser, astronomy lecturer at Dowling College and principal designer of the Dowling College Planetarium-Observatory.

Presentations: "Comet Kohoutek," "How to Photograph a

---

653 Cunard Line, "Two New Comet Cruises for *Queen Elizabeth 2*," news release.

654 "Seaport, Hayden, Goddard, Earth Society reach for stars via Kohoutek," newspaper article.

655 Hayden Planetarium, "Holiday Comet, 1973," promotional paper.

656 Ibid.

657 Hayden Planetarium, "The Voyage of the Comet," program 5 January 1974.

Comet," "The Sky Tonight," "Nature and Behavior of Comets," "Comets," "Another View of the Universe."
Comet Watch on the stern decks nightly. Closed-circuit television replays for viewing taped passage of Comet Kohoutek.

"Comet Kohoutek Cruise Program," 5-19 January 1974

Speakers and Topics:
Edwin "Buzz" Aldrin, astronaut – "The View from the Moon"
Dr. Ralph Cooper, associate division leader of the Laser Systems Division, Los Alamos Scientific Laboratory – "Potential for Limitless Energy"
Dr. Kenneth L. Franklin, astronomer, television commentator on Apollo space flights, chairman of American Museum-Hayden Planetarium, and co-discoverer of Jovian radio emission – "The American Museum-Hayden Planetarium at Sea"
Dr. William Glenn, director of research at CBS Laboratories, designer of reconnaissance satellite systems, and developer of color television projection systems – "Exotic Energy Production and Conversion Techniques"
Dr. Albert Hibbs, project scientist at NASA Jet Propulsion Laboratory and the "voice" of Mariner Control – "Mariner 10, the First Two-Planet Mission to Venus/Mercury"
Richard C. Hoagland, coordinator of special projects and public affairs at American Museum-Hayden Planetarium – "The Voyage of a Comet"
John McConnell, president of Earth Society – "Earth Day: Three Years After"
Dr. Marvin Minsky, director of the Artificial Intelligence Laboratory at Massachusetts Institute of Technology – "Artificial Intelligence: Totally Automated Manufacturing"
Dr. Carl Sagan, director of the Laboratory for Planetary Studies at the Center for Radiophysics and Space Research at Cornell University – "Mars: 90-Day Revolution"
Presentations and Discussions (individual or multiple presenters): "How to Photograph the Comet"; "Kohoutek, Visitor from the Dawn of the Solar System"; "Energy: Return to Simplicity, the Fork in the Road"; "The Most Exciting Six Months in the

History of the Solar System"; "The Future of Space Exploration"; "Kohoutek and the Southern Sky: Intelligence in the Universe"; "Thinking Big, a New Brand of Courage"; "Comet Kohoutek, Closest Approach to Earth, 75 Million Miles!"; "Tomorrow, End or Second Golden Age?"; "Where Do We Go from Here?"
Exhibits: Man and the Stars; Great Expeditions of the Sea; The Voyage of the Comet
Entertainers: Burl Ives; pianist Deirdre O'Donahue; synthesizist Robert Mason
Comet Watch on the stern decks nightly

In addition, on two mornings prior to the first cruise, Saturday and Sunday, 8-9 December 1973, the South Street Seaport Museum hosted gatherings on its Pier 16 along New York's East River between the Brooklyn Bridge and the southern tip of Manhattan Island. These programs, which began five weeks of celestial observation from that location plus an exhibit called "Man & A Star," featured a Comet Chowder Breakfast, served at 5:00 a.m., a presentation by Kenneth L. Franklin, astronomer and chairman of the American Museum of Natural History's Hayden Planetarium, musical performances, and a minute of silent meditation led by John McConnell. [658]

The idea for these events at the South Street Seaport Museum originated with John, who, for this endeavor, became an unpaid "employee" of the museum. Marion Gaines handled the promotion, a responsibility that suited her talent as a radio and television actress whose roles included the "Dragon Lady" on *Terry and the Pirates.* [659] Frank O. Braynard, who was the museum's program director, granted office space and use of phones to John and his assistant, George Soerensen. Braynard also sent a letter to museum members in September 1973, seeking funds on John's behalf for a phone line, a secretary and operating capital. This request was not new to museum supporters as Braynard had made a similar appeal, and he had established a special John McConnell fund, prior to the previous Earth Day. [660]

The Earth Society benefited from the cruises through publicity and

[658] Earth Society, "Earth Society Salute to Kohoutek," news release.

[659] Marion Gaines biography.

[660] John McConnell, interview by author, Denver, Colorado, August 2004.

income. Newspapers and electronic media promoted the event, the Earth Flag flew atop *QE2*, and the ship's operators, the Cunard Line, paid the Earth Society twenty percent of gross fares that resulted from the society's promotional efforts in addition to giving one free ticket for every twenty fares booked through John's endeavors. [661] Anna praised Cunard, saying it provided "wonderful accommodations and meals in the ship's most exclusive restaurant with two waiters per table, who enjoyed helping us feed Christa." [662]

John took advantage of every opportunity to encourage passengers to participate in Comet Kohoutek lectures. "Unlike traditional explorers, whose goal was purely geographical, we are going Nowhere to seek astronomical knowledge, heavenly fun, and escape from Everyday," he wrote in a letter distributed aboard the ship during the first voyage. [663]

For promotion and curiosity during the second voyage, John and others attached an Earth Flag and a pickle bottle with a note inside to a pole that was equipped with flotation devices. The bottle contained a message, written in English, Spanish and French: "An Earth Flag for the finder of this bottle." Penned on Earth Society notepaper, it identified the organization as "Sponsors of Comet Watch." After they released the apparatus from the stern of *QE2*, John noted, "It was visible for some time. … We expected it to go ashore somewhere and be reported. But we were disappointed. We never got a message that it had been seen or found." [664]

John hoped Comet Kohoutek would be, to the world, "a signal for the rescue and renewal of Planet Earth." [665] Yet, near the end of the second cruise, he made a dismal comparison between life aboard *QE2* and life on the planet; "The *QE2*, sailing the Caribbean, reminded me of our Earth Ship in its voyage through the seas of space. The *QE2* was rather crowded with people more interested in momentary pleasure and creature comforts than in finding and harmonizing with the universal process of Life, the

[661] John McConnell, letter to William C. North, Cunard Line.

[662] Anna McConnell, manuscript review with author, Denver, Colorado, October 2005.

[663] John McConnell, letter to *QE2* passengers, 9 December 1973.

[664] John McConnell, handwritten notation on the back of a photograph of the Earth Flag launching.

[665] John McConnell, "Earth Society Salute to Kohoutek," news release, December 1973.

source of greatest joy. Less than 100 of the 1,500 passengers attended the exciting workshops on energy, biology, astronomy, ... [and] Earth Values. No more than a few dozen joined the sky watch for inspiring explanations of stars and their workings by Ken Franklin. Only a few attended the Pickle Bottle ceremony and watched the fantastic sunset that followed. And still, in conversation with the uninterested, it was evident that personal conversation and explanation aroused their interest and led to participation. The problem on the *QE2*, and on planet Earth, is communication. Not manipulative promotion, but somehow to let the voices of the thoughtful & concerned be heard. Other analogies could be drawn: the difficulty of even the speakers having different meanings for the words they used; the excessive waste of food & energy aboard the *QE2* (though it might be argued it is good occasionally to be pampered – a specialty of the *QE2*). On the positive side, seeds were planted, opinions modified & prejudices reduced. I personally feel I have a better understanding of thinking & feeling of the artist & scientist because of this voyage. Perhaps we, who are constantly seeking and searching for answers, will 'turn on' to life and to one another more completely – and thereby release the energy needed to 'turn on' a majority of humankind to the care & real enjoyment of Earth and its wonderful web of life." [666]

With that sentiment, John hoped Comet Kohoutek would serve as "a reminder of the beauty and order of the Universe," [667] and would draw people's attention and actions toward better human relationships and more positive outcomes.

As an example, John wrote on 11 October 1973, as he was beginning to promote the Comet Kohoutek cruises: "Vice-president [Spiro] Agnew has just resigned. The new war is raging between Israel and her Arab brothers in Syria and Egypt, in spite of the recent, dramatic détente between the big powers who supply the arms. The Watergate hearings continue with ever new confessions of corruption in high places, with important but inadequate efforts for change. The Alaska Pipeline, opposed by leading environmentalists, has obtained approval of Congress. While there are thousands of new environmental groups and programs, the public support that followed Earth Day has diminished. Without more support, our Planet will die.

---

666 John McConnell, handwritten letter to Sue Citron, 14 January 1974.

667 John McConnell, "Earth Priorities 1974," essay, 31 December 1973.

"In the Eastern sky a new comet has been discovered, Comet Kohoutek. In its bright visit to our solar family, does it portend doom? Or can we, by our actions, make it a symbol of hope? We have enough answers to begin the rescue and renewal of Earth. Our problem is our race with time. The false values and habits of the past two hundred years, which, with the aid of mindless systems and machines that are now destroying our billion-year biosphere, are relentlessly pushing us toward the precipice: the point of no return.

"Last night I walked with my wife from our apartment in Brooklyn to a meeting about a drug addiction program in our neighborhood. The meeting was conducted by the local planning board and was several blocks away at St. Leonard's Church. It had probably been over a year since we last walked along this street, and it was encouraging to see the street much cleaner, more growing plants and trees, and several three-story multiple homes newly remodeled and decorated. This was the work of the local Block Association working against terrible odds in an area of poverty, drug addiction and despair.

"At the meeting there were emotional flare-ups between residents who felt threatened by the location of a drug treatment center on their street and those who were undergoing treatment at the center. I could not help but think of the similar angry words being exchanged at that moment at the United Nations Security Council. A young man from the drug treatment center stepped to the microphone and said that 'this Earth belongs to all the people, and we have got to remember that and work together.'

"... I am now convinced that we have a chance; that we can be that other, better planet; that midst the rancor, hate, greed and despair are individuals everywhere who see a better way. As we take action to become aware of one another, the new vision of Earth will quickly spread. The guidelines exist. The priorities are clear. The means are at hand. The time for total effort is now." [668]

[668] John McConnell, "Prologue," essay, 10 October 1973.

17
Earth Rights and Responsibilities
(1974 to present)

This is for young and old who care about the Earth, its air, water, land and living things. We must change the attitudes and actions now destroying the Earth into those that will heal and build our planet.
– John McConnell, 1974

In 1968, John McConnell wrote his "Planetary Inheritance Declaration," a profound document "concerning the rights and responsibilities of all people with respect to Earth's land, sea, minerals, oil and other natural resources." [669]

Then he set the concept aside, giving priority instead to the Earth Flag, WE, Inc., Earth Day, and love for his bride and care of his young children. But, in the early 1970s, with the Earth Society serving as a structural foundation, John resurrected the planetary inheritance idea, labeling it variously as "Planetary Rights" or "Earth Rights." He spoke of "Earth Responsibilities" and the need to "move people's actions from Earth Kill to Earth Care." [670]

While compiling these thoughts, John found inspiration in the *Bible*. "In praying about questions in my mind and asking God's help in understanding, I would occasionally close my eyes and open the *Bible* to wherever my thumb fell on the page. In this case, I had written 'planetary

[669] John McConnell, "Planetary Inheritance Declaration," 1968 and 1970.
[670] John McConnell, "Earth Kill vs Earth Care," definitions.

inheritance' and wondered if there was something in the *Bible* that would help me understand. I prayed. Then I opened the *Bible*, and I found 'The heavens are the Lord's, but the earth he has given to the children of men.' [671] That verse told me the Earth is for the whole human family." [672]

Thus motivated, John wrote a speech, titled "Earth's Resurrection," which he gave at the United Nations Church Center on Easter Sunday 1974. In the speech, John outlined three global objectives in the areas of ecology, justice and love. Ecology, he proposed, "[requires] education and action that will convert our desire and our practice to the care of Earth ... [and] the preservation and enhancement of its marvelous ecosystems." Justice, he said, "[involves] equal individual rights to the use of Earth and its raw materials and equal responsibility for the care and preservation of Earth's natural bounty." Love, he suggested, "[relies upon] encouragement and reward for the attributes and values and actions that, in spite of limiting dogmas and institutional barriers, have nourished the great religions and all humanitarian endeavors." [673]

John found most people easily understood his ideas for ecology and "care of Earth" as well as his advocacy of altruistic love. But his message regarding justice was harder to comprehend. This was caused, at least in part, by adherence to the Code of Hammurabi, written eighteen centuries before the birth of Christ, which defined justice as an "eye for an eye and a tooth for a tooth." In contrast, John described that as "legalized revenge."

Indeed, when John spoke of justice, he meant "economic justice," which he defined as "an equal sharing in all the world's natural resources." In his "Planetary Inheritance Declaration," John wrote, "Among the equal rights of men is the right to an equal share in nature's bounty, a right of each man to his planetary inheritance – his share of land, water, minerals, or an appropriate equivalent in food, housing or other benefits." And correspondingly, "No one can, by any compact, deprive or divest their posterity, or any other man's posterity, of the right to his portion of Earth." [674] John firmly believed that implementing the concept of economic justice, as he envisioned it, would

---

[671] *Bible*, Psalm 115:16.

[672] John McConnell, manuscript review with author, Denver, Colorado, October 2005.

[673] John McConnell, "Earth's Resurrection," speech, 14 April 1974.

[674] John McConnell, "Planetary Inheritance Declaration," 1968 and 1970.

eliminate poverty throughout the world. [675]

In part, John drew this opinion from American political economist and social reformer, Henry George who worked as a printer in San Francisco in the mid- to late-1800s and was as well known as his contemporaries, Thomas Edison and Mark Twain. George originated the idea of a single tax, based solely on the ownership of land. Writing in his most influential work, *Progress and Poverty*, which he published in 1879, George espoused that land was a free gift of nature, that all people have an equal right to use the land, and that it was unfair for a few to acquire great wealth by holding land that increased in value merely due to the passage of time or according to the buildings constructed upon it. George prescribed that unearned income from the property's increased value should be the sole source of all taxation, thus doing away with other government-imposed taxes on merchandise sold, stamps purchased and so on. This tax, imposed on land owners, would then subsidize all social programs for the benefit of those not privileged to own land. [676]

George's philosophy caused John to wonder about natural resources beneath Earth's surface. "The land owners didn't make the gold. That's the common property of the whole human family," John stated. "Nobody made the oil. The same would apply to silver and coal and soil and other treasures that nobody makes, like [virgin] timber and water. It's the property of everybody." Nobody should make a profit on things that God made, John summarized. [677]

John took his message to the United Nations Ad Hoc Committee on Raw Materials and Development, which met in a special session of the General Assembly in April 1974. John averred, "I speak, not for one country, nor for any partisan ideology, creed, or vested interest … [but] for Earth, its life and its unborn children." [678]

---

[675] John McConnell, interview by author, Denver, Colorado, August 2004.

[676] Agnes George de Mille. January 1979. *Who Was Henry George?* [online]. Henry George School of social Science [cited 14 August 2005]. Available from www.henrygeorgeschool.org/whowashg.htm. Also, *Henry George* [online]. World Book Encyclopedia [cited 14 August 2005]. Available from www.aolsvc.worldbook.aol.com/wb/Article?id=ar221300&sc=-1.

[677] John McConnell, interview by author, Denver, Colorado, August 2004.

[678] John McConnell, "Earth Rights," proposal to United Nations Ad Hoc Committee on Raw Materials and Development, 16 April 1974.

His message was similar to that spoken by Pope Paul VI at the UN on 9 April 1974 when the Holy Father said, "We are happy ... to send a message of support as the General Assembly embarks on the study of the Problems of Raw Materials and Development. Our deep interest in these important aspects of man's life stems from our spiritual mission at the service of the whole man and of all men." [679]

Similarly, in a report on Earth Society programs, John wrote, "The increase in oil revenues should be used to organize a grand alliance of concerned people to preserve the Earth and fill the needs of its poorest inhabitants." [680] John then penned a letter to Sheik Ahmed Yamani, the petroleum minister of Saudi Arabia, who was attending the conference. In his missive, John suggested that fifty percent of his country's oil royalties be given to help the planet's "disinherited people" through organizations that feed the hungry and house the homeless, environmental programs to enrich Earth's natural resources, and a direct, equal distribution to all adults in any poor area of the world. [681]

John also spoke privately with Sheik Yamani during a conference recess. He, first, confirmed Yamani's religious beliefs that land and raw materials are common property. Then, John reiterated the essence of his letter, "Well, you should pay a royalty to the owners when you take out their oil. That would be all the people of the world." [682] John told reporter John Cuniff, who wrote about this incident in *The Phoenix Gazette* in March 1974, "Sheik Yamani ... agreed with me, but did not implement the ideas. Had he done so, the world would be far better off today." [683]

In the summer of 1974, a company in New Mexico flew John to their corporate offices to discuss establishment of a Planetary Inheritance fund

---

679 Pope Paul VI. 4 April 1974. *Address of the Holy Father Paul VI to the General Assembly of the United Nations Organization on the Problems of Raw Materials and Development* [online]. The Vatican [cited 17 December 2005]. Available from www.vatican.va/holy_father/paul_vi/speeches/1974/documents/hf_p-vi_spe_19740409_paesi-poveri_en.html.

680 John McConnell, "Seeds of Change," report on Earth Society programs, 1974.

681 John Cuniff, "Founders Mission: Change the World," *The Phoenix Gazette*, 19 March 1974.

682 John McConnell, interview by author, Denver, Colorado, August 2004.

683 John Cuniff, "Founders Mission: Change the World," *The Phoenix Gazette*, 19 March 1974.

but later chose not to proceed. John experienced the same result – occasional interest coupled with courteous replies but no cooperation – from meetings with oil companies at other times in the 1970s [684] and correspondence he sent to oil companies in later years. [685]

While most industry executives, especially those in the business of exploiting the world's natural resources, would have called John's idea wild and radical, John vehemently disagreed. "In the perspective of one billion years of life evolution, ... the first priority of industry ... is to quickly convert to products and services that meet environmental criteria and aid the process of life," John said. [686]

In effect, John was among those who served as an external conscience to industry. He spoke a similar, but stronger, message than that found in environmental legislation enacted by the United States government throughout the 1970s. The difference was that John idealistically hoped industry executives would take a righteous road above and beyond the environmental standards legislated upon them.

At the same time, John looked upon the United Nations as the logical institution of world government to establish and monitor a "Natural Resources Royalties Pool" that would collect money from any individual, corporation or country that might take an excess of their rightful portion, then distribute that money to the rest of Earth's people. John hoped and believed the United Nations could "encourage cooperation and individual initiative ... [that would] eliminate many economic sources of discord that lead to war." [687]

John was not alone on this issue. The Henry George Institute, founded in 1971, welcomed John's message at a seminar in May 1996. Promotional material for the event cited, "Mr. McConnell has long shared Henry George's vision of the earth as the common heritage of all people, and he advocates the public collection of land rent as a way to actualize this all-important relationship." The seminar honored John's co-authorship, with Alanna Hartzok of the International Union for Land Value Taxation, of a paper that

---

684 "Planetary Inheritance," item in Earth Society newsletter, October 1974.

685 John McConnell, letter to Peter B. Trinkle, Exxon Corporation, 4 October 1990.

686 John Cuniff, "Founders Mission: Change the World," *The Phoenix Gazette*, 19 March 1974.

687 John McConnell, "Planetary Inheritance Declaration," 1968 and 1970.

advocated tax reform in Hartzok's home state of Pennsylvania. [688]

Another significant ally was Walter J. Hickel, governor of Alaska from 1966 to 1969 and from 1990 to 1994 and U.S. secretary of the interior under President Richard Nixon. Hickel devoted his life to making Alaska, of which nearly ninety percent is government-owned land, a place where the "commons" is managed for the betterment of all. In his book, *Crisis in the Commons: The Alaska Solution*, published in 2002, Hickel stressed the need to manage the commons as a means to prevent poverty. By standing strong against corporations that would ravage pristine places, Alaska, under Hickel's leadership, took mutual prosperity to new heights, becoming, to use the governor's words, "a state with an outstanding quality of life, celebrating a glorious natural environment and a robust, healthy economy." [689]

While not as well organized as the Georgists or as politically prominent as Hickel, John McConnell, nevertheless, persisted in promoting his dualistic message of Earth Rights and Earth Responsibilities. In more humble ways, John printed and distributed his definitions of Earth Kill and Earth Care, which, in that order, read: "Any action that causes the degradation or disruption of healthy Earth-life organisms, processes, diversity, interactions and environments ... [and] any action that helps the well-being of Earth, its life and its people." [690]

With modest epistles such as this, John became like a Biblical David winging paper airplanes at corporate and nationalistic Goliaths. In the late 1970s, he drew up plans for a seven-year Earth Care Campaign. He called upon individuals to form neighborhood alliances, organizations to come together to support the campaign, businesses and labor unions "to take new bold initiatives for clean energy, eco-development ... and eco-marketing," and for governments "to realize the Earth Care Campaign is more important to their future than any war they have ever fought." [691]

History has shown that individuals have formed neighborhood

---

[688] "John McConnell to Explain 'Earth Trustee Economics' at HGS," Henry George Society, 1996.

[689] Stan Pitlo. 19 May 2002. *Hickel blames poverty on mismanagement of 'commons'* [online]. Alaska Journal of Commerce [cited 17 December 2005]. Available from www.alaskajournal.com/stories/051902/vie_hickel_poverty.shtml.

[690] John McConnell, "Earth Kill vs Earth Care," definitions.

[691] John McConnell, "Earth Care Campaign."

or community alliances of various sorts, especially when a perceived environmental threat, such as a new landfill, was to be built nearby. Some environmental organizations have cooperated with each other while others have fought to hoard their memberships and dues. Some businesses, with or without encouragement, have implemented better ecological practices while others have flaunted environmental legislation. And key federal governments, especially the United States, have expanded military arsenals at great expense while reducing money and efforts to improve environmental and social conditions.

Thus, history reminded John McConnell that the grassroots of the environmental movement, while embedded, must continue to grow stronger and louder if it were to reach the ears of those who make decisions at the highest levels within industry and government. John McConnell, with his concept of planetary inheritance, was one necessary voice in the movement to implement change from the ground up.

18

Sea Citizens

(1974 to 1982)

Who 'owns' the sea? You do! And your property is being vandalized, stolen, destroyed. What are you doing about it?
– John McConnell, "Who Owns the Sea?" 1975

Not surprisingly, John McConnell included the seas in his Earth Care Campaign. And he did so because the world's view of the oceans was changing drastically in the 1970s.

In 1609, Dutch jurist Hugo Grotius wrote, "[The ocean] is common to all, because it is so limitless that it cannot become the possession of anyone. ... [It] can neither be seized nor enclosed." [692] For the next 350 years, the so-called "cannon shot rule" prevailed as nations abided by the agreement that all waters beyond the range of a cannon ball shot from shore were international waters, free to all nations and belonging to no one. [693]

But by the middle of the twentieth century, missiles, whether fired from shore or from military naval vessels, had greatly extended their range, as had fishing fleets and oceanographers. Potato-sized nodules of manganese, cobalt, copper and nickel, worth hundreds of billions of dollars, had been found in shallow waters off continental coasts, as had sand deposits of

---

[692] Brian J. Brown, "Staking Out the Oceans: Who Owns What," TIME Education Program, 1956.

[693] *United Nations Convention on the Law of the Sea* [online]. Wikipedia [cited 17 August 2005]. Available from en.wikipedia.org/wiki/United_Nations_Convention_on_the_Law_of_the_Sea.

titanium and magnetite and huge five-carat diamonds; more treasures, the explorers believed, lay in deeper fathoms. [694] Bathymetric technology had revealed that the ocean benthos, hidden by relatively flat water surface, was actually a topographic grandiosity of mountain ranges taller than Everest, chasms deeper than the Grand Canyon and volcanoes more powerful than Etna. People of vision had come to view the planet's vast seabed and ocean floor as another continent. [695]

In 1956, the United Nations held its first Conference on the Law of the Sea (UNCLOS I) in Geneva, Switzerland. UNCLOS I resulted in four treaties, signed in 1958, that established conventions regarding the territorial shelf and its contiguous zone, the continental shelf, the high seas, and fishing and conservation of living resources of the high seas. UNCLOS II, held in Geneva in 1960, produced no international agreements. [696]

Then, on 1 November 1967, Arvid M. Pardo, Malta's ambassador to the United Nations, addressed the General Assembly with a powerful message that urged the UN to enact "an effective international regime over the seabed and the ocean floor beyond a clearly defined national jurisdiction." [697] Pardo warned, "Ocean technology was fast outstripping ocean politics and new international laws were needed to avoid armed conflict over the rights of marine food supplies, resources and space." Pardo's words sparked a process that culminated with adoption of the Convention of the Law of the Sea fifteen years later, and he was nominated for the 1974 Nobel Peace Prize for his continued efforts to insure fairer distribution of underwater resources. [698] But, in the interim, the steps toward international convention were numerous and laborious.

In 1968, the United Nations General Assembly established a Committee on the Peaceful Uses of the Seabed and the Ocean Floor beyond the Limits

---

694 Clark M. Eichelberger, "The Promise of Seas' Bounty," *Saturday Review*, 18 June 1966.

695 Brian J. Brown, "Staking Out the Oceans: Who Owns What," TIME Education Program, 1956.

696 *United Nations Convention on the Law of the Sea* [online]. Wikipedia [cited 17 August 2005]. Available from en.wikipedia.org/wiki/United_Nations_Convention_on_the_Law_of_the_Sea.

697 "Constitution of the Sea Brings Order to the Oceans," *United Nations* (2002): 9.

698 Dr. Arvid M. Pardo, "Perspectives on the Law of the Sea Negotiations," speech, University of Southern California Sea Grant Institutional Program.

of National Jurisdiction. Two years later, the General Assembly adopted the committee's Declaration of Principles, which stated the seabed and ocean floor, beyond the limits of national jurisdiction, were to be the common heritage of mankind. That UN decision led to the Third Conference on the Law of the Sea (UNCLOS III), held in New York City in 1973, followed by a second session in Caracas, Venezuela, in 1974. [699]

UNCLOS III produced a draft resolution that was presented to delegates from over 160 countries, many of them landlocked, [700] at a third session in Geneva, Switzerland, in 1975. Then, over the next seven years, the world's nations negotiated and revised the draft, turning it into an agreement, which was ratified by 130 countries on 30 April 1982. [701]

Into this environment, John McConnell birthed the Sea Citizen concept. In part, he did so because of commonly felt frustration over the lack of progress at UNCLOS III in Caracas, which John viewed as an example of "every man for himself." He explained in Earth Society literature, "The world is making the same land rush mistakes in the ocean that led to cruel wars and the creation of deserts on the Earth. ... Without a strong, independent International Sea Authority, funded by the revenues derived from licensed, environmentally correct exploration of the ocean, there will be no way to effectively stop pollution of the deep oceans by reckless oil and mineral ventures, no way to conserve commercially valuable fish, and no way to protect from harm the small organisms that produce the oxygen we breathe." [702]

He saw the problem as "uninhibited sovereignty, with neither compelling authority nor commitment that would temper the ambition, greed and selfishness of individual states and of their leaders." And he believed this problem was exacerbated by "the feeling most people have that they are not being treated fairly." [703]

John's position was supported by Russell W. Peterson, former governor of Delaware and chairman of Save Our Seas. Peterson spoke at the Earth Day

---

699 "Constitution of the Sea Brings Order to the Oceans," *United Nations* (2002): 9.

700 Brian J. Brown, "Staking Out the Oceans: Who Owns What," TIME Education Program, 1956.

701 "Constitution of the Sea Brings Order to the Oceans," *United Nations* (2002): 9-10.

702 John McConnell, "The Sea... some thoughts on its future," Sea Citizen brochure.

703 John McConnell, "Loyalty to our Planet," essay.

ceremony in 1973 of the seas being "under rising pressure from technology [with] new ocean uses ... new dangers from pollution ... [and] new dangers from human encroachment and anarchy." [704] French underwater explorer Jacques Cousteau called the rhetoric in Caracas "egotistical nationalism," [705] and a publication titled "Staking Out the Oceans" published by TIME Educational Program, called the conference "a huge failure" in its attempt to set fair ground rules and equitably divide the riches of the ocean. [706]

John's writings of January 1975, within months of the Caracas session, complemented Pardo's words and the UN's intentions but, in addition, espoused the Earth Rights concept, as applied to the sea. "Since vast regions of the Sea had not been assigned as the property of any one nation-state, or combination of states, it [the sea] offered a special opportunity for Earth Right claims in behalf of the true owners," which, John meant to be all people of the world. As a result of discussions with delegates at the UN Conference on Raw Materials and Development in April 1974, the Earth Society created a subsidiary Sea Citizen Organization in December 1974 "to claim these rights for all who will register as Sea Citizens." [707]

John's idea to solicit registration in a privately run organization was a departure from his Earth Rights campaign, which suggested, and would have relied on, United Nations actions to implement. Rather, to counter the nationalistic mindset prevalent at the time, John envisioned the Sea Citizen Organization would "seek to register the poor, both in this and other countries, obtain for them dividends from their ownership of the Sea, and describe the responsibilities inherent in ownership."

He imagined a Sea Heritage Trust Fund that would "come from individuals and institutions interested in perpetuating the life and bounty of the Sea." This trust fund would "seek and accept royalties from Sea ventures that acknowledge Sea Citizens' claims and distribute them equally to all registered Sea Citizens." John saw that royalties would be paid "gladly" by

---

704 Russell W. Peterson, "Man and the Oceans: A Declaration of Interdependence," speech, 20 March 1973.

705 Brian J. Brown, "Staking Out the Oceans: Who Owns What," TIME Education Program, The Classroom Service of TIME, The Weekly Newsmagazine, 1956.

706 Ibid.

707 John McConnell, "The Care and Management of Planet Earth: a practical approach to our global crisis," 25 January 1975.

"corporations and governments interested in long-term exploitation ... as they come to understand the great advantage of ... a program effectively working for uniform rules and regulations to maintain and increase the life and wealth of the Sea." [708] This concept of companies paying royalties had precedent. "A disbursement of royalty payments is common practice for the leasing of oil fields and other [land-based] ventures," John pointed out. [709]

John wanted to run advertisements in leading newspapers "to tell people what is happening to their property." While a full-page ad in *The New York Times* would have cost $11,000, John assumed "thousands of people will respond to its message." [710] Having put together a letter requesting funds, he hoped for initial support from a few individuals and governments then, later, from an international authority – theoretically, the United Nations. [711]

As John communicated with various people, he received donations, generally $10.00, from Sea Citizen registrants. He also received advice, some of which conflicted with his idea. Astronomer Carl Sagan, for example, wrote to John in July 1974, "I do not think a full page ad in the NY Times is the most efficient investment of $11,000 for your purposes. For $11,000 you could finance two years of graduate education of a lawyer or ecologist or oceanographer who could devote his life to preventing the vandalizing of the oceans." [712]

Many letters, in reply to John's requests, conveyed the sender's choice to decline participation, either financial or temporal, due to desire to study the issue further, employment within a related government agency, involvement with other interests, or simply busyness. Paul Moore, the Episcopalian bishop of New York, for example, wrote, "Whatever impact I might have will be blunted if I am identified with too many reform efforts, however earnest and worthy." [713] John Gardner of Common Cause penned, "My name has appeared as sponsor of so many worthwhile activities that my associates have asked me to cut down the number – and I am trying to do so." [714]

708 Ibid.

709 John McConnell, "Sea Citizen campaign launched," news release 10 December 1974.

710 John McConnell, form letter to contributors, 16 July 1974.

711 John McConnell, "The Sea... some thoughts on its future," Sea Citizen brochure.

712 Carl Sagan, letter to John McConnell, 31 July 1974.

713 Paul Moore, letter to John McConnell, 23 October 1974.

714 John Gardner, letter to John McConnell, 22 July 1974.

And adventurer Lowell Thomas replied with one sentence, "Your letter and enclosures came just as I am taking off on another long journey abroad." [715]

At the same time, people who sent money included the names of others for John to contact. In a letter dated 22 July 1974, Mark Hatfield confirmed his recent telephone conversation "in which I indicated that you may use my name in promoting the Sea Citizen program as you see fit." [716] Folksinger Pete Seeger simply penned, "Dear John, you can count on me." [717] And Margaret Mead spoke on behalf of Sea Citizens at the 1975 Earth Day celebration at the UN.

The large volume of correspondence John mailed to earn support, whether verbal or financial, reminded him that grandiose plans required magnanimous funding. "It takes money and staff," [718] he said. And often, the money was not there – for neither expensive newspaper ads nor for salaries.

Yet staff continued to work without pay. The Earth Society newsletter for December 1974, which Anna wrote in the style of personal correspondence, contained a special plea for money to be given to "two young men who have worked without salary in years past on Earth Day [and are] willing to help us this year. However, they need salary. Tom Dowd has a 2 year old boy and since his wife is no longer teaching must have a salary. Bob Rosensweet … and his wife need funds to sustain them, also." [719]

In spite of this financial situation, John was excessively optimistic. "There's nothing wrong with a little idealism. After all, the founding fathers had a little when they wrote the Constitution. Their ideals seem to have been an improvement over the forms of government that existed in 1776," John stated in an interview about Sea Citizens. Then he added, "Of course, ideals mean nothing when they are just dreams. In the case of the oceans, some good men in the United Nations convinced some hard-headed politicians several years ago that they should declare the seabed the common heritage of all mankind. From the idea of the common heritage of the seabed's bounty, it is only a small practical step to saying that each individual on Earth has a

---

715 Lowell Thomas, letter to John McConnell, 7 October 1974.
716 Mark Hatfield, letter to John McConnell, 22 July 1974.
717 Pete Seeger, postcard to John McConnell, 10 January 1975.
718 John McConnell, interview by author, Denver, Colorado, August 2004.
719 Earth Society newsletter, March 1975.

right to some actual share of the wealth derived from the oceans." [720]

With his inherent idealism and enthusiasm, John persisted with ideas for an ocean management program that would "require a grand alliance of scientists, governments and industry." He envisioned that environmentalists and oceanographers would "provide the guidelines and basis for regulations" that would be enforced by governments through an International Sea Authority. He called for industry to "carefully divide and organize the work, [using] their best management skills. ... But best of all," John wrote, "involving people directly as individuals in a new relationship with the Sea, giving to its care and receiving its bounty, can assure public support and provide real protection and cautious harvesting and management of the Sea. This will be the task of Sea Citizens." [721]

While John sought grassroots support, he envisioned "recruiting individuals from international institutions, representing science, art, culture, religion, economics and business management." He sought participation in the U.S. Congress, the United Nations, environmental organizations and multinational corporations. "They, along with all of us, have much to gain," John wrote. [722]

He announced his Sea Citizen campaign on Tuesday, 10 December 1974, at both the UN and within the U.S. government. [723] At the UN Plaza, John hosted a press conference that featured a performance by singer Don McLean [724] and the presentation of the first Sea Citizen certificate to Lauren Ganz, a twelve-year-old science student at the United Nations International School. [725] On the same day, Mark Hatfield told the U.S. Senate, "The Sea Citizen Organization is the affirmation that the world ocean is the common heritage of mankind, not the special providence of coastal nations or those business enterprises most technologically able to exploit the resources of the sea. The Sea Citizen Organization," Hatfield said, "will ensure the access of

---

720 John McConnell, "The Sea... some thoughts on its future," Sea Citizen brochure.

721 John McConnell, "The Care and Management of Planet Earth: a practical approach to our global crisis," 25 January 1975.

722 John McConnell, "The Care and Management of Planet Earth," May 1975.

723 "'Sea Citizens' Campaign Is Launched," *Journal of Commerce*, 12 December 1974.

724 "A campaign to begin registration of Sea Citizens to protect the Global Sea," flyer, Earth Society, December 1974.

725 *Delegates World Bulletin*, 13 January 1975.

future generations to the bounties of the sea."[726]

While crediting John McConnell as the founder of Earth Day to his audience of political peers, which presumably included Gaylord Nelson, Hatfield quoted Norwegian explorer Thor Heyerdahl, who had testified earlier before the U.S. Senate Commerce Committee, "The world ocean ... is a large sink with no drain. Into the sink flows most of the world's pollution, and none of it leaves. It only swirls around with the ocean currents that ultimately distribute it to all reaches of the global sea."[727]

Hatfield announced to his fellow senators the names of the Sea Citizen Organizing Committee: John McConnell; Arvid M. Pardo; Harold Taylor, former president of Sarah Lawrence College and chairman of the U.S. Committee for the United Nations University; Frank O. Braynard; Louise Eggleston, former president of the International Literacy Foundation; and himself. Voicing no objection to his motion, the Senate agreed to print the Sea Citizen Declaration, written by the Sea Citizen Organizing Committee, into the Congressional Record.[728]

Hatfield's comments were consistent with earlier legislation, specifically Senate Resolution 222, that the Senate adopted on 19 February 1974. That legislation authorized the Commerce Committee "to undertake a comprehensive analysis of national ocean policy and Federal ocean programs." Focusing on "both legislative and executive approaches to ocean policy, [the study was] to identify ocean issues and raise them to a higher level." But perhaps because the policy study lacked a specific schedule,[729] Hatfield hoped his comments about the Sea Citizen campaign would heighten discussion among his colleagues.

Buoyed by this support from Hatfield, Pardo and others, John took the Sea Citizen message to the third session of UNCLOS III in Geneva, Switzerland, in 1975. Because the Earth Society was not registered with the UN as a non-governmental organization at that time, John attended as a delegate of the International Movement for Fraternal Union among Races and Peoples.[730] Yet, John spoke as Earth Society president and Sea Citizen

---

726 *Congressional Record*, 93rd Cong., 2nd sess., 10 December 1974, Vol. 120, No. 171.
727 Ibid.
728 Ibid.
729 *Senate National Ocean Policy Study*, post 19 February 1974.
730 "List of interested non-governmental organizations having consultative status with

advocate to many of the 5,000 attendees. Among them were Alfred van der Essen, chairman of the Belgian delegation, who became the first conference delegate to register his name as a Sea Citizen; Henrik Beer, secretary-general of the International Red Cross; and Hassan Ahmed, legal advisor to the UN Environment Programme. [731]

John attended this conference because of donations from people whom Anna described in the March 1975 Earth Society newsletter as "two praying members who sent John a total of $625, which enabled him to obtain a round-trip ticket, plus have approximately $150 for expenses. ... He left in faith that our Lord will supply his needs for the four to five weeks that he will remain at the Conference." Because the Earth Society was not yet an official nonprofit organization, the newsletter asked for additional donations to be sent to The Cathedral of St. John the Divine, where John's office was at that time, along with "a note stating that the contribution is to help finance Mr. McConnell's trip." [732]

This conference began on 17 March, four days prior to the fifth Earth Day. To benefit from that connection, John proposed the Earth Day theme should be "Share the Sea." He encouraged Earth Society members to enlist "ships around the world to join the celebration."

Acknowledging the Sea Citizen campaign as a tall order, especially for a newly formed organization with a minimal staff of volunteers, John persisted in his belief, "Yesterday's impossible stories are today's headlines: 'Man on Moon,' 'President Resigns,' etc." He suggested, "The following headlines are not impossible dreams for tomorrow: 'Japan Approves Sea Citizen Claims,' 'India Helps Register Sea Citizens in Bangladesh,' 'IBM Data Bank to Serve Sea Citizen Information Center,' 'HEW Computerizes Sea Citizen Dividends,' '*QE2* Joins Sea Citizen Fleet,' 'New York Times Advertising Converted to Earth Care Catalogue.'"

"Our planet is dying," he postulated. "The patient is weak, dirty, but still beautiful. Man has the scientific knowledge to save her. It was his unknowing

---

the Economic and Social Council, Addendum," United Nations, 17 April 1975. (John McConnell's name is handwritten as a delegate of the International Movement for Fraternal Union among Races and Peoples.)

[731] John McConnell, "Sea Citizen Idea Wins Support at Law of Sea Conference," news release, Earth Society, 9 May 1975.

[732] Earth Society newsletter, March 1975.

neglect and estrangement that brought her to death's door. Will he be moved by new appreciation and love to act in time?" John didn't offer his answer. Rather, he simply stated, "You will decide …" [733]

[733] John McConnell, "The Care and Management of Planet Earth," May 1975.

19

Earth Society Foundation

(1976 to present)

> *The Earth Society Foundation is a facilitating organization. It seeks to stimulate governments, communities and individuals to pursue their own appropriate methods and programs ... of Earth Care.*
> – "Earth Society Foundation Fact Sheet"

WITH MOMENTUM from the Comet Kohoutek cruises and the Sea Citizen campaign, John McConnell saw the benefit of surrounding himself with like-minded influential people. Margaret Mead, who was concerned that he worked solo too much, [734] agreed. Seeing John's perennial lack of funds, she told him the Earth Society needed tax exempt status, as defined by U.S. law, in order to accept charitable donations. John followed her advice and established the Earth Society Foundation (ESF) as a 501(c)(3) nonprofit corporation in the State of New York in January 1976. The initial directors did not include Mead, as many people have since stated, but were John McConnell, Frank O. Braynard, and Anthony Q. Keasbey, who was a teacher, sailor and volunteer tour guide at The Cathedral of St. John the Divine. [735]

John accepted Mead's advice, in part, because he liked her practice of not using the article "the" prior to the proper noun "Earth," as was common practice. "She reminded us that planet Earth isn't just something removed

---

[734] Helen Garland, telephone interview by author, 29 September 2005.

[735] *Certificate of Incorporation of The Earth Society Foundation, Inc.*, 1976.

from us, but it is our nest in the stars with its wonderful web of life on which we all depend." he said. [736]

Likewise, Mead expressed her belief in John's global vision. "John is the only person I know who thinks of planet Earth as a whole," Mead told Anna McConnell in one of their early encounters. [737] Mead expressed her dedication to John's cause when she wrote in 1977, "Earth Day at the March Equinox will be the universal planetary celebration, inaugurating a season of environmental activity culminating in UNEP's World Environment Day [5 June], during which such local or single events as Sun Day [circa 3 May] and Earth Week [circa 22 April] can be fitted in." [738]

Margaret Mead joined the ESF board of directors in September 1976 [739] and rang the Peace Bell for the Earth Day ceremonies in 1977 and 1978, making her one of only two people to ring the bell twice on the vernal equinox. [740] Mead was chairperson for the Earth Day ceremonies in those years, attracting notable persons to serve on the American Committee for Earth Day in 1977 [741] and formal support from thirty-three Nobel Laureates, [742] some of whom wrote eloquent endorsements. [743]

In Mead's 1978 Earth Day speech, she said, "Earth Day is the first holy day that transcends all national boundaries, yet preserves all geographic integrities, spans mountains and oceans and time belts and is devoted to the preservation of the harmony of nature and yet draws upon the triumphs of technology. Earth Day draws upon an astronomical phenomenon in a new way – which is also the most ancient way – using the Vernal Equinox, when the sun crosses the Equator, making night and day of equal length in all parts of the Earth. Earth Day begins with the striking of the Peace Bell at the United Nations, joined by gongs and bells ringing around the world. The

---

736 John McConnell, interview by author, Denver, Colorado, August 2004.

737 Anna McConnell, telephone interview by author, 25 July 2005.

738 Margaret Mead, letter to Mr. and Mrs. A. Maitland Edey, 22 December 1977.

739 Margaret Mead, letter to John McConnell, 7 September 1976.

740 Robert Muller also rang the Peace Bell twice at Earth Day ceremonies in 1985 and 1986.

741 "Members of the International Committee for Earth Day, 1977," Earth Society Foundation, 1977.

742 "Earth Day International and the Earth Society Foundation," historical summary, Earth Society Foundation.

743 "Statements of Support from Nobel Laureates," Earth Society Foundation.

celebration offends no historical calendar, yet it transcends them all." [744]

American Committee for Earth Day 1977

Georgia State Senator, Julian Bond; Professor Rene J. Dubos of Rockefeller University; Dr. Paul R. Ehrlich of Stanford University; Dr. Luther H. Evans, former Librarian of Congress; United States Senator Mark Hatfield of Oregon; Professor Patrick Horsbrugh of Notre Dame University; Dr. Richard H. Pough, President of the Natural Area Council, Inc.; Dr. Carl Sagan of Cornell University; Dr. David R. Brower, President and Founder of the Friends of the Earth; Stewart Brand, former publisher of Whole Earth Catalogue; R. Buckminster Fuller, design scientist, Frank O. Braynard, director of Operation Sail 1976 and New York Chairman for Earth Day 1977; and Margaret Mead, International Earth Day Chairwoman.

Nobel Laureates who supported the Earth Society Foundation

Oscar Arias, Julius Axelrod, Walter R. Brattain, Leon N. Cooper, Carl F. Cori, Sir J. W. Cornforth, Francis Crick, Christian De Duve, Werner Forssman, Murray Gell-Mann, D. A. Glaser, Ragnat Granit, H. Keffer Hartline, Odd Hassell, B. D. Josephson, Alfred Kastler, Arthur Kornberg, Hans Krebs, Wassily Leontief, Salvador E. Luria, Edwin M. McMillan, Rigoberta Menchu, Eugenio Montale, William P. Murphy, Philip Noel-Baker, Max F. Perutz, James Rainwater, Burton Richter, William H. Stein, Albert Szent-Gyorgyi, Harold C. Urey, Ulf von Euler, George Wald, James D. Watson, Patrick White

Helen Garland, an activist who appreciated the progressive politics of Eleanor Roosevelt and John F. Kennedy, was another influence on John at that time. Garland initially went to Earth Society Foundation meetings on Mead's behalf when the anthropologist was not able to attend. "I was the go-between with her and all the positive moves," Garland said. Of John, she commented, "He had this spiritual vision … and everybody admired that. No matter who he spoke to, whether the NGOs or the astronauts, that was

[744] Margaret Mead, speech, Earth Day, 20 March 1978.

always his focus."

Garland served ESF in various ways, including stints as board chairperson, for more than thirty years. During that time, she demonstrated her advocacy for international cooperation with the United Nations and her skepticism of people who, she felt, falsely presented themselves as environmentalists. [745]

Other supporters included UN Under-Secretary-General C. V. Narasimhan, Robert Muller, and several influential people who were active in the arena of environmental improvement, social justice and cultural change. Among these were Saudi Arabian ambassador Jamil Baroody, U.S. ambassador Allard Lowenstein, Bill Johnson of the New York City Federation of Block Associations, actress Gloria Swanson, inventor and humanitarian Harold Bostrom, civil rights activist the Rev. Sloane Coffin, and president of the Council on Religion and International Affairs Philip A. Johnson.

Another rising figure on the environmental scene was Claes Nobel, a great grand nephew of Alfred Bernhard Nobel who had established the Nobel Prizes in 1901. Claes Nobel was an environmentalist, humanitarian and businessman in his own right. He championed social and environmental corporate practices and drafted "The Nobel Laureates Declaration on the Survival of Mankind" in 1974, which was signed by seventy-eight Nobel Laureates. On 13 March 1975, he incorporated the Earth Aid Society (EAS) in the State of Wisconsin.

The Earth Aid Society's purpose was "promotion of study, research and public education in ecology and other natural sciences relating to man and his relationship to and preservation of his environment; and the support, both economically and administratively, of existing organizations ..." created for the same cause. [746] EAS promoted itself as "an organization of concerned people, like yourself, dedicated to inform all mankind of the fragility of the life support systems of our Only Earth and the necessity of developing and maintaining equilibrium between man and nature." Its board of directors included top ranking officers in The International Oceanographic Society, National Audubon Society, National Wildlife Federation, The Wilderness Society, World Wildlife Fund, and The Nobel Foundation. [747]

---

[745] Helen Garland, telephone interview by author, 29 September 2005.

[746] *Earth Aid society, Inc. Articles of Incorporation,* State of Wisconsin, 25 February 1975.

[747] "Earth Aid Society, Equilibrium between Man & Nature," brochure, Earth Aid

In June 1977, Harold Oram was doing public relations work for Earth Day when he arranged for John and Nobel to be introduced. This resulted in a three-day meeting that John described as "an exciting time, discovering our common goals and parallel efforts in reaching for them." [748] This discussion led to a six-hour conference of the two organizations' boards of directors at The Cathedral of St. John the Divine in New York City only one month later. And that resulted in a joint resolution to merge organizations under the name Earth Aid Society, thus foregoing the Earth Society Foundation appellation. [749]

Nobel documented his enthusiasm in a letter to John on 15 June 1977, writing, "It is always a very good feeling to get to know fellow crusaders who dedicatedly and unselfishly are working for the most critical issues that ever have faced Mankind, that is, our very own Survival." [750] And to a colleague, Nobel wrote, "This accomplishment is most pleasing to me and will greatly strengthen the mutual performance and programs of the two organizations." [751] ESF and EAS agreed to work together "to establish and promote the Earth Care Ethic" [752] through Earth Day (with the words being combined to form "EARTHDAY"), establishment of EARTHDAY Awards, and creation of an EARTHDAY Almanac. [753]

EARTHDAY was to continue on the vernal equinox. The EARTHDAY Awards were to be modeled after the prizes given by the Nobel Foundation with annual awards of $5 million that would require a capital endowment fund of over $100 million. [754] The EARTHDAY Almanac was to be "an annual yearbook citing progress and deterioration in the fields affecting Mankind's Future." Information was to be gathered from multiple established sources and compiled into what was hoped to be "an annual best-seller, …

Society.

[748] John McConnell, letter to Claes Nobel, 15 June 1977.

[749] "Merger Resolution," Earth Society Foundation and Earth Aid Society, 18 July 1977.

[750] Claes Nobel, letter to John McConnell 15 June 1977.

[751] Claes Nobel, letter to Matthew Rosenhaus, 22 November 1977.

[752] "Merger Resolution," Earth Society Foundation and Earth Aid Society, 18 July 1977.

[753] Margaret Mead, Claes Nobel, Patrick Horsbrugh, "Meeting Minutes," 25 June 1977.

[754] Earth Society Foundation and Earth Aid Society, "Meeting Minutes," 15 August 1977.

its words and advice will be recognized and followed by the laymen and decision makers of Earth." [755]

While this merger appeared to be a blessing for both organizations, two early indicators surfaced within the prenuptial period that may have led to a failure to sign the accord. One indicator was John's unwillingness to forfeit control of his organization, a sentiment he subtly indicated in his initial correspondence to Nobel in June 1977. "It is my feeling that our basic values and purposes are so deeply in accord that we can join forces without inhibiting the freedom to each act in our own unique way in supporting them," he wrote. [756] Years later, in a general statement about partnerships, John echoed his innate autonomy. "Once in a blue moon, you get a group of people who are really in tune, who are fully supportive of the idea of a united way. But most of the time, you're putting up with differences," he said. [757] The second indicator was the newness of both organizations and their dependence upon volunteers, who, as Nobel wrote in November 1977, would employ an arduous task of "face-to-face contact … in the solicitation of membership." [758] Plus, both organizations lacked money. [759]

Yet, hope and determination reigned. The boards of directors planned fundraising events in New York and Wisconsin for the fall of 1977. [760] John began to use EAS letterhead and business cards before the merger was confirmed, even to promote Earth Day. And in a letter dated 30 July 1977, Nobel wrote to his imminent partner, "John, we are taking on an enormous assignment. With perseverance and faith, we shall achieve!" [761]

In October 1977, Harold Bostrom, who gained fame for his invention of the hydraulic seat for highway trucks and farm tractors as well as his personal campaign to stem the world's rising population, reported that an EAS article in *The New York Times* had overwhelmed his office with supportive correspondence. He recommended volunteers be enlisted through the efforts of John McConnell, who would contact Protestant churches; University of

755 Claes Nobel, letter to Rene J. Dubos, 25 July 1977.
756 John McConnell, letter to Claes Nobel, 15 June 1977.
757 John McConnell, interview by author, Denver, Colorado, August 2004.
758 Claes Nobel, letter to Matthew Rosenhaus, 22 November 1977.
759 Ibid.
760 Earth Society Foundation and Earth Aid Society, "Meeting Minutes," 15 August 1977.
761 Claes Nobel, letter to John McConnell, 30 July 1977.

Notre Dame professor Patrick Horsbrugh, who would garner effort and support from students and wealthy parents; Fred Burrous, who would make media contact; Robert Muller, who would use his position at the UN to assemble a global assessment of population management; and a task force of people in developing countries, especially India. [762]

Bostrom was a frequent financial contributor to John's efforts and was instrumental in organizing an EAS conference in New York City that included John McConnell, Claes Nobel and Margaret Mead. He introduced John to K. V. Sundaram of India who, years later, drew upon inspiration from John to direct the Bhoovigyan Vikas Foundation, of which he was chair, to "awaken the Indian society to the need for protecting the Earth." [763]

The merger between ESF and EAS didn't happen, however. Its demise came as a result of a dinner, attended by nearly fifty people in New York City in December 1977, that Bostrom arranged as part of the organizations' campaign to raise $200,000. Nobel had told Bostrom he would make the first donation, in the amount of $5,000, and Bostrom passed that good news on to Mead. "He made his pledge, but afterward he told us that he had no intention to donate the money," John reported. "He said he did that to get others to donate. Margaret Mead was furious. Nobel locked horns with the wrong person. She told me, 'Get rid of him. Don't have anything to do with that man.'" [764]

At that time, Margaret Mead had contracted pancreatic cancer, and she died a year later on 15 November 1978. In 1979, she posthumously received the Presidential Medal of Freedom, the United States' highest civilian honor. Like the rest of the world, John McConnell felt her loss deeply. "Margaret Mead was going all out and devoting effort to make Earth Day a success," John recalled. "She was a dynamo. I believe without any question, if Margaret Mead had lived, the Earth Society Foundation would have had a better structure and a million dollars." [765]

Five days after Mead died, her friends paid a tribute to her in the Japanese Peace Garden at the United Nations. Mead's protégé, Jean Houston,

---

[762] Harold W. Bostrom, letter to Fred Armstrong, 11 October 1977.

[763] K. V. Sundaram, e-mail to John McConnell, April 2001.

[764] John and Anna McConnell, manuscript review with author, Denver, Colorado, October 2005.

[765] John McConnell, interview by author, Denver, Colorado, August 2004.

a scholar and researcher on human capacities, spoke of Mead's philosophies, which paralleled John McConnell's, saying, "[Mead] was proud to be made chairman of Earth Day." [766] Secretary-General Kurt Waldheim stated, "As a great anthropologist, she knew the importance of symbolism for the Earth community and summoned support on such occasions as Earth Day, World Environment Day and United Nations Day." [767] Robert Muller added, "Seldom has anyone cared so much for our planet." [768] And when John McConnell spoke at the ceremony, he complimented Mead's "inner fire and brilliant intellect ... combined with intuition." Then, he iterated her wish "that Earth Day goes around the world." [769] The program included ringing of the Peace Bell and a recording of Margaret Mead's Earth Day speech in 1977 in which she said, "I have lived long enough ... to know that we have only one Earth and ... all the people ... are one species. ... Earth Day is ... the first completely international holiday that the world has ever known." [770]

Throughout the following years, the Earth Society Foundation proved to be both a bane and a blessing to John and Anna McConnell – as well as to some of their banner carriers. Motivated by desire and generally consisting of well-intentioned people, the board grasped opportunities and created accomplishments while hampering itself with internal strife and personality conflicts.

Typically, board meetings began with a prayer, led by John. Anna brought cookies that she had baked, and others provided tea and coffee. Financial reports ranged from "we have enough to pay our bills" to "we have a minimal amount – less than $50 – in our checking account." [771] John contributed to these conditions with his penchant to be in charge.

Michael Geoghegan, an economist and development consultant at the

---

[766] Jean Houston, speech, Margaret Mead memorial ceremony, United Nations, 20 November 1978.

[767] Kurt Waldheim, speech, Margaret Mead memorial ceremony, United Nations, 20 November 1978.

[768] Robert Muller, speech, Margaret Mead memorial ceremony, United Nations, 20 November 1978.

[769] John McConnell, speech, Margaret Mead memorial ceremony, United Nations, 20 November 1978.

[770] Margaret Mead, speech, Earth Day, 20 March 1977.

[771] Earth Society Foundations, "Meeting Minutes."

United Nations and who served as ESF chair, confirmed John's impact on the board. "John was very, very strong willed," Geoghegan said. "He got his way by preaching, but he was always intact with his integrity and with his ideals. He preached good things for humanity." [772]

John's and ESF's actions were best summarized in a Feasibility Study of Fund-Raising Potential that the Earth Society Foundation contracted with PACE Consulting Service in late 1980. PACE's report consisted of thirty-one questions posed to thirty-seven people, the majority of whom knew John McConnell and were aware of, or associated with, ESF. These respondents advised the board to control John McConnell so he wouldn't engage in "tangents that could diminish the organization's purpose." PACE told the board to reorganize itself and to accept only board members who would make a significant annual financial contribution. Survey questions pertaining to Earth Day elicited answers that ranged from "poorly organized" and "ineffective" to "worthwhile," "positive," "symbolic environmentalism," and "a good thing to be promoted." [773]

The board and John chose not to act in accordance with PACE's recommendations, and fractionation continued. Annual budgets showed rosy black predictions, but year-end financial reports conveyed the reality of red five-digit deficits. Board member Hannah Wasserman wrote to John on 24 November 1980, "We, the Board, must take a much more active role in the functioning of the Society. We have been remiss in determining policy, keeping up with the day-to-day activities of the Society, and even in overseeing the collection and disbursement of funds." [774]

About the same time, new key people entered the organization. Following her husband John Drysdale, who joined ESF in 1978, Mary Carlin became an active volunteer in 1980. "I would tag along with John McConnell as he moved through the UN, passing out materials," Carlin said. "It was intriguing just to be a part of it." [775] Carlin's enthusiasm helped her rise to the position of ESF executive assistant and to serve as perennial secretary and treasurer. As a writer, photographer and United Nations journalist, Carlin promoted ESF through public speaking engagements and at conferences and

772 Michael Geoghegan, interview by author, New York, New York, 19 March 2005.

773 PACE Consulting Service, "Earth Society Foundation Feasibility Study, 1980-81.

774 Hannah Durlach Wasserman, letter to John McConnell, 24 November 1980.

775 Mary Carlin, interview by author, New York, New York, 3 February 2006.

seminars. Each year, she sent Earth Day notices to local and national network media with the notation, "Radio and television are requested to provide live coverage." [776] While this invitation was usually honored only by New York media, if at all, feature newsman Charles Kuralt carried the ceremony on the *CBS Sunday Morning* show in 1988. [777]

Throughout the 1980s, John persisted in his attempts to convey his spiritual approach to world peace. He wrote letters to business people, government officials in many countries, and ambassadors at the United Nations to promote an "Earth Line" telephone service through which callers could hear comments on peace and environmental progress by world leaders. [778] He initiated an "Earth Bounty" program and developed new ways to promote previous endeavors. [779]

In the mid to late 1980s, the ESF board sought to better involve their inner core of members, improve their relations with the United Nations, increase Earth Flag sales, and resurrect the Star of Hope concept by means of one million one dollar donations. Minutes of an ESF board meeting on 16 September 1986 noted, "Many of the new ideas currently getting attention are actually spin-offs from seeds he [John McConnell] planted in the '70s, such as 'Minute for Peace,' which led to Million Minutes for Peace, World Peace Day, etc." The minutes expressed the board's desire that the Earth Society Foundation "be the catalyst that will further all these other activities." [780]

To that end, in 1990, ESF established the Earth Trustee Environmental Award, which they gave at Earth Day ceremonies to individuals and organizations. The decision to grant awards to few corporations, and only those with sound environmental practices, displayed a philosophical distinction between ESF and Earth Day USA, an organization that Gaylord Nelson and environmental business consultant Bruce Anderson founded in the mid-1990s to promote the 1995 April 22 "Earth Day." Environmental magazines, such as *Outside* – and even Denis Hayes – ripped Earth Day USA

---

776 Ibid.

777 Earth Society Foundation, "Meeting Minutes," 23 March 1988.

778 John McConnell, "Dial 900 Earth Line 'Hope' Network," newsletter, 26 January 1986.

779 John McConnell, "Earth Bounty Program."

780 Earth Society Foundation, "Meeting Minutes," 16 September 1988.

for selling its logo, at $30,000 per donation, to corporations ranked among the world's major polluters. [781]

Earth Trustee Environmental Award recipients

1990: Greenpeace International, for environmental activism; Clean Air Technologies International, Inc., for developing a catalytic converter to reduce diesel pollution; William Dean Kilpatrick, sculptor, for creating the Earth Day Sculpture.

1991: Lou Gold, founding member of Siskiyou Project, for saving the Klamath-Siskiyou old-growth forests of Oregon and California; Gary Null, health activist and nutrition expert (honorary award); Paul McRae, Canadian Parliamentarian, for working for rights of native Intuits.

1992: Al Gore, U. S. Vice-President, for authoring *Earth in the Balance* (honorary award); David Depner, Trees for the Future, for thirty years of tree planting; Fred Burrous, for Young Earth Trustees; Glen and Mildred Leet, founders of the Trickle Up Programme.

1993: Rigoberta Menchu, Guatemalan Nobel Prize Laureate, working on indigenous rights.

1994: Bianca Jagger, human rights activist; Dr. Arvid M. Pardo, for the International "Law of the Sea" (honorary award).

1995: American Chestnut Foundation, for restoring native chestnuts; Robin Hood Oak Society, for micro propagation of Sherwood Forest oak trees, Nottingham, U.K.

1996: Vito Mazza, Hunger Relief Project, for providing relief aid and supplies worldwide; Rainforest Alliance, for saving rainforests; Herbert Johnson, botanist, for plant identification at Gateway National Recreation Area, New York (posthumous award); Lisa Henry MacNaughten, artist, for creating "One Heart" endangered species poster.

1997: Abolition 2000, peace and nuclear disarmament activists; Dr. Helen Caldicott, Australian activist, for promoting nuclear

---

[781] Bill Gifford. April 1995. *Environment: No, Uh, Cooperation in Defense of Mother Earth* [online]. Outside (magazine) online [cited 1 February 2006]. Available from outside.away.com/outside/magazine/0495/4di_envr.html. Also, *A Corporate History of Earth Day* [online]. Also, The Green Life [cited 1 February 2006]. Available from www.thegreenlife.org/earthdayhistory.html.

safety; David Horowitz, UN journalist, for 50 years of reporting; Dr. Anitra Thorhaug, marine biologist, for coastal ecosystem restoration; Aveda Corporation, manufacturers and distributors of cosmetic products that use plant-derived ingredients; Healthy Properties, New York, for employing "green building" technologies.

1998: Island Expeditions, Bahamian adventure company, for ecology and marine studies; *The Huntsville Times*, Alabama newspaper, for coverage of environmental issues; Father Thomas Kocherry, India, for organizing fishers and harvesters; Wyland, marine artist and educator, for using art to teach children about marine ecology; Ocean Arks International, U.S. company, for producing ecological wastewater treatment systems.

1999: Thor Hyerdahl, Norwegian explorer and author (honorary award); Special Eyes on the Environment, New Jersey, for helping disabled persons photograph the environment; Alexandra de Nigris, student from Bethel, Connecticut, an "Earth Trustee Town"; Richard Pough, co-founder of The Nature Conservancy; Captain Paul Watson, founder of Sea Shepherd Conservation Society; Startech Environmental Corp., Connecticut, for using plasma technology to process hazardous waste; Captain Grigory Pasko, Russian military journalist, for exposing nuclear waste dumping; Vortec Corporation, Pennsylvania, for research to reduce nuclear waste; Lama Gangchen, Tibetan healer and teacher and founder of the World Peace Foundation.

2000: Dr. W. C. Swanson Family Foundation, Utah, for working on children's health issues; Jeff Hornacek, environmental film producer, for working to save gray whales in Mexico; Judy Mitoma, director of the University of California, Los Angeles, Center for Intercultural Performance, for directing the World Festival of Sacred Music; Roko and Adrian Belic, filmmakers, for the movie *Genghis Blues* about blind blues musicians; Cheryl Magill, for studies regarding sonar and marine life; Lorna Salzman, environmental activist, writer and lecturer on food safety, for working to ban genetically modified food; Fina Oil and Chemical Corporation, Texas, for marine restoration.

2001: Dr. Helena Benitez, Philippines environmentalist; Dr. Birute

Galdikas, for working with orangutans; Findhorn Foundation, Scottish educational group and founder of the Global Ecovillage Network; Dr. Harold Wanless, Florida marine geologist, for working to restore the Everglades; Dr. Jackie Giuliano, Washington State University professor and author of *Healing our World*.

2002: Nane Annan, author, children's advocate and wife of UN Secretary-General Kofi Annan; Lisbet Palme, the Swedish Committee for UNICEF and wife of late Prime Minister Olof Palme; Norwegian Nobel Committee and Nobel Foundation, on the 100th anniversary of the Nobel Peace Prize; Goran Ohlin, Swedish economist and UN Assistant Secretary-General (posthumous award); Dag Hammarskjöld, UN Secretary-General (posthumous award). Linz-Pichling, Austria, for being a "Solar City" (special mention); Gary Braasch of Blue Earth Alliance, photographer, for documenting global climate change.

2003: Christopher Swain, swimmer, for promoting cleanup of the Columbia River; Tom Louie, tribal elder of the Noisy Water People; Captain Peter Marston, Massachusetts educator and environmentalist, for involvement with the PBS' *Voyage of the Mimi*; Erin Brockovich and Ed Marsten, environmental activists, for working on clean water issues; Grandmothers' Circle, Connecticut peace group; Lydia Gumbs, Anguilla, West Indies, UN peace activist (posthumous award); Patrick Horsbrugh, founder of Environic Foundation; Valdas Adamkus, Lithuanian political and environmental leader.

2004: Lawrence Anthony, South Africa, for saving animals at the Baghdad Zoo; Peter Sis, Czechoslovakian artist, for creating *The Tree of Life*; Bill Yotive, project manager, UN Global Teaching and Learning Project, for CyberSchoolbus Internet program; Liu Qing, China, Water Kids Foundation, for working with youth on water education; Charles Moore, captain of the catamaran *Alguita*, and Hideshige Takada, environmental geochemist, Tokyo University, for alerting the public to the gyre of plastic in the North Pacific Ocean.

2005: Dr. Armando Barrionuevo, Honorary Ambassador for Cuzco, for Children's Earth Charter; Marcia Brewster, Task Manager of UN Interagency Task Force on Gender and Water;

> Margot Walstrom of Sweden, European Union's Environment Commissioner; Jose Ramos Horta, Timor L'Est, Nobel Peace Prize Laureate; Jan Egeland, UN Under-Secretary-General for Humanitarian Affairs, for 2004 tsunami relief; Wangari Maathai, Kenya, Nobel Peace Prize Laureate; Green Belt Movement, for planting trees in arid lands; Dennis Meadows, co-author of *Limits to Growth* (1972), *Beyond the Limits* (1992), and *Limits to Growth: The 30-Year Update.* [782]

In an attempt to gain operating capital, the Earth Society Foundation, in the early 1990s, entered into a morass of overlapping agreements for marketing and public relations services. The first was with Mobius Systems International, a firm owned by John Drysdale, to develop a suitable organizational identity. On 1 May 1991, the ESF board enlisted the services of JT Earth Day, Inc., to conduct fundraising campaigns. Six months later, on 7 November 1991, ESF expanded that agreement into a three-way contract by adding another firm, Earth Day Marketing, to publish, promote and sell fine art, posters and prints that celebrate Earth Day. In the interim, on 1 August 1991, ESF signed a similar agreement with EMMI, Inc., a company in California that specialized in creation, development and marketing of media events and products.

The board received pro bono financial and marketing assistance from Watermark Communications, Inc., which provided office space on Fifth Avenue and funding for Earth Day events. This arrangement came about because John McConnell walked into the firm and introduced himself as the man who started Earth Day. Charles Donnelly, Watermark's owner, said, "ESF was in dreadful financial condition. John was not reimbursed for his time as most people would expect to be, and it was as though he and Anna had taken a vow of poverty. Their goal was to save the planet and integrate society." [783] As a result, Kurt Koenig, Watermark's financial manager, became ESF's chief financial officer in the fall of 1992. [784]

---

[782] In 2005, the Earth Society Foundation consisted of two factions; one faction initiated a separate Earth Day award, named after Meadows' deceased wife, Donella Meadows. Dennis Meadows was the first recipient of this award.

[783] Charles Donnelly, telephone interview by author, 14 February 2006.

[784] Kurt Koenig, telephone interview by author, 28 December 2005.

New York businessman Dennis Dubin became involved at that time. Through personal gifts to John McConnell and donations he acquired from corporations such as TRW and RCA Telecom, he brought several thousand dollars into ESF. He also paid the expenses of Nobel Laureate Rigoberta Menchu to attend the Earth Day ceremony in 1993 and for John and Anna to travel from Denver to New York when John rang the Peace Bell in 2004. [785]

"Things were really popping at that time [in the early 1990s]," Anna recalled. "We had money coming in. And the people thought John's ideas were good. But by the mid-1990s, they seemed to support only John's idea of the Earth Day ceremony and not his other ideas for peace, justice and the care of Earth." [786]

Koenig's recollections complemented Anna's. "The Earth Society Foundation was fractious," he said. "Different parties were involved, all with different ideas and little unification. John, in his frustration with the society's inability to organize around a common purpose, entered into a lot of those arrangements [in 1991] on his own. That's why there was duplication of effort." That duplication created, as Koenig described, "Business deals that were distracting the society from its mission. People were trying to cash in and creating problems." [787]

Over the same period of years, the Earth Society Foundation experienced leadership challenges. In March 1990, ESF president Ed Brennan, who was president of Earth Flag Corporation and responsible for marketing Earth Flags, recommended that John McConnell, who was then 75, become chairman emeritus. Brennan suggested John assume an honorary "Father Figure" position that would "connote both symbolically and realistically his future role." [788] The board approved Brennan's recommendation. Then, in late 1991, the board challenged Brennan for marketing irregularities regarding the Earth Flag and for not renewing the flag's trademark. [789]

In addition, an embarrassing situation occurred when Brennan mailed a

---

[785] Dennis Dubin, e-mail to author, 19 January 2006.

[786] Anna McConnell, manuscript review with author, Denver, Colorado, October 2005.

[787] Kurt Koenig, telephone interview by author, 28 December 2005.

[788] Ed Brennan, memo to Earth Society Foundation board of directors, 29 March 1990.

[789] "Assessment of Ed Brennan record with ESF," Earth Society Foundation, 17 September 1991.

letter, not authorized by the board, [790] to Seminole Chief James Billy inviting him to ring the Peace Bell at the Earth Day ceremony in 1992. [791] Minutes of board meetings in that period indicated Chief Billy had been discussed as a potential candidate for that honor but no decision was made to extend the invitation. [792] Brennan resigned in the wake of those two events, but, interestingly, the board allowed him to continue marketing the Earth Flag. [793]

Leadership faux pas occurred in 1994 when pollster George Gallup, Jr., was nominated and elected to be ESF chairman of the board [794] and, again, in 1995 when Sir James Murray, a former British Consul General, was nominated and elected as president and chief executive officer [795] without either man's prior knowledge or approval. [796] [797]

Then, in the first years of the third millennium, two men, Tom Dowd and Stan Cohen, claimed to be ESF president. Both men had supporters, and both factions posted web sites: www.earthsocietyfoundation.org and www.earth-society.org. The former identified John McConnell and Margaret Mead as founders, [798] and the latter excluded John McConnell's name. [799]

On the positive side, a major accomplishment occurred on 2 July 1991 when the United Nations approved the Earth Society Foundation as a non-governmental organization of the UN Department of Public Information (DPI). This approval was in response to a request to become an NGO submitted by John McConnell, Helen Garland and Monica Getz, an international lecturer on human ecology and widow of jazz saxophonist Stan Getz, on 6 March. [800] The NGO status allowed ESF to designate one

---

[790] John McConnell and Gregory de Sousa, letter to Robb Tiller, Native American Save the Earth Festival '92, 3 September 1991.

[791] Ed Brennan, letter to Robb Tiller, 20 August 1991.

[792] Earth Society Foundation, "Meeting Minutes," various.

[793] Earth Society Foundation, "Meeting Minutes," 17 September 1991.

[794] *Earth Journal*, newsletter, Summer 1994, Earth Society Foundation.

[795] Earth Society Foundation, "Meeting Minutes," 18 September 1995.

[796] Earth Society Foundation newsletter editor, letter to members, Summer 1994.

[797] Hans Janitschek, letter to Earth Society Board of Directors, 15 September 1995.

[798] Earth Society Foundation [cited 25 February 2006]. Available from www.earthsocietyfoundation.org.

[799] Earth-Society.org [cited 8 October 2005]. Available from www.earth-society.org.

[800] Miss Oca, United Nations NGO Resource Center, telephone interview by author, 15 December 2005.

primary representative and one alternate representative to attend DPI/NGO weekly briefings as well as open meetings of the General Assembly, its committees, the Economic and Social Council (ECOSOC) and other bodies. In addition, ESF was allowed access to a wealth of information housed in the UN NGO Resource Centre. As an NGO, the Earth Society was expected, according to the UN letter of acceptance, "to increase public understanding of the principles, activities and achievements of the United Nations and its Agencies." [801]

In addition, in 2004, ESF attained "ECOSOC Special Consultative Status," a higher honor with a greater degree of privilege. [802] With ECOSOC status, the Earth Society Foundation was permitted to participate in, rather than merely attend, meetings of the Economic and Social Council, an important UN body that dealt with world social and economic issues relating to standards of living, health and human rights.

Late 1992 and 1993 brought more opportunities and accomplishments through the efforts of high-profile figures who became members of the Earth Society Foundation. These included publisher, editor and writer Ed Grosvenor, who, as John McConnell complimented, "did yeoman service for us 15 years ago," [803] career diplomat John McDonald, United Nations Assistant Secretary-General Robert Muller, and professor Timour Timofeyev of the Russian Academy of Sciences. These joined Anna McConnell, who was elected to the board for the first time; Helen Garland, who served as chair; Monica Getz as vice chair; Hans Janitschek as president and CEO; Kevin Sanders as vice-president; and Mary Carlin as secretary/treasurer.

Ann Charles learned about the Earth Society Foundation by writing an article about Earth Day and came to appreciate John McConnell's energy in front of a crowd, which she described as astounding. "That's when his greatness comes to the surface," she said. [804] In turn, Anna praised Charles for bringing Earth Day to the Baltic States of Latvia, Estonia and Lithuania. "She really worked to get those countries to celebrate Earth Day on the equinox," Anna said. [805]

---

801 United Nations, letter to Edward L. Brennan, president, ESF, 2 July 1991.

802 United Nations Reference Team, e-mail to author, 15 December 2005.

803 John McConnell, "Report from John McConnell," 8 December 1992.

804 Ann Charles, telephone interview by author, November 2004.

805 Anna McConnell, manuscript review with author, Denver, Colorado, January 2006.

The Earth Society Foundation also attracted people of environmental and scientific expertise. Notable among them was marine biologist Anitra Thorhaug. Based in Florida, Thorhaug was active in restoration of the Everglades and other coastal ecosystems, which involved planting sea grass, mangrove and coral. She was honored by the United Nations in 1997, the same year she received the Earth Trustee Environmental Award. [806]

Another environmental expert was Michael Dichand, a pioneer in organic farming who converted his ranch in the Austrian province of Burgenland into a well-known training center for what he termed "the care of Earth and its plants." Dichand often referred to John McConnell as his "inspiration and mentor." [807]

Simon Reeves brought a Southern Hemisphere voice to the Earth Society Foundation. As author of the New Zealand chapter of the *International Encyclopedia of Environmental Law*, he saw value in historical documents and, therefore, encouraged John McConnell to entrust his Earth Day Proclamation to the United Nations. "That Proclamation should be framed and permanently attached to the wall near where the Peace Bell is rung because it cements the moment when the environmental movement split into those who saw Earth restoration as a fundamental, if not spiritual, urgency for all people and those who saw it as an issue that could be resolved by political activity and continued economic growth." [808]

Physically strong and mentally sharp into his late 70s, John McConnell found an opportunity to take his message to the world in the summer of 1993 when he flew to Vienna to attend the UN World Conference on Human Rights. John went there, as he reported to the ESF board, "to see our Earth Trustee ideas serve the purpose of the conference, aid the efforts for peace in nearby war-torn Bosnia, and obtain vigorous support for our Earth Day and Earth Trustee 'Battle for Earth.'" John's task was daunting due to the vast number of delegates from 1,500 NGOs who were, in his words, "Trying to get attention, too often pushing their own agenda on each other, throwing down on the table their own self-interest. … With a little luck and a lot of

806 Anitra Thorhaug (1987 Laureates) [online]. Global 500 Forum [cited 13 February 2006]. Available from www.global500.org/news_58.html.

807 Hans Janitschek, e-mail to author, 14 February 2006.

808 Simon Reeves, telephone interview by author, 22 February 2006.

love, most of them could benefit from our Earth Trustee Formula. … Most everyone I contacted showed interest in our ideas and literature." [809]

A highlight of that trip was a children's concert, sponsored by the Earth Society Foundation, in the castle of Viennese Prince Alfred von Liechtenstein. The concert was arranged on short notice by Hans Janitschek and conducted by Pulitzer Prize winner Marvin Hamlisch, composer of the musical, *A Chorus Line.* [810] The singers were refugee children from war-torn Kosovo who had been brought to Austria under dangerous conditions in a truck by peace activist Assim Burger. [811] John described the concert, which received television coverage and a front-page article in Vienna's *Neue Kronen Zeitung* newspaper, as "the Balm of Gilead [with] beautiful music that brought tears to eyes, including my own. … When he [Hamlisch], a Jew, put his arms around a Muslim boy, we seemed to feel a new faith in the future." [812]

On Sunday, 20 June 1993, while in Vienna, John awoke at 3:00 a.m. with an urgent desire to know the exact moment of the summer solstice. He attributed this awareness to having seen a ceremony the day before by Indians from Canada who were living in teepees and observing a three-day fast and ritual to honor the mid-summer geo-celestial event. Learning the moment of solstice would occur at 8:00 a.m. local time, he went to the Austrian Center where the entrance was marked by great stones from different continents and flags from nations throughout the world. With a young woman who happened to join him, John stood next to a stone from Europe and sang and recorded the "Minute for Peace" song, which he had previously written.

Later in the day, he played the recording for sponsors of the children's choir who had performed under Hamlisch's direction. They agreed to bring a few children to meet John at the same stone at 4:30 that afternoon to celebrate the solstice. When a mixup in the children's schedule nearly prevented them from participating, Ann Charles, who attended the conference as a reporter, prevented the bus from leaving and brought the children to the great stones where they sang the lyrics: "One mighty voice, crying aloud for wars to end. Peace among men." In his report to ESF, John told of one little girl who added, "And women." Austrian television broadcast the event that day,

809 John McConnell, "Vienna Report," 8 June to 1 July 1993.

810 "Der Komponist von 'Chorus Line' in Wien," *Neue Kronen Zeitung*, 17 June 1993.

811 Hans Janitschek, e-mail to author, 17 December 2005.

812 John McConnell, "Vienna Report," 8 June to 1 July 1993.

and CNN News included it on a 4 July program called "Earth Matters, International." [813]

"Minute for Peace" song

From nations a wind is rising
Carrying a message above.
Let's join our voices together
In a minute of peace and of love,

Together we'll join for the joy of the world
Our countries will have no fear
A moment of peace will engulf the world
One minute each day of the year.

Rise up and stand on your feet one and all,
Join with your friends as they answer the call,
One mighty voice, crying aloud for wars to end.
Peace among men.

At the conference, John relished the advent of computer technology by receiving instructions on how to access conference data banks. In addition, he, Janitschek and a Russian expatriate, whom Janitschek had met through Norman Mailer, employed a videophone, provided by American Telephone and Telegraph (ATT), to facilitate discussions between high-ranking United Nations officials in New York and representatives from Balkan States and Asian countries, who were in Vienna. The UN officials had come to the Earth Society Foundation office in New York, [814] and the representatives from Bosnia, Herzegovina, Croatia and Nepal were gathered at the Janitschek residence in Vienna. [815] John dubbed the occasion a "Global Tea Party," [816] and Janitschek called it "an historic event, the first time that a videophone connection between New York and Vienna had taken place." He added, "It

[813] Ibid.

[814] At Watermark Communications, Inc.,

[815] Hans Janitschek, e-mail to author, 17 December 2005. Also, Videoconference flyer, 23 June 1993.

[816] John McConnell, "Vienna Report," 8 June to 1 July 1993.

was a great success, technologically speaking, and prepared the ground for a permanent videophone link between UN Headquarters at New York and Vienna." [817]

John then attended a three-day congress, hosted by Globally Integrated Village Environment (GIVE), at Vienna University of Technology that advocated "Architecture & Urban Planning in the Age of Telecommunication" as a means for "linking ecological and technological issues in the field of new types of settlement, lifestyle, work, education and production." [818]

The mechanisms for global unity represented by GIVE pleased John because it characterized a change in economic, social and political thinking. GIVE promoted, and John embraced, the idea that information can be given away without being lost. "When I give information, we both have it. More GIVE thinking and less SELL thinking can benefit everyone," he wrote to ESF. [819] And he, like the GIVE people, believed in the need to renew sustainable rural areas rather than abandoning them for overcrowded cities. [820] Therefore, John foresaw, "Through new interactive technology, people in a village can efficiently work from anywhere for a distant company." [821] That concept, later, became known as "telecommuting" and evolved into a practice that, by the millennium, would allow fifty percent of people in developed countries to work within their homes.

GIVE's founder and leader was Franz Nahrada, a researcher and developer of efficient mechanisms for village renewal through telecommunications technology. Nahrada provided John with a suite and office amenities in his father's hotel, The Karolinenhof. Influenced by John, Nahrada and his wife Minoo Fararooei initiated an Earth Day committee in Austria that led to John ringing the United Nations Peace Bell in Vienna three years later in 1996.

"Everywhere, I see a growing desire to find common ground where honest, important consensus is possible," John journaled regarding his 1993 trip to Vienna. "There are many important programs and holidays observed by different countries and some are sponsored by the United Nations – World

817 Hans Janitschek, e-mail to author, 17 December 2005.
818 John McConnell, "Vienna Report," 8 June to 1 July 1993.
819 Ibid.
820 Franz Nahrada, e-mail to author, 5 December 2005.
821 John McConnell, "Vienna Report," 8 June to 1 July 1993.

Peace Day, World Environment Day, United Nations Day, etc. They call attention to *parts* of our concern. Earth Day brings attention to *the whole*. Using the March Equinox, nature's symbol of unity and balance and history's longest recorded holiday, Earth Day expresses the best human concern and commitment to a future of peace, justice and the care of Earth." [822]

Embracing that spirit, the Earth Society Foundation conducted a host of activities in 1993 and 1994 that displayed its inclination to promote peace in the international arena. Chief among these was the first Margaret Mead Memorial Lecture, held in a private dining room at the United Nations on 3 November 1993. The featured presenter was Emma Bonino, leader of the Transnational Radical Party in Italy and speaker of the House of Representatives in the Italian Parliament. She spoke on the topic, "After Rio – Chaos or Paradise?" in reference to the United Nations Conference on Environment and Development in Rio de Janeiro in June 1992, also known as the Rio Earth Summit. [823]

Three weeks before the Margaret Mead Memorial Lecture, on 11 October 1993, John McConnell and Prime Minister G. P. Koirala of Nepal planted a tree in New York City's Central Park. The tree memorialized Koirala's late brother, B. P. Koirala, a Nepalese national hero. They also attended the unveiling of a life-size bronze sculpture of an African elephant by U.S.-Bulgarian artist Mihail on United Nations grounds; the sculpture was arranged by Janitschek, chair of the Sleeping Elephant Trust, and sponsored by the governments of Nepal, Kenya and Namibia. [824]

Also in late 1993, Kurt Koenig persuaded movie producer Steven Spielberg to arrange a special screening of the movie *Jurassic Park* in the General Assembly Hall of the United Nations and negotiated a European telecast of an International Concert with American singer Eartha Kitt. On the same occasion, Ann Charles helped organize an International Fashion Show that featured performances by Zairian bandleader, guitarist and vocalist Dominic Kanza as well as aboriginal dancers from Panama and Portugal. [825] Michael Dichand provided fashion models, organic food and non-alcoholic

---

[822] Ibid.

[823] *Earth Journal*, newsletter, Vol. 1, No. 2, Fall 1993, Earth Society Foundation.

[824] Ibid.

[825] Ibid.

champagne for the event's 200 guests. [826]

The following spring brought the second Margaret Mead Memorial Lecture at which Israeli Foreign Minister Shimon Peres spoke. The event, held on 23 May 1994, followed a profound thirty minute ceremony in the Japanese Peace Garden during which Peres, Secretary-General Boutros Boutros-Ghali, and John McConnell sounded the Peace Bell three times to mark the bell's fortieth anniversary. Guests at the ceremony included James P. Grant, director of the United Nations International Children's Emergency Fund (UNICEF), and delegates from over twenty-five countries.

In his remarks at the Peace Bell ceremony, Boutros-Ghali identified Peres as "a long-standing architect of peace ... between Egypt and Israel." And in his speech, given without notes in the UN's Dag Hammarskjold Auditorium, Peres affirmed his belief in the bond between peace and environmental justice. "We discovered that the things we were fighting for are not as important, and all the things that are important you cannot achieve by wars," Peres proclaimed. "The Lord has provided us with two commodities, free of charge. One is fresh air, and the other is real freedom. Nobody has to pay for it, and yet we have corrupted both of them." [827]

While many people contributed to these efforts, John McConnell was the prime motivator, even at age 78 and 79. Kurt Koenig's 1993 Earth Day report, as an example, acknowledged, "John rescued us when, only three days before Earth Day, he stormed the offices of UNESCO and procured the necessary paperwork and authorization to put the various UN departments into motion for Earth Day." The report stated, "John arranged for the President of Ecuador [Sixto Duran-Ballen Cordovez] to ring a bell at the moment of Equinox, obtained an official statement from the ambassador of Iran, obtained an Earth Day proclamation from the Mayor of Seattle [Washington], and inspired [jazz bassist and composer] John Leaman to compose an original musical arrangement entitled 'Oasis,' which he arranged to perform at our ceremony as well as at a benefit on our behalf later that evening." [828]

But even greater than these accomplishments was John's rectification

[826] Hans Janitschek, e-mail to author, 6 January 2006.

[827] *Earth Journal,* newsletter, Vol. 1, No. 4, Summer 1994.

[828] Kurt Koenig, "Earth Day 1993 Report," *22* March 1993.

of a discovery, two weeks before Earth Day, that Nobel Laureate Rigoberta Menchu's aide had failed to schedule her participation at the ceremony at the United Nations. Koenig reported, "John placed a phone call … and by the next day we had a confirmed commitment from Senora Menchu's aides that she would attend." [829]

Clearly, the telephone was a major communications component in John McConnell's life. It was his link of persuasion with the rest of the world, and he generally rang up monthly phone bills of $150 or more, especially prior to Earth Day celebrations. Who should pay the bill was a perennial point of debate within the Earth Society Foundation. The situation came to a head during the summer of 1992 when John and board president Gregory de Sousa argued over this matter. While they presented opposing opinions, a check from a donor that would have covered a current bill remained undeposited and John's phone was disconnected. This outraged John, who told de Sousa, "I was absolutely appalled when I got through to the [telephone company] supervisor and found that the person responsible for my standing out in the sun [at a pay phone] day after day with quarters trying to find out why our phone wasn't connected, that the person who was responsible for the difficulty was you." [830]

When Hans Janitschek became president of the Earth Society Foundation in November 1992, he instituted a policy through which John McConnell received a monthly stipend of $500 from the board as well as payment of his phone expenses. "John requested and often got his telephone bill refunded by the board," Janitschek related, "but there was often a fight. You could divide the board between those who were in favor of paying John's phone bill and those who were against it. It was unbelievable." Janitschek felt it was important for John to have an income, as a matter of dignity. In addition, Janitschek felt a responsibility to Anna who, as he said, "was taking care of so many things."

Interestingly enough, during Janitschek's presidency, John sometimes gave extra money that he earned back to the board. "He often got invitations to speak or to lecture, and occasionally he got a fee," Janitschek explained. "I

---

829 Ibid.

830 John McConnell, "Record of Statements by Gregory de Sousa Regarding July 1992 Phone Disconnect," memo to Earth Society Foundation, 8 October 1992.

can remember at least three or four times when he came back and gave the check to the Earth Society. As long as his basic needs were being taken care of and as long as he could make phone calls whenever he wanted and could make a contribution to [his and Anna's] house expenses, he was okay."

But Janitschek's paradigm didn't prevail, and, in 1995, he resigned in anger over a board decision to suspend John's stipend. Janitschek surmised some board members were afraid of John. "The phone was his best weapon. John, with making a few phone calls, could achieve a lot. And he could cause a lot of trouble. But I felt that was his right; it was his duty, as a matter of fact. The Earth Society Foundation was always about him. ... We needed him. I needed him. He was inspirational. He was a great leader." [831]

[831] Hans Janitschek, telephone interview by author, 25 February 2005.

PUZZLES
for
everyone
PLACE THE NUMBERS 1, 2,
3, 4, 5, 6, 7, 8, 9 IN THE
CIRCLES SO THAT ANY
THREE NUMBERS IN A
STRAIGHT LINE ADD UP
TO 15. ANSWER IN LOWER RIGHT
HAND CORNER.
B
C
A
WHICH OF THE TWO LINES
IS THE LONGER—A TO B
OR A TO C? DECIDE, THEN
MEASURE TO FIND OUT!
START WITH ANY LETTER.
MOVE ALONG THE LINES TO SPEL
WORD. THEN START WITH THE LA
LETTER USED AND GO ON TO SPE
ANOTHER WORD LETTERS CAN
USED AGAIN AND AGAIN, BUT IT M
BE A NEW WORD EACH TIME. TAK
TURNS WITH SOMEONE. THE ONE
SPELLS THE LAST WORD IS THE W

Texas Restaurant 1971

Earth Trustee
Repairing, planting
conserving, and in
every other way seeking
to protect and improve
the part of Earth where
I live.

Earth Trustee
Helping protect & take care
of Earth – its air,
water and life.
land

Earth Trustee
Registry
To Save Our Earth

Earth Trustee: Seeking to find and do those things that will protect, nurture and improve Earth's life and destiny.

John McConnell's handwriting appears on the back of a placemat from a Texas restaurant on which he captured his Earth Trustee concept in 1971. The front of the placemat (opposite page) contained puzzles and games.
John and Anna McConnell

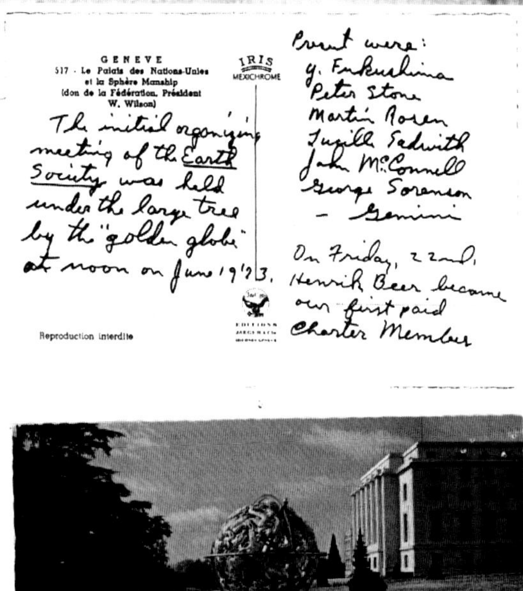

A post card with John McConnell's handwriting documents the founding of the Earth Society in Geneva, Switzerland. The image on the card's face is: "Le Palais des Nations-Unies et la Sphere Manship." John's inscription reads: "The initial organizing meeting of the Earth Society was held under the large tree by the 'golden globe' at noon on June 19, 1973. Present were: Y. Fukushima, Peter Stone, Martin Rosen, Lucille Sadwith, John McConnell, George Soerensen, [given name unknown] Gemini. On Friday, 22nd, Henrik Beer became our first paid Charter Member." *Swarthmore College Peace Collection*

Anna McConnell, Louise Eggleston, Christa McConnell, Alice Powell and John McConnell board the ***Queen Elizabeth 2*** for the December 1973 Comet Kohoutek cruise.
John and Anna McConnell

Passengers aboard the *Queen Elizabeth 2* hold a pole, equipped with flotation devices and an Earth Flag at the top, that they released from the stern of the ship during the January 1974 Comet Kohoutek cruise.
Swarthmore College Peace Collection

John McConnell works with volunteers to register concerned individuals as Sea Citizens in 1975. John and the Earth Society collected hundreds of registration forms at various venues, including schools.
Swarthmore College Peace Collection

John McConnell, Margaret Mead and Mark Hatfield participate in a news conference in Washington, D.C. on 17 March 1976. Hatfield's inscription at the bottom read: "To John McConnell, the wide awake keeper of the Earth."
John and Anna McConnell

Congressional Record

United States of America

PROCEEDINGS AND DEBATES OF THE 93^d CONGRESS, SECOND SESSION

Vol. 120 WASHINGTON, TUESDAY, DECEMBER 10, 1974 *No. 171*

Senate

SEA CITIZENSHIP

Mr. HATFIELD. Mr. President, today, Human Rights Day, I would like to bring to the attention of my colleagues in the Senate and my fellow Americans everywhere the formation of an international organization that will be devoted to the stewardship of the sea. Like the Earth Society, which founded Earth Day and sought to heighten awareness among our citizenry for the environmental destruction going on in our land, the Sea Citizen Organization will seek to focus our attention on an environmental matter that should be of direct concern to us all—the threat to the global sea and to the stake each one of us has in the resources of the sea.

The founding principle of the Sea Citizen Organization is the affirmation that the world ocean is the common heritage of mankind, and not the special province of the coastal nations or those business enterprises most technologically able to exploit the resources of the sea. We all own the sea. We all have a tremendous stake in its future. We, the people of the world, have a right to demand responsible management of the sea resources.

The Sea Citizen Organization will promote formation of an international sea authority which will establish the kind of guidelines that will insure the
access of future generations to
bounties of the sea. Without coordin
international attention, the ocean
its resources will become despoiled.
is already happening. Sea Citizens
try to sound alarms before it is too
They will try to focus public pressur
governments and corporations to
destructive exploitation of the sea.

Nations are faling to control the
lution that threatens the estuaries
shallow coastal waters where sea li
most abundant and where the repro
tive cycle of many fish and other
animals is carried out. Coastal coun
are failing to stop the destructio
natural wetlands that support sea
and shellfish. The fishing fleets of m
nations are overtaking the abilit
many sea species to regenerate. It is
that these problems are global in s
and need cooperative multinati
solutions.

I vividly recall the testimony of
Heyerdahl before the Senate Comm
Committee following his *Ra I* and *R*
voyages several years ago. He dem
strated in those Atlantic expeditions,
in the Pacific *Kon Tiki* expedition be
them, that our concept of "territo
water" is very mistaken. The w
ocean, he said, is a large sink wit
drain. Into the sink flows most of
world's pollution, and none of it le
It only swirls around with the ocean
rents that ultimately distribute it t
reaches of the global sea. Pollu

dumped into the "territorial waters" of Japan often reaches the west coast of the United States; Moroccan pollution reaches the Caribbean, as *Ra II* demonstrated; Peruvian pollution reaches Polynesia, as *Kon Tiki* demonstrated. The inescapable conclusion is that whatever one nation does with its "territorial waters" affects *other nations*, other people, and, in fact, the whole world ocean. The people of the world who fear for the future of the ocean must somehow influence these countries' governments, and the Sea Citizen Organization affords them the opportunity.

The members of the Sea Citizen Organizing Committee are Mr. John McConnell, founder and president of the Earth Society; His Excellency Dr. Arvid Pardo, former chairman of the U.N. Seabed Committee; Mr. Harold Taylor, former president of Sarah Lawrence College and chairman of the U.S. Committee for the United Nations University; Mr. Frank Braynard, general manager of Operation Sail '76 and author of 11 books on the sea; Ms. Louise Eggleston, former president of the International Literacy Foundation; and myself. Today we are presenting the first Sea Citizen Certi-

rents, enjoyed the marine environment on which the whole web of life on Earth depends.

We urge education, developmental guidelines and essential environmental regulations be provided by the United Nations to encourage careful stewardship and management: in the harvesting of fish, Sea plants and other marine sources of protein for the world's hungry; in the protection of individuals and nations that depend on the Sea for their living; in obtaining oil and minerals from the sea-bed; in the operation of ships that ply the Sea. We support programs that will preserve for future generations the healing balm of clean salt water and blue seas, with their benefits to the mind, body and spirit, and to all who swim, sail, or fish.

We seek recognition of the Sea and its bed as the common heritage of mankind, and affirm that the borders of the Sea shall extend to the highwater mark and to the *farthest reach* of brackish waters in rivers, inlets and bays. Management of coastal resources (fish, seaweed, oil, minerals) should conform to guide-lines established by a global Sea authority. These guide-lines should set forth how nations can best take responsibility for the care and protection of adjoining tidelands. Efforts to expand national sovereignty further into the Sea by increasing navigation and economic boundaries, should be taken as an encroachment on the rights and property of all Sea Citizens, and all Earth's children, as a threat to the wholeness and *future of the Sea.*

We support the formation of an International Sea Authority, with appropriate safeguards to national and individual interests, which will safeguard the common heritage of the Sea for the benefit of all Earth's life.

The members of the Sea Citizen Organizing Committee are Mr. John McConnell, founder and president of the Earth Society; His Excellency Dr. Arvid *Pardo, former chairman* of the U.N. Seabed Committee; Mr. Harold Taylor, former president of Sarah Lawrence College and chairman of the U.S. Committee for the United Nations University; Mr. Frank Braynard, general manager of Operation Sail '76 and author of 11 books on the sea; Ms. Louise Eggleston, former president of the International Literacy Foundation; and myself. Today we are presenting the first Sea Citizen Certificate to a young student of the United Nations International School at a ceremony in New York.

The U.S. Congressional Record shows that Senator Mark Hatfield introduced the Sea Citizens Declaration to his Congressional colleagues on 10 December 1974, Human Rights Day. John McConnell, founder and president of the Earth Society, and other members of the Sea Citizens Organizing Committee were named in the second column.

Swarthmore College Peace Collection

Photos of Earth and John McConnell grace the cover of the original 75 Theses on the Care of Earth, 1985.
Swarthmore College Peace Collection

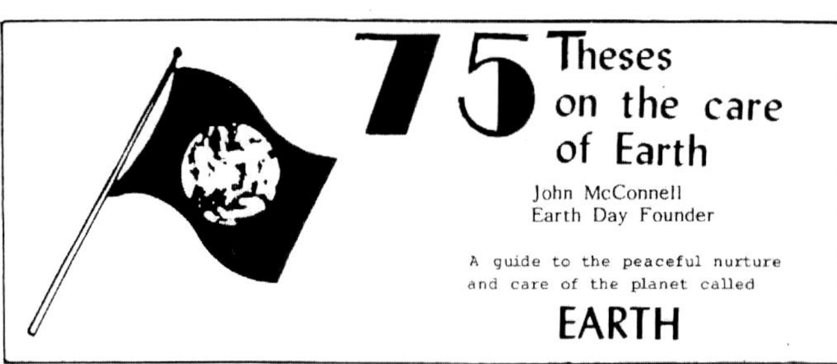

Dear John,

I have read and re-read your 75 Theses.

They are just wonderful and so much to the point.

I believe that most of them are already accepted by a large segment of people and will some day be accepted by all.

I will disseminate them.

With loving thoughts,

s/ ROBERT MULLER

Robert Muller
Assistant Secretary General, United Nations.

For 75 THESES send $1.00 to EARTH SOCIETY FOUNDATION
585 Fifth Avenue, New York, NY 10017

Assistant Secretary-General Robert Muller's picture appears on the inside cover of John McConnell's 77 Theses on the Care of Earth along with Muller's assessment, "They are just wonderful and so much to the point."
John and Anna McConnell

This poster, compiled by John Drysdale, incorporates ***The Ancient Days*** by artist William Blake and a NASA image of Earth to attract attention to John McConnell's Earth Charter. The poster contained this image on the front and the entire Earth Charter on the back. It hung in many locations at the United Nations in the early 1980s.
Swarthmore College Peace Collection

John McConnell and American journalist and former Beirut hostage Terry Anderson enjoy conversation during a radio interview at the Museum of Television & Radio in New York City in 1991. The interview, which was broadcast coast-to-coast, linked speakers McConnell and Anderson in New York and environmental entertainer Paul Tracey in Los Angeles, California, with radio talk show hosts Paul Gonzalez in Tampa, Florida, and Gerry Coffey in Decatur, Alabama.
John and Anna McConnell

John McConnell and Canadian Member of Parliament Stan Darling enjoy the festivities of an April 22 Earth Day celebration in Ottawa, Quebec, in 1990.
John and Anna McConnell

Donnerstag, 17. Juni 1993 / Nr. 11.884, S 8,-

Abend-ausgabe
Neue Kronen Zeitung
UNABHÄNGIG

Der Komponist von „Chorus Line" in Wien

„Chorus Line"-Komponist Marvin Hamlisch ist mit seiner Frau Terre in Wien eingetroffen. Auf Initiative des Journalisten Hans Janitschek (mit Bart) wird er auf dem Rathausplatz ein Benefiz-Musical mit Kindern geben (siehe ADABEI).

Foto Klemens Groh

A children's concert in Vienna, organized by the Earth Society Foundation and presented on 17 June 1993, receives front page coverage in one of Europe's major newspapers. Shown are composer Marvin Hamlisch, who conducted the concert, his wife Terre Hamlisch and ESF member Hans Janitschek
Neue Kronen Zeitung (Vienna)

Franz Nahrada, John McConnell, Minoo Fararooei and Hannes Wolf hold an original Earth Flag during a reception in Vienna in June 1993. The person in the background is Heinz Klaus, chancellor of the Austrian Mission to the United Nations in Geneva.
John and Anna McConnell

John McConnell and West German Chancellor Willy Brandt share ideas at a reception given by the German government to honor Brandt in Washington, D.C. in 1993.
Swarthmore College Peace Collection

Israeli Foreign Minister Shimon Peres presents a message at the Earth Society Foundation's Margaret Mead Memorial Lecture in 1994. Also at the speakers' table are Kevin Sanders of ESF, Israeli ambassador Gad Yaacobi, Japanese ambassador Hosadi Owada, and Hans Janitschek and John McConnell of ESF.
Hans Janitschek

John McConnell and Hans Janitschek pose at the United Nations Peace Bell prior to the Earth Day ceremony in 1995.
John and Anna McConnell

John McConnell celebrates his 80th birthday at a party at the New York home of Hans Janitschek. With him are Anna McConnell, who was 64, and long-time associate Tom Dowd. At the party, the Earth Society Foundation presented John with the Earth Trustee Environmental Award, symbolized by the gold medal and blue lanyard around his neck.
John and Anna McConnell

Kevin Sanders, John McConnell and Fred Burrous participate in an award presentation at the Earth Day ceremony in 1995.
Travis Photography

Anna and John McConnell, Ann Charles and Dennis Dubin pause for a photograph at an Earth Society Foundation reception for John in 1996.
John and Anna McConnell

Hans Janitschek, John McConnell and Lama Gangchen share their mutual appreciation at the Lama Gangchen World Peace Foundation's Fifth International Congress in Madrid, Spain, 24 May 1996.
John and Anna McConnell

Students sit on a stage at Bethel Middle School in Bethel, Connecticut, to hear words of Earth wisdom from John McConnell on 2 October 1998.
John and Anna McConnell

John and Anna McConnell pose for a casual photograph within the hallway of Waynesboro Elementary School, Waynesboro, Pennsylvania, where John spoke to an assembly of children in 1998.
Swarthmore College Peace Collection

John McConnell and Angela Alioto pull on a bell cord that rings a steeple bell at the Shrine of St. Francis as part of the thirtieth anniversary Earth Day celebration in San Francisco in 2000. This photo was taken two days before John's 85th birthday. *Swarthmore College Peace Collection*

Anna and John McConnell proudly display the Earth Flag, which flies from a standard near the front door of their Denver, Colorado, home in 2004. *Robert M. Weir*

John and Anna McConnell take their grandchildren Hannah Rose and Bethany Anne for a stroll around Kentucky Circle Village, the modest senior apartment complex where they live in Denver, Colorado, in 2004.
Robert M. Weir

This 5-foot by 12-foot mural panel of Anna and John McConnell, created by Joanne Tawfilis and Cady Macasa, is part of the Art Miles Murals project in Denver. The project, which stretched for nearly 11,000 feet in an attempt to break the world record for the largest outdoor mural, was unveiled on 23 April 2005.
Fouad Tawfilis

20

Earth Charter

(1979 to present)

> *We who sign this pledge advocate that in the year 2000 a worldwide Bi-millennium Celebration be held, to be preceded by two decades of unparalleled thinking, perception, inspiration, love, planning and work for the achievement of a just and peaceful human society on Earth.*
>
> – John McConnell, "Bi-millennium Celebration of Life," August 1979

In 1979, John McConnell crafted the Earth Charter. In nine succinct paragraphs, he set forth principles that had become themes in his life as well as precepts that would become watchwords for people in the future: Earth Care, Earth Rights, The Human Spirit, Education, Production, Trade/Marketing/Advertising, Consumption, Renewable Resources, and Communications. Then, in Article 10, he advocated continuing the annual celebration of Earth Day on the March equinox and, looking twenty-one years into the future, he stated his desire for "a Bi-Millennium Celebration, graduating to a larger, richer destiny for our planet and its people." [832]

"I was greatly inspired by the space program. We set out to explore space and discovered Earth," John said. Then, ruminating about the Latin and Greek origins for the English words for paper, character, chart and charter, he

---

[832] John McConnell, "Earth Charter," 1979.

determined, "I felt the 'charter for the future' should be an Earth Charter." [833]

For form and title, John looked to the Magna Carta, the "great character of English liberties," written in 1297 under the rule of English King Edward I, that has come to be synonymous with fundamental laws, rights and liberties.

For content, he drew upon ideas he had written earlier in his essay titled "Bi-Millennium Celebration of Life," a document with eleven brief precepts, in which he called upon people to "pledge our hearts, minds, time and talents over the next two decades as active participants in the creation of a more human world order." Thus, he hoped the world would celebrate the year 2000 with "the inherent dignity of every person within our interdependent, planetary family … [and] the inherent value of the earth itself and all the life forms it supports." He urged that change-of-millennium celebrations, which he had the foresight to perceive would be a grand global event, be "rooted in the values of justice, peace, and ecological balance." [834]

John took his Earth Charter to communities, universities and the United Nations. In April 1980, Bridgeton, New Jersey, became the first community to embrace the principles enunciated in the Earth Charter. [835] Speaking at Princeton University, John called the Earth Charter "an outline that might provide connections and … a broad consensus to help people see the difference between Earth Kill and Earth Care." [836] And through the assistance of John Drysdale, the Earth Charter became a display item at the UN.

Drysdale applied his art knowledge and persuasive skills to the creation of a two-sided poster. On one side, Drysdale, a commercial artist and advertising manager of Revlon cosmetics, combined a NASA photograph of Earth with the painting *The Ancient Days* by early Romantic artist William Blake (1757-1827). On the other side, he typeset the 1,130-word Earth Charter text. Drysdale then convinced Primary Metal & Mineral Corp. to print and donate several thousand copies. For the next few years, he and John

---

[833] John McConnell, e-mail to author, 7 December 2005.

[834] John McConnell, "Bimillennium Celebration of Life," essay, August 1979.

[835] Donald H. Rainear, mayor of Bridgeton, New Jersey, letter to Jerry Fitzgerald English, New Jersey Department of Environmental Protection, 7 April 1980.

[836] John McConnell, "Earth Care Campaign," speech, Princeton University, 8 December 1982.

McConnell obtained permission to tape the posters to windows and walls within the United Nations in conjunction with Earth Day celebrations. [837]

John's futuristic vision was most evident in Earth Charter articles 5, 6 and 7, in which he espoused principles the United Nations General Assembly crafted into its Millennium Development Goals (MDGs) two decades later in 2000. Yet, in spite of that, the Earth Charter proved to be another example of John's vision that was adapted, without recognition, by others.

In 1987, the United Nations World Commission on Environment and Development asked for creation of a charter that would set forth fundamental principles for sustainable development. That request began a process, lasting more than ten years, that involved committees at the Rio Earth Summit in 1992, Maurice Strong and Mikhail Gorbachev of Green Cross International in 1994, formation of a UN Earth Charter Commission in 1997, and a UN Earth Charter Secretariat to continue monitoring the project. Hailed as the creation of civic groups worldwide and a universal declaration of human responsibilities, [838] the final UN product is much lengthier and more complex than John McConnell's simple document. [839]

"I get so upset when I see all these United Nations conferences that are selling an earth charter. They never used those words before I wrote an Earth Charter," John said. He noted, "[The newer version] does not mention there had been a previous charter [840] ... [and] it doesn't have any reference to Earth Day." [841] These two omissions perplexed John even further because he received correspondence from Maurice Strong about the content and progress of the UN's new Earth Charter in December 1997. In that correspondence, Strong wrote, "Of course, the [UN] Earth Charter initiative embodies many of the ideas of Earth Day. Though they each have their specific objectives, I feel that they would greatly benefit from closer collaboration and interaction." [842]

---

837 John McConnell, "History of the Earth Charter."

838 *Frequently Asked Questions* [online]. The Earth Charter Initiative [cited 7 December 2005]. Available from www.earthcharter.org/innerpg.cfm?id_menu=38.

839 *The Full Earth Charter* [online]. The Philadelphia Earth Charter [cited 7 December 2005]. Available from www.earthchartercitizens.org/earthcharterpreamble.htm/.

840 John McConnell, interview by author, Denver, Colorado, August 2004.

841 John McConnell, manuscript review with author, Denver, Colorado, October 2005.

842 Maurice Strong, fax to John McConnell, 30 December 1997.

John McConnell's "Earth Charter"

EARTH CHARTER INTRODUCTION

A Key to Earth's Survival

Here is a world view with incentives for our Earth's physical and spiritual regeneration. It calls for heroic efforts to achieve a critical common goal: To save our planet. Genuine cooperation to save Earth will lead to mutual understanding and trust – a true basis upon which to forge lasting peacekeeping accords.

Disarmament can become a reality, economic order and opportunity can spread, and a spirit of cooperation can grow as we work together. The power of these ideals will make our Earth a healthy, peaceful planet – a harmonious home for all our children to enjoy.

We can begin now, with a major effort this year and in each succeeding year, to become responsible custodians and benefactors of Earth's amazing web of life. With progress reported each year on Earth Day, we can, by the year 2000, observe a two year Bi-millennium to celebrate our triumph over fear and greed, graduating to a larger, richer destiny for our planet and its people.

In this year 1979, many people around the world realize that we are the first generation to determine the life or death of the planet we have inherited.

This Earth Charter is intended to help define our new role and responsibility and to strengthen the many efforts that are moving in this direction. It is intended to inspire unity and cooperation in our task that we may preserve, restore and increase Earth's beauty and bounty for our own and future generations.

People of all ideologies and religions can, and must, unite in pursuing this vital purpose. To many religious people, stewardship is a divine obligation: subjecting oneself to the will of God creatively and comprehensively. To humanitarians, stewardship is a moral imperative.

Every community on Earth is invited to ratify this Earth Charter and support it by their words and deeds.

EARTH CHARTER

Preamble

In order for us as one human family to effectively assume our new role as the custodians of Earth and as people who care about Earth's future, we will strive to act in accordance with the following principles and guidelines.

We are the first generation to determine the life or death of the planet we have inherited. The care of Earth is now our most important task. The Earth Charter defines our new role and responsibility and strengthens our efforts. It inspires unity and cooperation in our task so that we may preserve, restore and increase Earth's beauty and bounty for our own and future generations. People of all ideologies and religions can, and must, unite in pursuing this vital purpose.

A massive communications effort is needed to publicize every program or product that improves the care of Earth. We must no longer condemn others, but each seek what we can honestly praise. In this way we can obtain public support and enthusiasm for Earth Care action and motivate people everywhere to practice Earth Care.

We believe that a vigorous united effort to understand, protect and revive our planet will at the same time promote mutual trust and accommodations needed for creating a peaceful future. The signers urge individuals and communities throughout the world to endorse and ratify this Earth Charter. Together we can save our planet.

Principles

– Article 1. Earth Care

The natural bounty of land and sea is the inheritance and responsibility of all Earth's people. Each person's help is now needed for the care of Earth and each person can benefit from that care. We must each act responsibly to help nurture and care for our planet – in our block, our neighborhood, our vocation and in the new policies, formulated within all institutions and governments, that affect the future of Earth. The fact of Earth's existence, and the nature of the live web of life, of which we are all a part, should form the basis for all future actions.

– Article 2. Earth Rights

We hereby determine that in pursuing the goal of Earth's renewal, opportunity will be provided every person on Earth to share in its future. More important than property rights and the rights of sovereignty is the fundamental right of each person's claim to a portion of our planet: and opportunity for every person, who will contribute to the care of Earth, to have a portion of land, a home, a job and the means to learn the skills needed to live a wholesome life.

– Article 3. The Human Spirit

The greatest contributions to human progress – whether in art, music, science, religion or philosophy – have come from tapping the inner resources of the human spirit. To many religious people stewardship is a divine obligation: subjecting oneself to the will of God creatively and comprehensively. To humanitarians, stewardship is a moral imperative. To foster a global spirit of cooperation, it is essential that we recognize our common desires for love, truth, beauty, justice and freedom, and that we are all inter-dependent members of one human family.

– Article 4. Education

In order to carry out our responsibility as custodians of Earth, we must all learn how to produce, trade, consume and create without damaging the delicate fabric of life; to practice an Earth Care Ethic. An Earth Care Curriculum is now the first requisite for a good education.

– Article 5. Production

We must walk the soft path that meets human needs without endangering the many interdependent Earth life forms that exist throughout our biosphere. So urgent is this task that we must now achieve the same kind of massive innovation that nations have demonstrated in time of war. Decentralism and self-help programs are urged for grass roots participation everywhere. Eventually, all mass-produced products must conform to Earth Care criteria: (1) long life; (2) easy repair: (3) non-polluting in production and use; (4) energy efficient; and (5) recyclable.

– Article 6. Trade/Marketing/Advertising

Our goal in Earth's renewal is to provide fair and equal access to credit, raw materials, exchange and trade. Economic policies and incentives must reward those who provide basic human needs instead of those who, out of mindless shortsighted greed, unfairly exploit their neighbors. For this purpose a stable medium of exchange can and must be created, as well as an accessible means of mass transportation. Advertising should inform, not deceive.

– Article 7. Consumption

Every consumer should realize each product he buys and uses can affect Earth for good or bad. An Earth Care Ethic will foster in our buying habits and personal conduct, choices that will avoid pollution and waste. Each person will be an educated consumer. The present practice of Earth Kill will be supplanted by Earth Care.

– Article 8. Renewable Resources

The preservation, improvement and renewal of soil, water, air, wild life and vegetation must be a primary goal in our research and planning. All the basic physical needs of society must be obtained in ways that will increase rather than destroy Earth's renewable bounty. To this end a rapid transition is needed to greater conservation and use of renewable resources: to tracking and recycling scarce non-renewable raw materials, to new land use policies for clean water, healthy soil, parks, gardens and creative human settlements. Sustainable population goals and sustainable solar energy are all essential for our survival.

– Article 9. Communications

The new Earth Care Ethic is best communicated person-to-person. Each individual who makes Earth Care a major goal can contagiously spread the excitement and adventure to be enjoyed as caretakers of our planet. Communicators in all media can also make a vital difference. Headlines for heroes who are caring for Earth and about Earth Care alternatives can create a sense of high purpose and adventure in young and old.

– Article 10. Earth Day: A yearly Celebration to unite the World in the Care of Earth

To strengthen the efforts described in this Earth Charter, and to call attention to yearly progress in these efforts, we will celebrate

Earth Day each year on the day of the March Equinox. In the week preceding Earth Day, we will help give an accounting of the state of the Earth – in every part and as a whole. Earth Day will then be a time to celebrate Earth's life and progress, a time to come together in renewed dedication to its care, a time to rejoice, sing, dance and play, a public holiday shared by all people of Earth. Every community, city, state and nation is invited and urged to plan their own special ceremonies and participation in this annual event.

To forever commemorate our task and our challenge, we will in the year 2000, begin a two-year Bi-Millennium Celebration, graduating to a larger, richer destiny for our planet and its people.

21

Alone in Iran

(1979 to 1981)

> *I hope the meanings and purposes of Noruz will be given the highest possible support in your country. This will inspire many countries to resurrect similar practices from their own history and culture.*
> – John McConnell, message to Mr. Gamaroodi, assistant to Iranian President Abolhassan Banisadr, March 1980

Having made strong connections with people of the Middle East through the United Nations, John McConnell remained highly cognizant of ongoing strife between Israel and Palestine as well as other international tensions in that part of the world. Then, like many Americans, he watched in anguish as a situation known as the Iran Hostage Crisis erupted in Iran in late 1979 and prolonged for 444 days until early 1981.

For several decades, the United States had supported the rule of Mohammed Reza Pahlavi, the Shah of Iran, with military and economic aid in exchange for a continuous supply of oil and a strategic presence in the Middle East. People in Iran who were opposed to the Shah and his opulent, westernized lifestyle led a social and religious coup that overthrew the Shah in January 1979. The Shah fled to the U.S. where he received medical treatment for lymphoma, a situation that angered revolutionary Iranians.

The new Iranian leader, Ayatollah Ruhollah Khomeini, encouraged demonstrations against the United States, which motivated thousands of Iranian students to gather outside the U.S. embassy in Tehran, Iran's capital city, on 1 November. Three days later, a thrust of several hundred students stormed past a token guard of U.S. Marines, entered the embassy and took sixty-six American diplomats and citizens hostage.

In February 1980, Iran issued a demand that the U.S. return the deposed Shah and issue an apology. President Jimmy Carter sought negotiation through Switzerland, a third-party government. In April 1980, he also authorized a secret rescue mission that failed and another, later, that was aborted. [843]

Amidst this international intrigue, John perceived that he, as a missionary of global peace and founder of Earth Day, should intervene. John knew that Iranians and other nations in central and west Asia celebrated Noruz, their new year, on the spring equinox. "They have special food and meals with friends and neighbors in celebration. It's a time when they take special care of their animals and property and show respect for wildlife and trees and shrubs and plants," John said. "At the moment of the equinox, Iranians are to be home with their families and God. So, it's a time for worship and a time for commitment to the care of our planet and good relations with neighbors." Noting the beauty of this holy day, John added, "I wish the whole world would celebrate Earth Day that way. It would really make a difference." [844]

John spoke with Mark Hatfield about this relationship between Earth Day and Noruz. "The way to open up a little bit of understanding with your enemy is to praise something that you honestly approve of," he told the senator. "That doesn't mean you support things that are wrong, but you can commend what's good and try to cooperate with what you're applauding. You can look for honest agreement, a common ground." [845]

Following a comparable approach, United Nations Secretary-General Kurt Waldheim created a Commission of Inquiry, which undertook a fact finding mission in Tehran. By hearing Iran's grievances, Waldheim hoped for an early solution, but by mid-March 1980, the hostage crisis had already lasted more than 130 days.

Likewise, John believed if he could go to Iran and meet with Iranian President Abolhassan Banisadr, he would point out that Noruz and Earth

---

843 *Iran hostage crisis* [online]. Wikipedia [cited 8 December 2005]. Available from en.wikipedia.org/wiki/Iran_hostage_crisis.

844 John McConnell, interview by author, Denver, Colorado, August 2004.

845 Ibid.

Day both occur on the spring equinox. Knowing the Iranian custom of being especially kind to neighbors on that day, he hoped to persuade Banisadr to release the hostages. With Hatfield's assistance, John obtained a visa as a journalist. He scraped together some money and departed on 18 March 1980.[846] "I got enough money to pay for my ticket there and back, with just a little beyond that," he recalled.

John remembered Hatfield telling him, "You know, you're totally on your own, John. The government's not backing you." John replied, "I know, but I think this might open up communication and understanding." And, of course, John did not have an appointment, nor was he expected by anyone in Iran.

"I was praying all the way there," he stated, "and when I arrived in Iran, I was really praying at the airport. I wondered, 'What in the world do I do now?' I looked around the counters, and I liked the appearance on the face of a man behind the counter. So, I said a little prayer and went over to him, explained to him why I was there and asked if there was any way to get to Banisadr. And he said, 'Oh, my cousin is his top assistant. I'll get you to him.'"

Through that miraculous connection, John met with a man whom he referred to only as Mr. Gamaroodi, who was Assistant to the President. John complimented Gamaroodi on the manner in which Iranians celebrate Noruz. "If we could make that a global holiday," John told his host, "it would further understanding and peace all over the world." Then John told Gamaroodi about Earth Day celebrations at the United Nations and reminded him of the Iranian custom to release some prisoners on Noruz as a symbol of forgiveness. "If you would release the hostages now in commemoration of Noruz and Earth Day, I believe it would do so much good for your own country and for the whole world," John said. Gamaroodi became emotional and agreed that was a good idea, but noting the time, he replied, "Noruz is only four hours away and I must be home and alone with my family and God." And with that, Gamaroodi ended the meeting.[847]

In the days after his meeting with Gamaroodi, John went to the American embassy where the hostages were held. He took with him an audio

---

[846] John McConnell's visa.

[847] John McConnell, interview by author, Denver, Colorado, August 2004.

tape he had recorded while planning for his departure and which he played for himself on the airplane "to help with my prayer and thinking." [848]

The words on the tape were "The Beatitudes" from the Christian *Bible*. [849] John had found comfort knowing Jesus Christ had spoken that message about the Kingdom of Heaven in the part of the world he was about to visit. At the embassy gate on the afternoon of 25 March, five days after astronaut Edward Gibson had rung the Peace Bell at the United Nations, John engaged an Iranian student guard who spoke English. John told the guard, whose name was Achbar Zadeh, "The way to peace is described on this tape." Zadeh took the tape, promising to give it back the next day. But when John returned, Zadeh said he liked the message and wanted to keep it, and John let him. "So, that tape is somewhere in Iran," John said years later. [850]

"The Beatitudes"

Blessed are the poor in spirit, for theirs is the kingdom of heaven.
Blessed are they who mourn, for they will be comforted.
Blessed are the meek, for they will inherit the land.
Blessed are they who hunger and thirst for righteousness, for they will be satisfied.
Blessed are the merciful, for they will be shown mercy.
Blessed are the clean of heart, for they will see God.
Blessed are the peacemakers, for they will be called children of God.
Blessed are they who are persecuted for the sake of righteousness, for theirs is the kingdom of heaven.
Blessed are you when they insult you and persecute you and utter every kind of evil against you (falsely) because of me. Rejoice and be glad, for your reward will be great in heaven.

Even though John stayed in Tehran until 7 April, a week beyond the period allocated on his visa, [851] he was not able to meet with Gamaroodi

848 Ibid.

849 *Bible*, Matthew 5:2-12, Luke 6:20-26.

850 John McConnell, interview by author, Denver, Colorado, August 2004.

851 John McConnell's visa.

again, nor with any other Iranian official.[852] "I really believe that if I had gotten there sooner, or had I been able to stay longer, I would have come back with the hostages," John claimed.[853]

"Statement in Tehran, Iran," 22 March 1980

As the founder of Earth Day, I have directed my thoughts to a global view, seeking a strategy that might avoid total destruction of life on our planet.

It does little good to solve a crisis in Iran, South Africa, the U.S.A., or any other place, if in spite of local success the whole world goes down the drain – an ever increasing danger that frightens many of the most thoughtful and informed people in the world.

In Iran there exists a unique opportunity to save our planet. It is this possibility that I want to discuss. But first I must set forth some basic facts that go to the heart of our global problem.

Whether it is inflation, pollution, poverty, or clashes of group against group and nation against nation, efforts to solve the problem ignore the basic cause of the problem.

The reason for our difficulty is greed and selfishness. Many people recognize this but there seems to be a total disinterest in doing anything about it. It is assumed that nothing can be done, that in the world of business and politics, greed and gain will decide the future.

The cause of this corrupt worldview is a false basic assumption – sinister, secret and taken for granted – that in the hard world of reality, stimulating greed and selfishness is the dynamic that will bring the greatest prosperity – an ingenious lie that must be exposed.

Basing an economy on the stimulation of greed and acquisition does bring material wealth and affluence – but with it a loss of morality, meaning and integrity, which are essential for the well-being of the body, mind and spirit in the total person – and for the healthy functioning of a community or society – which is also determined by the degree of morality and integrity.

By morality is meant the honest pursuit of what is good and the

852 John McConnell, message to Mr. Gamaroodi, March 1980.

853 John McConnell, interview by author, Denver, Colorado, August 2004.

rejection of what is evil; the practice of the Golden Rule, love of neighbor. Now, with our new awareness of our whole planet and the vital necessity to understand its man-made problems – to act as custodians for its protection and care – the best definition of morality is: To seek the well-being of our planet and its people.

The United States is a prime example of what has gone wrong. The irresponsible drive for "me, mine, more" has dramatically increased production, affluence, superficial pleasures and creature comforts. But while people say they are "increased with goods and have need of nothing," inside they are 'wretched, miserable, poor, blind and naked." [854] Inflation, crime and corruption is a part of the terrible toll they must pay. Worst of all, the house of the future in which their children must dwell is poisoned, polluted and crumbling. The spacious skies are filled with smog, the amber grain with chemicals, the purple mountains scarred by ill-planned roads and houses have lost their majesty – and their forests. The fruited plain is paved. The next generation will never know the natural bounty of the once beautiful land called America.

Any plans to save our planet must include a return to morality. There must be a massive mobilization of science, psychology and religion to achieve this goal. Major guidelines for this purpose are given in the Earth Charter – which, while broad in its approach, can obtain universal support and provide direction for global efforts.

However, to achieve the massive changes needed in attitudes, values and conduct, it is vital that we make the challenge clear and evoke the same energetic response that has fueled support for wars and revolutions.

In the United States, in 1941, Pearl Harbor triggered an energetic response. Citizens from every walk of life stopped their greed and selfishness to help save their country. A clear effective challenge today could obtain a similar response to save our planet and avoid catastrophe for our children. It must be made clear that the threat to our planet is such that we cannot wait for the catastrophe to trigger our response – for then it will be too

---

[854] *Bible,* Revelations 3:17.

late. There can be no response to atomic war, the death of the oceans, or the destruction of the ozone layer that protects us from the Sun's radioactivity, just a few of the dangers we face because of our short-sighted greed and selfishness and our misdirected technology.

To escape the ultimate catastrophe, I suggest we turn to the world of theatre, of imagination for the answer. Napoleon said, "Imagination rules the world." While the world is made of mind and matter, it's mind matters most.

Shakespeare told us, "All the world's a stage." At present the playwrights and producers of our global drama are the world leaders who are masters of money, guns and communications. They call the shots and keep the players puppets to their passions and pride – all for lucrative profits and with amazing ability to rationalize their actions. The play is a bad play, a terrible play.

But we can change all that. Following is a way we can close the show and provide in its place a grand epic, an heroic epic, in which people who love their fellow man – who want to save their planet – will be the producers, playwrights and principal actors.

The conjunction of Earth Day, Iran's New Year, the hostages at the American Embassy, and the meetings of the Revolutionary Council provide an unprecedented opportunity.

Let the hostages be freed now. Connect their release with Earth Day and Iran's New Year. Announce support of the Earth Charter and plans to implement the Charter in the new government. (This need not all be done at one time.) State your commitment to make your revolution an Earth Care Revolution; to be the first country dedicated to the care of our planet as described in the Earth Charter – that in striving to obey the moral law, choosing the good and refusing the evil, you will seek the well-being of our planet and all its people.

By your example you will let the people of the world know they can be the producers instead of the puppets. More and more the seekers and doers, the people who love their fellow man, will take action in their own way to further the Earth Care Revolution. Succeed in this grand endeavor and future generations will sing

> your praises. You can succeed. After all, this world is made for music, not for madness.
> Without the unique circumstances regarding the hostages, the kind of action I suggest would be largely ignored by media. But given the present situation, it will create a media shock wave with continuing coverage of efforts and results.
> Why not end the bad play? Ring down the curtain! LET A NEW PLAY BEGIN!

John then spoke of another aspect of the story. "I don't know what part this played," he related, "but the enigma is that Jimmy Carter was President, and I tried [via mailgram in early March 1980] to get him to issue a proclamation in support of Earth Day on the equinox. [855] We had a proclamation from President [Gerald] Ford [Carter's predecessor], but we needed to bring it up to date. Well, I failed to connect with President Carter, and he issued a proclamation for April 22. [856] I'm thoroughly convinced that had I connected with him or had he backed my effort for Earth Day, I might have gotten the hostages released and he would have continued [been elected for a second term] as President." [857]

Then John said, "There's more to this crazy enigma. When I came back to the United States, I had gotten a little publicity, and I was invited by one of the reporters of the *New York Post* to have lunch with him. He wanted to talk with me about my trip to Iran. He asked me for a quote, and I said that I would like to go back, that I still thought we could bring about better relations with Iran." John failed to remember the reporter's name but he did recall the reporter invited him to meet at a nice restaurant.

When John arrived, the reporter had another guest with him. "He said his guest was a millionaire and would be glad to provide the money for me to return to Iran and get the hostages. The guest gave me his card with his [New York City] address and phone number. He said he was totally obligated at that point but, if I would wait a few days, he would get back to me." John said, "I waited and waited and never got a call. Finally, I called the number on the card, and it wasn't any good. So, I went to the address on the card and

---

855 John McConnell, mailgram to Jimmy Carter, 6 March 1980.
856 Jimmy Carter, *Proclamation 4710*, 1 January 1980.
857 John McConnell, interview by author, Denver, Colorado, August 2004.

there was no one by that name living there." Then, John stated, "I learned the man who had arranged the lunch meeting wasn't a reporter but was on the committee – one of the prime people – promoting [Ronald] Reagan for President. I think he was making sure that I didn't get back to Iran and Carter didn't [get credit for the release of the hostages and] remain as President. I have no documentation, but it certainly made sense to me." [858]

John's assertion made sense in light of the fact that Iran finally released the hostages on 20 January 1981, Inauguration Day in the U.S., and only twenty minutes after Reagan's inaugural address. The timing of these two events gave rise to what became known as the "October Surprise Conspiracy," an alleged plot that representatives of Reagan's 1980 presidential campaign, including former director of the Central Intelligence Agency George H. W. Bush, conspired with Iranian leaders to delay the release of the hostages until after the 1980 presidential election and not during the last month's of President Carter's administration. [859] The U.S. Senate and House of Representatives investigated this allegation in the 1990s and concluded there was no evidence to support any claims of wrongdoing. [860]

Later, in an essay titled "The Enigma of How President Reagan Defeated Jimmy Carter," John referred to Ronald Reagan as "the Hollywood Communicator." Of Reagan's election, John wrote, "The War Department Dealers in Death (who make billions from devilish weapons of war) were delighted. They were able to continue their propaganda for 'Peace through Strength.' Ever since then, the peacemakers, who follow the way of nonviolence, have been ignored. Now the whole world is infused with the lust for power of weapons." [861]

While John's actions in Iran were far beyond the norm of what almost any other United States citizen would have done, he was not alone. Ten Americans, including Ramsey Clark, who had been attorney general under President Lyndon B. Johnson and later became an antiwar activist, flew to

---

858 Ibid.

859 *Iran hostage crisis* [online]. Wikipedia [cited 8 December 2005]. Available from en.wikipedia.org/wiki/October_surprise_conspiracy.

860 *Iran hostage crisis* [online]. Wikipedia [cited 8 December 2005]. Available from en.wikipedia.org/wiki/Iran_hostage_crisis.

861 John McConnell, "The Enigma of How President Reagan defeated Jimmy Carter and the turn toward global peace that Carter had initiated," essay.

Tehran to participate in the Crimes of America conference in Tehran in June 1980. [862]

John's trip to Iran was one of several audacious steps he took to establish dialogue with persons of the Middle East. Two years earlier, in April 1978, John met with Prince Faisal of Saudi Arabia at the hotel where the prince was staying while attending United Nations business in New York City. When John called to confirm an appointment, he was told the prince was at the Waldorf Astoria hotel, and John went there to make personal contact. Finding the prince surrounded by other distinguished looking gentlemen who were being photographed, John introduced himself, and the prince said, "Yes, I understand we have an appointment this afternoon."

At that meeting, Prince Faisal expressed sympathy for John's Earth Rights initiatives but remained skeptical about rapid change. "He thought I was ahead of my time," John said. "He thought that while we have had great material changes, there has been no moral improvement for hundreds of years."

John commented to Prince Faisal about his conversation with Sheik Yamani in 1974 in which John told the Sheik he must pay a royalty to the world's people for oil extracted from under Arabian soil, and Prince Faisal concurred that the Muslim faith does not recognize property rights. "We are agents for God," the prince told John, "and have no say in how our property is to be disposed of after our death." John considered that Muslim belief to be in harmony with his attempts to encourage people to be custodians of Earth. He gave Prince Faisal an Earth Flag and asked for a financial contribution of $120,000 to facilitate his efforts, [863] which he did not receive. [864]

In another attempt to be part of Middle East dialogue, John invited Egyptian President Anwar Sadat to ring the Peace Bell at the Earth Day celebration in 1979. Via telegram, Sadat replied his appreciation "for your kind invitation," but added, "I would have gladly accepted had I not been

---

[862] *The Daily News – June 1980* [online]. The Eighties Club: The Politics and Pop Culture of the 1980s [cited 8 December 2005]. Available from eightiesclub.tripod.com/id100.htm.

[863] John McConnell, "Met Prince Faisal – 1978," activity log entry, 18 April 1978.

[864] John McConnell, manuscript review with author, Denver, Colorado, October 2005.

preoccupied in the peace process." [865] The peace process to which Sadat referred was a series of negotiations between Egypt and Israel, known as the Camp David Peace Accords worked out between Sadat, Israeli Prime Minister Menachem Begin and U.S. President Jimmy Carter. These led to agreements, which news reports deemed "more necessary and pressing than ever," [866] that Sadat and Begin sealed with a handshake on the White House lawn on 26 March 1979. [867]

In the following decade, John continued communication regarding ongoing international conflict in that part of the world. He sent messages to Mideast leaders, [868] King Hussein of Jordan, [869] President Mikhail Gorbachev of Russia, [870] evangelist Billy Graham [871] and others.

He extended an invitation to Kamal Kharrazi, Iranian ambassador to the United Nations, to participate in the Earth Day ceremony in 1993. [872] Kharrazi attended and provided a table of Iranian food. Then, after the ceremony, John and Anna joined Kharrazi and his delegates for a private ceremony in the Iranian Mission. [873] Kharrazi participated more fully at the Earth Day ceremony in 1997, reading a statement that honored both Noruz and Earth Day as "a celebration of the God given gifts and bounties of the earth." [874]

A year later, Hadi Nejad Hosseinian, another Iranian ambassador to the UN, commemorated Noruz and Earth Day as a "celebration focusing on prayer for peace and prosperity for all ... irrespective of national boundaries, race or creed." [875] In 1999, Hosseinian spoke again, saying, "In the threshold

---

865 Mohamed Anwar El Sadat, telegram to John McConnell, 23 March 1979.

866 *European Community, Venice Declaration on the Middle East, Venice European Council,* 12-13 June 1980 [online]. Europa [cited 8 December 2005]. Available from europa.eu.int/comm/external_relations/mepp/decl/.

867 *1979: Israel and Egypt shake hands on peace deal* [online]. British Broadcasting Corporation [cited 8 December 2005]. Available from news.bbc.co.uk/onthisday/hi/dates/stories/march/26/newsid_2806000/2806245.stm.

868 John McConnell, "A Message for Mid-East Leaders," 10 September 1990.

869 John McConnell, letter to King Hussein, 10 September 1990.

870 John McConnell, letter to Mikhail Gorbachev, 14 September 1990.

871 John McConnell, letter to Billy Graham, 5 September 1990.

872 John McConnell, letter to Kamal Kharrazi, 24 February 1993.

873 John and Anna McConnell, manuscript review with author, Denver, Colorado, October 2005.

874 H.E., Dr. Kamal Kharrazi, speech, Earth Day, 20 March 1997.

875 H.E. Hadi Nejad Hosseinian, speech, Earth Day, 20 March 1998.

of the third millennium, celebration of Earth Day finds a renewed meaning and importance. The need for a new and global understanding of the earth's fragility and man's destructive power and habit is all the more present." [876]

As the world moved into the third millennium, John received support from David N. Rahni, professor of chemistry and physics at Pace University in New York, who encouraged him to continue communicating with Kharrazi as well as Iranian ambassador Javad Zarif. [877]

John enjoyed friendship with Najeeb Halaby, who was one of the speakers for the WOR television broadcast in 1972. Halaby, who was born in Texas of Syrian and Lebanese ancestry, was a former CEO of Pan American World Airways, one time head of the U.S. Federal Aviation Administration, and former deputy assistant secretary of defense. He was the father of Elizabeth Najeeb Halaby who married Jordan's King Hussein in 1978, taking the name Queen Noor. Queen Noor and King Hussein sent John and Anna Christmas cards for many years. [878]

John also engaged in correspondence with Middle Eastern individuals of common means. Among them was Mohammad Amin Alipour, a student of software engineering at Tarbiat Modares University in Tehran. In November 2004, Alipour sent an e-mail to John in which he said he had proposed that Iran celebrate a "Peace Day" on the first day of spring in response to a claim by U.S. President George W. Bush that Iran was part of an "Axis of Evil." Amin Alipour told John the Iran Ministry of Foreign Affairs had accepted his idea and wanted him to compose a letter to President Mohammad Khatami, and, for that, Alipour sought John's opinion. He posed a question, "How can we hold two nations – Iranians and Americans – together?" [879]

John, who was then 87, sent a reply e-mail on the same day, "The only hope for the future is to reach the hearts and minds of people in every country with the message that we have only one planet. We must work together for peace, justice and a sustainable future." [880] Through this correspondence and other communiqués with dignitaries and ordinary citizens, John did all he could to "connect with the right people."

---

876 H.E. Hadi Nejad Hosseinian, speech, Earth Day, 20 March 1999.

877 David N. Rahni, e-mail to John McConnell, 2003.

878 John McConnell, interview by author, Denver, Colorado, August 2004.

879 Mohammad Amin Alipour, e-mail to John McConnell, 24 November 2002.

880 John McConnell, e-mail to Mohammad Amin Alipour, 24 November 2002.

John's sentiment was founded in his faith in Jesus Christ and in scientific knowledge that ancient people in that part of the world may have planted the seeds from which all civilizations grew. He found further hope in a verse that Alipour, a Muslim, sent about the light of Christ: "Peace is prerequisite for safety and health. I Am the Light of the Heart shining in the darkness of Being and changing all into the golden treasury of the mind of Christ. I Am projecting my love out into the world to erase all errors and to break down all barriers. I Am the power of Infinite Love amplifying itself until its victorious World without end!" [881]

[881] Mohammad Amin Alipour, e-mail to John McConnell, 26 November 2002.

22
Formula for Earth Care
(1985)

> *We need a formula that will provide a double helix of the mind and spirit that will foster creative altruism in the care of Earth.*
> – John McConnell, "Earth Rejuvenation Formula," 11 December 1981

In 1985, at age 70 and seeing that "money and political power took the Earth Charter name away from me," John McConnell desired to write another document he hoped would attract attention of global leaders, media and the world's people. He considered the "Disputation of Doctor Martin Luther on the Power and Efficacy of Indulgences," commonly known as "Luther's 95 Theses," which the founder of the Lutheran Church wrote in 1517. From that inspiration, John developed 75, then, 77 Theses on the Care of Earth.

Each thesis was a simple, one-sentence statement formatted under twenty-two topics. John found these short, numbered paragraphs to be "a good way to communicate important thoughts and ideas. When I put them down, I aimed for 75, then I wrote a couple more. I like the number 77. I am influenced by Ivan Panin and his study of Bible numerics and the significance of numbers in nature and history. Seven is the number of perfection." [882]

John published these in a small twenty-four page booklet, the size of a

[882] John McConnell, manuscript review with author, Denver, Colorado, October 2005.

religious tract on attractive salmon-colored recycled paper stock that bore the subtitle "A guide to the peaceful nurture and care of the planet called Earth." The booklet contained a portrait of John, looking very distinguished with an image of Earth in the background, and a brief, two-sentence introduction by Robert Muller, "Dear John, I have read and reread your 77 Theses. They are wonderful and so much to the point." [883]

"77 Theses on the Care of Earth," 1985

A Guide for Earth Trustees

Principles and Policies that will foster the peaceful nurture and care of the planet Earth.

The world of tomorrow is not foreordained to be either good or bad. Rather it will be what we make it. In these 77 Theses, I have tried to present the essential ideas needed to achieve an historic global change – from mindless exploitation, with increasing danger of worldwide catastrophe, to the peaceful nurture of our home, Planet Earth.

PROLOGUE – Earth Trusteeship

The 77 Theses are especially for people who will think of themselves as Trustees of Earth and who seek to do the things about ecology, economics and ethics that foster peaceful progress on our planet.

Earth's rejuvenation can best be realized by individuals and small groups of people (preferably 5 to 15 each) who will make their own special commitment to projects for the care of Earth. And, who at the same time, affirm a common world view about the protection and care of Earth – which they share with other Earth Trustee groups – a view and commitment which hopefully will soon spread to include all, or practically all, of Earth's people. The Earth Trustee concept can provide the measure of unity in our diversity needed for achieving Earth's rejuvenation.

A useful analogy is the way each cell in the body has its specific task, but has within it the genetic code – or pattern – for the whole body.

The problem is to determine the items in the Earth Trustee world view that can be accepted and shared voluntarily by people of

---

[883] Robert Muller, "75 Theses on the Care of Earth," introduction.

every clime and culture, of every ideology, religious belief and temperament.

To accomplish this it is important to separate the vital facts on which most people can agree (2+2=4, etc.) from the items of belief that deal with uncertainties or differing viewpoints in politics, religion, economics, education, social justice, etc.

The 77 Theses can obtain general support for a broad Earth Trustee world view. With this as a common template that all approve – not in details of implementation, but in general purpose – rapport and appropriate bonds between groups can be established. Earth Trustees will recognize their independence and points of difference. The purpose they will share is the care of Earth.

The objective then in each group will be to obtain information that will assist their choices and the pursuit of their Earth Care project, or projects. Computer networks, data banks and flow of communication about what others are doing will serve this purpose.

With the above in mind, Earth Care Handbooks* in every language will provide an Earth Trustee world view and orientation, plus guidelines for finding and choosing Earth Care projects – carefully avoiding the partisan issues that cause disagreement. Our goal is a global consensus on the care of Earth.

*Handbooks can be produced independently, with common guidelines.

Part of the program – and basis of eventual success – will be a practical determined effort by each person and group to share their enthusiastic interest with friends and thereby bring about a rapid doubling – each month if possible – of individuals joining or organizing Earth Care projects.

In these efforts a key to success will be the sense of community, or spirit of cooperation that is engendered. Special emphasis on reverent prayer, worship, dedication to and emphasis of moral and ethical values in the terms acceptable to each group will make a vital contribution.

The most important inner point of unity in the care of Earth is our love of Earth, its life and its people – especially our nearest neighbors.

The most important outer point of unity is the simultaneous celebration of and dedication to the care of Earth on each Earth Day, March 20-21, and will be aided by observance each day on radio and TV of global Earth Minutes. Religious groups are especially invited to participate – each in its own way. In this, there is no compromise or watering down of their particular faith or belief. The point of unity is neither doctrinal nor ideological belief, but dedication to the care of Earth and inner love of our planet and its people.

I can engage in this united action in spite of strong differences with people of other religions or political beliefs. Loyalty to country, which exists in spite of differences with other citizens, must now be equaled and transcended by loyalty to our planet and dedication to its care.

A sign of participation can be the flying of the Earth Flag.

EARTH DANGER

1. RECOGNIZING: That ignorance and neglect of our planet, combined with the folly of international rivalries, has now endangered all life on Earth;

2. That our planet's life is threatened by policies and actions that cause massive pollution of air, water and soil and dangers of chemical, biological and nuclear disaster;

3. That mutual trust is necessary in order to counter these threats;

MUTUAL TRUST

4. That only by open communication and joint action, for a great common good, can mutual trust develop;

5. That the one thing we have in common is our planet;

CAMPAIGN FOR EARTH

6. That a campaign for the care of Earth will create relationships leading to mutual trust and ultimately to reciprocal disarmament and stable peace;

7. That in pursuing peace, it is important to identify and emphasize vital matters and the extent and nature of our accord, and to build on this accord;

8. That peaceful actions beget peace;

9. That in a world of instant global communications, a strong, informed public opinion in all nation's dedicated to peace and care of Earth could become the greatest deterrent to war and to local violence;

10. That the greatest challenge in history is the present challenge of destiny involving all humanity, a challenge to reclaim the Earth for all peoples and to free them from the fear of war and want;

11. That accepting this challenge will bring the measure of trust needed to achieve these goals;

WHOLEHEARTED DEDICATION NEEDED

12. That the peaceful care of our planet cannot be accomplished through half-hearted or insincere efforts, but will require the dedication of all humanity;

13. That in seeking the basic change in the conduct of governments and their peoples, we acknowledge the failures of all previous efforts to achieve a peaceful world;

14. That investments worldwide in instruments of destruction endangers the human race;

15. That excessive destruction of trees, vegetation, and wildlife, from ancient times to the present has decimated or destroyed numerous species and degraded Earth's potential for nurturing life, and that the current acceleration of this process will bring global catastrophe if it is not soon brought to a halt;

HUMANITY'S SPACE AGE CHOICE

16. That world peace requires a basic long-term commitment to change attitudes and conduct and to develop structures and programs that will foster peaceful progress in the care of Earth and in our relationships with each other;

17. That new factors in the quest for peace are Space Age global awareness and deep concern everywhere that something must be done;

18. That we owe to untold generations in our past and future a firm decision for peace and care of Earth;

19. That it is time for humanity to take charge and take care of their planet;

NURTURE OF EARTH

20. That the campaign for Earth requires ideas and attitudes

conducive to the nurture and care of Earth;

21. That loyalty to community, bioregion, and planet is essential for the healing of our planet and people;

22. That a patriotism embracing people and planet as well as nations is necessary now;

23. That loyalty to our planet will not hurt, but instead will help our lesser loyalties;

ALLEGIANCE TO EARTH

24. That while national governments use police force to coerce allegiance when needed, their long-term strength depends on voluntary support by their citizens;

25. That loyalty to our planet can best be achieved through voluntary efforts to understand its life systems and processes, and then with love for our planet to help nurture and sustain the amazing web of life that covers our globe;

26. That global communication and education to foster Earth's care can provide the measure of enlightenment needed to justify and assert the authority of humanity in the management and care of Earth;

GLOBAL COMMUNITY OF CONSCIENCE

27. That voluntary support of Earth Care and person-to-person communication about Earth Care can provide a global communication of conscience dedicated to Earth's protection. This will bring inner peace and global peace;

28. That constraints and requirements for Earth Care will then permeate society and provide our global conscience with moral authority and influence greater than that of national governments;

29. That as we develop a strong community commitment of individuals and governments to the care of Earth and to one another and are aided by world public opinion filled with hope instead of fear, we will establish peaceful relationships and make any war unthinkable and impossible;

30. That the management and care of Earth by the people of Earth can only be achieved by their willing support;

31. That the willing support of people throughout our world can only be obtained by providing equitable, fair benefits in return

for their services;

32. That it is necessary to determine the rights and responsibility of individuals in the care of Earth;

RIGHTS TO THE USE OF EARTH

33. That religions teach and philosophers aver that the Earth is for all people. The Psalms state, "The Earth hath He given to the children of men";

34. That, whether considered the gift of God, or the bounty of Nature, every individual has an equal claim, or right to Earth's natural bounty – to a portion or benefit from their share of Earth's land, raw materials and natural resources;

35. That every country should provide a free homestead for each family that lacks one, or the means to obtain one. Every person who wishes to receive this basic inheritance in their planet should be given a secure habitable shelter, or be provided the purchasing capacity or land and materials;

FAIR BENEFITS FROM EARTH

36. That expenses of government and public needs they serve can best be met by land use fees, or single tax, based on the value of the land (not on improvements or labor);

37. That every individual, regardless of circumstances or lack of resources, should be assured an opportunity for basic nutritious food, or practical means for procuring it;

38. That raw materials – oil, coal, minerals – are the inheritance of all Earth's people. As they are mined, sold, or used, at least 2 percent of their value should be equally distributed as royalties to everyone. These unearned assets in the ground, the inheritance of all Earth's people, should be carefully mined, conserved and recycled by the owners or managers and used by consumers in ways that will increase the Earth's natural bounty and benefit Earth's people;

RESPONSIBILITY FOR THE CARE OF EARTH

39. That rights to the bounty of Earth must be equaled by responsibility for its care;

40. That every individual should be taught from childhood the requirements for Earth Care by instruction and experience in caring for gardens, animals, and birds. Later instruction should include

Earth Care criteria and guidelines for land use, manufacturing, recycling, energy, design of homes and communities with sustainable goals in population and development; preservation of wildlife and wilderness areas are ways to diminish pollution of air, soil and water;

MONEY AND TRADE

41. That equitable trade and development requires a fair honest medium of exchange;

42. That money should not be a product, controlled by special interests and sold to the highest bidder, but instead should be a free medium of exchange, based on things to be exchanged, and made available through collateral loans in percentages needed to facilitate trade and exchange without inflation;

43. That amply secured loans should not require payment of interest, only the cost of paper work. Usury (interest) is condemned by major religions. It can cause inflation and results in unearned and unnecessary income by manipulators;

44. That in high-risk loans to individuals or firms, security provided by the borrower should be of equal value to money provided by the bank, and both should share equally in any losses or profits; in this case money is actually an investment instead of a loan;

PRODUCERS AND CONSUMERS

45. That control of capital should be widely dispersed and prevented from being used to take unfair advantages of individuals or corporations with legitimate need for money;

46. That public disclosure should be required in the management of any business or the sale of any stock setting forth the company's adherence to Earth Care criteria: such as what is being done to avoid pollution in production and use of products or services; energy efficiency; design for easy repair, service and recycling of products; fair wages and benefits to employees. Reports of standards adopted and adherence should be provided by appropriate independent authorities;

47. That leaders in church, state and entertainment should urge support of Earth Trustee efforts and provide examples of an Earth Trustee conscience in investments, purchases and life style;

48. That individuals who invest for greatest profit with no

regard for how the money is made – bombs for poor misguided countries, production lacking environmental safeguards, unfair poverty wages for employees – should be made aware of the harm they are causing. Companies responsible for such Earth Kill practices should be exposed, penalized and their products shunned until they convert to Earth Trustee conduct;

49. That the media should be the guardian of the public's long-term interest and could serve this purpose by exposing gross Earth Kill examples and by headlining Earth Trustee solutions and programs;

GREED AND WHAT TO DO ABOUT IT

50. That a major cause of injustice, of crimes against Nature and people, is the way we have accepted and institutionalized greed, particularly greed for private profit from the land and natural resources of the Earth;

51. That most successes in selling products are presently achieved by advertising and promotion that increases greed, lust and vanity. Subtle motivational techniques are used to deceive and corrupt and thereby make greater profits: For example, in the promotion and sale of cigarettes;

52. That to attain a viable Earth Trustee future, it is essential that designers, inventors, planners, producers, consumers, and advertising executives all learn the necessity of Earth Trustee constraints. A massive educational program in schools, churches and voluntary agencies is needed to expose Earth Kill kinds of promotion and products and instead promote public awareness of Earth Trustee values and choices;

EDUCATION

53. That an Earth Trustee curriculum in schools is urgently needed. Earth Trustee studies can provide the best unifying purpose for education;

54. That it is essential for children to learn more about the wonders of Earth and that our generation can become trustees, custodians and caretakers of our beautiful planet;

55. That to accomplish these goals, effective use must be made of every means of communication – print, fax, radio, TV, telephone, satellite, computer networks;

MEDIA

56. That the general knowledge about how the world works should be constantly presented by media – in news and special programs. For example, the role of light, soil, water, air and living organisms in nurturing the thin skin of life that covers our globe; the diversity of plants, trees, animals, birds, insects – all necessary to the delicate balance of life-giving nutrients on our planet;

TECHNOLOGY

57. That technology must be used to foster Earth's care. The present mindless use of technology in ways that poison, pollute and disrupt Nature's ecosystems must be halted. Instead of a destroyer, technology can and must become a harmonious extender of Nature's bounty;

RIGHT SIZE FOR EVERYTHING

58. That there is a right and wrong size for everything. Finding the right size is essential to the lasting success of any product, system, arrangement, institution or endeavor;

59. That everything should be as small as possible, unless there is a good reason for it to be larger. In many cases communities and businesses should be smaller – providing more intimate, humane services to smaller groups of people;

60. That constant growth of a city or a business will eventually lead to disaster. Exponential factors decree this. Cities and towns can avoid this by providing laws that only allow new construction which replaces old structures. New Earth communities using interactive technologies can relieve congestion;

61. That once a community or business reaches an optimum size, progress should be sought, not through an increase in size or profits, but through improved quality of services and products. In a small business where the employees are close to owners with a personal interest in each employee, a shared understanding of the operation and its purpose brings better give and take, the pursuit of excellence and efficiency. Given a level playing field of competition, when a business gets too big, its smaller competitors will be the ones to increase sales. Also, cooperatives will be given a better chance to prove their worth;

ETHICS OF RELIGION

62. That a sense of responsibility and the practice of Earth Trustee ethics is an essential requirement for the future;

63. That major religions, philosophies and ideologies teach the "Golden Rule" – to do unto others as you would have them do unto you;

64. That while some people of faith are engaged in works of peace and works of charity, many religious people show in their actions bigotry and hypocrisy;

65. That the majority of people fail miserably to live up to their intentions;

66. That moral responsibility and ethical behavior is for the most part found in people of deep, religious faith – reflected in their compassion, fairness and charity;

67. That most conflict over religious and ideological beliefs has its roots in different hypotheses about the unknown. Does God exist? What is the nature or purpose of reality?;

KEY TO BASIC ACCORD

68. That in the question of what life is all about, we face profound mysteries and unanswerable questions. Who can imagine the Universe never having a beginning or ever having an end?;

69. That there is in the human spirit a desire for meaning in life. Religious belief, especially belief in a loving God, provides a more promising hypothesis about the unknown. While belief in God or life after death cannot be scientifically proven, there are phenomena that suggests its possibility; for example, answers to prayer and reports by people who were briefly dead;

70. That the value and test in the here and now of religious faith or philosophical belief is its good effect on the believer; the measure of confidence, virtue, integrity and the practice of the Golden Rule;

VIRTUE

71. That in the present crisis of our planet, the greatest virtue or moral imperative is the care and rejuvenation of Earth and securing the right of all people to its natural bounty;

A NEW GOLDEN AGE

72. That every adherent of ethics or religious faith should act

as a responsible Trustee of Planet Earth: join the global Earth Trustee Effort and assist some Earth Care project;

73. That every municipality or community should form an independent Earth Trustee Committee, which will discuss the 77 Theses and then form their own program to help the Earth Campaign, initiating or assisting projects that eliminate poverty and pollution and benefit humanity;

74. That radio stations and TV need to program one or more daily Earth Minutes – at 0300, 1100 or 1900 GMT*. These simultaneous global "minutes without words" can be produced independently by any radio or TV station, with views and sounds of nature, children, music, bells, our planet;

75. That to foster the vital unity needed in our diversity, all individuals and institutions will celebrate Earth Day each year on the March Equinox – Nature's Day, March 20 or 21; the first day of Spring (Fall in the Southern Hemisphere);

76. That global acceptance of responsibility for the protection and care of Earth can usher in a new golden age of opportunity for all humanity;

77. THEREFORE, LET US PLEDGE OUR LIVES AND FORTUNES TO AID THE GREAT TASK OF EARTH'S REJUVENATION AND, WITH CONFIDENCE AND FAITH, EACH DO OUR PART AS A TRUSTEE OF EARTH TO TAKE CHARGE AND TAKE CARE OF OUR PLANET.

*Whenever people hear an Earth Minute on radio or TV, they will add their thought or silent prayer. A growing multitude are praying and working for Earth's rejuvenation: for the prosperity that harmony with nature and neighbors will bring.

23
Earth Magna Charta
(1995)

We need to find ideas that can generate the greatest cooperation for the greatest good on our planet. That's what I tried to do with Earth Day, the Earth Trustee Agenda, Minute for Peace and the Earth Magna Charta.
– John McConnell, interview by author, Denver, Colorado, August 2004.

AT AGE 80, A DECADE AFTER he wrote his 77 Theses on the Care of Earth, John McConnell continued to propose his philosophies in formal documents. "Words are imperfect vehicles of human feeling and thought," he said. "It's very natural for people to put the same ideas or what they feel about ideas into different words." [884]

The vehicle John chose in 1995 was his Earth Magna Charta. "I thought about the history of England's Magna Carta, which I admired. I thought about 'magna,' which means 'large' or 'great.' I thought there was a need for a new document. ... We have the United States, which are states united. We have the United Nations, which are nations united. But we don't have a united world. I believed uniting the world would be such an awesome task that the best chance of success would be to post on the [World Wide] Web, or wherever we can in major media, an edited version of the Earth Trustee

---

[884] John McConnell, manuscript review with author, Denver, Colorado, October 2005.

Agenda and urge that every municipality issue a proclamation in support of this. If the Earth Magna Charta were implemented in universities, why, we would see such tremendous benefit that it would excite people all over the world. And we would have a more creative state of mind." [885]

John was not alone in this assertion. Pollster George Gallup, Jr., critiqued, "John McConnell's inspiring and carefully crafted document, the Earth Magna Charta, could serve as a vital global rallying cry at this moment in history." [886]

A year later, in August 1996, Yehudi Menuhin gave a concert at New York City's Avery Fisher Hall that John and Anna attended. Afterward, Menuhin signed John's Earth Day Proclamation, and, in doing so, suggested John stress the importance of music in furthering peace. John agreed, then added a paragraph to the Earth Magna Charta that read: "The exercise of arts and crafts – especially in the form of singing, dancing, mime acting and music making – is the most effective antidote to violence and crime. Let us ensure that every child from the very first year will NEVER be deprived of the aural and physical experience on which its whole life and the future of humanity depends." [887]

In 1999, during an online Internet conference on Global Ethics, Sustainable Development and the [United Nations] Earth Charter, which the UN was still crafting and processing, Steven Rockefeller, the chairperson of the Earth Charter Drafting Committee, posted a statement of praise and support for John's Earth Magna Charta. "Over the past three decades since the first Earth Day celebration and the UN Stockholm Conference on the Human Environment, over 150 declarations and people's treaties have been issued by various NGO and religious groups. Many of these documents involve inspiring visions and calls to action. One of the best NGO documents of this nature has been prepared by John McConnell and is called the Earth Magna Charta, … which is very much in the spirit of the [United Nations] Earth Charter." [888]

Using the same forum, Robert Muller, speaking for himself as well as

---

[885] John McConnell, interview by author, Denver, Colorado, August 2004.

[886] George Gallup, Jr., introductory statement to Earth Magna Charta, 1995.

[887] John McConnell, "Yehudi Menuhin Adds Music to Purpose of Earth Day," news release, 11 August 1996.

[888] Steven Rockefeller, "Excerpts from the Earth Forum," 7 April 1999.

his wife Barbara, posted a statement of praise for John McConnell, the man. "As usual over so many years, starting with the first Earth Day in human history, you are a great visionary and proposer of timely action," Muller wrote. "I would recommend that all of us who have read your [Earth Magna Charta] message consider ourselves from this day on to be Earth Trustees. We could even put it under our name when we write letters. Barbara joins me [in this sentiment] and reminded me of my exhortation 'Decide To' which I repeat here for the readers. 'Decide to Network. Use every letter you write, every conversation you have, every meeting you attend to express your fundamental beliefs and dreams.'" [889]

Reflecting on these statements of support, John said, "There are many different perspectives, but the thing we should come back to over and over again is how we can cooperate and work for peace, justice and the care of Earth. I've suggested that we need to have 'the moral equivalent of war' – that was the term I used many years ago when speaking in San Francisco.

"If people of every religion, of every faith, and businesses and schools, especially the colleges, adopted the Earth Trustee Agenda, as explained in the Earth Magna Charta, as a basic formula for educating people and students in everything they do, that would be so important. And, of course, it would be marvelous if our governments were fashioned after the principles Christ provided as far as freedom and opportunity are concerned. Freedom, justice and opportunity. These things can be a part of the community, of a person, of an institution, of a country. If our country adopted the Earth Magna Charta, why, we wouldn't sell and have things that pollute and corrupt, and we would start moving the whole world in a better direction." [890]

"Earth Magna Charta," 1995

Prelude

The people of planet Earth have the raw materials, natural resources, and technology for all to enjoy a life of quality. But they are still restricted by the evil that has dominated history. They lack the vision of the great future now possible and how to attain it. As a result, the world is filled with confusion and conflict.

---

889 Robert Muller, "Excerpts from the Earth Forum," 7 April 1999.

890 John McConnell, interview by author, Denver, Colorado, August 2004.

This Earth Magna Charta provides the needed vision and the way. Individuals and institutions can now be trustees of Earth, seeking in ecology, economics and ethics policies and decisions that will benefit people and planet. In the present state of the world, this Space Age trustee concept has a chance of tapping the best in human hopes and aspirations and providing a healthy, innovative and fulfilling future for our planet and its people. In this new future, deeds will demonstrate what is best in creeds. Young Earth Trustees will lead the way.

Our Miracle Planet

In this Magna Charta we will consider what we have, as a human family, on this miracle planet we call Earth. To understand the possibilities and how we can each participate in realizing them, we need to think about basics. Actions good or bad begin in the mind.

To plan and achieve the best future, we must look at our assets and liabilities. Experts will confirm the abundance of raw materials and natural resources on our planet. (They have a value of hundreds of trillions of dollars.) There is more than enough to provide and maintain a healthy lifestyle for everyone, with more for those with greater ability and initiative.

This is possible now because of our advanced technology. A major problem is how to restructure the social institutions of money, credit and property rights so that there will be a level playing field where rights and responsibilities will be recognized and realized. The Earth Magna Charta provides guidelines to achieve these goals – recognizing that people with different cultures and creeds will apply them in different ways. But all can warmly support the goals presented here. Aided by the sense of connectedness and the spirit of cooperation engendered by thinking of themselves as Trustees of Earth, all benefit.

Harmony with Neighbor and Nature

The people of Earth can have a great future by working together for a global goal all can approve. Here is a basic goal that most enlightened people of every religion, clime and culture will support. Here is a principled purpose that will quickly reduce the terrible chaos and conflict that troubles civilization. Here is an idea that will bring ever increasing harmony with neighbor and nature and bring peaceful progress in the human adventure.

The Earth Magna Charta describes the most important points of general agreement about the physical world – and the common view of human rights and responsibilities that naturally follow.

Rights and Responsibilities

We are all members of one human family that has inherited a planet rich in resources. We each have an equal claim to its land, minerals and raw materials. None of us produced them. We all need them or what they provide. We all have need for their sustainable development and use. To assure equitable benefits, every individual and institution should seek to balance rights and responsibilities.

The long term goal must be to restructure social institutions so that there is equitable return for services, efficient balance of supply and demand, and fair benefits from our mutual claims to Earth's natural bounty.

One possible way to equitable benefits is for those who own land, oil, gold or other minerals to pay a 2% royalty each year on their income from these resources to a fund that will then provide the homeless their inheritance or stake in their planet. All will then join in responsible care of Earth.

The digital economy will make it possible to eventually replace money and credit as we know it with new, fair methods of trade and exchange.

Global Goal: Every Person a Trustee of Earth

In regard to the physical world, we all can agree that we have only one Earth – a miracle planet teeming with life. With our amazing new technology and awareness of Earth's raw materials and natural resources, we know that poverty and pollution, the breeding ground of crime and corruption, can quickly be eliminated. All that is needed is the will.

Here is the way: First, as Earth Trustees, leaders will focus on the many solutions that are being found around the world. At present, too many accent the negative and have no clear objective. You cannot be objective without an objective. The objective is now the rejuvenation of Earth.

Then we must rally and inspire a grand Effort for Earth, an Earth Campaign that will eliminate poverty and pollution and bring new freedom, order and opportunity. This will happen as every individual and institution chooses to act as a responsible Trustee of Earth.

Ethics and Moral Values

While there are many differences about race, religion, money control and power – and conspiracy theories throughout history – we can agree that institutional policies and actions of greed and deception are unfair, defeat the common good, and should be corrected. While laws are needed and passed, without a strong spirit of community and cooperation, their measure of success is limited. The Earth Campaign will meet this need.

The great periods of progress in history have resulted from religious fervor for universal ideals of honesty, freedom, justice and creative altruism or divine love. A recent example was the Civil Rights Movement of Martin Luther King, Jr. Its essence is described in his book, *Strength to Love*. The Campaign for Earth needs to tap the deepest and the best in our religious faith or inner feelings.

Metaphysical Mysteries

People of different cultures can agree on basic moral values and deeds though they may differ on creeds that relate to the great mysteries of life. For honest agreement and cooperation we need to separate our creeds and their claims about life and death from the ideas and actions in which we can all agree. We can agree on the need for deeds that nurture people and planet, though we differ on creeds warmly held about mind and spirit and the ultimate mysteries of the cosmos and its creator. Of course the best evidence of the value of our creed is the love it produces in our lives. Common to every major religion is the Golden Rule – treat others as you would like to be treated. Now we have a new common ground: Awareness of our planet and our responsibility to take care of it.

How to be an Earth Trustee

"Actions good or bad begin in the mind." Think, pray, talk and write about how you can be an Earth Trustee. Help your neighborhood or town to be an Earth Trustee community. Spread the word about recycling, planting trees, neighborhood gardens, composting and saving energy, healthy diet, sleep and exercise. When you buy or invest, make choices that diminish pollution and poverty – that increase sustainable development. Join or form a group that will further these purposes. As a start, register with the EarthSite and become an Earth Trustee.

Young Earth Trustees

Arts and Crafts

The exercise of arts and crafts – especially in the form of singing, dancing, mime acting and music-making – is the most effective antidote to violence and crime. Let us ensure that every child from the very first year will NEVER be deprived of the aural and physical experience on which its whole life and the future of humanity depend."

Organization

There is no official Earth Trustee authorizing organization. Anyone is welcome to use the name as long as they base their effort on the principles set forth in this document. Any existing organization that adopts these purposes can be an Earth Trustee business, school, church or temple. Any neighborhood, city or state can form an independent Earth Trustee Committee to further these purposes in their own way. All are invited to share what they are doing with others.

Communications

Our global communications with its Information Superhighway can, under this Charter, bring rapid change to heal, nurture and improve life on Earth. To accomplish this requires a radical change in attitudes and policies of mass media. They must seek in every way possible to define and further Earth Trustee goals. While plans and methods for achieving goals will differ, affirming points of accord will increase harmony and accommodation. The new policy will be, "Accent the positive, headline solutions, pursue excellence. Give honest assessment of things as they are and then with creative vision, aided by computer data, show the better future that intelligent decisions will bring – with follow-up on actions taken and their results."

Earth Campaign:
A Global "Effort for Earth"

To this end, every radio, television station and newspaper that endorses this Earth Magna Charta will join the Campaign for Earth, reporting problems and progress; radio and television stations will carry daily non-verbal Earth Minutes at designated times – 0300, 1100 and 1900 GMT. These non-verbal minutes of inspirational music, views of children and natural wonders, will remind us we are all connected and working for one goal – Earth's rejuvenation. Simultaneous and world-wide, they will deepen our awareness.

Earth Day

Each year on Earth Day, March 20-21, the Peace Bell at the United Nations will ring at the moment spring begins. As this occurs, a celebration of life will cover our globe as bells ring in every community and people join in heartfelt love and devotion to the care of this nest in the stars: Earth, our wonderful home.

24
John McConnell, Octogenarian
(1995 – 2005)

Dear Heavenly Father, we pray that, as I reach near the end of my sojourn here, whatever your mission for me is that I might clearly understand how I can make a difference in changing the global state of mind and providing a way to continue the human adventure.
– John McConnell, prayer at the beginning of interview with author, 26 August 2004.

In 1995, at age 80, John McConnell taught himself how to operate a computer. "Somebody gave him an old computer," Anna explained. "'Of course,' he said, 'This is what I need because I can get around the world on it.' I'm amazed at my husband. He just keeps going, going, going. It's because of his mission." [891]

The computer was a gift of Carlo and Meeja Parisel, owners of an investment development company in Connecticut that catered to the entertainment industry. At the time, John was considering an agreement through which the Parisels would promote him as a public speaker. Carlo and Meeja also contributed time and money for John to travel to the Earth Day celebration in Vienna in 1996. "Your gift of a Packard Bell Computer and Printer has been of special value," John wrote in a letter of gratitude. "I am learning how to … benefit from its many advantages. I can now personally

[891] Anna McConnell, interview with author, Denver, Colorado, August 2004.

prepare copy for my web site." [892] As he learned, John's mind played with "www," the acronym for World Wide Web. With the global communications network now at his fingertips, he saw that "www" also stood for "World Without Walls" and "World Without War." [893]

To speed his learning, especially with the Internet, John called on computer-literate friends who came to John and Anna's home and offered private instruction. One of those friends was Hank Waxman, who provided the service of a member of the Information Technology department of his recycling company. [894] John sought assistance, specifically for his web site, earthsite.org, from Gillette Global Network (GGN), an electronic communications company in New York City. GGN, then later, Eureka Network, so believed in John's concepts that the company's president and chief executive officer Raul Martynek chose to design, then host, John's web site at no charge. [895]

In October 1997, John was surfing the Internet when he discovered the web site of Carmen Colombo, wowzone.com, on which she promoted the concept that humans should "Wish Only Well" for each other. John liked Colombo's message, so he telephoned her and introduced himself. "To love one another is the only thing that all religions have in common. That's the Golden Rule," John told her. Colombo recalled she was shaking when she realized who was on the line. "It was incredible, getting a call from the founder of Earth Day," Colombo said. "It was like getting a call from the Buddha."

Further conversations led to Colombo, a resident of Montreal, Quebec, Canada, attending the Earth Day celebration at the United Nations in 1999. She was the guest of John and Anna at their tiny Queens apartment for five days surrounding that event. "He's like a walking encyclopedia. He's an amazing man," she said of John and his knowledge.

Over breakfast on 22 March, John's 84th birthday, he told Colombo, "Until I was 80, I never thought of death." Colombo expressed her surprise, saying, "But you saw combat even as a war resister. And you've traveled so much. You've had to see people die." John looked at her in earnest and told

---

892 John McConnell, letter to Carlo and Meeja Parisel, 18 September 1996.

893 John McConnell, interview by author, Denver, Colorado, August 2004.

894 Hank Waxman, telephone interview by author, 7 November 2005.

895 Raul Martynek, telephone interview by author, 5 January 2006.

her, "My goodness, you're right. I wonder why I had never thought about death before."

By the time of that visit and conversation, Colombo had assumed responsibility for being John's web master. She performed that pivotal role until 2004 when she turned those duties over to John Munday, Jr., a professor at Regent University in Virginia Beach, Virginia. [896]

Like Colombo, Munday met John McConnell via the telephone. "He would call *The 700 Club* and seek to have his message put on the air," Munday said, explaining that Regent University was the site of religious broadcasts of conservative evangelist Pat Robertson. "John McConnell wanted to talk about Earth Day or promote his Minute for Peace and other ideas," Munday stated. Although Munday was not associated with *The 700 Club*, he was known on campus as a scientist concerned about the environment and public policies, thus, the show's producers forwarded John's calls to him. "He was so persistent, and I became impressed with his limitless energy, so I spent more and more time talking with him," Munday added. [897]

While Colombo, then Munday, gifted John with their time and talent in the digital realm, John Tandana provided a tribute to John in the analog world with an Earth Clock that Tandana designed. "I did it on the silver anniversary of Earth Day in 1995," Tandana explained. "I met John and Anna, and I was very sympathetic with John's idea and dedication to save the Earth from man-made destruction. I felt honored to meet the Earth Day founder, so I made the clock to commemorate the silver anniversary." Tandana said he got his inspiration from the Earth Flag and used an image of Earth for the design. Tandana, who is of Oriental descent, created a prototype then had a quantity of clocks produced in Hong Kong. He presented the Earth Clock to John and Anna the following year, and they proudly hung it in the kitchen of their apartments in Queens, New York, and Denver, Colorado. [898]

In 1996, at age 81, John traveled to Europe three times, visiting four countries. In March, he, along with former United Nations Secretary-General Kurt Waldheim and Japanese ambassador Nobutoshi Akao, rang the

---

896 Carmen Colombo, telephone interview by author, 5 January 2006.

897 John Munday, telephone interview by author, 3 January 2006.

898 John Tandana, e-mail to author, 24 December 2005.

Peace Bell for the first Earth Day ceremony in Vienna. In May, John was the guest of Lama Gangchen Rinpoche, a Tibetan healer and teacher, in Madrid, Spain. From there, he went to a UN habitat conference in Istanbul, Turkey, where he spoke at the International Youth Caucus. And in October, he flew to Budapest, Hungary, where he met Ervin Laszlo of the Club of Budapest and the Dalai Lama. [899]

The trip to Spain followed by one year the first meeting between John and Lama Gangchen, who had established the World Peace Foundation through which he instituted more than 100 inner peace education centers and self-healing study groups around the world. In June 1995, these two visionaries met at a celebration to honor the United Nations' fiftieth anniversary. They encountered each other a second time at a reception on 22 March 1996 at the home of Hans Janitschek on the night of John's 81st birthday. At that event, Lama Gangchen became an Earth Trustee and invited John to the Lama Gangchen World Peace Foundation's Fifth International Congress in Madrid.

The purpose of the International Congress was to present, what Lama Gangchen called, "a Grand Peace concert to increase Inner and World Peace, Physical and Mental Health and Healing, and for Making Peace with the Environment Now and Forever." John McConnell was among the honorees, receiving the Lama Gangchen World Peace Foundation Peace Plaque "for his invaluable contribution as one of the 20th century great Social Motivators [and for being the] founder of Earth Day." Also honored were Bawa Jain, a leader of the interfaith movement, and Hans Janitschek for their contributions to world peace. In turn, Janitschek bestowed upon Lama Gangchen the United Nations Society of Writers and Artists' Award of Excellence, and John McConnell gave the Tibetan an Earth Flag. [900] John recalled that Lama Gangchen referred to him as "the grandfather of the program," and had him sit in a place of honor. "Lama Gangchen is a very dynamic, outgoing person. He's very positive," John said. "When he introduced me, he made it sound like I was really something. He has charisma."

In 1999, Lama Gangchen rang the Peace Bell at the Earth Day celebration

---

[899] John and Anna McConnell, interview by author, Denver, Colorado, August 2004.

[900] Lama Gangchen Rinpoche, e-mail to author (via Lama Gangchen's aide Ishtar D. Adlar), 12 January 2006.

along with Franciscan priest Fr. Ignacio Harding, a combination of bell ringers that delighted John because of the diverse spiritual faiths represented by these two men. At the ceremony, Lama Gangchen received the Earth Trustee Environmental Award from the Earth Society Foundation.

On 13 August 1997, at age 82, John had a heart attack and Anna rushed him to Roosevelt-St. Luke's Hospital in New York City, saving his life. "It was pretty bad. We were told he wasn't going to live," Anna said. [901]

Lying in a hospital bed a few days after the heart attack, John recorded his thoughts. "I had a severe heart attack last Wednesday. ... My plans were very much upset. Things that I'd hoped to get attention for will have to be delayed. ... But I felt that I might put on my tape recorder, try to sum up what's been going through my mind. ... Through the last part of my life, I have been able to think more globally, to see the whole picture and to be aware of everything that's going on, not in detail. I'm a terrible detail person. But if there's a breakthrough in science or in politics or in health or in philosophy, you name it, I seem to pick up the thing that is right on the cutting edge. ... Also, I find that much of the time I've come up with ideas that are later brought out by others. The best example of that, to date, was my being the person who started Earth Day." The rest of John's thoughts on that day revolved around "the very nature of the mystery of life," "conditions on this planet that are so appalling," his experiences as "an evangelical Christian," and his belief that "we have such great possibilities through the Earth Trustee Agenda." [902]

A year after John's heart attack, Anna had a mastectomy. "The cancer didn't go to the lymph nodes, so I didn't have radiation. I was praising the Lord," she said. "The doctor came in and said, 'I've never seen you look so beautiful. You don't look like you had surgery.' I said, 'It's all the people praying.'" [903]

John and Anna both recovered. John initially started walking short distances in his neighborhood and worked his strength and stamina to the point where he could walk two or three miles. [904]

With improved strength, John resumed his campaign for "peace, justice

901 Anna McConnell, interview by author, Denver, Colorado, August 2004.

902 John McConnell, audio recording, 17 August 1997.

903 Anna McConnell, interview by author, Denver, Colorado, August 2004.

904 Anna McConnell, manuscript review with author, Denver, Colorado, January 2006.

and the care of Earth." He was the keynote speaker at an environmental event on Sunday, 19 April 1998, in the community of Waynesboro, Pennsylvania. The theme was "Looking Ahead," and a newspaper article described John's impact on the students assembled before him. "McConnell was kept busy for more than an hour after his speech, signing copies of his 'Earth Magna Charta,' a document stating his philosophy on sharing the Earth's resources," the *(Hagerstown, Maryland) Morning Herald*, reported. [905]

John encountered a similar experience at Bethel Middle School in Bethel, Connecticut, in October 1998. After speaking to 700 students at an assembly, a handful wanted to learn more. With their principal's permission, they gathered around John on the auditorium stage as he continued to expound on his philosophies and ideas. [906]

At age 85, John celebrated Earth Day 2000 in San Francisco where he joined civil rights trial attorney Angela Alioto, daughter of former mayor Joseph Alioto. Like her father, Angela was a former member of the San Francisco Board of Supervisors and had devoted her life to community politics. For this thirtieth anniversary of Earth Day, she and John rang a steeple bell at the Shrine of St. Francis. Copies of the city's original Earth Day proclamation, which her father had signed in 1970, were sent to newspapers across the nation, many of which published it. [907]

When John and Anna moved from Queens, New York, to Denver, Colorado, in 2002, it was primarily Anna's decision, based on her desire to be near their grandchildren. They found a modest, two bedroom apartment at Kentucky Circle Village, a senior citizen complex funded, in part, by three Denver churches: Calvary Baptist Church, First Plymouth Congregational Church, UCC, and Green Mountain Presbyterian Church. The couple, with Anna's charm and John's charisma, became instant friends with residents as they took their meals once a week in a community dining hall and walked the quarter-mile circle through the heart of the village property.

John was pleased to be in Denver with its abundant sunshine, even during winter. He recalled being in that city with his parents as a young

---

[905] Don Aines, "Inspirational day shaky for ED pioneer," *(Hagerstown, Maryland) Morning Herald*, April 1998.

[906] John McConnell, notations on back of Bethel Middle School photographs, October 1998.

[907] Angela Alioto, e-mail to author, 12 June 2005.

child. "My father built a church here. He taught the men how to lay bricks," he said. And in fashion similar to his father's, John made his residence in the Mile High City known among Denver's governmental leaders. Through contacts with mayor Wellington E. Webb, then his successor mayor John W. Hickenlooper, John hoped Denver would "lead the world to a better future by going all out and helping prepare for Earth Day by getting radio, TV stations, colleges and churches talking about how we can work for peace." [908]

Webb honored John as one of Denver's "Mile High Legend-Unsung Heroes" in a reception in city hall on 15 July 2003. The mayor's invitation stated that the award honors "our diverse citizens, history and culture" by paying tribute to individuals who "displayed outstanding commitment and dedication to the 'Mile High' City of Denver through volunteerism and community involvement." The letter concluded, "Mr. McConnell, you have undoubtedly justified your worthiness of this honor." [909]

Then, through association with Hickenlooper, John spoke at both the opening and the closing ceremonies of Denver's Earth Fair on 19-22 April 2004. With dynamic voice, John complimented his new home community for organizing the well-attended event, which he identified as "an amazing opportunity for the city to get the attention of the world and get the cities of the world to take action where the nations have failed." His message capitalized on the themes of his life – Earth Day, the Earth Magna Charta, 77 Theses, Earth Kill versus Earth Care, and "peace, justice and the care of Earth" – all presented in a self-effacing manner as "a way to turn the world right side up." Speaking with enthusiasm, John encouraged Denverites to act as Earth Trustees every day, saying, "It will affect the way you travel, what you buy, and how you invest. But, more and more, we will turn our attitudes and our actions toward a future that can be left to our children with pride."[910]

Hickenlooper signed a proclamation, designating March 20, 2004 as the day "that the people of Denver will celebrate Earth Day." [911] The city and the mayor followed this with another proclamation, a year later, that specified

[908] John McConnell, interview by author, Denver, Colorado, August 2004.

[909] Wellington E. Webb, letter to John McConnell, 1 July 2003.

[910] John McConnell, speeches, Denver Earth Fair, 19-22 April 2004.

[911] *Earth Day Proclamation*, Denver, Colorado, 20 March 2004.

March 20, 2005 as "Denver's Earth Day in Honor of John McConnell." [912]

This official attention came about because John spoke out on issues of the day. Upon his arrival in Denver, John began to submit letters to the editor of *The Denver Post*. In one, he attacked the media as "the key cause of terrorism ... with stories of violence and all the worst that is happening." [913] In another, he encouraged investment in "major universities that were established by devout Christians and originally taught the moral values that nurtured justice and peaceful progress." [914]

These caught the attention of columnist Dick Kreck who wrote an article in March 2003 that included John's assessment, "War is not inevitable, even if our President is hellbent on unleashing the dogs," as well as John's belief that prayer "can turn the tide." After listing John's accomplishments, Kreck asserted, "McConnell ... moved to Denver with his wife, Anna, in October, to relax in retirement. He is, after all, 87 years old. Instead, he's laboring for peace, on a Social Security budget." The article included John's statement, "It is governments' lust for power, building up armies, that lead to war. The most guilty party of all is the United States. We spend billions for the military and pennies for peace." Then, Kreck posed the question, "Does he ever get weary, laboring in the vineyards for peace when war seems so close?" John replied, "I have moments of discouragement. I pray to the Lord to keep me going." [915]

In 2003, John, who was a lifelong Republican, encouraged John Buchanan to run for presidency of the United States on the Republican ticket. Buchanan, promoting a platform to reduce military spending and limit corporate lobbying, was one of fourteen Republican candidates, including President George W. Bush, whose names appeared on the New Hampshire primary ballot. Buchanan garnered 836 votes, the third highest total behind Bush and the former mayor of Berlin, New Hampshire, Richard Bosa, [916] who was Buchanan's campaign advisor. [917]

---

[912] *Earth Day Proclamation*, Denver, Colorado, 20 March 2005.

[913] John McConnell, "The Key Cause of Terrorism," letter to editor, *The Denver Post*, 24 July 2002.

[914] John McConnell, letter to editor, *The Denver Post,* 4 August 2002.

[915] Dick Kreck, "Peace lover fights wars with prayer," *The Denver Post*, 5 March 2003.

[916] *New Hampshire Primary* [online]. Answers.com [cited 31 March 2004]. Available from www.answers.com/topic/new-hampshire-primary.

[917] John Buchanan, telephone interview by author, 31 March, 2004.

In a seemingly serious tone, Buchanan asked John to be his running mate. When Anna heard of this, she exclaimed, "What? Absolutely not! He'd never have a wife if that happened. I'm sorry. Wow!" [918] John agreed, "Well, it would be a little ridiculous having an 88-year-old vice-president." But John did express a latent desire to be a consultant to anyone elected to the White House. At the same time, he vehemently vocalized his disdain for incumbent Bush and Democratic challenger John Kerry, sardonically calling the candidates "war Christians." [919]

During the debates between Bush and Kerry in the summer of 2004, John criticized both men for claiming they would use war to "win the peace in Iraq." [920] With brilliant recall, John contrasted the candidates' childishness with quotations by men whom John admired: Albert Einstein, "Peace cannot be kept by force; it can only be achieved by understanding;" John F. Kennedy, "Peace is a daily, weekly, monthly process gradually changing opinion, slowly eroding doubts, quietly building new structures;" UN Secretary-General Dag Hammarskjöld, "The greatest prayer of man asks not for victory, but for peace;" and UN Secretary-General U Thant, "There is no peace in the world today because there is no peace in the minds of men." [921]

But when Bush was re-elected in November 2004 and with the war that Bush initiated in Iraq continuing to flare, it was obvious that opinions of peace-oriented persons would not be heard or heeded by executives in the Bush administration. In times like that, John McConnell expressed his disgust with nationalism and his appreciation for the United Nations. [922]

In the early days of the third millennium, the UN was comprised of 191 Member States – all but three countries in the world. In theory, at least, that world body strove for peace, although ambassadors often disagreed on how to obtain peace. Advising the UN Member States were thousands of civil society organizations (CSOs), many of them non-governmental organizations, like the Earth Society Foundation. One CSO was We, The

---

918 Anna McConnell, interview by author, Denver, Colorado, August 2004.

919 John McConnell, interview by author, Denver, Colorado, August 2004.

920 George W. Bush and John Kerry, presidential debates, August 2004.

921 Albert Einstein, John F. Kennedy, Dag Hammarskjöld, U Thant, "You are invited to express yourself on the subject of 'A Minute for Peace,'" John McConnell's compilation of comments on peace.

922 John McConnell, telephone interview with author, 5 November 2004.

World, founded by visionary Rick Ulfik in 1998. In September 2004, We, The World inaugurated a convergence of events called 11 Days of Global Unity to promote international peace and sustainability. 11 Days involved more than 200 citizen activities, including concerts, festivals and web casts, in over eighty countries. These celebrations culminated with the UN's International Day of Peace on 21 September, the autumnal equinox, at which Secretary-General Kofi Annan rang the Peace Bell. John McConnell was one of the honorary co-chairs for 11 Days of Global Unity, joining other notable social advocates such as Jane Goodall, Deepak Chopra, Irene Khan, Marianne Williamson, Robert Thurman, Hazel Henderson, Barbara Marx Hubbard and Riane Eisler. John was an elder of this group. [923]

In early 2005, Colene Riffo of Santa Clarita, California, brought John a gift of communications technology, in the form of an "Earth Trustee pilot project," that allowed him, in Denver, to communicate with the West Coast for an Earth Day event on 21 March 2005. The event was part of the Digital Storytelling Festival and Youth Ambassador Cyber Fair, an "edu-tainment" program broadcast via community public television. [924]

To participate, John and Anna visited the office of Tom Rapp, director of the Retired and Senior Volunteer Program in the Denver area. John had telephoned Rapp after having read his column in a senior newspaper. That conversation motivated Rapp to have John speak at a senior recognition luncheon. "I was impressed with the scope of his work and the extensive contacts he made over the years," Rapp said. "I was impressed with the passion John has been able to maintain for his Earth Day project." Through Rapp, John later made an appearance on a local senior television program.

Further discussion led to John mentioning his need for assistance with a web cam for Riffo's telecast. Tom's wife Jean, who was an information technology specialist at the U.S. Bureau of Land Management, set up the computer and web cam interface for John. [925] The audience in California consisted of youths from various high schools and city officials involved with urban forestry, housing development, environmental planning, water and sustainability. His image and message were also videotaped, edited and

---

[923] Rick Ulfik, e-mail to author, 13 February 2006.

[924] Colene Riffo, e-mail to author, 29 June 2005.

[925] Tom and Jean Rapp, e-mail to author 28 December 2005.

rebroadcast in segments at a later date.[926]

Others online with John, via web cam, were Julia Morton-Mahr of International Holistic Tourism Education Centre in Canada, who provided technical support for the videoconference link; John Southworth of the Lab School Distance Learning Enrichment Programming at the University of Hawaii; peace activists Heiner Benking and Eric Schneider in Germany; and me. As John's biographer, I was given the privilege of introducing him to the California audience.[927]

Riffo classified her motivation for producing this real-time, multi-party video conference as a way of honoring John, whom she described as "an underdog achieving great things even if he didn't get proper credit." Of John's role in the videoconference, Riffo said, "I feel a sense of purpose in people's interactive destinies. Individuals, who are Helpful Hannas, Engineer Bills, Mr. Rodgers, etc., are all karmic adjusters, transpiring to a higher value that uplifts consciousness and transcends the deed. [Their] impact becomes ten-fold or more, showing how people can rally in numbers with a spark of hope and become ablaze in social reconstruction."[928]

A month later, Joanne Tawfilis honored John and Anna by including their painted visages in an elaborate art project that connected more than 900 murals, each five feet high and from twelve to over 100 feet long, in a collection that stretched for 10,912 feet. The project was an attempt to break the world record, as documented in the *Guinness Book of Records*, for the "longest painting in the world." Many of the murals were created by students from 150 Denver schools as well as children in after-school programs, members of clubs and organizations, and individuals. Some murals came from the eastern part of the United Sates and others from Egypt and Austria. Tawfilis, who was co-founder, with her husband Fouad, and executive director of the Art Miles Mural Project, displayed them in a Denver park on 23 April 2005.

The mural of John and Anna contained images of planet Earth, the Earth Day Proclamation and the Gospel Car. It was the work of master muralist Cady Macasa, who was the art director for the project, and it proved

---

926 Colene Riffo, e-mail to author 15 December 2005.

927 Author's participation, Swarthmore, Pennsylvania, 21 March 2005.

928 Colene Riffo, e-mail to author, 29 June 2005.

to be the last mural Macasa painted because he died unexpectedly while delivering it to Tawfilis, who had sketched its conceptual design. Tawfilis, who painted signature murals of celebrities such as Cher, Elizabeth Taylor and Lindsay Wagner, said she intended to paint another mural of John and Anna that would incorporate more of their personal life, including Christa, Hannah Rose and Bethany Anne. "There is no one who has the soul and spirit of John McConnell," she said. "He did such great things and lives so simply and humbly with his devoted wife." [929]

Athena Buchanan brought her expertise in Internet marketing to John later in 2005. After having achieved success creating revenue-generation programs for technology companies in Silicon Valley, Buchanan (no relation to John Buchanan) founded DotOrg Marketing in 2001. She knew, as John McConnell had learned, that e-mail was the most powerful communications tool among Internet users. Through her company, Buchanan assisted environmental nonprofit organizations. Her clients included The Gorilla Foundation, Just Think Foundation, The Dian Fossey Gorilla Fund International, The Orangutan Foundation International, and Campaign for Old-Growth.

While surfing the web, she discovered earthsite.org and decided she wanted to create a new Earth Trustee web site for John. Initial phone calls confirmed her assumption that her efforts would be pro bono, but she found his zeal to be commanding and proceeded anyway. On 5 October, she and a video crew flew to Denver and invested a day taping John. The footage consisted of his recitation of a thirty second announcement and longer recording of John expounding his philosophies for humanity's better future. [930]

Buchanan's goal in developing www.earthtrustee.org, she said, "Is to have a legacy site, providing a historic perspective of the Earth Day founder and presenting the opportunity for people to take up the cause." [931] Explaining her motivation, Buchanan continued, "The world needs its icons, and John McConnell is a living human icon who has created other icons – Earth Day and the Earth Flag. His story must be told." [932]

John's image as a Star of Hope persisted in newspapers and magazines

[929] Joanne Tawfilis, e-mail to author, 14 May 2005.

[930] Author's participation, Denver, Colorado, 5 October 2005.

[931] Athena Buchanan, e-mail to author, 21 November 2005.

[932] Athena Buchanan, e-mail to author, 28 November 2005.

in the Denver area. "Can one person's vision of peace and humanity spread hope to others?" asked an article in the October 2005 issue of the *Glendale News Cherry Creek Chronicle*, a paper serving the Denver suburb where John and Anna resided. "Ninety-year-old John McConnell, the creator of Earth Day, the Minute for Peace and one of the world's first environmentalists, answers this question with a resounding yes," the article said. [933]

John not only spoke a "resounding yes" to the local reporter, he continued to work five to eight hours each day, communicating his message via telephone calls and e-mails. [934] Anna, who encouraged John to walk one mile every day, said his routine consisted of being in touch with old friends and making new acquaintances. [935]

John's e-mails contained one to three of his previously written essays, generally customized, and a request for the recipient take advantage of an upcoming date to promote peace and justice: Star of Hope on Christmas (25 December) and the feast of St. Francis (4 October); Minute for Peace on the anniversary of President John F. Kennedy's assassination (22 November) and the original Minute for Peace broadcasts (22 December); and Earth Trusteeship as "the way to peace and prosperity on planet Earth" on Earth Day (vernal equinox).

He continued to employ symbolism associated with particular events: New Year's Day (1 January) as an opportunity to make a personal resolution to end war; U.S. Memorial Day (last Monday in May) as a time to forgive soldiers for being taught to kill; Christmas as a season to value natural resources and end excessive consumerism; and any occasion to follow his "Formula for the Future – Doomsday or Opportunity."

In tune with current events, he employed the Republican National Convention (29 August to 2 September 2004) to speak out against America's emphasis on war and money; U.S. Inauguration Day (20 January 2005) to decry President George W. Bush as "the chief example of fakery" for proclaiming to be a Christian while transforming Jesus' message of "love thine enemies" [936] into kill thine enemies; the passing of Pope John Paul II (2

[933] "Star of Hope," *Glendale News, Cherry Creek Chronicle*, October 2005.

[934] Author's observation, Denver, Colorado, January 2006.

[935] Anna McConnell, manuscript review with author, Denver, Colorado, October 2005.

[936] *Bible*, Matthew 5:43.

April 2005) to commit to the teachings of Jesus; and the passing of Gaylord Nelson (2 July 2005) to expose "the world's biggest lie" in regard to Earth Day.

He advocated that U.S. Independence Day (4 July) be celebrated with peaceful bell ringing rather than firecrackers that emulate the sound of bombs. He promoted 4 October 2007, the upcoming fiftieth anniversary of the launch of Sputnik 1, as a "a perfect time to launch a Star of Hope satellite." [937] And he dreamed that a Peace Bell and Earth Day ceremonies at all UN facilities, especially at the United Nations Office at Geneva, [938] would join those ongoing traditions at UN Headquarters at New York and the UN Office at Vienna. [939]

Gary Arvidson, a writer in North Carolina who published an article about John, said, "At his age, I find no diminishment of his desire to help mankind. By this time, most men would have completely retired or given up this high level of humanitarian pursuit. John has never given up, but only continues in a stronger effort ... [trying to change the world] from that of destruction to upbuilding." [940]

On the day after Christmas 2005, John continued to speak out. By means of the telephone, John, in Denver, was the guest of Gary Goldman, president and founder of International Quality Leadership Institute and host of *A Voice for America's Youth Radio Show* in Chicago, Illinois. "I was very impressed by John's clarity and compassion and commitment to the idea of peace within and peace throughout the world, and with his breadth

---

937 John McConnell, e-mails to author, 2004 and 2005.

938 In 2001, Hans Janitschek, knowing John McConnell's desire for a Peace Bell at the United Nations Office at Geneva, proposed that idea to Vladimir Petrovsky of Russia, the director general of the UN Office at Geneva. Petrovsky pledged his support. Also in 2001, Janitschek, through communications with Heinz Klaus, chancellor of the Austrian Mission to the UN at Geneva, obtained support from Wolfgang Petritsch, the Austrian ambassador to the UN Office at Geneva. Petritsch offered to sponsor the bell's inauguration. Janitschek then engaged U.S.-Bulgarian sculptor Mihail, who had cast the African elephant sculpture at United Nations Headquarters at New York, to design the bell. In 2004, Tibetan healer and teacher Lama Gangchen agreed to finance creation and placement of the bell. Peace Bell III is scheduled for inauguration for either the autumnal equinox in 2006 or the vernal equinox, Earth Day, in 2007. Source: Hans Janitschek, e-mail to author, 17 February 2006.

939 Hans Janitschek, interview by author, New York, New York, 8 June 2004. Also, Hans Janitschek e-mails to author 12 and 13 January 2006.

940 Gary Arvidson, e-mail to author 31 October 2005.

of experience with various well-known people," Goldman said. The radio host noted John's ability to dialogue with the live studio audience, who were teenagers ranging in age from 16 to 20. "They agreed with John that it's important for young people to be working for peace, and they want to be heard. There was a perfect communication bridge between the younger generation and the older generation," he added. [941]

I began to write John's biography in July 2004, but the seed was planted in 2001 when my church, Unity of Blue Water in Port Huron, Michigan, asked me to be the presenter for the Sunday service on 22 April. The theme was ecology. Through writing assignments for government agencies and environmental organizations, I was well-versed on topical issues in the Port Huron area as well as the Great Lakes. And while I knew about Earth Day on April 22, I had never heard of John McConnell. But Internet research led me to John's web site. There, I read his essays and was impressed. More importantly, I learned about the original vernal equinox Earth Day, and when I spoke of that at my church, the congregants expressed their surprise, too.

Through earthsite.org, I sent an e-mail to John in which I expressed my appreciation for his philosophy, which I had included in my speech. Two days later, John telephoned me. Near the end of a thirty minute conversation, he asked if I would write his biography. I said no. I was in the midst of caring for my aging dad, who, like John had been born in 1915. But when my dad passed in May 2003, I considered John's request.

The process began with an exploratory three-day visit to John and Anna's home in Denver in January 2004. Sated with Anna's delicious meals and impressed with stories by both John and Anna, I promised to write the book. I was especially impressed with a comment from Anna, "John's vision is 'Everything at peace.' The world needs men like him because, it's as Christa's pediatrician in Brooklyn in the 1970s said one day, 'If men like you stopped working, we would be in hell.'" [942]

In June, I scouted the John McConnell Document Group at the Swarthmore College Peace Collection. The volume of papers was daunting. In late July, I went to Denver again, staying at Kentucky Circle Village for

941 Gary Goldman, telephone interview with author, 29 December 2005.

942 Anna McConnell, interview by author, Denver, Colorado, January 2004.

six weeks. During that time, John and I met almost every day. At John's suggestion, each meeting began with a prayer. When not conversing, I transcribed our recorded conversations, pored over printed documents from John's office, and conducted Internet research.

Then, in the seven months from November 2004 through May 2005, I invested all but six weeks at the Peace Collection. Working alone in the quiet archives for over 800 hours, I weighed John's prediction from our initial meeting in January, "Well, putting the whole story together would be a gigantic task, but it would be worth it." [943]

In retrospect, I realized I went about my task in the best possible manner. From John and Anna, I received oral history. At Swarthmore, I found corroborating details plus nuances. And through conversation with their peers, I added human insight into John's greatness and Anna's love and support.

To experience the venue in which John McConnell operated, I also attended Earth Day ceremonies at the United Nations in 2004 and 2005 and a program commemorating the fiftieth anniversary of the Peace Bell on 8 June 2004. At these events, I met members of the Earth Society Foundation. Notable among these was Hans Janitschek, who owned a publishing company, Swan Books. He agreed to publish John McConnell's biography, thus bringing invaluable personal knowledge and enthusiasm to the project.

We considered several titles for the book, focusing on John's role as a global visionary and as the Earth Day founder. Finally, we landed upon *Star of Hope*. "That's it!" Janitschek exclaimed. "Yes, *Star of Hope*. The Star of Hope editorial was John's first international accomplishment, but more importantly John McConnell *is*, himself, a Star of Hope!" [944]

---

[943] John McConnell, interview by author, Denver, Colorado, August 2004.

[944] Hans Janitschek, manuscript review, New York, New York, September 2005.

Index

A

B

C

F

G

H

I

L

M

N

O

P

T

U

V

W

Y

Z

Acknowledgements

Never doubt that a small group of thoughtful committed people can change the world: indeed it's the only thing that ever has!
– Margaret Mead, (1901-1978)

I want to thank:

John and Anna McConnell for their vision, information, hospitality, encouragement and wisdom.

Wendy E. Chmielewski, curator of the Swarthmore College Peace Collection, and her staff Barbara Addison, Mary Beth Sigado, and Anne Yoder, and student interns, who organized John and Anna's vast materials into archival boxes by subject and chronology.

Hans Janitschek, publisher of Swan Books for his enthusiasm and knowledge.

And Ishtar Adler, Yolanda Alacort and Chris Hollinsed, Angela Alioto, Bonnie Alkema, Diane Allen, Gary Arvidson, Ridgway Banks, Heiner Benking, Anatoly Berezovoi, Ian Betts, Frank O. Braynard, Ron Brinkley, Penny and Rick Briscoe, Athena Buchanan, Fred Burrous, Mary Carlin, Carol Carter Marks, Ann Charles, Gerry Coffey, Stan Cohen, Carmen Colombo, Mike Connell, Norman Corwin, Ardyce Curl, Dave and JoAnne Davies, Clarence Davis, Charles Donnelly, Tom Dowd, John Drysdale, Dennis Dubin, Margaret Fikoris, George Gallup, Jr., Helen Garland, Michael Geoghegan, Monica Getz, Gary Goldman, Wilfrid Grey, Linda Grover,

Steve Hansen, Alanna Hartzok, Patrick Horsbrugh, Anji Janitschek, Friedl Janitschek, Jim and Clare Keating, Kurt Koenig, Don Koff, G. P. Koirala, Al Korn, Lama Gangchen Rinpoche, Ann Lane, Holley Lantz, Christa (McConnell) and Paul Mason, Cary McConnell, Evan McConnell, John and Christel McDonald, Rigoberta Menchu, Lee Merrick, Marcia Anne Meyer, Linda Misek-Falkoff, Mark Monroe, Julia Morton-Marr, Barbara and Robert Muller, John Munday, Jr., Franz Nahrada, Bob Nelson, Arren Nguyen, Marleen Nobell, Joe Novara, Otto Ota, Deb Owen, Andrea and Clarkson Palmer, Melinda Pillsbury-Foster, Karen Porter, Jean and Tom Rapp, Dorothy Reeder, Colene Riffo, Darrin Rodgers, Tony Roisman, Erling Saevarsson, Kevin Sanders, Edwina Sandys, Dawn Sawyer, Ann Seeger, Pete Seeger, Helen Shaskan, Ruth Short, Robert Alan Silverstein, S. Fred Singer, Maris Soule, John Southworth, Alison Sparks, Ernie and Marguerite Stenquist, Jeffrey Stine, Maurice Strong, John Tandana, Helen Tang, Joanne Tawfilis, Aye Aye Thant, Will Thompson, Kristina Tomczak, Odin Toness, Narelle Townsend, Rick Ulfik, United Nations Reference Team, Ida Urso, Wilson Van Dusen, Ruth VanVoorhis, Kurt Waldheim, Dala Walters, Hank Waxman, Marti Weir, Veronica Weygand, Kit Whittington, Monica Willard.

And especially Robin Harper, a fine Quaker gentleman and ice cream lover who took me into his home for most of the six months that I researched documents at Swarthmore College.